The
MOFFATT
NEW TESTAMENT COMMENTARY

Based on *The New Translation* by the
REV. PROFESSOR JAMES MOFFATT, D.D.
and under his Editorship

THE GOSPEL OF LUKE

THE
GOSPEL OF LUKE

BY

WILLIAM MANSON
D.D.

Professor of New Testament Language
Literature and Theology
New College
Edinburgh

HARPER AND BROTHERS PUBLISHERS
NEW YORK AND LONDON

EDITOR'S PREFACE

MOFFATT'S NEW TESTAMENT COMMENTARY

THE aim of this commentary is to bring out the religious meaning and message of the New Testament writings. To do this, it is needful to explain what they originally meant for the communities to which they were addressed in the first century, and this involves literary and historical criticism ; otherwise, our reading becomes unintelligent. But the New Testament was the literature of the early church, written out of faith and for faith, and no study of it is intelligent unless this aim is kept in mind. It is literature written for a religious purpose. ' These are written that ye might believe that Jesus is the Christ, the Son of God.' This is the real object of the New Testament, that Christians might believe it better, in the light of contemporary life with its intellectual and moral problems. So with any commentary upon it. Everything ought to be subordinated to the aim of elucidating the religious content, of shewing how the faith was held in such and such a way by the first Christians, and of making clear what that faith was and is.

The idea of the commentary arose from a repeated demand to have my New Testament translation explained ; which accounts for the fact that this translation has been adopted as a convenient basis for the commentary. But the contributors have been left free to take their own way. If they interpret the text differently, they have been at liberty to say so. Only, as a translation is in itself a partial commentary, it has often saved space to print the commentary and start from it.

As everyman has not Greek, the commentary has been written, as far as possible, for the Greekless. But it is based upon a first-hand study of the Greek original, and readers may rest assured that it represents a close reproduction of the original writers' meaning, or at anyrate of what we consider that to have been. Our common aim has been to enable everyman to-day to sit where these first Christians sat, to feel the impetus and inspiration of the Christian faith as it dawned upon the minds of the communities in the first century, and thereby to realize more vividly how new and lasting is the message which prompted these New Testament writings to take shape as they did. Sometimes people inside as well as outside the church make mistakes about the New Testament. They think it means this or that, whereas its words frequently mean something very different from what traditional associations suggest. The saving thing is to let the New Testament speak for itself. This is our desire and plan in the present commentary, to place each writing or group of writings in its original setting and allow their words to come home thus to the imagination and conscience of everyman to-day.

The general form of the commentary is to provide a running comment on the text, instead of one broken up into separate verses. But within these limits, each contributor has been left free. Thus, to comment on a gospel requires a method which is not precisely the same as that necessitated by commenting on an epistle. Still, the variety of treatment ought not to interfere with the uniformity of aim and form. Our principle has been that nothing mattered, so long as the reader could understand what he was reading in the text of the New Testament.

JAMES MOFFATT.

PREFACE

THE present Commentary conforms to the general design of the
series of which it is a part, and aims to furnish the English reader
with literary and historical guidance towards the understanding
of the text of Luke. Severe restriction upon space has precluded
the discussion of many questions connected with the pre-literary
history of the evangelical tradition, but where the understanding
of an episode or of a saying has seemed to demand the raising of
such questions, the latter have not been entirely ignored.

The reader of the gospels should remember that for a generation after Christ the tradition of his life and teaching circulated
in a form in which, as yet unfixed by writing, it was freely adapted
to the evangelistic and missionary ends of the Christian society
and underwent modification, partly by reference to the changing
historical circumstances of the time, and partly through the
Church's need of giving fuller and preciser expression to its
experience of Christ. The recognition of such modifications,
which were retained when the tradition was put into literary
shape by the evangelists, is the justification of historical criticism
as applied to the gospels. The reader must not assume that
every episode or saying has come down to us just in its original
form or context. Interpretative and symbolical elements have
been added, now under the influence of Old Testament prophecy
and type, now through the Church's need of defining its conceptions more clearly to itself. But if the reader is not thus at
liberty to feel absolved from questions going deeper than to the
mere understanding of the text, he will scarcely fail to be com-
pensated by the closer approach to the mind and work of Christ
to which this method of study invites him, nor will he lack
guidance. For the collective tradition is of such a character
that at no vital point is the authentic voice of the Master inaudible
or his lineaments obscure.

Luke's is the richest and most voluminous of our gospels, and
this quality it owes to the incorporation in it of the highly varied
matter of its Special or L Source. This source was Judean.
Visiting Palestine in the company of Paul between the years
A.D. 57 and 59, the Gentile evangelist fell under the spell of the
Mother Church of Jerusalem and of the special tradition which
he found there, and to the inspiration of this experience we may
trace the genesis of his idea of writing a gospel. To the same

inspiration may be ascribed many of the well-defined characteristics of the work. Paradoxical as it seems, the Gentile writer
Luke in some respects reflects the spirit of Judaic Christianity
more fully than any of his peers.

In the present Commentary the main emphasis is laid on the
teaching of Jesus and on those passages which seem to interpret
the purpose of his mission. Here attention is directed primarily
to the historical conception of the Kingdom of God which Jesus
took up and carried forward, and I have taken the view that the
imminence of the Kingdom in his teaching is to be connected
throughout with his consciousness of bringing to his nation
a final revelation of the redeeming will of God. Jesus offers to
his nation, not a new doctrine of the Kingdom, but a conception
of the will of God which, if received, brings the goal indicated
by the Kingdom into measurable, and, indeed, immediate, relation with the lives of men. On close approach we find that
loving enemies, meeting evil with good, dying to self, and
becoming by a new birth sons of God, constitute the central
and vital datum, the ' mystery ' which Jesus reveals to men.

Among other works on Luke, I owe a particular debt to the
Commentaries of Easton and Klostermann, and to the great
thesaurus of Strack and Billerbeck. Had space permitted,
the last-named work would have been laid still more fully under
contribution. My thanks are also due to Prof. G. S. Duncan,
St. Mary's College, St. Andrews, and to the Rev. James Manson,
M.A., Broughty Ferry, who kindly read the following pages in
proof and assisted me with many helpful suggestions.

W. MANSON.

NEW COLLEGE, EDINBURGH.
Jan. 25, 1930.

*

CONTENTS

INTRODUCTION

COMMENTARY

APPENDICES

INTRODUCTION

I. General Character of the Gospel Narratives

The Gospel which is the subject of the present commentary was composed some forty to fifty years after the Crucifixion, and probably about the year A.D. 75. The unanimous tradition of the following century affirms that its author was Luke, a companion of Paul, whom that apostle mentions in certain of his later epistles. A less unanimous but not improbable tradition assigns the composition of the work to Greece.

It is important that the modern reader should understand clearly what a gospel is. For more than a generation after Jesus the story of his life and death was transmitted solely by word of mouth. His deeds and words formed the material upon which the missionary and preacher drew, and by which the truths of Christianity were illustrated and enforced. Shortly before or after A.D. 70 written gospels arise, beginning with Mark, and with these the tradition of the Saviour's life acquires a certain fixity. But neither in the earlier nor in the later period did the word ' gospel ' signify the history of Jesus or the books in which that history had come to be written down. Signifying ' good news ' or ' tidings of joy,' the word invariably referred to the redemption offered to the world in Jesus Christ. Yet, because the proclamation of this redemption involved continual allusion to the earthly history of the Redeemer, the word gospel acquired in time a substantive character with reference to that story, and towards the close of the second century, though not at first without a certain hesitation, it was transferred to the books in which the story was embodied.

The early history of the gospels is indeed the record of a process by which only very slowly and gradually a living spoken tradition was superseded in popular esteem by written manuals. Christians clung to the free tradition handed down by word of mouth from the apostles, and were not at first inclined to countenance the replacement of this tradition by authoritative books. Nevertheless, the transference of the name ' gospel ' to our evangelical treatises had a distinct literary fitness. In the gospels Christianity had created a literature which had no exact analogy in any contemporary type of memoirs or biography.

In the first place our gospels represent a popular literature. Written not in the artificial idiom of the literary schools but in the language of the street and market, they are intended to reach the ordinary man. Here Luke, the most accomplished artist among our evangelists, stands essentially on the same plane as Mark. His Greek is that in which, as we now know from papyrus writings discovered in Egypt, ordinary individuals exchanged ideas and conducted their daily business and correspondence. There is no attempt to rival the studied graces of contemporary writers such as Philo or Josephus.

In the second place, the gospels are distinctively religious. They are written not to please, nor even only to instruct, but to persuade, to convert, to redeem. No contemporary literary types, the Stoic diatribe, the idealized lives of philosophers, the hortatory exercises of moralists like Dion Chrysostom, are here really parallel. For what the gospels present is not the reasonableness or the truth of ethical and spiritual ideas, nor even the holiness and beauty of a life, but the testimony of a religious society to one in whom redemption has been experienced, and for whom faith, obedience, love, and worship are unqualifiedly claimed.

Even in other respects the gospels differentiate themselves from contemporary forms of memoir or biography. While Justin Martyr (*c.* A.D. 150) describes and quotes our gospels as ‘ Memoirs of the Apostles,’ they differ from ordinary memoirs by incorporating not the personal reminiscences of their authors but the collective tradition of a society. Whatever part the personal testimony of apostles and others played in the formation and building up of the evangelical tradition, the material handled in our gospels has behind it the faith of the Church. Only once does any of our evangelists speak of himself, and then it is merely to indicate his literary method, and to reveal that his material is not personal but an authoritative tradition received by him from others (Luke i. 1–4).

Once more, in biography as a current literary type, the human interest of the story is paramount. The actions of the hero are presented in relation to his ‘ ethos ’ or character, and this in turn is variously exhibited by reference to his ancestry, birth, upbringing, and environment. The gospels present Jesus with only a minimum of reference to any of these things. Mark says nothing about Jesus before his call to public service. The human interest of the story, great as it is, is subordinated to the higher purpose of discovering in him the Messiah, the Son of God, the agent of divine redemption. The unity of the story lies not in the human evolution of the character but in the presence and operation within that character of a superhuman purpose. The 'character' of Jesus is simply his self-manifestation as the Messiah-Son of God. His actions are a part of that self-manifestation, so that the norms of ordinary biography are in part exceeded and in part ignored.

Not different, finally, is the judgment to be passed on the relation of these narratives to history. The gospels are historical works in so far as the episodes of which they treat formed part of a series of events belonging to the life of Jesus in the past. But the impulse to recall or reconstitute the past for its own sake was not the motive which inspired their composition or which dictated what they should and what they should not contain. The spoken tradition from which the gospels sprang was inspired from the beginning by a definitely practical and missionary purpose. Events were recalled not because they filled out and preserved an outline of the past, but because they ministered to the religious needs and realities of the present, and because through them Christ was announced as Saviour. The written gospels likewise are to be received and read primarily as evangelical and missionary deliverances. They are written 'out of faith and for faith,' to present Jesus as Lord, and their contents are to be interpreted in the first instance as aids to religious life.

II. SOURCES OF THE GOSPEL OF LUKE

The Prologue to Luke (i. 1-4) asserts that, before its author took up the pen, other writers had started on the task of reducing the evangelical tradition to written form. The evangelist does not indicate what these earlier 'essays' were, nor whether he laid any of them under contribution in the composition of his own narrative. But here literary criticism comes to our aid with a partial answer to the first of these questions and a complete answer to the second. It is now established beyond reasonable doubt that one of the sources of Luke was the gospel of Mark, and that besides Mark he used at least one other written source, containing teachings of Jesus, which was also used by the writer of Matthew, and which modern scholars name Q, from the German word *Quelle,* meaning ' source.'

A. *Luke's use of Mark*

Mark, the earliest of our gospels, was written, probably at Rome, between A.D. 65 and 70, and is our primary source for the historical outline of the Saviour's life. Based, according to tradition, on the teaching of Peter, it supplies, though not a full, a representative conspectus of the events in and through which the life of Jesus had become ' gospel ' or ' glad tidings ' for mankind. It falls into two parts, in which are shewn respectively (1) how the Christian society came to its confession of Jesus as the Messiah (Mark i. 1–viii. 29), (2) how there was revealed to it the mystery of the Messiah's death (viii. 30–xvi. 8). The fact that, as literary criticism has convincingly shewn, Mark was used as a source by the writers both of Matthew and of Luke, inspires the highest confidence in its simple and vivid record. Plainly these later evangelists would not have used it unless they considered that, whether based on Peter's teaching or not, Mark represented in a reliable and authoritative form the common tradition of the Christian community regarding its Saviour and Lord.

The following sections of Luke reveal Mark as basis :

iv. 31–44	Drawn from Mark i. 29–39.
v. 12–vi. 19	,, ,, ,, i. 40–iii. 19.
viii. 4–ix. 50	,, ,, ,, iv. 1–ix. 40.
xviii. 15–43	,, ,, ,, x. 13–52.
xix. 29–xxii. 13	,, ,, ,, xi. 1–xiv. 17.

An examination of these sections will shew that Luke owes to Mark a very great part of his knowledge of the ministry of Jesus both in Galilee and in Jerusalem. The derived sections begin with the first Sabbath of Jesus in Capernaum and extend to the last day of his life on earth. Actually Luke has reproduced more than half of Mark's 666 verses. As Luke contains 1,151 verses, these borrowings from Mark represent 30 per cent. of his total work. Among his omissions are the passages Mark iv. 26–29, vi. 17–29, vi. 45–viii. 26, x. 35–40, xiv. 3–9.

INTRODUCTION

That Luke should freely incorporate large portions of Mark's gospel is not surprising when we reflect that this first of written gospels would not be regarded either by its author or by its readers as literary property in the strict sense, but only as a compendium of the public tradition of the Church.

Within the limits of what he has borrowed, Luke adheres to Mark's order. He condenses the narrative and improves the language and style, but he does not add notes of time or place where Mark does not give them. His treatment of his source is objective. This consideration is important because of its bearing upon Luke's use of sources which, unlike Mark, have not been preserved.

B. *The Q Sections of Luke*

Mark is deficient in point of the *teaching* of Jesus, and here the writers of Matthew and Luke fell back upon another source. The existence of this source, commonly called Q, is inferred from the occurrence in Matthew and Luke of a large number of common sections (not paralleled in Mark) of which the close resemblance in language suggests that they go back ultimately to a single document.

The Q sections in Luke are as follows :

	Luke	*Subject*	*Matthew*
1.	iii. 7–9, 16–17.	Preaching of John.	iii. 7–10, 11–12.
2.	iv. 1–13.	Temptation of Jesus.	iv. 1–11.
3.	vi. 20–23.	Four Beatitudes.	v. 3, 4, 6, 11, 12.
4.	vi. 27–36.	Love the Law of the Kingdom.	v. 38–48.
5.	vi. 37–42.	Against Censoriousness.	vii. 1–5.
6.	vi. 43–49.	Deeds, not Words, the Essence of Religion.	vii. 16–27.
7.	vii. 1–10.	Healing of Centurion's Servant.	viii. 5–10, 13.
8.	vii. 18–35.	The Baptist's Question, and Words of Jesus about John.	xi. 2–19.
9.	ix. 57–60.	Warnings to Candidates for Discipleship.	viii. 19–22.
10.	x. 2–12.	Instructions for Mission Work of Disciples.	ix. 37–38, x. 7–16.
11.	x. 3–15.	Chorazin and Bethsaida Denounced.	xi. 21–23.
12.	x. 21–24.	Exultation of Jesus, and Blessing of the Disciples.	xi. 25–27, xiii. 16–17.
13.	xi. 2–4.	The Lord's Prayer.	vi. 9–13.
14.	xi. 9–13.	Promises to Prayer.	vii. 7–11.

Reviewing the above list of Q sections, we notice that Nos. 1–7 occur in relatively the same order in Matthew and Luke, and consequently this will have been their order in Q. Nos. 8–10 also have the same sequence except that Matthew has placed the

Baptist's question last, not first. Again, Nos. 11, 12, 15, 16, and 17 exhibit the same order except for Matthew's inversion of the last two. Finally, the same order may be perceived in Nos. 38–41.

A glance at the above passages will also shew the range and character of the Q source. It consisted mainly of memoranda of the Sayings of Jesus with a few strands of narrative such as the healing of the centurion's servant and the sending of messengers by John. Q contained but few parables and reported no miracles, though alluding to such in one passage (Luke vii. 21–22). Looking at the contents of the parallel sections we see the needs which the Q document, originally drawn in Aramaic probably between A.D. 40 and 50 and afterwards translated into Greek, was designed to serve. Christians, especially after the scattering of the original community which followed Stephen's death and the persecution of the Church by Herod Agrippa I (Acts viii. 1, 4, xi. 19–21, xii. 1, 24), were acutely conscious of the need of a guidance adequate to the augmented problems of their daily existence, and were thus flung afresh upon the teachings of the Master. What did Jesus say about inheritance in the Kingdom of God ? To whom had he promised it, and what constituted discipleship to himself ? What did he say about prayer and the power of faith, about earthly cares and temptations, about loving and forgiving others, about leaving everything for his sake ? What did he say about his own mission relatively to that of John, whose followers were still holding aloof, unwilling to cross the line to Christ ? What did he say about the Father, about his own personal relation to God, about the final coming of the Kingdom and the appearance of the Son of Man ? These were the questions to which Q sought to provide an answer. It began by narrating the call of Jesus, and closed with solemn predictions of his coming in glory as the Son of Man.

Luke, in view of the closeness with which he has elsewhere followed Mark, may be presumed to have reproduced Q with equal fidelity. The free, unconstrained sequence of the Q elements in his narrative bears out the opinion that he did so. As to the place of Q's origin we are wholly in the dark. The proposal is made by Canon Streeter to assign it to Antioch, but we have really no sufficient evidence upon which to build a judgment.

C. *Luke's Special Material*

Much of Luke's material is special to himself, and may be presumed to have been drawn by him from a third source (or group of sources) to which the symbol L is ordinarily annexed. L accounts for about one-half of the total bulk of Luke, and includes the following passages :

1.	iii. 10–15.	Details of John's Preaching.
2.	iv. 16–30.	Sermon of Jesus at Nazareth.
3.	v. 1–11.	The Call of Peter.
4.	vii. 11–17.	Raising of the Widow's Son at Nain.
5.	vii. 36–50.	The Penitent Woman in Simon's House.
6.	viii. 1–3.	Women who Ministered to Jesus.
7.	ix. 51–56.	Rejection of Jesus by the Samaritans.
8.	x. 1, 17–20.	Mission and Return of the Seventy.
9.	x. 29–37.	Parable of the Good Samaritan.
10.	x. 38–42.	Mary and Martha.
11.	xi. 5–8.	Parable of the Friend at Midnight.
12.	xii. 13–21.	Parable of the Rich Man's Death.
13.	xii. 49–56.	Jesus came to Kindle Fire.
14.	xiii. 1–9.	The Massacred Galileans.
15.	xiii. 10–17.	Healing of the Cripple Woman.
16.	xiii. 31–33.	Jesus Warned by Antipas.
17.	xiv. 1–6.	The Man with the Dropsy.
18.	xiv. 7–14.	Table Talk of Jesus.
19.	xiv. 28–33.	On Counting the Cost of Discipleship.
20.	xv. 1–3, 8–10, 11–32.	Parables of Lost Coin and Lost Son.
21.	xvi. 1–15.	Parable of the Unjust Steward. Use of Mammon.
22.	xvi. 19–31.	Parable of Dives and Lazarus.
23.	xvii. 7–10.	Unprofitable Servants.
24.	xvii. 11–19.	Healing of the Ten Lepers.
25.	xvii. 20–21.	The Kingdom is in your Midst.
26.	xviii. 1–8.	Parable of the Unjust Judge.
27.	xviii. 9–14.	The Pharisee and the Publican.
28.	xix. 1–10.	Conversion of Zacchaeus.
29.	xix. 39–44.	Tears of Jesus on beholding Jerusalem.

Certain of the above items may have come from Q, though in the absence of Matthew-parallels this derivation cannot be proved. To the above passages must be added a number of episodes peculiar to Luke's narrative of the Passion and Resurrection (xxii. 14–xxiv. 53), of which the following are the most remarkable :

30.	xxii. 15–18, 27– 30a, 31–38.	Words of Jesus at the Last Supper.
31.	xxiii. 6–16.	Jesus before Antipas.
32.	xxiii. 27–32.	Words to the Women of Jerusalem.
33.	xxiii. 40–43.	The Penitent Thief on the Cross.
34.	xxiv. 13–35.	The Disciples going to Emmaus.
35.	xxiv. 36–49.	Appearance of Jesus to the Eleven in Jerusalem.
36.	xxiv. 50–53.	The Ascension.

While Luke has also made use of Mark in his narrative of the Passion, the inclusion in that narrative of so many special items, combined with the fact that his order shews a dozen transpositions of events as compared with Mark, makes it plain that Mark did not supply the foundation of Luke's Passion history.

To glance at the above lists is to realize how deeply the total narrative of Luke is coloured by this special material, and how indelibly our thought of Jesus is stamped by parables and incidents derived from this source alone. Of the items listed above as belonging to L, Nos. 9, 11, 12, 20, 21, 22, 26, 27 are parables, some of them the most memorable in the whole teaching of Jesus. Nos. 4, 15, 17, 24 are miracles not elsewhere recorded. Nos. 2, 3, 5, 20, 27, 28 are illustrations of the graciousness of Jesus to the penitent. Nos. 9 and 24 reveal his interest in Samaritans. Nos. 12, 21, and 22 treat of the right uses of wealth. Nos. 11, 26, and 27 emphasize prayer. Nos. 4, 5, 6, 10, 15, 32 contain references to women whom Jesus helped or restored to God or otherwise comforted, or who ministered to him.

What then was the source of the L material ? As it is for the most part found in the same sections of the gospel as the Q sayings, the question resolves itself into the form, Did the evangelist find the Q and L material already combined in some *written* source, or did he collect the L material by personal research and himself combine it with Q ? The first theory has been widely supported, but it seems to reduce Luke's part in the composition of the gospel to the insignificant rôle of a mere editor of existing documents. Consequently, the other theory has found advocates, and has recently been revived in an interesting form by Drs. Streeter and Vincent Taylor. These scholars consider that Luke collected the L material from oral and written sources at Caesarea and other centres in Palestine, combined it with the Q sayings, and originally intended this Q and L compilation to serve as a gospel by itself. Afterwards, however, becoming acquainted with the gospel of Mark, he enriched his narrative with copious extracts from that writing, with the result that his completed narrative unites three streams of tradition, traceable respectively to Antioch (Q), Caesarea or Jerusalem (L), and Rome (Mark). To the original draft of the gospel, consisting of Q and L without Mark, Dr. Streeter gives the name ' Proto-Luke.' It comprises iii. 1–iv. 30, v. 1–11, vi. 12–viii. 3, ix. 51–xviii. 14, xix. 1–27, 30–44, and xxii. 14–xxiv. 53, *minus* the Markan elements in the last section.

Whatever may be thought of this literary theory, the special or L material of Luke can with confidence be traced to a Judean or Jerusalem source. This is proved (1) by the acquaintance which this material shews with personalities belonging to the original circle of Jesus (viii. 3, x. 38–42), (2) by its peculiar emphasis on poverty and wealth in Jesus' teaching (see page xxv. f.), and (3) by its localizing of the post-Resurrection history entirely in Jerusalem and its vicinity. The L material everywhere reflects a Jewish-Christian point of view, and is a valuable witness to Christianity in its original home.

D. *The Birth-Narratives*

In the birth-narratives of Luke i.–ii. we have demonstrably a tradition which Luke derived from Judean sources. Here, as against Prof. Adolf von Harnack, the majority of scholars believe that Luke founded on a written document, and this seems to be the more probable view. The origin and character of the narratives are briefly discussed in the commentary and in Appendix II. Luke apparently was not satisfied to begin, like the older tradition embodied in Mark, with the baptism and call of Jesus. He wished to go as far back as existing tradition reached, and thus to make his gospel a complete record of events ' from the beginning ' (i. 3). Then, having prefixed the birth-stories to the main body of the narrative, he composed the prefatory dedication to Theophilus, calling attention to the completeness of his work, and to the extensiveness of the sources which he had explored and utilized.

III. HISTORICAL AND RELIGIOUS VALUE OF THE WORK

If Theophilus, whom the evangelist addresses under the courteous title of ' Your Excellency,' was, as is usually assumed, a Roman official of rank who was interested in Christianity, the Lukan writings may be regarded as the earliest apology for the Christian religion. In other words, it may be contended that Luke hoped by his presentation of the Christian facts to abolish in official circles the suspicion which, since Nero's days (A.D. 64), had fallen on the hapless Christians of the Empire, and to win for the followers of Christ the same measure of toleration as was already granted to the Jews. That such was one of the principal motives of the Acts of the Apostles need not be questioned. The author of that work dwells consistently on the friendliness of the Roman officials to Paul (Acts xiii. 12, xviii. 12–16, xxiii. 29, xxv. 25–27, xxvi. 32), and in turn on the friendliness of Paul to the Roman authority (Acts xxiv. 10, xxv. 8, xxvi. 2 f., 25 f.). In addition, he stresses the fact that Christianity is in the direct line of descent from ancestral Judaism (Acts xxiv. 14–21, xxvi. 4–8, 22–23, 27, xxviii. 20), and so seeks to win for the new religion the toleration which was granted to the old.

In the case of the gospel the same apologetic intention is naturally not so manifest. Nevertheless, here too its presence, if admitted, would help to explain a number of features. In particular, Luke's resolve to narrate the Christian facts ' from the beginning,' i.e. from the birth of Christ, would acquire a new point if what he wished to shew was that Christianity, as originating in the most hallowed traditions of Jewish piety, was the legitimate descendant of Judaism (i. 78–79, ii. 29–32) and not, as its enemies alleged, a break-away from that religion. To the same motive we might ascribe the omission of a number of legal controversies recorded in Mark which, superficially regarded, might prejudice Christianity's claim to represent the religion of the fathers, e.g. the discussions of purity in Mark vii. 1–13 and of divorce in x. 2–12. Finally, the same apologetic intention might be invoked to explain a feature of the evangelist's delineation of the trial of Jesus. Luke represents the Jewish Sanhedrin as giving to the charge against Jesus a maliciously political and anti-Roman complexion (xxiii. 2, 5) which Pilate, however, refuses to accept (xxiii. 4, 14–15). It would appear that the evangelist desired to exculpate the procurator and to put the Roman authority, so to speak, on the side of Jesus.

But while an apologetic interest may to some extent be admitted, it forms but an undercurrent or sub-intention of the work. The evangelist's main purpose is to present the facts of Christianity so as to serve the religious end which gives these facts their real significance in history. When therefore we speak of Luke as historian we must do so in the sense required by a proper respect for his evangelistic aim. In recent years the historical value of the Lukan writings has been highly appraised by scholars who, like Sir W. M. Ramsay, have been impressed by the correctness of the references in Acts to contemporary institutions and forms of government in the Asian and Macedonian cities. The standards, however, by which we judge the historian of Acts must be of a somewhat different character from those which we apply to the evangelist. In the gospel we are dealing not with an eyewitness of the events but with an investigator and reporter of tradition. Obviously we must not everywhere demand of him the kind of evidence which is possible in matters of personal observation. His claim to be a true evangelist will be properly enough sustained if he has faithfully reproduced the statements which have been credibly attested to him by his authorities or which have been elicited in response to his inquiries. This, we have reason to believe, Luke has most carefully done.

The substantial character of Luke's service as historian of the evangelical tradition is shewn by the voluminousness, richness, and conspicuous merit of the special matter which he has handed down as the fruit of his researches. His gospel rests not only on Mark but, as we have seen, on other earlier sources (Q and L) which he deemed to be of equal authority and value. From his use of Mark we may judge that in reporting these other sources Luke followed an objective principle, not adding to or subtracting from what he received. The objectivity of his testimony must not be impugned because, for example, he gives to miracle an importance which it does not possess for our modern system of thinking. When we judge Luke as an historian, we must allow for the presence in the historical personality and work of Jesus of elements transcending all normal human experience. His power over the physical as well as the spiritual nature of man we are not in a position to define too narrowly. At the same time we have to remember that the world-view of Luke's age, both in Jewish and in Hellenistic quarters, was saturated with the belief in miracle, so that many events to which we would to-day assign a natural or normal causation were interpreted as direct interpositions of the supernatural. Hence the frank and eager interest with which Luke reports this element in the tradition must not operate to the exclusion of his claim to be within his proper limits a conscientious historical witness. In a number of cases a certain materialistic bias may be detected in his work. We cannot be sure that his source for the baptism or for the resurrection of Jesus contained the expression ' in bodily form ' (iii. 22) or all the details with which the Risen One's appearance is set forth in xxiv. 36–43. But narratives like the raising of the Widow's Son at Nain (vii. 11–16) would come to Luke among his data. Whether such traditions owed anything to an earlier materializing of spiritual events is of course a separate question. The tendency to impart a miraculous colour to this or that event in the primitive tradition was doubtless strong, but it was not ungoverned. Had it been so, there is no explaining why an event like the healing of the Epileptic Child in Mark—compare especially the words, ' And he became as one dead, with the result that most people said, He is dead ' (Mark ix. 26)—should not have been transformed into an actual raising from the dead. The tradition clearly shews a certain reserve in regard to the miraculous, and we may be certain that Luke, open as he was to the idea of the supernatural, did not introduce this element where he did not find it.

In considering the historical value of Luke's record we have further to take account of that primary purpose in writing which he shares with all the evangelists. He is not primarily an historian but an exponent of the ' gospel ' in history. His business is to state his facts, not as an external eye might behold them but weighted with all that passionate significance which they have come to possess for the redeemed society. Thus Jesus is to Luke divine Saviour, Son of God, Lord : not, as the Jewish opponents of the faith might contend, a Galilean visionary deceived by a Messianic dream. The Christ of Luke takes up into himself all the sublime features which the Christ of Mark and the Christ of Q already possessed. Supernatural ' Son of God,' vanquisher of demons, ransomer from death, mighty to save, whom heavenly voices call and whom mysterious divine forces lead onwards to the Cross—this Christ of Mark is at the same time the meek and lowly ' Servant ' whom Q delineates, who incarnates in himself the wisdom and the love of God. The earthly history of Jesus has significance for Luke only as it becomes the vehicle and instrument of this passionate faith in the divine Lord.

In his religious presentation of Jesus and of Christianity Luke has been guided by a selective principle of his own. He has largely passed over those elements in our Lord's teaching which had particular reference to Jewish prepossessions and interests, and he dwells by preference on the universally human aspects of Christ, his grace to the poor and outcast, his forgiving tenderness to the penitent. Typical here is the passage where in the house of Simon Jesus defends the penitent woman who had bathed his feet with her tears :

And, turning towards the woman, Jesus said to Simon, Dost see this woman ?

I came into thy house, thou gavest me no water for my feet : but she with tears has drenched my feet, and wiped them with her hair.

Thou gavest me no kiss : but she, since she came in, has not ceased to lavish kisses on my feet.

Thou didst not anoint my head with oil, but she has anointed my feet with precious unguent.

Wherefore I say to you, Her sins, her many sins, are pardoned : for great has been her love.

But while the gospel is thus adapted to the larger needs of humanity, it nevertheless, by its elimination of the more Jewish aspects of Jesus' teaching, hardly brings out to the full the intensely intellectual as well as spiritual reaction to Judaism in which the religion of the Master was grounded. Luke is less intellectual and less theological than Matthew. His version of the Sermon of Jesus in vi. 20–49 follows Q, and represents perhaps more closely than Matthew's ' Sermon on the Mount ' the actual words which Jesus spoke. But as an indication of the epoch-making character of Jesus' deliverances in Galilee Luke's sermon cannot compare with the great composite discourse which we have from the other evangelist. This observation perhaps touches Luke less as historian than as theologian, though in the writer of a gospel the two functions are not to be disjoined. On the other hand the Lukan gospel is inspired by a spontaneity of feeling, an emotional and at times a lyrical quality to which Matthew is a stranger. In the special matter of the gospel, where Luke's selective instinct was perhaps specially free to move, these qualities are at their maximum.

A gospel which has at the heart of it such parables as the Good Samaritan and the Lost Son, and such incidents as the defence of the woman in Simon's house and the conversion of Zacchaeus, is peculiarly fitted to appeal to the whole human heart of the world. Such incidents and teachings reveal the very core of evangelical religion, and here Luke has done more for us perhaps than all our other evangelists put together. ' The Spirit of the Lord is upon me : for he has consecrated me to preach the gospel to the poor, he has sent me to proclaim release for captives ' (iv. 18). There, and in such words as ' I am among you as a servant ' (xxii. 27) or ' This word of scripture must be fulfilled in me : he was classed among criminals ' (xxii. 37), the Lukan keynote is struck. Yet curiously enough this gospel which so closely identifies Jesus with the saving of sinful humanity omits, as it happens, all direct reference to the theological necessity of his Death. Luke's original narrative of the Supper is limited, as we shall see in the commentary to the words xxii. 17–19a. Neither cup nor bread is there interpreted as pointing to a sacrifice made or to a covenant established by the Redeemer's blood. Luke also has no parallel to the great word : ' The Son of Man came not to be served but to serve, and to give his life as a ransom for many ' (Mark x. 45). Such omissions, doubtless accidental, in their own way reveal that theological interests were not paramount in the mind of Luke. If he was truly a companion and friend of Paul, he shews but little distinctive appreciation of the profounder ideas of that apostle. His leaning is towards the emotional and practical aspects of religion, towards the elements of feeling and action.

We have still to speak of one other aspect of Luke's selective instinct as applied to his material, viz. his marked social sympathies. An intense interest in the humbler members of society and a certain severity towards wealth and its possessors characterize many sections peculiar to his gospel. The sentiment is revealed variously in the Song of Mary (i. 51–53), in the preaching of John (iii. 11–13), in the opening words of the Saviour's discourse at Nazareth (iv. 18–19), in the Lukan form of the Beatitudes and in the Woes attached thereto (vi. 20–26), in the parables of the Rich Man's Death and of Dives and Lazarus (xii. 13–21, xvi. 19–31), and in various words and admonitions of Jesus (xii. 33, xiv. 12–14, xvi. 9, 14–15). It is not for a moment suggested that the material in question was not derived

by Luke from Jewish-Christian sources inspired by the sentiment, so characteristic of Jewish pietism, that the ' rich ' are
the godless and the ' poor ' the faithful and good. Such uses of
the terms poor and rich are frequent in the Psalter and in the
post-canonical anthology of religious pieces which is known as
the Psalms of Solomon. But with all allowance for sources,
whether oral or written, we may assume that special sympathies
of the evangelist co-operated to give the social element in
Christ's teaching the remarkable prominence which it has received in this gospel.

It seems to the present writer that Luke has here fallen under
the spell of the Mother-church of Jerusalem and of the particular
Christian tradition which he found in that centre. The early
chapters of Acts reveal the ardour of his sympathy for the suffering ' saints ' in Judea. And it is just possible that Luke has
taken over the language of these Christians without sufficiently
marking the native shades of their thought. For in Palestine
the terms ' poor ' and ' rich ' had not only an economic but a
religious import. The poor are the faithful who in their devotion
to God suffer human injustice and the loss of earthly goods.
Wealth on the other hand implies the disregard of both God and
man. In both cases the conditions of Oriental life are presupposed, for Oriental life knew little of real justice. Read in
this way, the Beatitudes and the parable of the Rich Man and
Lazarus no longer necessarily yield the idea that poverty *per se*
gives entrance to the Kingdom of God and that wealth *per se*
excludes. Luke has not so carefully guarded his language as
Matthew, but his meaning is not really very different. The
fact that in Acts his references to the renunciation of property
are all connected with the church of Jerusalem shews that an
intense appreciation of the special history of that church rather
than a doctrinaire idea of the uses of wealth in general explains
the special features of the social teaching of his gospel. On the
other hand, we must not forget that solemn warnings of the perils
of riches and an ardent espousal of the cause of the poor are
authentic and primordial features of the Master's teaching.
Jesus renounced possessions, and going up to Jerusalem called
on the Twelve and on all who would follow him to do the same
(Mark viii. 34–37, x. 17–31, Luke ix. 57–58, xii. 33–34, xiv. 33,
etc.). He made his last appeal to Israel as one divested of every
earthly interest. Luke has specially underlined the Master's

example and teaching at this point, and thereby revealed an interesting aspect of his own human sympathies.

We need not linger over other special features of Luke's gospel, such as its emphasis on prayer (iii. 21, vi. 12, ix. 18, 29, xi. 1, 5–8, xviii. 1–8, xxii. 31–32), its inculcation of humility and faith (xviii. 9–14), its inclusion of Gentiles in God's eternal purpose of salvation (ii. 29–32, iii. 6, iv. 25–28, xxiv. 47). Here, as everywhere else, in the endeavour to give to Theophilus and to the world an ordered statement of the Christian testimony to Jesus, Luke has cast his net wide, and produced a gospel the most voluminous and varied, the most vibrant and sympathetic, the most beautiful and sweetly reasonable of all that we possess.

IV. The Author of the Gospel

Hitherto in referring to the gospel and to its author we have used without prejudice the traditional name of Luke. It is now necessary to consider the evidence on which this traditional ascription rests. Here little or no help is to be obtained from the Gospel itself. Only once is the writer's personality revealed, and that is where, stepping for a moment before the curtain, he states in the Prologue the motive with which he takes up the pen.

From this statement, however, it would appear that the evangelist was not a personal witness of the life of Jesus. On the other hand he claims (1) to have been in touch with such witnesses, (2) to have at command or to know the work of predecessors in the art of gospel-writing, and (3) to have made a thorough personal study of the facts. Such evidence, indirect as it is, appreciably clears the ground for the discussion of the authorship question.

The tradition that the evangelist was Luke, a companion of Paul, mentioned in Colossians iv. 14, Philemon 24, and 2 Timothy iv. 11, goes back to the second century. While not all second-century ascriptions of this kind can be relied upon, strong grounds exist for regarding this particular tradition as trustworthy, all the more so because the man to whom it assigns the gospel was not otherwise a prominent figure in the apostolic church. The authorship of the work by a member of an apostle's staff tallies sufficiently with the Prologue's statement as to the writer's relation to men and things, but there exist preciser grounds for regarding the tradition as sound.

These grounds are found largely in conclusions drawn from certain sections of Acts where the writer, who must in any case by the evidence of language and style be identified with the author of the gospel, uses the first personal pronoun plural ' we,' thereby seeming to indicate that he was at certain times an associate of Paul and a witness of events (Acts xvi. 10–17, xx. 5–15, xxi. 1–18, xxvii. 1–xxviii. 16). It is scarcely credible that if he did not himself witness the events in question, but merely derived them from the diary or travel-notes of another person, he would have failed to delete the personal pronoun of his source. The argument does not of course prove that the witness in these passages was Luke, but the proximity in which Luke stood to Paul at other times in the apostle's career (Colossians iv. 14, etc.) renders it probable enough that ' the beloved physician,' a Gentile by birth, was indeed the unnamed companion of the ' We-sections,' and in any case some deference is due to the ancient tradition that he was so. The arguments by which the evidence for and against the tradition is finally balanced cannot be presented here, but are briefly stated in Appendix I. There it is shewn that while the Lukan authorship of Acts and, by implication, of the gospel cannot be regarded as absolutely proved, it claims a greater probability than attaches to any other hypothesis, and may be reasonably assumed.

The identification of the evangelist with Luke, the companion of Paul, makes it possible to form some fairly accurate conception of his experience and, in particular, of his opportunities of obtaining knowledge of ' the established facts ' of Christianity. Apart from Paul, he had in A.D. 50 the company for a time of the Jewish-Christian Silvanus (Silas), who was excellently qualified to speak of the early days of the Jerusalem church (Acts xvi. 10 f.; cf. xv. 22, 27, 32, 40). Moreover, he spent the years A.D. 57–59 in Palestine, chiefly at Jerusalem and Caesarea, and his opportunities of investigating not merely the early history of the Church but the current traditions of the Saviour's life would be abundant. In Jerusalem he was present with Paul at interviews with James, the Lord's brother, and with the presbyters of the Church (Acts xxi. 17–18). At Caesarea he lodged in the apostle's company at the house of Philip the evangelist (Acts xxi. 8–9), where also he met Agabus the prophet from Judea. Such information is valuable as shewing how and where Luke may have obtained much of the matter incorporated in his gospel. At another period, either at Ephesus or at Rome, Luke formed one of the same circle with the Jerusalem Christian John Mark (Colossians iv. 10, 14, Philemon 24), the follower and friend of Peter and Paul, to whom our Second Gospel is traditionally ascribed. It harmonizes with the relations so established that Luke should at a later date supplement his own researches from the narrative of his friend.

What more can be made out regarding the evangelist ?

According to a reading occurring in certain ancient authorities for Acts xi. 27, the personal contact of the evangelist with Christianity might be traced back to Antioch, about the year A.D. 46. The reading is : ' In those days prophets came down from Jerusalem to Antioch. And there was great exultation : and *when we had assembled*, one of them, by name Agabus, spoke, etc.' The italicized words would, if genuine, give us a ' We-passage ' of earlier date than any of those above enumerated. But the reading is doubtful. We cannot build securely on such foundations.

Nevertheless, the Antiochian extraction of Luke may be regarded as highly probable. Much of the early history of Acts revolves round the church of Antioch, and it will be noticed that from the moment that Antioch is first mentioned, Luke's narrative acquires a new fullness and circumstantiality. He mentions Antioch some thirteen times, and such references as Acts xi. 19–27 and xiii. 1 f. are striking in their wealth of detail. The earliest explicit testimony to Luke's Antiochian origin occurs, however, in Eusebius and in Jerome. Eusebius describes him as ' an Antiochian by birth, a physician by profession.' Jerome writes : ' Luke the physician, by birth a Syrian of Antioch, was the third (of the evangelists) to compose a volume.' Such evidence is meagre, and shews no source independent of the New Testament. As for the place where the gospel was composed, some MSS. have a footnote assigning it to Rome. Others state that it was written at Alexandria. Jerome, however, and the document known as the Monarchian Prologue to Luke connect it with ' the parts of Achaea,' i.e. with some district of Greece. The evidence is too indistinct for definite conclusions in these matters. Enough that a Gentile Christian was believed to have written the gospel and to have written it for the Gentile Christian world.

INTRODUCTION

Among works referred to or quoted by the authors' names in the present Commentary the following should be mentioned :

Easton, B. S. : *The Gospel According to St. Luke* (1926).

Klostermann, E. : *Das Lukasevangelium* (1919).

Montefiore, C. G. : *The Synoptic Gospels*, 2 vols. (1927).

Zahn, Th. : *Das Evangelium des Lukas* (1920).

Strack-Billerbeck : *Kommentar zum Neuen Testament*, by H. L. Strack and P. Billerbeck (1922, 1924, etc.).

Bultmann, R. : *Die Geschichte der synoptischen Tradition* (1921).

Cadbury, H. J. : *The Making of Luke-Acts* (1927).

Foakes-Jackson and Lake : *The Beginnings of Christianity*, ed. by F. J. Foakes-Jackson and Kirsopp Lake, 3 vols. (1920, 1922, etc.).

Harnack, Ad. von : *Luke the Physician* (1907), *The Acts of the Apostles* (1908), etc.

Ramsay, Sir W. M. : *Was Christ Born at Bethlehem ?* (1898), etc.

Robinson, T. H. : *The Gospel of Matthew* (Moffatt Commentary, 1928).

Streeter, B. H. : *The Four Gospels* (1924).

Taylor, V. : *Behind the Third Gospel* (1926).

Smith, Sir G. A. : *Historical Geography of the Holy Land* (1894).

Berguer, G. : *Some Aspects of the Life of Jesus* (1923).

Case, S. J. : *Jesus : A New Biography* (1927).

Dalman, G. : *Jesus-Jeshua : Studies in the Gospels* (1929).

Denney, J. : *Jesus and the Gospel* (1908).

Holtzmann, O. : *The Life of Jesus* (1904).

Klausner, J. : *Jesus of Nazareth* (1925).

Schürer, E. : *The Jewish People in the Time of Jesus Christ* (English translation in 5 vols., 1894, etc.).

Box, G. H. : *The Ezra-Apocalypse* (1912). A Study of Chapters 3–14 of 2 Esdras.

Charles, R. H. : *The Book of Enoch* (1912).

Taylor, C. : *Sayings of the Jewish Fathers* (1897).

THE GOSPEL OF LUKE

THE AUTHOR'S PROLOGUE (i. 1-4)

Inasmuch as a number of writers have essayed to draw up a 1
narrative of the established facts in our religion exactly as 2
these have been handed down to us by the original eyewitnesses who were in the service of the Gospel Message, and 3
inasmuch as I have gone carefully over them all myself from
the very beginning, I have decided, O Theophilus, to write 4
them out in order for your excellency, to let you know the
solid truth of what you have been taught.

LUKE'S exordium is unique in the Gospel-literature, since nowhere else does an evangelist speak to us in the first person or
declare the nature of his aims. The disclosure made with regard
to the author's sources of knowledge and to the methods of his
work is important, and has received attention in the Introduction
to the present work. In prefixing a dedication to his book the
evangelist follows a fashion of his day. Close parallels can be
cited from Josephus and other historians, and from Greek medical
writers such as Dioscorides.

The evangelist's allusion to **a number of writers** as having
already made a start with the literary codification of the gospel-
tradition is in no sense disparaging. There is no suggestion that
these writers had gone to work with inadequate knowledge or,
as Origen inferred, 'without the grace of the Holy Spirit.'
Rather does Luke find in the admitted success of these previous
experiments an incentive and omen of good augury for a fresh
venture of his own. If, selecting his terms carefully, he speaks
of his predecessors—who must in any case have included Mark—
as having **essayed to draw up a narrative**, it is because of the
difficulties which inevitably beset the first efforts to reduce to
literary shape the floating materials of the oral tradition. This
was no easy task when, as so often happened, the order or the
sense of the incidents and sayings composing the tradition had
been forgotten or obscured. Moreover, it was a daring thing,

and at first somewhat of an innovation to propose to substitute writings for the spoken word on which the Church had hitherto depended. Christians clung to the living word, and time was necessary to prove the superiority of the written document. Nevertheless, Luke considers that where other writers have led the way he need not hesitate to follow.

The subject handled in the earlier gospels was the **established facts** of the Christian religion as recorded in the tradition of the Church. These would include the call of Jesus as Messiah, his ministry, teaching, miracles, death, and resurrection. The authority to which everything was referred was the testimony of **original eyewitnesses who were in the service of the Gospel Message**, and this would extend normally from the baptism of Jesus to the day when he was taken up (Acts i. 21). It is clear that, so far as Luke's knowledge went, no apostle or original eyewitness had himself committed anything to writing. But that all who had written had founded upon apostolic testimony is definitely asserted, and is corroborated by the second-century tradition that Mark derived his material from the preaching of Peter (Eusebius, *History*, iii. 39).

Luke's purpose in publishing a Gospel of his own now follows. He has **gone carefully over** the facts,[1] and is in a position to give Theophilus a revised and consecutive narrative. What his special opportunities of knowing the truth were we have considered in the Introduction, Sect. IV. Three points are here made : (1) Luke has traced the entire course of authentic tradition regarding the Saviour ; (2) he has recorded it **from the beginning,** i.e. from the Saviour's birth, thus going a stage farther back than Mark, who started with Jesus' baptism ; (3) he has aimed **at order** or consecutive narration in place of the haphazard presentation of facts which was only too common in that age. He may have known from private sources that the versions of Christian history which had previously reached Theophilus left something to be desired.

The word **Theophilus** means ' dear to God,' and may or may not be the actual name of the person to whom the work is dedicated. The form of address, **your excellency,** points to official rank, and suggests that Theophilus held procuratorial

---

[1] Professor Milligan, in his *Vocabulary of the Greek Testament*, takes Luke's expression here to mean that he has acquired such familiarity with the facts that his witness is practically contemporary witness.

or other office in some province of the Empire. That he was a professing Christian is unlikely, since in that case Luke would have exchanged the honorific style of ' your excellency ' for the Christian appellation of ' beloved ' or ' brother.' We may think of Theophilus, however, as belonging to some cultured and earnest circle of Gentile ' God-fearers ' who were interested in Christianity, and to whom the evangelist wished to present that religion in the fullest, clearest light, and with the hope of thus commending it to official toleration and respect (Introd., Sect. III). Amid much prejudice and ignorance there was a genuine desire in such circles for solid truth in the matter of religion, in this case for reliable evidence that the Jesus of whom the Christians spoke was ' no mere Jewish Messiah, but a World-Saviour, the founder of a world-religion.' Christianity was on its trial, and competing with other religions for a hearing both in the Jewish and in the Gentile worlds. Professor C. C. J. Webb says in fact of the contemporary age : ' We have reached a period in the history of philosophy in which men came to demand of philosophy that it should provide them with a religion, or, if it could not do this, should stand aside, and let religion provide them with a philosophy ' (*History of Philosophy*, p. 78).

I. THE BEGINNINGS (i. 5-ii. 52)

In accordance with his purpose to set out the facts ' from the beginning,' Luke opens his gospel with narratives of the births of Jesus (i. 26-56, ii. 1-40) and of his forerunner John (i. 5-25, 57-80). As it is not his method in using sources to supply connectives between events where his authorities do not give them (Introd., page xv), we infer from his interweaving of the two narratives, that in the tradition upon which he drew the births of John and Jesus were already associated. In other words, Luke's authority for these narratives was *Christian*. While the John-narrative may owe something to beliefs current among the followers of that prophet, Luke found it already part of a Christian tradition relating to Jesus, and this tradition he has taken as a basis for chaps. i.-ii.

The origin of the birth-narratives is enveloped in an obscurity which can never be wholly penetrated. In Appendix II the character of Luke's source is briefly examined, and the view taken that the evangelist drew upon Judean traditions which had consolidated in the quiet years preceding the Roman war of A.D. 66–70. To the shaping of these traditions various factors, including the study of Old Testament prophecy and the poetic-creative impulse which lay at the heart of early Christianity, have freely contributed. From an historical point of view the primary value of the narratives lies in their spontaneous testimony to the transcendent place belonging to the personality of the Redeemer in primitive faith and worship. Christ, who came to make men by a new birth sons of God, is himself not only from God but of the very nature of God. From a literary point of view the same narratives serve to present Christianity as the crowning phase of the Jewish religion. The Messiah comes as God's answer to the faith and expectation of His saints (i. 13, 30, 54–55, 68–75 ; ii. 26, 29–32, etc.).

One other observation it is proper to make at this stage. It was stated in the Introduction that the evangelical tradition presents its facts not as a dispassionate external observer might describe them but with all that added weight of passionate religious significance which they have come to possess for the faith of Christian men. This consideration is not out of place at the approach to narratives which, herein largely differing from the rest of the evangelical history, record visitations of angels, predictions of coming events, and songs of heavenly choirs. A mode of narration which involves such elements can scarcely be judged free of the instinct of religious minds to clothe in poetic form the truths in which they believe and which they are out to proclaim to the world. But from the imaginative symbolism of the narrative we will necessarily distinguish the fundamental religious realities from which the representation proceeds. The appearing of angels and the singing of the heavenly host over the Judean fields conceivably represent a poetic-religious form of narrative which takes over and continues the traditional religious symbolism of the Old Testament. That John came from God to turn His nation to righteousness and that God was in Christ reconciling the world to Himself are experienced realities of the Christian faith without which there is no gospel to proclaim. Bearing this in mind, and recollecting always that the faith which inspires the entire representation is a faith created and sustained by Christ himself, we need not shrink from the demand at times to distinguish form and substance in these narratives. The distinction will at any rate be so far valid as

4

to permit of the primary emphasis being laid less on the external
and pictorial symbolism of the story than on the deeply experienced religious values from which the symbolism starts.

i. 5-25 : The Annunciation to Zechariah

In the days of Herod king of Judaea there was a priest called 5
   Zechariah, who belonged to the division of Abijah ; he had
   a wife who belonged to the daughters of Aaron, and her
   name was Elizabeth. They were both just in the sight of 6
   God, blameless in their obedience to all the commands and
   regulations of God ; but they had no child, for Elizabeth was 7
   barren. Both of them were advanced in years.

Now while he was officiating before God in the due course of his 8
   division, it fell to him by lot, as was the custom of the priest- 9
   hood, to enter the sanctuary of the Lord and burn incense,
   the mass of the people all remaining in prayer outside at the 10
   hour of incense. And an angel of the Lord appeared to him, 11
   standing on the right side of the altar of incense. When
   Zechariah saw him he was troubled, and fear fell on him ; 12
   but the angel said to him, ' Fear not, Zechariah, your prayer 13
   has been heard ; your wife Elizabeth will bear a son to you,
   and you must call his name John.

    It will be joy and gladness for you,   14
      and many will rejoice over his birth :
    for he shall be great in the sight of the Lord,   15
    he will drink neither wine nor strong drink,
    he will be filled with the holy Spirit from his very birth ;
    he will turn many of the sons of Israel to the Lord their God, 16
    he will go in front of Him with the spirit and power *of Eliah* 17
      to turn the hearts of fathers to their children,
    turning the disobedient to the wisdom of the just,
    to make a people ready and prepared for the Lord.'

Zechariah said to the angel, ' But how am I to be sure of this ? 18
   I am an old man myself and my wife is advanced in years.'
   The angel replied, ' I am Gabriel, I stand before God ; I have
   been sent to speak to you and to tell you this good news. But 19
   you will be silent and unable to speak till the day this happens, 20
   because you have not believed what I told you ; it will be
   accomplished, for all that, in due time.'

Now the people were waiting for Zechariah and wondering that 21

22   he stayed so long inside the sanctuary. When he did come
out he could not speak to them, so they realized that he had
seen a vision in the sanctuary ; he made signs to them and
23   remained dumb. Then, after his term of service had elapsed,
he went home.
24 After those days his wife Elizabeth conceived ; and for five months
25   she concealed herself. 'The Lord has done this for me,' she
said, 'he has now deigned to remove my reproach among men.'

The opening section of the Gospel sets the dawn of Christianity
in impressive contrast to contemporary political conditions.
John, the morning-star of the new era, appears just when the
reign of Herod, king of Judea from 37 to 4 B.C., is setting towards
its tragic and hopeless close. In the priest Zechariah and his
wife Elizabeth we have a bright counterfoil to the general spirit
of the age. The purest Jewish piety has kept its flame alive in
their consecrated and blameless walk with God. Childless, however, and far advanced in years, they dream not what joy awaits
them and the whole nation through the gift of God in John.
The narrative-form which the tradition employs—visions of
angels are in Jewish literature ascribed to saints who like Simon
the Just lived close to God—indicates the Christian consciousness
of a divine purpose preceding and finding fulfilment in John.
Zechariah is engaged in the service of the altar when the vision
comes. The division of Abijah, to which he belongs, is the
eighth of the twenty-four classes in which the priests were listed
for service (1 Chronicles xxiv.). The divisions served in the
temple by turns, the duties of the individual ministrant being
assigned to him by lot. Incense (Exodus xxx. 7–8) was an
invariable accompaniment of every morning and evening sacrifice. The ascending smoke symbolized the offering of the
nation's devotion, and to the assembled worshippers in the
outer court of Israel it served as a call to prayer.

Thus ministering at the altar, Zechariah receives in answer to
prayer the supernatural promise—here the poetic-religious form
of the narrative comes clearly to expression—of a son whose
birth will bring gladness to Israel and will prelude the Messianic
era. The representation is from the Christian standpoint where
John is seen as the Lord's messenger of whom prophecy had
spoken, and for whom Israel was waiting : compare Malachi iii.
1, iv. 5 : 'Behold, I will send you Elijah before the great and

terrible day of Jehovah come.' For the statement, virtually identifying John with the Nazirites, that **he will drink neither wine nor strong drink,** see Numbers vi. 1–8. Asceticism was a pronounced feature of John's historical character and left an impress on all his work. The other prediction that **he will be filled with the holy Spirit** relates to the unique sanctity of John and to the power with which he swayed the hearts of men. His function, for which as the Lord's messenger he receives **the spirit and power of Elijah,** is to inaugurate the Great Repentance of Israel, and since the foundation of religious life in Israel is the home, this task takes the form (Malachi iv. 6) that he will **turn the hearts of fathers to their children,** i.e. unify and consolidate Israel again upon the basis of its religious hope, redirect a discordant nation to the vision of the Messianic future, and so create a spiritually alert and expectant nation, **a people ready and prepared for the Lord.**

The same poetic-creative impulse which, working upon the achieved historical results of John's career as seen from the Christian standpoint, has freely moulded the above narrative, operates also in the sequel in which Zechariah's bedazed incredulity is said to produce a state of aphasia lasting till John is born (cf. Psalm xxxix. 9 f.). Is there any suggestion here that the coming of John first silenced and then awoke to blessing and praise those saints in Israel who said that the Lord no longer visited his people by messenger or prophet? On the Jewish belief in angels of the Presence see Tobit xii. 15 and Enoch xx. 1–8, where the names of the seven are given as Uriel, Raphael, Raguel, Michael, Saraqael, Gabriel, and Remiel. To **Gabriel** belonged special functions in revelation, Daniel viii. 16, ix. 21.

i. 26–38 : THE ANNUNCIATION TO THE VIRGIN MARY

In the sixth month the angel Gabriel was sent by God to a town 26 in Galilee called Nazaret, to a maiden who was betrothed to 27 a man called Joseph, belonging to the house of David. The maiden's name was Mary. The angel went in and said to 28 her, 'Hail, O favoured one ! the Lord be with you ! ' At 29 this she was startled ; she thought to herself, whatever can this greeting mean ? But the angel said to her, ' Fear not, 30 Mary, you have found favour with God. You are to conceive 31 and bear a son, and you must call his name Jesus.

32 ' He will be great, he will be called the Son of the Most High,
and the Lord God will give him *the throne of David* his father ;
33 *he will reign* over the house of Jacob *for ever,*
and to his reign there will be no end.'
34 ' How can this be ? ' said Mary to the angel, ' I have no husband.'
35   The angel answered her, ' The holy Spirit will come upon
you, the power of the Most High will overshadow you ;
36   hence what is born *will be called holy*, Son of God. Look,
there is your kinswoman Elizabeth ! Even she has conceived a son in her old age, and she who was called barren
37   is now in her sixth month ; for *with God nothing is ever*
38   *impossible.'* Mary said, ' I am here to serve the Lord. Let
it be as you have said.' Then the angel went away.

The narrative now passes to the annunciation of a greater
birth, and here too the promise comes through a divine *nuncio*
or messenger.   According to Luke's source, Nazaret is the home
of Joseph and Mary.   The migration to Bethlehem is due to
exceptional causes (ii. 1–5).   The statement that Mary was
betrothed to Joseph, a man belonging to the house of David,
establishes the necessary connexion between the birth of Jesus
and the Messianic hopes attaching to the royal line (2 Samuel
vii. 12 f., Psalm lxxxix. 29), and has sometimes been supposed
to indicate that in the Judean source of Luke's narrative Joseph
was not the putative but the actual father of Jesus.   It is a
different interpretation, however, which Luke in accordance
with the higher thought of his time puts upon the event.   Jesus
is born not of a human father but by the supernatural operation
of the holy Spirit.   This thought does not, however, appear
expressly until ver. 34.   In ver. 28 the angelic salutation,
' Hail, O favoured one ! the Lord be with you ! ' implies simply
the singular grace bestowed on Mary in that she is selected among
the daughters of Israel to become the Mother of the promised
Messiah, a purpose which to her startled mind is further defined
in the words, recalling Isaiah vii. 14, ' You are to conceive and
bear a son, and you must call his name Jesus.'   This prophecy,
while it claims for the Messiah's birth the character of a divinely
purposed event, does not as yet exclude the fulfilment of the
event in the natural course through marriage.   Note that
nothing said of Mary here or elsewhere supports the patristic
assumption that she as well as Joseph was of Davidic descent.

Rather does ver. 36 suggest that like Elizabeth she came of a Levitical line.

The promises in vers. 32-33 that Jesus will be great and **will be called the Son of the Most High**, and that **the Lord God will give him the throne of David his father**, constitute an admirable summation of the thoughts and hopes called up in simple Jewish minds at the mention of the Messiah. There was in Judaism another line of Messianic thought which started not from the promise to David but from the prophecy in Daniel vii. 13 f. of one ' like a son of man ' who would come with the clouds of heaven, and to whom the Ancient of Days would give an ever-lasting kingdom. As we shall later see, this more transcendent conception of the Messiah's person was constantly before the mind of Jesus. But in popular Jewish and Jewish-Christian circles the Messianic hope continued to retain an anchor in the promise made to David's line. In the present passage **Son of the Most High** involves as yet no physical conception of the Messiah's relation to God, but presents him simply as supreme object of the divine love and favour. The promise that **the Lord God will give him the throne of David his father**, and will uphold his reign everlastingly, might conceivably be spoken of one who connected with the house of David merely in the natural way. But the throne and the reign here spoken of must be understood spiritually. Jesus was not king of Israel in the political sense, and the Jewish hope sometimes conceived the Davidic Messiah as reigning only for a limited term, after which a new supernatural era—the Kingdom of God—would replace the present world.

In vers. 34-35 the prediction enters on a higher phase. A Jewish maiden, apprised that she would become the mother of the Messiah, would naturally think of this destiny as to be ful-filled through marriage, and Mary's marriage was not yet actual. But it is now explained that God's purpose is immediate, and comes about not by human laws or processes but through the power of the holy Spirit. Hence what is **born of Mary will be called holy, Son of God**. It is obvious that in this context ' Son of God ' is to be explained no longer in a purely spiritual but in a physical or hyperphysical sense. Jesus is Son of God because a new constitutive principle, the creative energy of God, enters into and determines his nature before he is born. And for sign or proof of the supernatural power of God here spoken of, Mary is pointed to the case of Elizabeth, to whom also, though in a

9

different way, it has been shewn that **nothing is ever impossible
with God.** Hence the submission of faith expressed in the assent
of the *ancilla Domini*, the theme of so much later art and poetry,
' **I am here to serve the Lord. Let it be as you have said.** '

Such is Luke's explanation of the mystery of the Saviour's
personality. The entrance of Christ into history involves the
setting aside of the ordinary laws of generation and an independent operation of the Creative Spirit. Such an idea would not
be strange to the Greek world, for which Luke was writing. One
of the greatest of Greek literary men of the age says expressly
that ' it is not impossible for the spirit of God . . . to engender
certain beginnings of birth ' (Plutarch, *Numa*, 4), and certainly
Luke's explanation is in keeping with the belief prevalent in the
Christian circles in which he moved. But some uncertainty
exists as to whether the Virgin-birth was asserted in the Judean
source from which the rest of the birth-narratives is derived. It
will be observed that, except for vers. 34–35 and the phrase ' as
people supposed ' in iii. 23, Joseph appears without prejudice
as one of the parents of Jesus (ii. 27, 33, 41, 43, 48). Doubtless
the source might so speak of him without implying that he was
actually the father of Jesus. But many scholars consider that
vers. 34–35, or at anyrate the words **I have no husband** in 34b,
represent an overlaying of the idea in the source by another idea
which was given to Luke by the environing medium of thought in
which he lived. On this view : (1) the source spoke of a divinely
promised birth but not yet of a Virgin-birth, and (2) Mary's perplexity in 34a and in 36–37 was inspired purely by the incredible
wonder that the Messiah should be born of her. But, even so,
the Judean source would not cease to be a witness to the supernatural character of the birth of Jesus. Jesus would still be more
than the product of an historical development and more than the
culmination of an ethical process in humanity. Jesus comes from
God in fulfilment of the agelong promise of redemption, and
Luke's addition, if it be an addition, touches only the mode in
which, according to the presuppositions of an age in which the
spiritual was commonly defined in physical or supraphysical
terms, the entrance of Jesus into history was rendered possible.

i. 39–56 : THE VISIT OF MARY TO ELIZABETH

39 In those days Mary started with haste for the hill-country, for a
40   town of Judah ; she entered the house of Zechariah and

saluted Elizabeth, and when Elizabeth heard the salutation 41
of Mary, the babe leapt in her womb. Then Elizabeth was
filled with the holy Spirit ; she called out with a loud cry, 42
' Blessed among women are you, and blessed is the fruit of
your womb !
What have I done to have the mother of my Lord come to me ? 43
Why, as soon as the sound of your salutation reached my ears, 44
the babe leapt for joy within my womb. And blessed is she 45
who believed that the Lord's words to her would be fulfilled.'
Then Mary said   46

> ' *My soul* magnifies *the Lord,*
> my spirit *has joy in God my Saviour :*   47
> for *he has considered the humiliation of his servant.*   48
> From this time forth all generations will call me blessed,
> for He who is Mighty has done great things for me.   49
> *His name is holy,*
> *his mercy is on generation after generation,*   50
> *for those who reverence him.*
> He has done a deed of might *with his arm,*   51
> *he has scattered the proud* with their purposes,
> *princes he has dethroned* and *the poor he has uplifted,*   52
> *he has satisfied the hungry with good things* and *sent the* 53
> *rich away empty.*
> *He has succoured his servant Israel,*   54
> *mindful of his mercy—*
> *as he promised our fathers,*   55
> *to have mercy on Abraham and his offspring* for ever.'

Mary stayed with her about three months and then returned 56
home.

The visit of Mary to Elizabeth follows upon the sign given
to her in ver. 36. The visit enables the narrator to bring out the
pre-existing harmony of divine events constituted by the births
of John and Jesus. The unborn child of Elizabeth salutes the
Mother of the Messiah, and Elizabeth herself is supernaturally
inspired to utter the greeting in vers. 42–45. Here again we
have to recognize an idealizing interpretation of history. In the
actual order of events John did not recognize the Messiahship
of Jesus until the close of his own career (Matthew xi. 2–3 ;
Luke vii. 18–19), or, according to another tradition, until the
day of Jesus' baptism (Matthew iii. 14 ; John i. 32–34). Never-

theless, in the eternal order a prenatal harmony is seen to govern the relation of the two personalities, and it is the purpose of the present narrative to bring this harmony out.

The hymn, known from its opening word in the Latin Vulgate as the *Magnificat*, follows upon the verification of the sign given to Mary, and celebrates in an exalted poetic strain the now certain coming of the Messiah. A few Western MSS. and authorities assign the psalm to Elizabeth, but the textual support for the reading **And Mary said** is better, and such a prediction as ' **From this time forth all generations will call me blessed** ' obviously refers to the Virgin herself. ' **My soul magnifies the Lord,** ' etc. The *Magnificat* is based in large part on the Song of Hannah in 1 Samuel i. 11, ii. 1–10. As God is magnified or glorified wherever His grace is seen and acknowledged, so the singer dwells on the divine condescension in granting the Messiah to be born of the lowly Jewish maiden, thus rendering her name for ever blessed, and for ever proving the saving interest of God in His people. (For the expression **my Saviour** applied to God compare Psalm xxiv. 5, xxv. 5.) In vers. 51–55 the Messianic hopes of the purest elements in Judaic society break into flame. Israel has lain crushed under the foreign despotism of Rome, but will be brought by the Messiah into the liberty of the Kingdom of God. The **proud**, the **rich**, the **princes** are, according to the Jewish conception, those who oppose themselves to God. The **humble**, the **poor**, the **hungry** are the objects of His compassion and righteous vindication. Hence redemption is envisaged as a drastic revolution by which the mighty are dethroned, the rich dispossessed, and the proud humiliated. This language, though it is not to be taken literally but in a spiritual sense, shews how intimately in Judaic Christianity the coming of Christ still stirred the chords of national hope.

As to the origin of the hymn, it has sometimes been proposed to regard it with its companion-piece, the *Benedictus*, as a free composition of the evangelist. But it is more likely that Luke found it in his source. Possibly a Jewish Messianic psalm, founded on the Song of Hannah, constituted its basis. It may, however, be a purely Christian creation celebrating, by aid of Hannah's words, the community's sense that ' To us a Child has been born, to us a Son has been given ' (Isaiah ix. 6). In either case, the ascription of the hymn to the Mother of our Lord would have a distinct literary fitness.

i. 57–80 : THE BIRTH OF JOHN

Now the time for Elizabeth's delivery had elapsed, and she gave 57
birth to a son.   When her neighbours and kinsfolk heard of 58
the Lord's great mercy to her they rejoiced with her, and on 59
the eighth day came to circumcise the child.   They were
going to call it by the name of its father Zechariah, but the 60
mother told them, ' No, the child is to be called John.'   They 61
said to her, ' None of your family is called by that name.'
Then they made signs to the father, to find out what he wanted 62
the child to be called, and he asked for a writing-tablet and 63
wrote down, ' His name is John,' to the astonishment of all.
Instantly his mouth was opened, his tongue loosed, and he 64
spoke out blessing God.   Then fear fell on all their neighbours, 65
and all these events were talked of through the whole of the
hill-country of Judaea.   All who heard of it bore it in mind ; 66
they said, ' Whatever will this child become ? '   For the
hand of the Lord was indeed with him.

And Zechariah his father was filled with the holy Spirit ; he 67
prophesied in these words,

' *Blessed be the Lord the God of Israel*,   68
     for he has cared *for his people* and wrought them *re-*
     demption ;

he *has raised up a strong* saviour for us   69
     in the house of his servant David—

as he promised of old by the lips of his prophets—   70
     to save us from our foes and from the hand of all *who hate* 71
     us,

to deal mercifully with our fathers   72
     and *to be mindful of his* holy *covenant*,

of the oath he swore to Abraham our father,   73
     that freed from fear and from the hand of our foes   74

we should worship him in holiness and uprightness   75
     all our days within his presence.

And you, my child, shall be called a prophet of the Most 76
     High ;

for you shall go *in front of the Lord to make his ways ready*,

to bring his people the knowledge of salvation   77
     through the remission of their sins—

by the tender mercy of our God,   78
     who will make the Dawn visit us from on high,

79 *to shine on those who sit in darkness and in the shadow of death,*
to guide our steps into the way of peace.'
80 And the child grew, he became strong in the Spirit and remained
in the desert till the day when he made his appearance before
Israel.

A prominent motive here is to re-emphasize the religious
significance of the name, meaning ' Jehovah is gracious,' which
John receives at birth. This name, already communicated to
Zechariah (i. 13), and now discerned and pressed by Elizabeth
despite the opposition of kinsfolk and friends, is finally decided
by appeal to Zechariah, who recovers his speech the same instant.
The circumcision of the child follows on the eighth day (cf.
Genesis xvii. 12). In ver. 65 there occurs a statement which is
of great interest as revealing the region in which these birth-
traditions were first diffused. These events were talked of through
the whole of the hill-country of Judaea, the dwellers in which had
been awestruck by the birth and by the visible signs of grace
which attended the child. Ver. 66 refers to the youth and not
merely to the birth of John. The extraordinary religious
endowments of the child—the hand of the Lord was indeed with
him—portended from the start an exceptional destiny. Hence
Zechariah is moved to utter the prophetic psalm of thanksgiving
(vers. 68–79), which from its opening word in the Latin Vulgate
we call the *Benedictus*.

The *Benedictus* starts with praise to the God of Israel for
sending redemption to His people through a strong Saviour, the
Messiah (vers. 68–69). This Saviour arises in the house of David,
and his historic task is conceived as national deliverance in
terms of the oath which God swore to Abraham (vers. 72–73).
With this prospect of national deliverance there goes the hope
of religious peace enabling a pure worship and observance of the
Law to be established as the permanent rule of life in Israel
(vers. 74–75). The hope of being freed from fear and from the
hand of our foes reflects an age of peace, and thus assigns the
hymn to a date before the war of A.D. 66–70. ' The concept of
redemption is much the same as in the *Magnificat*, but with
greater emphasis on the ceremonial worship. . . . Palestine will
be devoted to the pure observance of the Law, free from the
interference and defiling influence of Gentiles ' (Easton). Both
in the *Magnificat* and in the *Benedictus*, therefore, the national

14

hope of deliverance from Rome shews through, but the deliverance is to be effected spiritually. At ver. 76 a distinctively Christian thought enters. The child John will be the Lord's forerunner, and will bring to his people the knowledge of salvation through the remission of their sins. The words are based on the historical work of John, and lead to the thought of the new Christian era as the Dawn from on high which God makes to break on a darkened world (vers. 78–79). For the thought of the Messianic era as Sunrise-time after the world's night compare Isaiah ix. 2, lx. 1, and especially Malachi iv. 2 : ' Unto you that fear my name shall the sun of righteousness arise with healing in his wings.' The evangelist, as he wrote these words, cannot but have thought with gratitude of the effects produced by the preaching of Christ in his own Gentile world. He had known the deep spiritual darkness of that world, and its longing for religious certainty, for the assurance of immortality, and for the peace of forgiveness, all of which things had come to it through Christ. For the contemporary pessimism of the Greek world see Professor Gilbert Murray's *Five Stages of Greek Religion*, chap. iv.

Like the *Magnificat* the hymn came doubtless to Luke as part of his Judean source. Drawing its language very largely from the Psalter (cf. Psalms cxi. 9, cxxxii. 17, cvi. 10, cv. 8–9, etc.) it reflects the Christian estimate of John's personality and work (vers. 76–77), and represents doubtless a Christian composition. The only alternative would be to suppose that a Jewish psalm celebrating the coming of Elijah has been worked over in Christian circles in such a manner as to harmonize with John's career. On either view the hymn would naturally become associated with the tradition of the prophet's birth.

ii. 1–20 : THE BIRTH OF CHRIST

ii.

Now in those days an edict was issued by Caesar Augustus for a   1
census of the whole world. (This was the first census, and   2
it took place when Quirinius was governor of Syria.) So   3
everyone went to be registered, each at his own town, and as   4
Joseph belonged to the house and family of David he went
up from Galilee to Judaea, from the town of Nazaret to   5
David's town called Bethlehem, to be registered along with
Mary his wife. She was pregnant, and while they were there   6

15

7   the days elapsed for her delivery ; she gave birth to her first-
born son, and as there was no room for them inside the khan
8   she wrapped him up and laid him in a stall for cattle.   There
were some shepherds in the district who were out in the fields
9   keeping guard over their flocks by night ; and an angel of
the Lord flashed upon them, the glory of the Lord shone all
10   round them.   They were terribly afraid, but the angel said
to them, ' Have no fear.   This is good news I am bringing
you, news of a great joy that is meant for all the People.
11   To-day you have a saviour born in the town of David, the
12   Lord messiah.   And here is a proof for you : you will find
13   a baby wrapped up and lying in a stall for cattle.'   Then a
host of heaven's army suddenly appeared beside the angel
extolling God and saying,
14   ' Glory to God in high heaven,
and peace on earth for men whom he favours ! '
15 Now when the angels had left them and gone away to heaven, the
shepherds said to one another, ' Let us be off to Bethlehem
16   to see this thing that the Lord has told us of.'   So they made
haste and discovered Mary and Joseph and the baby lying in
17   the stall for cattle.   When they saw this they told people
about the word which had been spoken to them about the
18   child ; all who heard it were astonished at the story of the
19   shepherds, and as for Mary, she treasured it all up and mused
20   upon it.   Then the shepherds went away back, glorifying
and extolling God for all they had heard and seen as they had
been told they would.

The dating of the Messiah's birth by a census or enrolment
imposed by Augustus was part of the tradition which Luke
found in Judea.   The language of ver. 1 is, as popular language
often is, somewhat inexact, for no enrolment would extend to
the whole world or even to the entire Roman section of the
world.   Possibly the original expression in the source was not
world but ' folk,' meaning Israel, the Aramaic term 'amma
(folk) being mistaken for 'alma (world).   We know from Egyptian papyri that from A.D. 20 onwards a census by households at
intervals of fourteen years was a feature of the imperial administration of Egypt.   A similar census of the province of Syria,
including Palestine, took place in A.D. 6, and if the fourteen-
year cycle applied to Syria, there may have been a previous

census there in 8 B.C., which some scholars consider not too early a date for the birth of Christ.

Ver. 2, stating that the ordinance in question was the first census imposed on Judea, and took place when Quirinius was governor of Syria, is probably an amplification of the source by Luke. We know from Josephus that P. Sulpicius Quirinius carried out an enrolment of Judea in A.D. 6, which provoked a desperate rising under Judas of Gamala (*Antiq.* xviii. 2. 1). The date—A.D. 6—is settled for Josephus by the express statement that the census occurred thirty-seven years after the battle of Actium (31 B.C.). But as A.D. 6 is an impossibly late date for the birth of Christ in view of i. 5, 26, it has usually been held that Luke's statement assigning the census at the birth of Christ to the governorship of Quirinius is a chronological error. It appears, however, by inscriptions that for two years between 10 and 7 B.C. Quirinius, though not at the time governor of Syria —the governor from 9 to 6 B.C. was C. Sentius Saturninus—was engaged in military operations on the northern frontiers of Cilicia. If this means that he held some administrative commission in the province of Syria, a situation exists in which the carrying out by Quirinius, though not as governor, of such a census as Luke describes becomes a possibility. So at anyrate Sir W. M. Ramsay and some other scholars have argued. But could a census in the years 8-6 B.C. be imposed on Judea which, under Herod (i. 5), was still semi-independent ? The answer is that normally it would not, but Herod, whom the disordered state of affairs in Judea had rendered suspect in Roman eyes, probably deemed it wise to come into line with Roman policy, or Quirinius may have forced his hand. Josephus indicates that a swearing of allegiance to Augustus and Herod was required of ' all the people of the Jews ' about this time (*Antiq.* xvii. 2. 4 ; Ramsay, *Was Christ born at Bethlehem ?*, pp. 179-80), and some see in this census of loyalty the enrolment with which the tradition connects Jesus' birth. It will be seen, however, that this reconstruction of the facts involves many conjectural elements. The precise value of Luke's statement regarding the census which led to the Saviour's birth at Bethlehem remains indeterminable.

Normally a census such as the tradition implies would include the names, households, and property-qualifications of the enrolled. An Egyptian census-notice of the year A.D. 104 obliges ' all who for any cause are outside their own districts to return to their homes that they may fulfil the customary requirements of the enrolment and attend to the husbandry-duties which pertain to them' (Deissmann, *Light from the Ancient East*, p. 268). Conditions of land-tenure in Egypt were exceptional, and regulations in force there would not apply to Herod's dominions. Nevertheless, a Herodian census in Palestine being assumed, ' it would be quite like Herod's skill in governing Jews to disguise the foreign nature of the command by an appeal to tribal patriotism' (Easton). In any case, such a journey was given by Luke's Judean source as the event which brought about the Saviour's birth at Bethlehem, and if the journey coincided with one of the stated festivals at Jerusalem, the statement that there was no room for them inside the khan explains itself. All hostelries were thronged with pilgrims.

The narrative of the Shepherds, which forms the centre-piece of the section, condenses in poetic form the significance which the Messiah's coming has for pious hearts in the original Judean home of Christianity, and forms an interesting counterpart to Matthew's story of the Magi which reveals the significance of the same event for the missionary church of Antioch, where probably Matthew was written. To the dwellers in Judea, a simple folk keeping guard over their flocks, comes the supernatural good news or 'evangel' that a Saviour is born in the town of David. The name 'Saviour' indicates for Luke the character in which Jesus is destined to make his appeal to sick and suffering humanity, particularly in that section of the world which lay beyond Israel, and which, as we know from Asclepius-worship and other therapeutic cults of Hellenism, was peculiarly attracted to the thought of a Healer-divinity. The words which follow identify this World-Saviour with the Jewish Messiah of whom the prophets of Israel had spoken. Jesus is the Lord Messiah. As ' Messiah ' he fulfils the hope of Israel and brings the Kingdom of God ; as ' Lord ' he summons the wider world to worship and adore. Over his birth therefore the host of heaven's army—the phrase is sometimes used of the stars (Acts vii. 42)—is represented as chanting the story of a world's deliverance.

The content of the hymn follows. Glory is ascribed to God in high heaven because the coming into the world of Jesus Christ marks the culmination of the divine self-revelation to humanity. With this goes peace on earth for men whom God favours. How earnestly the world was looking for peace at this time appears by inscriptions set up in Asia Minor and elsewhere in honour of the Emperor Augustus. The nations had received the *pax Romana*, but, as a philosopher was to say before the century was out, while Caesar may give peace from war on land and from piracy on the seas, he cannot grant peace from passion, from sorrow, from envy (Epictetus, *Dissertations*, iii. 13. 10). Over against this merely civil peace therefore the same philosopher sets what he calls ' the peace not preached by Caesar but preached by God,' and it is this peace which is the burden of the Christian ' evangel.' Our ancient authorities differ as regards the reading in the second half of the angels' song. The majority of MSS. read, ' Peace on earth, goodwill towards men.' A group of the best, however, have ' Peace on earth towards men of goodwill,' i.e. towards men as the objects of God's goodwill. The goodwill or favour belongs in both readings to God. It is He who initiates salvation.

With the visit of the Shepherds to Bethlehem the sign given in the angelic ' evangel ' (ii. 10) is fulfilled by their beholding the divine Child. In vers. 17–18 the words all were astonished at the story of the shepherds hint that the shepherd folk of Judea formed the circle from which the birth-narratives were drawn. Ver. 19 is of difficult interpretation. Does the statement that Mary treasured up these ' things that the angels had told her and the shepherds had said ' mean that she had a secret to reveal in later days to the Church ? It is possible, but the sense of the words is not entirely clear. (See Appendix II.)

ii. 21–38 : CIRCUMCISION AND PRESENTATION OF THE HOLY CHILD

When the eight days had passed for his circumcision, he was 21 named Jesus—the name given by the angel before he had been conceived in the womb.

When the days for their purification in terms of the Mosaic law 22 had elapsed, they brought him up to Jerusalem to present him to the Lord (as it is written in the law of the Lord : *every* 23 *male that opens the womb must be considered consecrated to the Lord*) and also to offer the sacrifice prescribed in the law of 24 the Lord, *a pair of turtle-doves or two young pigeons*. Now 25 there was a man in Jerusalem called Symeon, an upright and

26 devout man, who was on the outlook for the Consolation of Israel. The holy Spirit was upon him ; indeed it had been revealed to him by the holy Spirit that he was not to see death
27 before he had seen the Lord messiah. By an inspiration of the Spirit he came to the temple, and when the parents of the child Jesus carried him in to perform the customary regula-
28 tions of the law for him, then Symeon took him in his arms, blessed God, and said,

29 ' Now, Master, thou canst let thy servant go,
 and go in peace, as thou didst promise ;
30 for mine eyes *have seen thy saving power*
31 which thou hast prepared *before the face of all the peoples,*
32 *to be a light of revelation for the Gentiles*
 and *a glory to* thy people *Israel.*'

33 His father and mother were astonished at these words about him,
34 but Symeon blessed them, and to his mother Mary he said, ' This child is destined for the downfall as well as for the rise of many a one in Israel ; destined to be a Sign for man's
35 attack—to bring out the secret aims of many a heart. And your own soul will be pierced by a spear.'
36 There was also a prophetess, Hannah the daughter of Phanuel, who belonged to the tribe of Asher ; she was advanced in years, having lived seven years with her husband after her
37 girlhood and having been a widow for eighty-four years. She was never away from the temple ; night and day she
38 worshipped, fasting and praying. Now at that very hour she came up, and she offered praise to God and spoke of him to all who were on the outlook for the redemption of Jerusalem.

The circumcision of the child takes place, like that of John, on the eighth day, and then too the pre-natally revealed name of Jesus (' He saves ') is bestowed on him. The scrupulousness with which this rite and the other requirements of the Mosaic law are said to have been observed reminds us not merely that Christ was ' born under the law,' but that Christianity is the fulfilment of Judaism. While the redemption of the first-born did not require a visit to the temple, such a visit would be natural on occasions of pilgrimage and for parents residing near Jerusalem. The sacrifice of ' a pair of turtle-doves, etc.,' brought for purification—possibly the original text in ver. 22 was ' her,' not ' their ' purification—indicates that the parents were poor (cf. Leviticus xii. 8). The redemption of the Child would include the payment of five shekels as prescribed by the law (Exodus xiii. 1–2, 11–15 ; Numbers xviii. 16).

The centre of interest in the section lies in the predictions uttered concerning the Child by the aged Symeon, type of those Jewish saints whose eyes were continually turning towards the Messianic dawn, or consolation of Israel, as it was called (cf. Isaiah xl. 1). Symeon has received the supernatural assurance that he will live to see the Lord Messiah, and the song of praise which he utters in his *Nunc Dimittis* signifies that in the coming of Jesus the prayer of Israel's saints is answered, and they can depart with a satisfied mind. Symeon's vision of the Messianic age has the two features which characterize the Jewish hope at its highest. On the one hand the Messiah brings a light of revelation for the Gentiles (cf. Isaiah xlii. 6–7, xlix. 6–7), and so it actually proves in history. Through Jesus revealed religion spreads to the non-Jewish world (Matthew xxviii. 19, Acts i. 8, Colossians i. 27, Ephesians ii. 13–14). On the other hand he brings a glory to thy people Israel, and here too history is the proof. Never was such evidence delivered to the world of Israel's special function in revelation as was given in the character and work of Jesus. The utterance harmonizes with Luke's own conception of the Christian religion as bringing to the Greeks for the first time the ' sure word ' of truth for which they were waiting (i. 4), while at the same time it provides the final verification of Israel's ancient faith.

The further words of Symeon have a more oracular quality, revealing as they do a consciousness that an historical crisis is initiated by Christ. This child is destined for the downfall as well as for the rise of many. While the Messiah brings glory to Israel, it will be through the throes of a spiritual revolution. Moral issues will be intensified. Men will be depressed or exalted according to their attitude to the new revelation. Thus the Messiah becomes a challenge to his times, a sign for man's attack (cf. Isaiah viii. 14, xxviii. 16–17). In actual fact Jesus is accused of being in league with Satan (xi. 15), and Judaism still charges him with being a ' beguiler ' who ' led Israel astray.' But this must all be hazarded in order to reveal the full spiritual potentialities of the situation, the secret aims of many a heart. Finally, Symeon predicts the piercing sorrow which her Son's rejection and death will bring to the Mother. In all this the Messiah serves as the highest instance of the law that moral development comes by inspired personalities raising their generation to new levels of spiritual perception, at which their moral responsibility is heightened, and their capacity to suffer and to rejoice increased. ' The life of Christ,' says Professor A. N. Whitehead, ' has the decisiveness of a supreme ideal, and that is why the history of the world divides at this point of time ' (*Religion in the Making*, p. 47).

The mention of the aged Hannah the prophetess forms a suitable pendant to the ' recognition ' by Symeon.

ii. 39–52 : An Episode from the Boyhood of Jesus

39 When they had finished all the regulations of the law of the Lord,
40   they returned to Galilee, to their own town of Nazaret. And the child grew and became strong ; he was filled with wisdom,
41   and the favour of God was on him. Every year his parents
42   used to travel to Jerusalem at the passover festival ; and when he was twelve years old they went up as usual to the
43   festival. After spending the full number of days they came back, but the boy Jesus stayed behind in Jerusalem. His
44   parents did not know of this ; they supposed he was in the caravan and travelled on for a day, searching for him among
45   their kinsfolk and acquaintances. Then, as they failed to find him, they came back to Jerusalem in search of him.
46   Three days later they found him in the temple, seated among the teachers, listening to them and asking them questions,
47   till all his hearers were amazed at the intelligence of his own
48   answers. When his parents saw him they were astounded, and his mother said to him, ' My son, why have you behaved like this to us ? Here have your father and I been looking
49   for you anxiously ! ' ' Why did you look for me ? ' he said,
50   ' Did you not know I had to be at my Father's house ? ' But
51   they did not understand what he said. Then he went down along with them to Nazaret, and did as they told him. His
52   mother treasured up everything in her heart. And Jesus *increased* in wisdom and in stature, and *in favour with God and man.*

The return to Nazareth is followed by a reference to Jesus' growth and development. The wisdom which fills him is divine or religious insight, and the favour of God is revealed in singular endowments of mind and spirit. It is implied here and in ver. 52 that the development of Jesus proceeded according to the laws of human growth. The educative agencies which promote the spiritual life of humanity—home, parental instruction, nature, school, scripture, the life and worship of the synagogue— would all contribute to the moulding of his religious nature. Over this process, however, our records pass in silence, the visit of the boy Jesus to the Temple in his twelfth year being all that remains to indicate the direction of his mind. But this episode is of cardinal importance as shewing the ascendancy which at a particular crisis in adolescence the conception of God as Father had attained over his consciousness.

The occasion is a pilgrimage of the household to the **Passover** at Jerusalem. 'The three annual pilgrimages prescribed in Exodus xxiii. 14–17, etc., had generally been reduced to one, even in Palestine' (Easton). Jesus, who has stayed behind in Jerusalem at his parents' departure, is after three days of search discovered in the temple, sitting at the feet of the Rabbis, drinking in their words, and asking and answering questions. The climax is reached in the word spoken to his mother in reply to her reproaches, '**Did you not know that I had to be at my Father's house ?** ' [1]

The fascination which the House of God had for the boy : above all, his words **my Father** constitute the directive hint which the incident affords as to the spiritual youth of Jesus. It is true that God was the Father of all Israel, and that every Israelite in later Judaism was accustomed to speak of Him as such (cf. Tobit xiii. 4, Ecclesiasticus xxiii. 1, 4, Wisdom ii. 16, Aboth v. 30, Yoma viii. 9, etc.). Nevertheless, Jesus is already understood to use the name with a unique intensity of realization and with a corresponding consciousness of filial obligation and responsibility. If the journey to Jerusalem marked the time when Jesus assumed, like all Jewish youths, the obligation to keep the Law, a new light falls on the incident. The boy's visit to the Temple indicates the seriousness with which he has dedicated himself to the service of the God of Israel. In any case the consciousness of Jesus is in these years moving to the climax which it attains at his baptism. The words in which he expresses himself have

[1] Dr. Dalman considers that the original expression of Jesus means 'the things of my Father,' viz. the study of the Law and Scripture. The boy is drawn to the place where God's word was expounded.

at times an unfathomable quality passing his parents' comprehension. Nevertheless, at Nazareth he continues to live the life of obedience, giving his mother cause to treasure many hallowed memories, and revealing in ordinary intercourse a singularly gracious and attractive personality.

II. THE CALL OF JESUS (iii. 1–iv. 13)

iii. 1–2 : SIGNS OF THE TIMES. APPEARANCE OF JOHN THE BAPTIST

iii.

1 Now in the fifteenth year of the reign of Tiberius Caesar, when Pontius Pilate was governor of Judaea, Herod being tetrarch of Galilee, Philip his brother tetrarch of the country of Ituraea and Trachonitis, and Lysias tetrarch of Abilene,
2 during the high priesthood of Annas and Caiaphas the word of God came to John the son of Zechariah in the desert ;

At this point the narrative emerges into the clearer light of day, and joins the main stream of the older evangelical tradition which began not with the birth but with the baptism of Jesus. As the appearance of John was the event which under God led to this consecrating experience, the evangelist marks its importance by an elaborate sixfold synchronism. The material from iii. 1 to iv. 13 is largely from Q, and Canon Streeter sees here the original opening of the earliest draft of Luke's gospel, or ' Proto-Luke ' as he calls it. See page xix f.

The chronology of vers. 1–2 is based probably on the evangelist's personal researches. Augustus died in the autumn of A.D. 14, and therefore the fifteenth year of Tiberius would set in at the corresponding period of A.D. 28. But as Tiberius was colleague to Augustus in the government of the provinces as early as A.D. 12, it is possible that A.D. 26 is the year intended by Luke, when John began his ministry. The other synchronisms in the passage are too general to be of help to us on this point. Pontius Pilate was procurator of Judea A.D. 26–36, Herod Antipas tetrarch of Galilee and Perea A.D. 4–39, and Philip, the half-brother of Antipas, tetrarch of Iturea and Trachonitis A.D. 4–34. The districts of Iturea, Trachonitis, and Abilene lay outside of the Palestine of Jesus, but were incorporated with that country under the rule of Luke's contemporary, Herod

Agrippa II (A.D. 50–100), which may explain why Luke includes them in his survey. **Iturea** was a hilly country in the Anti-Lebanon range, inhabited by roving Arabs ; **Trachonitis** corresponds with the stony, lava-strewn district in Eastern Palestine now known as El-Leja ; **Abilene** lies north-east of Hermon, and near to Damascus. The ruler of Abilene is merely a name to us. The expression **the high priesthood of Annas and Caiaphas** is loose. **Annas** was high-priest only from A.D. 6 to 15, but as he was succeeded by various members of his family,[1] the best known being **Caiaphas**, who held office from A.D. 18 to 36, he exercised unofficial powers which were practically equivalent to full status.

iii. 3–6 : THE WORK OF JOHN

And he went into all the Jordan-district preaching a baptism of 3
    repentance for the remission of sins—as it is written in the 4
    book of the sayings of the prophet Isaiah,
      The voice of one who cries in the desert,
      * Make the way ready for the Lord,*
      level the paths for him.
      Every valley shall be filled up, 5
        every hill and mound laid low,
      the crooked made straight,
        the rough roads smooth ;
      so shall all flesh see the saving power of God.' 6
                         (Cf. Mark i. 2–4.)

The immediate cause of John's appearance as prophet is given in the simple words, **the word of God came to John in the desert.** Here, as elsewhere, the prophetic summons would be conditioned by contemporary events. What in John's case was the outward situation which, conspiring with the voice of God within his heart, forced him out of his hermit-like seclusion (i. 80) to preach repentance to Israel ? Our records do not here enlighten us, but it may be assumed that sinister tendencies in the social and political world, including perhaps the growing menace of a conflict between the Jews and Rome, convinced John that divine judgment was hanging like a cloud over Israel, and that the nation must be warned.

[1] ' The office seems to have remained almost " in commission " among them ' (Dr. C. Gore, *Jesus of Nazareth*, p. 26).

The appearance of John marks an epoch in contemporary Judaism. After the slumber of centuries prophecy revives and calls to men in the old accents, stabbing the nation awake with the message of an offended God. While to his contemporaries the Reign of God was an idea which, however dominant in imagination or in national hope, was remote from everyday life and conduct, to John it indicated immediate moral imperatives to which men must bend or perish. The Reign of God was a familiar conception. It signified on one side the inextinguishable protest of the Jewish spirit against the heathen empires under which Israel lay politically crushed. It signified on the other side God's purpose to save and sanctify His people. As, however, the incubus of Gentile domination seemed irremovable by earthly means, Judaism had come to think of salvation apocalyptically, as a deliverance to be ushered in by a miraculous act of God. Hence over wide areas of the national life the thought of the Kingdom of God had practically ceased to prescribe rules or laws for conduct. John insisted that this separation of religion from everyday affairs must cease. The coming of the Kingdom must once again become the object of individual conscience and concern. One feature of his mission was unique. Whereas idealists and visionaries in recent years had appealed to liberationist sentiment and had promised the Jews deliverance from Rome, John depressed these expectations. To him moral reformation was the one condition on which salvation was even to be conceived.

This peculiar emphasis was marked by John's ritual. In **preaching a baptism of repentance** he indicated that washing with water in token of conversion was the revealed means by which at this crisis **the remission of sins** was to be attained and the wrath of God averted. How did John attain this consciousness? Was he giving effect to Isaiah i. 16–17 : ' Wash you, make you clean, put away the evil of your doings from before mine eyes, etc.' ; or to Zechariah xiii. 1 : ' In that day a fountain shall be opened to the house of David . . . for sin and uncleanness ' ? Did he mean that Israel must now *re-enter* by baptism into covenant relation with God ? Apparently John's rite of baptism was a new thing, and to the Christian mind of a later day the prophet of the Jordan with his rigorous ultimatum, his fearless application of correction and rebuke to his times, and his vivid annunciation of coming Judgment, seemed an incarnation of the Voice which long ago the Exilic prophet had heard calling, Make the way ready for the Lord, etc., that the captives of Israel might return to Zion (Isaiah xl. 3 f.).

iii. 7-20 : THE TERMS OF JOHN'S PRONOUNCEMENT

To the crowds who came out to get baptized by him John said, 7 ' You brood of vipers, who told you to flee from the coming Wrath ? Now, produce fruits that answer to your repentance, 8 instead of beginning to say to yourselves, '' We have a father in Abraham.'' I tell you, God can raise up children for Abraham from these stones ! The axe is lying all ready at 9 the root of the trees ; any tree that is not producing good fruit will be cut down and thrown into the fire.' The crowds asked 10 him, ' Then what are we to do ? ' He replied, ' Let everyone 11 who possesses two shirts share with him who has none, and let him who has food do likewise.' Taxgatherers also came 12 to get baptized, and they said to him, ' Teacher, what are we to do ? ' He said to them, ' Never exact more than your 13 fixed rate.' Soldiers also asked him, ' And what are we to 14 do ? ' He said to them, ' Never extort money, never lay a false charge, but be content with your pay.' Now as people's 15 expectations were roused and as everybody thought to himself about John, ' Can he be the Christ ?' John said to them all, 16
   ' I baptize you with water,
   but after me one who is mightier will come,
   and I am not fit to untie the string of his sandals ;
   he will baptize you with the holy Spirit and fire.
   His winnowing-fan is in his hand to purge his threshing- 17
     floor,
   to gather the wheat into his granary
   and burn the straw with fire unquenchable.'
Thus with many another appeal he spoke his message to the 18 people. But Herod the tetrarch, who had been reproved by 19 him for Herodias his brother's wife as well as for all the wickedness that he, Herod, had committed, crowned all by 20 shutting John up in prison.

        (Cf. Matthew iii. 7-12, Mark i. 7-8.)

John's proclamation was denunciatory, a veritable preaching of coming Wrath. The threat and demand in vers. 7-9 (which are from Q) are addressed, not as in Matthew to Pharisees and

Sadducees, but to the general public. **Brood of vipers calls up** the picture of snakes wriggling from some burning field. The Wrath as John described it therefore left no escape for any except such as undertook the strictest reformation of life. John stripped from his Jewish hearers their mask of pride in national privilege, and forced them to contemplate the moral realities of the situation. Was not the **axe** of judgment laid at the root of the nation's life ? As for heirs to **Abraham**—many of John's hearers took cover under the promises given to the patriarch's seed—John answered that the preservation of the Jewish race was no necessity to God. God could summon a new nation from the desert-steppes, nay, create one out of the stones which strewed the waste.

Vers. 10–14 are peculiar to Luke, and illustrate what John meant by **fruits that answer to repentance.** On the ordinary public he urged the duty of sharing goods with their poorer brethren. From **taxgatherers** and **soldiers**—the reference to these classes shews how wide and far-reaching was the appeal of the desert prophet—he exacted pledges against rapacity, extortion, and blackmail. Professor Burkitt speaks of the ' rough practical ethics ' of the code of John, and indeed in inwardness and range the latter falls far short of the teaching of Jesus, who in calling men to ' seek the Reign of God ' asks for nothing less than the complete surrender of the soul to the indwelling power of the divine Spirit.

John's preaching created a powerful current of Messianic expectation, but when the crowds asked **Can he be the Christ ?** John answered with a disclaimer, and pointed to the coming of **one who is mightier,** who, in the vivid phraseology of ver. 16, **will baptize you with the holy Spirit and fire.** John conceived the Messiah therefore as one who would effect a more thorough sifting and purgation of the national life than he had been able to produce. Vers. 16–17 are from Q. Nothing suggests that John, when he thus spoke of the Messiah, knew or was thinking of Jesus of Nazareth. The picture is wholly traditional, drawn after the accustomed outline of Jewish Messianic expectation. John was delineating a Messiah familiar to the imagination of his hearers. For ' fire ' compare Isaiah iv. 4, where it is said that God will cleanse Israel ' by the spirit of justice and the spirit of burning.' For ' Spirit ' as a sign or concomitant of the Messianic times compare Joel ii. 28–29 and Isaiah xliv. 3 : ' I will pour water upon him that is thirsty and streams upon the dry ground : I will pour my Spirit upon thy seed.' Water, fire, Spirit, righteousness, are accordingly conceptions derived from Scripture. John's conception of the Messiah as *Judge* comes powerfully to the front in the statement : **his winnowing fan is in his hand.** The winnowing process consisted in heaving into the air the mingled grain and chaff of the threshing-floor. The wind carried off the chaff. The grain fell back and was gathered. John looks forward therefore to an ever deepening and increasing judgment upon the life of the nation. The final remnant of the righteous—the **wheat** of the Messiah—will be small indeed.

John's unsparing castigation of sin was at length to bring him to his doom. He reproved Antipas *inter alia* for his adulterous union with **Herodias,** the wife of Antipas' half-brother Herodes, and Antipas retaliated by imprisoning John in the Dead Sea fortress of Machaerus (Josephus, *Antiq.* xviii. 5, 2).

iii. 21–22 : THE BAPTISM OF JESUS

Now when all the people had been baptized and when Jesus had 21 been baptized and was praying, heaven opened and the holy 22 Spirit descended in bodily form like a dove upon him ; and a voice came from heaven,
> ' Thou art my son, the Beloved,
> to-day have I become thy father.' [1]

(Cf. Mark i. 9–11.)

The supreme service which John rendered in religious history was to summon to consciousness the spiritual forces which were latent at this time in the soul of Jesus of Nazareth.

The brevity with which the Baptism is narrated might disguise from the reader the historical importance which the tradition attaches to the event. Briefly this is that in baptism Jesus received his call as the Messiah or Messiah-elect of Israel. The call is doubly certified : (1) by the holy Spirit descending upon Jesus ; (2) by the voice from heaven proclaiming him the Chosen of God. To what extent the narrative rests on statements later made by Jesus, to what extent it presents inter-

---

[1] Reading ἐγὼ σήμερον γεγέννηκά σε, with D, the Old Latin, Justin, Clement, Tyconius, etc. In the other MSS. it has been altered, for harmonistic reasons.

pretative ideas by which the Christian community explained to itself and others the office and authority with which their Master was invested, must be left undetermined ; but that Jesus was anointed by God with the holy Spirit and power (Acts x. 38) is a governing conception of the tradition.

No reason is given why Jesus comes to John or why he is found among the sinners and outcasts at the Jordan. In view, however, of the estimation in which Jesus held the office and authority of John (vii. 24, 27–28, xx. 3–4 ; Mark ix. 11–13, etc.), he may be presumed to be acknowledging in the prophet's baptism a divine ordinance (Matthew iii. 15) to which he wished to make his submission, and the vision and the voice which come to him may be interpreted as evidence of the high emotional tension of the spirit in which his resolve was taken. Certainly this is how Luke presents the incident. The baptism of Jesus marks the highest, the climactic act in a national movement of obedience to the will of God. **When all the people had been baptized, and when Jesus had been baptized and was praying**—Luke alone mentions his prayer (cf. vi. 12, ix. 18, 29)— heaven opened above him, and Jesus knew himself called in a unique sense as ' Son of God.'

The language in which the experience is described rests upon traditional use of symbol. That **heaven opened** implies that the summons to Jesus had its source in supernatural revelation. That **the holy Spirit descended** indicates that the call is to a work for God. The comparison **like a dove** need not imply the still-ness with which the new vocation superimposed itself on the mind of Christ, for the similitude was familiar. The Rabbis explained the movement of the Spirit of God on the waters in Genesis i. 2 as like the brooding of a dove. Similarly the state-ment that **a voice came from heaven** reflects the Jewish con-ception of the ' Bath Qol ' or ' daughter of the voice,' and implies that what Jesus heard was the echo of a decree promulgated in heaven. Finally, the content of the Voice, ' **Thou art my son, the Beloved,**' indicates not merely that Jesus' mind was pos-sessed at this moment by an overwhelming sense of the divine love or Fatherhood, but that simultaneously he was invested by that love with an inalienable office or vocation.

Luke's account resembles Mark's except that, whereas the latter leaves it open to us to interpret the opening of the skies and the flight of the dove as the subjective content of a vision seen by Jesus (Mark i. 10), Luke objectifies the events, translating into outward and physical terms an inward and mystical experience. The effect is heightened by his addition of the phrase **in bodily form** to the description of the dove's descent.

The most distinctive feature of Luke's narrative, however, is in the Voice heard by Jesus if, following certain Western authorities, we adopt the reading, ' **Thou art my son, to-day have I become thy father.**' These words are a full quotation of Psalm ii. 7, and in the Psalm they embody the terms of a divine decree ratifying the royal office of the king of Israel on the day of his enthronement. In the present passage they signify that Jesus first attained his royal or Messianic status on the day of his baptism.

Such is the evangelical tradition of the Baptism of Jesus. Heaven opened above him at the Jordan, and his calling stood revealed. The narrative is undoubtedly symbolical, and some further consideration of its terms is necessary. First, there is the title ' son of God ' by which Jesus is denominated. In order to understand this designation the reader must set aside all explanations suggested by the birth-narratives, since, as we see by Mark i. 1–11, the first preachers of the gospel used the title without the kind of support which the birth-narratives afforded. The possibilities which here open before our minds are various. (1) ' Son of God ' may be explained as simply equivalent to ' Messiah.' In that case the baptismal narrative simply asserts the call of Jesus to Messiahship, and the Christian use of the title has a purely Messianic basis. But though the designation ' my son ' is bestowed in the Old Testament upon the king of Israel (2 Samuel vii. 14, Psalm ii. 7, lxxxix. 20–27), and was thus capable of extension to the Messianic king of the future, it does not follow that its application to the Messiah, as in Enoch cv. 2 and 2 Esdras vii. 28–29, proves ' son of God ' a mere *synonym* for Messiah. (2) The designation may be traced to a personal source in the unique sense of filial trust and fellowship with God which filled the soul of Jesus and which formed the sustaining ground of all his consciousness (cf. Matthew xi. 25–27, Luke x. 21–22). So understood, the title bears primarily a spiritual, not an official, sense. (3) Some scholars have asserted that the title goes back not to Jesus or to his first followers, but to the language of the Greek-speaking church beyond Palestine, which thereby indicated its sense of a divine or superhuman person having been manifested in Jesus. Setting aside the last hypothesis as taking us too far away from the well-documented facts of Jesus' own consciousness, we are left with two theories, which between them exhaust all the real possibilities of the case. In view, however, of the uncertainty whether ' son of God ' was in Jewish usage synonymous with Messiah, and of the fact that none of our gospels gives the voice heard by Jesus in the form ' Thou art the Messiah ' but all in the form ' Thou art my son, the Beloved,' it seems best to adopt the second alternative, and to conclude that the Christian title ' son of God,' while it includes Messiahship with reference to Jesus, has its origin and primary ground in the filial love toward God which possessed Jesus, and which at his baptism became charged with the quality of a supernatural revelation.

How, secondly, is the task to which Jesus now knows himself committed to be understood ? Here two features of the situation would need to be before us : (1) the exalted consciousness of knowing and loving God which thrills through Jesus' being, and forms the psychological ground of the voice ' Thou art my Son ' ; (2) the moving spectacle of the Jewish multitudes whom the longing for salvation has drawn to the Jordan. In the concurrence of these two factors it is not strange that a great resolve, based on his own apprehension and experience of God, should form itself in the mind of Jesus. This resolve is nothing less than instantly to proclaim the Reign of God, and to be himself the deliverer of his people. Conscious of possessing in himself the secret of all religious blessedness, he sees in the massing of Israel at the Jordan a dramatic revelation of the conditions under which his own experience may be propagated universally around him. Hence the decision immediately to proclaim the Kingdom. The Reign of God was a conception which varied with the quality and degree of the individual's religious insight. For some it signified merely the national glorification of Israel. For others it implied an apocalyptic event in the far future. For Jesus it derives its character and immediacy from the filial joy in God which is his possession. To make men sharers in his experience, to discover God afresh to their souls, to call Israel to an absolute acceptance of the Rule of God in the heart—this is the task to which, as by a rending of the skies, Jesus is called. The voice ' Thou art my son ' condenses and focuses the vision of an Israel committed and surrendered to personal, individual realization of the power and love of God.

Such a vision goes far beyond John's. John had concentrated on judgment, and contemplated that only a fraction of the nation would be saved. Jesus will seek to win the many, offering to all men ' the Father known as he knows Him . . . the Father served as he serves Him ' (Berguer). His message will be ' good news,' the good news of God's instant willingness to redeem His people.

The name ' Messiah ' has not been uttered. But in Jesus' singular sense of responsibility for the saving of his nation a consciousness is present which very soon, indeed at once, demands the Messianic idea for its measurement and expression.

iii. 23–38 : The Genealogy of Jesus

At the outset Jesus was about thirty years of age ; he was the 23 son, as people supposed, of Joseph, the son of Heli, the son 24 of Matthat, the son of Levi, the son of Melchi, the son of Jannai, the son of Joseph, the son of Mattathias, the son of 25 Amos, the son of Nahum, the son of Esli, the son of Naggai, the son of Maath, the son of Mattathias, the son of Semein, 26 the son of Josech, the son of Joda, the son of Joanan, the 27 son of Rhesa, the son of Zerubbabel, the son of Shealtiel, the son of Neri, the son of Melchi, the son of Addi, the son of 28 Kosam, the son of Elmadam, the son of Er, the son of Jesus, 29 the son of Eliezer, the son of Jorim, the son of Matthat, the 30 son of Symeon, the son of Judas, the son of Joseph, the son of Jonam, the son of Eliakim, the son of Melea, the son of 31 Menna, the son of Mattatha, the son of Nathan, the son of 32 David, the son of Jessai, the son of Jobed, the son of Boaz, the son of Sala, the son of Nahshon, the son of Aminadab, 33 the son of Admin, the son of Arni, the son of Hezron, the son of Perez, the son of Judah, the son of Jacob, the son of 34 Isaac, the son of Abraham, the son of Terah, the son of Nachor, the son of Serug, the son of Reu, the son of Peleg, 35 the son of Eber, the son of Sala, the son of Kainan, the son 36 of Arphaxad, the son of Shem, the son of Noah, the son of Lamech, the son of Methuselah, the son of Enoch, the son 37 of Jared, the son of Maleleel, the son of Kainan, the son of 38 Enos, the son of Seth, the son of Adam, the son of God.

The statement that Jesus was about thirty years of age when he began his ministry may be interpreted broadly, so that, on the hypothesis that the year in question was A.D. 28 or 26, the birth of Jesus may be allowed to fall anywhere between 8 and 4 B.C.

It will be noticed that Luke's genealogy occurs not like Matthew's as part of the birth-records, but in connexion with Jesus' baptism. It came therefore from a source (doubtless L) which started not with Jesus' birth but with his call as Messiah. Luke, however, inserts as people supposed in ver. 23 in order to harmonize the genealogy with the other account of Jesus' divine Sonship.

The Jews of post-exilic times were accustomed to keep genealogical records of families and of individuals prominent in religious history. Hence an interest in drafting the descent of Joseph may be credited to the early Christian community in Judea. If the Virgin-birth was an article of faith among those by whom the genealogy was framed, Joseph's relation to Jesus would, as in Matthew i. 16, be understood as that of *legal* paternity.

But the genealogies in Matthew and Luke are not, as they stand, reconcilable, for Joseph is in Luke the son of Heli, whereas in Matthew he is the son of Jacob. It does not remove this discrepancy to assume that the Lukan genealogy is that of *Mary*, and to understand the words the son, as people supposed, of Joseph, the son of Heli, to mean that Jesus (though nominally the son of Joseph) was actually (i.e. on his mother's side) the son (i.e. grandson) of Heli. The word ' son ' does not admit of two different meanings in the one sentence. Hence we must either suppose that Joseph, the legal father of Jesus, stood in a merely adoptive relation to either Jacob or Heli, or else give up the problem. As a matter of fact we do not know enough of the sources of such traditions to make the further discussion of the matter fruitful.

In Luke the names from Heli to Zerubbabel and Shealtiel (ver. 27) are all otherwise unknown, and so are those to Nathan and David (ver. 31). In Matthew Joseph connects with David not through Nathan but through Solomon, i.e. Matthew's genealogy follows the royal line. From David to Abraham Luke's genealogy follows Old Testament lists (2 Chronicles i.–ii.), agreeing, though not exactly, with Matthew's. Finally, from Abraham it is carried back to Adam, who also was the son of

God. Has Luke in his mind at this point Paul's thought of
Christ as the second Adam ? Certainly by carrying the genealogy
back to Adam he would seem to suggest the organic relation of
Christ to all humanity. The total number of names in the list
is 77 (7 × 11).

iv. 1–13 : THE TEMPTATION IN THE WILDERNESS

iv.

From the Jordan Jesus came back full of the holy Spirit, and for 1
forty days he was led by the Spirit in the desert, while the 2
devil tempted him. During these days he ate nothing, and
when they were over he felt hungry. The devil said to him, 3
' If you are God's son, tell this stone to become a loaf.'
Jesus replied to him, ' It is written, *Man is not to live on* 4
bread alone.' Then he lifted Jesus up and shewed him all 5
the realms of the universe in a single instant ; and the devil 6
said to him, ' I will give you all their power and grandeur,
for it has been made over to me and I can give it to anyone
I choose. If you will worship before me, then it shall all 7
be yours.' Jesus answered him, ' It is written, *You must* 8
worship the Lord your God, and serve him alone.' Then he 9
brought him to Jerusalem and placing him on the pinnacle
of the temple said to him, ' If you are God's son, throw yourself down from this ; for it is written, 10
    He will give his angels charge of you,
and 11
    They will bear you on their hands,
    lest you strike your foot against a stone.'
Jesus answered him, ' It has been said, *You shall not tempt* 12
the Lord your God.' And after exhausting every kind of 13
temptation the devil left him till a fit opportunity arrived.
(Cf. Matthew iv. 1–11.)

The Temptation of Jesus appears in the tradition as the
sequel to his baptism. The Spirit which fills him and
impels him into solitude is the Spirit which came on him at
Jordan, and the conflict which ensues turns upon the meaning
of the task to which the voice ' Thou art my son ' now points.
Much has been written on the subject of the Temptation narrative, and it has sometimes been proposed to regard it as a
' myth ' or purely symbolic representation intended to shew

why Jesus, though the Messiah, did not and could not answer to ordinary Jewish Messianic ideas. In working out the contrast, it is alleged, the Christian community fell back upon the analogy of the Exodus experience of Israel : ' The Lord thy God led thee in the wilderness, that he might humble thee to prove thee. . . . And he suffered thee to hunger, etc.' (Deuteronomy viii. 2 f.). But while the tradition incorporates symbolical features, there is no reason why it should not go back to an actual conflict in the life of Jesus. All depends upon the amount of historical reality which we allow to the Jordan experience when heaven opened over Jesus and his calling stood revealed. Was Jesus conscious at that moment of the call to save his nation ? Then the retirement into solitude, the fasting, the wrestling of soul, the temptation under stress of overborne feeling to solicit external proofs of his call, become intelligible. A psychological situation is created with which the features of the wilderness story are consonant enough.

The record is from Q (cf. Matthew iv. 1–11), and this of itself suggests that the Temptation, like the Baptism and the story of John's preaching, embodies teachings or revelations received from our Lord himself. The account in Mark i. 12–13 is brief, and throws no light on the character of the experience. In Matthew and Luke, on the other hand, the forty days' trial, details of which are not given, eventuates in three specific temptations, two of them introduced by the formula if you are God's son, and all turning on the question what it means for Jesus to assume and fulfil this rôle. This suggests that the conflict reached its *climax* in these particular solicitations. The source of the temptation is Satan—who appears no longer in his Old Testament rôle of accuser of the saints (Job i. 6–12, ii. 1–6 ; Zechariah iii. 1–2), but as the usurping enemy of God, who holds the world in thrall—and Jesus repels him by falling back upon higher intuitions of what God wills and what constitutes reverence for Him. In the background of the experience there undoubtedly lie the Messianic ideas of Jesus' race and time. ' In such an environment as his, the natural expression of the religious genius lay along the extended lines of Messianism ' (Berguer). But to Jesus, intent on following purely the will of God, these traditional Messianic ideas of his people appear not as divine inspirations, but as Satanic perversions of the truth, visions and dreams which tempt the soul to sin.

The first temptation (vers. 3-4) may be considered Messianic if we suppose that, because Moses had given Israel bread from heaven, the Jews of Jesus' day expected the Messiah to do no less. (Cf. John vi. 30 and Isa. xlix. 10, where the promise ' They shall not hunger nor thirst ' enters into the plan of the divine salvation.) But that which gives the temptation impact and power is the seeming contradiction in Jesus' own experience between the love of God which calls him to his task and the acute privation, the hunger and weakness, into which he has been brought. He has abandoned the carpenter's bench and the ordinary means of subsistence, and is committed to bring to his nation the Kingdom of God. Here surely is a situation in which the dream ' They shall not hunger nor thirst ' should be realized. From this temptation to seek a ' sign ' of his calling Jesus finds relief in the word spoken to ancient Israel, ' **Man is not to live on bread alone** ' (Deuteronomy viii. 3). Israel was God's son (Deuteronomy viii. 5), yet God disciplined it and suffered it to hunger ' in order to bring it into a more perfect relation to Himself. So Jesus will not doubt his calling because of the physical straits into which he is brought, nor interpret in miraculous terms the love of God to His ' son.'

It is not clear why Luke or his source gives the two remaining temptations in inverse order to Matthew. Possibly Luke's arrangement is due to the scene of his second temptation being geographically intermediate between the Jordan desert and Jerusalem. The narrative is of course symbolical. The devil is said to lift Jesus up—an inward imaginative experience is intended—and to **shew him all the realms of the universe in a single instant.** The temptation this time is definitely Messianic. Jesus is invited to construe his election by God in terms of a Messiahship founded on earthly rule. The suggestion is powerful, because Messiahship as thus construed not only answered to Jewish expectations but seemed promised in Scripture to Israel's future king (cf. Psalm ii. 7 : ' The Lord said to me, Thou art my son. . . . Ask of me, and I will give thee the nations for thine inheritance, etc.') But as this idea presented itself to the Jews, Jesus discerned in it not an asking of *God* but a capitulation to methods and aims—militarism, hatred, revolt against Rome—which signified only too clearly a surrender to the evil spirit which disputes God's government of the world. Therefore he rejects it. ' **You must worship the Lord your God and serve**

37

him alone ' (Deuteronomy vi. 13). The Kingdom belongs to God, through whose good pleasure alone it comes (xii. 32). Therefore it must be sought only in God's way, which Jesus will later define when he says, ' Love your enemies ' (vi. 27), ' Bless those who curse you,' ' Resist not him that is evil ' (Matthew v. 39).

Jesus therefore turns from the dream of an earthly Messiahship, but one temptation still remains. It is that a special calling from God will surely accredit itself by ' signs ' (vers. 9–12 ; cf. 1 Corinthians i. 22). The Ninety-first Psalm, which promises supernatural protection to the man who dwells in communion with God, seemed to support such a view, and is therefore cited by the Tempter. Here again the temptation is Messianic if we suppose that, the promises of the Psalm not being verified in ordinary religious experience, Judaism took them to refer to the Messiah and applied to him the words ' He will give his angels charge of you,' etc. (Psalm xci. 11–12). A Jewish Midrash contains a tradition which is sometimes quoted in this connexion. ' When King Messiah is revealed, he comes and stands upon the roof of the Holy Place : then will he announce to the Israelites and say, Ye poor, the time of your redemption is come ' (*Pesikta Rabba*, 162a). If such a tradition were current in the time of Jesus, it might well provide the basis of the suggestion here ascribed to the Tempter. The Messiah, by casting himself from the temple pinnacle on which he stood, would be a sign to the people to precipitate revolt against the enemies of Israel and of God. But, whatever the original meaning of this particular temptation may have been, Jesus rejects it as a violation of the commandment ' You shall not tempt the Lord your God ' (Deuteronomy vi. 16). He saw men being led astray by fanatical hopes, expecting interventions of divine power instead of reasonably submitting to the declared principles of God's spiritual government of the world, and this severance of God's power from the ethical nature of His holy will Jesus will not approve.

The meaning of the Temptation, as set forth in the above narrative, would therefore seem to be that Jesus, conscious of a singular responsibility to seek the redemption of his nation, has to meet the challenge of certain facts and ideas, all more or less connected with traditional conceptions of Israel's Saviour, by which the clear imperative of his call is threatened or obscured.

Over against these various forms of challenge, for all of which appeal can be made to the letter of Scripture, Jesus asserts unfalteringly his own fundamental reading of the Will of God. The fact that three times over he uses the language of Deuteronomy indicates that God's will for His people has been sufficiently declared in its ancient history. God has shewn that His will is not to be forced, but to be simply trusted and obeyed.

The story of the Temptation, as thus presented in the tradition, incorporates many symbolical ideas, but that it goes back in essence to statements made by the Lord himself, when speaking of the ' trials ' through which he had to pass (cf. xxii. 28), may be reasonably assumed. Here an interesting question arises. Jesus was throughout his whole ministry face to face with the popular craving for Messianic signs and wonders. The Galileans lacked bread in the wilderness. The Pharisees demanded a sign from heaven. Galileans, Pharisees, and disciples alike had an earthly vision of the Kingdom of God. Is the temptation-narrative therefore an epitome of the *whole* spiritual history of Jesus ? A circumstance favouring this idea within the narrative itself is the fact that the three special temptations occur *after* the forty days' trial is past (iv. 2). We might on the strength of this feature suppose that Jesus, narrating at some later time the story of an early experience in the desert, went on to describe other specific assaults which Satan made on him throughout his ministry, and that these have become conflated with the wilderness-experience. But while this hypothesis is attractive, it may well be that Jesus, already at the threshold of his ministry, had a vision of the future in which the subsequent issues of his work were fully precognized.

III. JESUS IN GALILEE (iv. 14-ix. 50)

iv. 14-30 : THE ANNOUNCEMENT AT NAZARETH

Then Jesus came back in the power of the Spirit to Galilee, and 14
the news of him spread over all the surrounding country.
He taught in their synagogues and was glorified by all. 15
Then he came to Nazaret, where he had been brought up, 16
and on the sabbath he entered the synagogue as was his
custom. He stood up to read the lesson and was handed 17
the book of the prophet Isaiah ; on opening the book he
came upon the place where it was written,

18   *The Spirit of the Lord is upon me :*
        for he has consecrated me to preach the gospel to the poor,
        he has sent me to proclaim release for captives
        and recovery of sight for the blind,
        to set free the oppressed,

19   *to proclaim the Lord's year of favour.*

20   Then, folding up the book, he handed it back to the attendant
        and sat down.   The eyes of all in the synagogue were fixed

21   on him, and he proceeded to tell them that ' To-day, this

22   scripture is fulfilled in your hearing.'   All spoke well of him
        and marvelled at the gracious words that came from his lips ;

23   they said, ' Is this not Joseph's son ? '   So he said to them,
        ' No doubt you will repeat to me this proverb, " Doctor, cure
        yourself ! " " Do here in your own country all we have

24   heard you did in Capharnahum." '   He added, ' I tell you

25   truly, no prophet is ever welcome in his native place.   I tell
        you for a fact,

            In Israel there were many widows during the days of Elijah,
                when the sky was closed for three years and six
                months, when a great famine came over all the land :

26   yet Elijah was not sent to any of these,
                but only *to a widow woman at Zarephath in Sidon.*

27   And in Israel there were many lepers in the time of the
                prophet Elisha,
                yet none of these was cleansed,
                but only Naaman the Syrian.'

28   When they heard this, all in the synagogue were filled with

29   rage ; they rose up, put him out of the town, and brought
        him to the brow of the hill on which their town was built,

30   in order to hurl him down.   But he made his way through
        them and went off.

                                        (Cf. Mark vi. 1-6.)

        What was the task to which Jesus now knew himself com-
        mitted ?   Luke answers by inserting at this point (from L) a
        deliverance which Jesus was stated to have given to his townsfolk
        at **Nazaret.**   That thereby he has anticipated a later event
        appears (1) by the fact that Mark definitely locates the earliest
        activities of Jesus in Capernaum, and records no visit to Nazareth
        until a comparatively advanced stage in the Galilean ministry
        has been reached (Mark i. 21, vi. 1) ; (2) by the allusion of the

Nazarenes in this very passage to a *previous* work of Jesus at Capernaum (ver. 23). On the other hand, the placing of the Nazareth episode here in accordance with the L source had literary advantages which Luke was not averse to utilizing. The incident serves as a frontispiece to the Ministry, presenting as it does the part played by Jesus in the history of Israel's religion and the crisis which his appearance created for contemporary Judaism.

The passage is interesting as affording an almost contemporary account of a synagogue service. The lesson from the prophets which Jesus reads would be preceded by the recitation of the Shema (Deuteronomy vi. 4–9, xi. 13–21), and by a passage from the Law read first in Hebrew and then orally translated verse by verse into Aramaic. The lesson from the Law was prescribed by a lectionary, but whether in the time of Jesus a similar regulation applied to the reading from the prophets is not known. The selection of the passage from the book of the prophet Isaiah may have been due to a local order for the day or it may have been due to the choice of Jesus. Ascending the platform at the invitation of the presiding leader, who was accustomed to extend such courtesies to visiting Rabbis or teachers, Jesus opens the book at the passage, **the Spirit of the Lord is upon me**, etc., and reads the commission there given to the prophet. Here as in a mirror we are meant to see a reflexion of the consciousness with which Jesus opens his ministry in Israel.

The passage as cited combines Isaiah lxi. 1–2 with some words from lviii. 6, and discovers not a Messiah after the national pattern but ' the Servant of God whose mission it is to bring to the poor and afflicted spiritual enlightenment and salvation ' (Montefiore). The coming of the Spirit upon the Servant answers to the baptism of Jesus. The declaration ' **He has consecrated me to preach the gospel** ' reflects the sense of vocation which since the baptism has filled Jesus' mind. The term ' gospel,' meaning ' good news,' was not unknown to the contemporary world. An inscription from Priene in Asia Minor, dated 9 B.C., speaks of the birthday of Augustus as marking ' the inauguration to the world of good news through him.' On Jesus' lips the ' good news ' has a purely religious import. What urges Jesus to preach and to become the deliverer of his nation is the sense that he has the secret of salvation and can offer it to others. The term **the poor** is to be taken in its inward spiritual sense

41

(see Introd., page xxvi, and below, on vi. 20–26), and similarly the expressions **captive, blind, oppressed** indicate not primarily the down-trodden victims of material force, such as Rome's, but the victims of inward repressions, neuroses, and other spiritual ills due to misdirection and failure of life's energies and purposes. To these Jesus is impelled to offer deliverance by the power of God, and so to bring in for Israel **the Lord's year of favour.** Returning the book to the sexton, Jesus opens his ministry by announcing ' **To-day this scripture is fulfilled in your hearing.** '

It will be noticed that in Mark i. 14–15 the opening announcement of Jesus takes the outwardly different form of proclaiming the approach of a new supernatural era, the Reign of God, which, though near, is not yet come. Here on the other hand he speaks in terms of a present redemption. The apparent discrepancy disappears if we consider what it is that inspires the announcement that ' the Reign of God is near.' Such a formula may well represent the manner in which in that age of expectant Judaism any great prophet or inspired teacher would call attention to a divine revelation granted to himself. It would be a signal that God had spoken in order to bring about the salvation of His people. In the case of Jesus, who is conscious of having received a supreme revelation (see above, on iii. 21–22), the message that ' the Reign of God is near ' indicates possession of the final secret of God. While his contemporaries are waiting for ' signs ' to be given or for ' times ' to elapse, Jesus declares God's will to save His people to be immediate. Not in a future age but *now* is the captive power of sin to be broken, communion with God to be established, and the will of God to be done. The ' throng of mental pictures ' which the traditional idea of the Kingdom called up in Jewish minds must not obscure from us the fact that for Jesus the redemption of God means *present* deliverance from sin, ethical renewal of the life forces, the sublimation and regeneration of the will.

The announcement is at first received with admiring approval, but this passes quickly into criticism as it becomes apparent that Jesus, not content to expound the promised redemption, takes to himself responsibility for bringing it to his nation.[1] The Nazarenes retort ' **Is not this Joseph's son ?** ' and Jesus

[1] See the brilliant exposition of this point by Dr. Dalman (*Jesus-Jeshua*, pp. 44–55).

answers by citing the proverbial sayings about the doctor and the prophet who returns to his native place. Apparently the Nazarenes would have it understood that Jesus has not as yet produced sufficient credentials of his high claim to religious authority. Jesus points to Elijah and Elisha as confirming his statement that the Jews reject their prophets. (For **Elijah** see 1 Kings xviii. 8-24; for **Elisha** 2 Kings v. 1-19.) These references to Gentiles shewing a readier faith than Jews in the messengers of God enrage the Nazarenes, and they wish to precipitate Jesus from some neighbouring cliff in accordance with the method of capital punishment by stoning (*Sanhedrin* vi. 4a). This would imply that Jesus is judged guilty of blasphemy, but from the consequences of this judgment he is delivered by the supernatural awe which his personality inspires.

It is unlikely that so acute a crisis was reached at the very beginning of Jesus' ministry. Everything points to a developed situation, when the prospect of his rejection by Israel had thrown its sorrowful shadow on his mind. But that Jesus, like the greatest prophets since the Exile, saw God to be interested in others besides the Jewish people, and that within his own nation he habitually spoke and acted with a tremendous sense of personal responsibility for bringing to pass the redemption which he preached, has simply to be admitted. Jewish criticism would fasten on both these features of his work.

iv. 31-44 : INCIDENTS AT CAPERNAUM

Then he went down to Capharnahum, a town of Galilee, and on 31 the sabbath he taught the people ; they were astounded at 32 his teaching, for his word came with authority. Now in 33 the synagogue there was a man possessed by the spirit of an unclean daemon, who shrieked aloud, ' Ha ! Jesus of 34 Nazaret, what business have you with us ? Have you come to destroy us ? I know who you are, you are God's holy One ! ' But Jesus checked it, saying, ' Be quiet, come out 35 of him.' And after throwing him down before them the daemon did come out of him without doing him any harm. Then amazement came over them all ; they talked it over 36 among themselves, saying, ' What does this mean ? He orders the unclean spirits with authority and power, and they come out ! ' And a report of him spread over all the 37

38 surrounding country. When he got up to leave the synagogue he went to the house of Simon. Simon's mother-in-
law was laid up with a severe attack of fever, so they asked
39 him about her ; he stood over her and checked the fever,
and it left her. Then she instantly got up and ministered to
40 them. At sunset all who had any people ill with any sort of
disease brought them to him ; he laid his hands on everyone
41 and healed them. From many people daemons were also
driven out, clamouring aloud, ' You are God's son ! ' But
he checked them and refused to let them say anything, as
42 they knew he was the Christ. When day broke he went
away out to a lonely spot, but the crowds made inquiries
about him, came to where he was, and tried to keep him
43 from leaving them. He answered them, ' I must preach the
glad news of the Reign of God to the other towns as well,
44 for that is what I was sent to do.' So he went preaching
through the synagogues of Judaea.

(Cf. Mark i. 21-39.)

Luke here begins the first of his extensive adaptations from
Mark. The present section reproduces Mark i. 21-39, and
consists of incidents falling on the first Sabbath of Jesus at
Capernaum. Capharnahum, ' village of Nahum,' the centre of
Jesus' work in Galilee, is usually identified with one or other of
the two sites, Tell-hum and Khan-Minyeh, which closely adjoin
one another on the north-west shore of the Lake.

The dominating idea of the section is the ' authority ' of Jesus.
People were astounded at his teaching, for his word came with
authority. This can only refer to the directness with which,
herein differing from the Scribes, Jesus speaks of God and of
divine things. Whereas the scribes leaned on precedent, and
based their judgments on the interpretations of earlier Rabbis
or theologians, Jesus speaks from immediate knowledge of the
living God, and his teaching, thus based on personal experience,
becomes the source of a new God-consciousness in his hearers.
Compare Justin Martyr's famous characterization of Jesus :
' Brief and concise came the words from him, for he was no
sophist, but his word was power of God ' (*Apol.* i. 14. 11). The
expression also brings out the positive and encouraging character
of our Lord's teaching as contrasted with the repressive and
minatory tone of the legalists. A second illustration of his

authority is provided by his exorcizing of a demon in the synagogue. Jesus shews an extraordinary power over disordered minds, and evil spirits depart at his word. A third example of the same authority is his declaration regarding forgiveness (v. 24) and the Sabbath (vi. 5). Jesus does not qualify his judgments on such matters, as do the scribes. The authority of Jesus is therefore the keynote to which everything in iv. 31-44 and v. 12-vi. 11 is subordinated.

Jesus, preaching in the synagogue, is interrupted by the wild cry of a demoniac ' Ha ! Jesus of Nazaret, what business have you with us ? ' The belief in demons or spirits plays little part in the Old Testament, but in later Judaism, through Babylonian and Persian ideas pressing in from without, it had become very prevalent, and in Galilee—as in all the surrounding Syrian, Egyptian, and Hellenistic countries—it was universal. The ' daemons ' under Beelzebub, Beliar, or other infernal potentate ' represent a kingdom of evil over against the Kingdom of God ' (Klostermann). They inhabit waterless places (xi. 24), graves (viii. 27), mountains (Mark v. 5), and the lower strata of the atmosphere (Ephesians ii. 2). Judaism sees in them the descendants of the fallen angels (Enoch xv. 8), or the spirits of the wicked dead (Josephus, Wars, vii. 6. 3), or the gods of the heathen who tempt men to idols (1 Corinthians x. 19-21, xii. 2). It is believed that the demons seek entrance into human bodies in order to corrupt and ruin them (see later, under xi. 24-26), and to their malign operation are attributed most of the nervous and mental disorders which we describe by terms like disassociation of personality. Such cases would be extraordinarily frequent, because of the extreme force of suggestion with which the belief was charged.

In the present case the sufferer, whose morbid condition probably owes something to rigours of conscience working upon the sense of an evil life, is moved by Jesus' preaching to an unexampled excitement. He hears Jesus proclaim that God's power is now put forth to end the reign of sin, and the word fills his mind with terror. ' Have you come to destroy us ? ' he cries ; ' I know who you are—God's holy One ! ' The man identifies himself with the demon, and dreads that Jesus, whose holiness of spirit lays on him a kind of supernatural spell, will send him to the perdition reserved for evil spirits. Jesus takes the man's obsession seriously. The belief in demons was far too

terrible a part of human ruin for him to regard it as delusion or
to separate himself from the full admission of its reality. Yet
underneath the story of the exorcism can be traced the process
by which Jesus leads a conscience-stricken soul back to God
and peace. We see him calming the man's spirit by saying to
the demon ' Be quiet, come out of him.' All utterances of
demoniacs were ill-omened or unpropitious, and therefore to be
discouraged. The cry of the man in ver. 34 need not with the
tradition be taken to mean that demoniacs actually confessed
Jesus to be the Messiah. They felt the extraordinary psychic
influence of his personality, and this the tradition interprets as
explicit recognition of his theocratic office.

In the succeeding incident (vers. 38–39) the power of Jesus
is again illustrated. Jesus does not seek the occasions presented
by the demoniac and by the sick mother-in-law of Peter. Confronted, however, by such cases, he is conscious of a challenge
to the redeeming power of God which he proclaims; and he
asserts that power victoriously. By word and touch he inspires
an extraordinary faith resulting in marvellous powers of physical
recovery. The day closes (vers. 40–41) with a succession of
healings wrought after sunset. The Jewish Sabbath ended at
6 p.m., which explains why crowds of sick folk began to be
brought to Jesus at that hour. If the statement that the
demons knew that he was the Christ could be taken literally,
the prohibition of their outcries would signify that Jesus discountenanced everything tending to inflame Messianic passions
among the Galileans. If what really underlies the statement is
the fact that demoniacs were extraordinarily sensitive to the
psychic power of Jesus, the prohibition will mean that all utterances of demons were considered unholy. At dawn on the
next day Jesus leaves the town in order, as Mark says, to pray—
Luke curiously omits this notice—and when the crowds come
desiring to retain him in their midst, he answers, ' I must preach
the glad news of the Reign of God to the other towns.' This
mission, conceived as Jesus conceives it, brooks no lingering in
any one place.

v. 1–11 : THE CALL OF THE FIRST DISCIPLES

v.

1 Now as the crowd were pressing on him to listen to the word of
2   God, he saw, as he stood beside the lake of Gennesaret,

two boats on the shore of the lake ; the fishermen had disembarked and were washing their nets. So he entered 3 one of the boats, which belonged to Simon, and asked him to push out a little from the land. Then he sat down and taught the people from the boat. When he stopped speaking, 4 he said to Simon, ' Push out to the deep water and lower your nets for a take.' Simon replied, ' Master, we worked 5 all night and got nothing ! However, I will lower the nets at your command.' And when they did so, they enclosed 6 a huge shoal of fish, so that their nets began to break. Then 7 they made signals to their mates in the other boat to come and assist them. They came and filled both the boats, till they began to sink. But when Simon Peter saw it he fell 8 at the knees of Jesus, crying, ' Lord, leave me ; I am a sinful man.' For amazement had seized him and all his com- 9 panions at the take of fish they had caught ; as was the 10 case with James and John, the sons of Zebedaeus, who were partners of Simon. Then said Jesus to Simon, ' Have no fear ; from now your catch will be men.' Then they brought 11 the boats to land, and leaving all they followed him.

(Cf. Mark i. 16–20.)

The present narrative is peculiar to Luke, and forms a sub- stitute for Mark i. 16–20. Its specific point is that the adhesion to Jesus of Peter and the sons of Zebedee was rooted not simply in the call ' Come and follow me,' but in powerful impressions of the holy and the supernatural awakened in their souls by Jesus. Jesus, who is followed by a throng of people intent on hearing the Word, sits down in Simon's boat, and instructs the audience on the beach. Thereafter he asks Simon to ' push out to the deep water ' and to lower the nets. If, as it is permissible to suppose, Jesus already knew something of these men (cf. John i. 35 f.), and wished to have them as his adjutants, his action is explained by his desire to give them a lesson in faith. They have ' worked all night and got nothing,' but not for that reason must they relax hope or effort. The astounding success which crowns the experiment carried out in obedience to the command of Jesus constitutes the sign or token by which Jesus now summons them to a higher service.

The centre of interest in the section is the profound moral crisis effected in the soul of Peter who, overwhelmed by the

supernatural prescience of this teacher of faith in the power
of God, cries 'Lord, leave me ; for I am a sinful man.' For
Peter and his companions the spiritual or holy is inseparably
associated with signs and portents, and with the more awe-inspir-
ing aspects of personality ; and that Jesus, by transcendent
qualities of mind and spirit, constantly evoked in his followers
the sense of the supernatural has simply to be admitted. Hence
a typical significance attaches to the present incident as shewing
the kind of experience in which the attachment of the disciples
to Jesus was rooted, and from which the summons to catch
men proceeded. It is interesting that Jesus goes for his first
assistants not to the visionaries or dreamers of Galilee but to
men whom patient toil had disciplined and inured to patience
and stedfastness. But the incident also reveals, by aid of
Peter's confession, and of the Master's reassuring word 'Have
no fear,' that the impression wrought by Jesus was profoundly
inward and moral. The disciples are stirred to the depths of
their nature by the transcendent qualities of the character of
Jesus, and there begins for them what can only be called a
reintegration of personality round a new centre.

The incident markedly resembles the post-resurrection story in
John xxi. 1–19. Both include (1) a wonderful catch of fish after
a night of failure ; (2) a crisis of penitence in the soul of Peter ;
(3) an apostolic charge to that disciple. Hence the narratives
conceivably present different settings of the same tradition.
Luke's source associated the story with the original call of
Peter.

v. 12–16 : The Cleansing of a Leper

12 When he was in one of their towns, there was a man full of
leprosy who, on seeing Jesus, fell on his face and besought
13   him, 'If you only choose, sir, you can cleanse me.' So
he stretched his hand out and touched him, with the words,
'I do choose, be cleansed.' And the leprosy at once left
14   him. Jesus ordered him not to say a word to anybody, but
to 'Go off and shew yourself to the priest, and offer whatever
15   Moses prescribed for your cleansing, to notify men.' But
the news of him spread abroad more and more ; large
crowds gathered to hear him and to be healed of their com-
16   plaints, while he kept in lonely places and prayed.

(Cf. Mark i. 40–45.)

Luke again follows Mark, but whereas Mark suggests that the incident took place in the open country, Luke locates it in one of their towns. This statement cannot, however, be pressed, for it is difficult to think that a man full of leprosy, i.e. at an advanced stage of the disease, would make his way into any populous centre. The law applying to ' the plague of leprosy ' is stated in Leviticus xiii.–xiv., and there also the requirements as to the segregation of the leper are specified. In the present narrative the coming of the leper to Jesus is not otherwise explained than as an act of faith. The suppliant appeals to the will of Jesus, and Jesus in whole-hearted consent extends his hand and touches him. The touch was the sign of healing, but in the case of a leper it betokens a special act of grace. The leper is required not to say a word to anybody— reverence should forbid any light speaking about the miracle of healing—but to shew himself to the priest, in accordance with the Law, and to make the prescribed offerings for his cleansing. The phrase to notify men admits of various inter- pretations : (1) Jesus wishes the man's cleansing to be duly confirmed or registered ; (2) he wishes the religious authorities to be satisfied that he upholds the Law ; (3) he wishes all to know—cf. 2 Kings v. 8—that the power of God is at work in Israel. The last interpretation would seem to be the best. Though Jesus enjoins secrecy on the leper, the report of the cure spreads, and Jesus can only find rest and time for prayer —Luke adds this touch here, though he omitted it in iv. 42— by withdrawing into the solitudes.

v. 17–26 : JESUS AND THE FORGIVENESS OF SINS

One day he was teaching, and near him sat Pharisees and doctors 17 of the Law who had come from every village of Galilee and Judaea as well as from Jerusalem. Now the power of the Lord was present for the work of healing. Some men came 18 up carrying a man who was paralysed ; they tried to carry him inside and lay him in front of Jesus, but when they 19 could not find any means of getting him in, on account of the crowd, they climbed to the top of the house and let him down through the tiles, mattress and all, among the people in front of Jesus. When he saw their faith he said, ' Man, 20 your sins are forgiven you.' Then the scribes and Pharisees 21

E   49

began to argue, 'Who is this blasphemer ? Who can forgive
22 sins, who but God alone ? ' Conscious that they were
arguing to themselves, Jesus addressed them, saying, 'Why
23 argue in your hearts ? Which is the easier thing, to say,
"Your sins are forgiven," or to say, "Rise and walk " ?
24 But to let you see the Son of man has power on earth to
forgive sins '—he said to the paralysed man, ' Rise, I tell
25 you, lift your mattress and go home.' Instantly he got
up before them, lifted what he had been lying on, and went
26 home glorifying God. And all were seized with astonishment ; they glorified God and were filled with awe, saying,
' We have seen incredible things to-day.'

(Cf. Mark ii. 1–12.)

This is the first of five consecutive incidents taken over from
Mark to illustrate the ' authority ' of Jesus in religious matters.
The connecting-links in Mark are loose, and the relation of the
incidents would seem to be logical rather than chronological.
The common motive is indeed to illustrate and defend the right
of the Christian society (1) to preach forgiveness of sins in the
name of Jesus ; (2) to associate with persons beyond the legal
pale ; (3) to feel dispensed from the Jewish fasts ; and (4) to
set aside the Sabbath-law. In every case the authority appealed
to is that of Jesus' word and example.

In Mark the first incident is laid in Capernaum, and the
witnesses who throng the house are ' certain scribes.' Luke
omits Capernaum, and transforms Mark's group of scribes into
an assembly of **Pharisees and doctors of the Law,** who had
come ' from every village of Galilee and Judaea as well as from
Jerusalem.' To Luke also we owe the notice that **the power
of the Lord was present for the work of healing,** a statement
which either looks back to the unusual challenge implied in the
presence of so many inquisitors or looks forward to the remarkable cure to be effected in the case of the paralytic. The
description of the incident is taken over with only a minimum
of change from Mark. The expedient resorted to by the friends
of the palsied man, their resolution in mounting the roof, and
their refusal to allow any obstacle to defeat their purpose,
impress Jesus, and give point to the statement : **When he saw
their faith, he said,** etc.

The point of the narrative is in the claim of absolving power

50

made by Jesus when he says, ' Man, your sins are forgiven you.'
Why does Jesus preface the act of healing with this declaration ?
We may of course appeal to the familiar connexion of ideas
stated in the Jewish saying, ' No sick man is healed until his
sins have been forgiven him ' (*Nedarim*, 41a), or we may suppose
that Jesus has been speaking to the company of faith as the
sole condition on which the power of God to end the reign of
sin can be appropriated, and that the dramatic irruption of the
stretcher-bearers with their friend has provided an unexpected
illustration of what he means.   But what the incident is intended
primarily to bring out is that the authority of Jesus in religion
starts with the forgiveness of sins.   He comes to deliver souls
from the paralysis of moral and spiritual energy, the neuroses—
to use a psychological expression—in which a misdirected life
has resulted, and from which the soul must be freed if the
power of God is to take effect in the lives of men.   This claim,
however, to forgive sins shocks the Pharisees, and they ask,
'Who is this blasphemer ? '   Here we have the primary protest
of Judaism against the Christian Church and gospel.   Not that
the Jewish teachers did not believe in divine forgiveness or
held it to be offered only upon conditions, e.g. the offering of
sacrifices.   But they protest against the assumption that any
human being is entitled to declare that forgiveness.   ' Who can
forgive sins but God alone ? '   Not even the Messiah was allowed
by the Rabbis to have such a prerogative, for did they not
read in Scripture : ' I, even I, am he that blotteth out thy
transgressions for my own sake ' (Isaiah xliii. 25 ; cf. xliv. 22) ?
To this the Christian answer is that Christ's forgiveness is fundamental, and has physical evidence to support it.   The fact
that divine power—in the present case the power to heal—is
with Jesus is valid ground for declaring that the authority
which he claims—in the present case the authority to declare
sins forgiven—has its source in God.   ' Which is the easier
thing,' etc. ?   To Jesus himself the power to restore a sufferer
was all the proof needed of his right to absolve his conscience,
and certainly this test carries conviction to the general audience,
who disperse, glorifying God and saying, 'We have seen incredible
things to-day.'

There remain the difficult words (ver. 24), ' To let you see the
Son of man has power on earth to forgive sins.'   Here suddenly
and without explanation we encounter the mysterious title

Son of man which, as occurring in the gospels some eighty or more times, and always on the lips of Jesus, must have borne a peculiarly solemn and emphatic significance for Jesus himself. How is this title to be understood ? It will not do to say that Jesus is emphasizing his human in distinction from his divine nature, for such a demarcation of ' natures,' though entering into later theological definitions of his personality, plays no part in his own teaching or in the language of his first reporters. Rather must we seek the source of the designation in Scripture or in contemporary Jewish thought. The evidence here is as follows.

(1) The term ' Son of man ' (= ' man,' creature of human form and destiny) occurs in Ezekiel upwards of ninety times, and denotes the prophet himself whom God has raised up and sent to the children of Israel to win them from disobedience to righteousness (Ezekiel ii. 1–3). This prophetic sense of the term would consort aptly enough with the fact that Jesus identifies himself with his nation in order to save it and bring it to God (see under iii. 21–22, iv. 14–30). Upon any explanation of the origin of the term it has for Jesus the value of conveying a sense of true humanity, of complete brotherhood with men. But certain peculiarities in Jesus' usage of the expression are against its derivation from Ezekiel.

(2) The term ' Son of man ' (again = ' man ') occurs in the famous vision in Daniel vii. 13 f., where the seer, after beholding the passing away of the world-empires under the symbolic forms of animals, beholds again in the night-visions : ' And lo ! there came with the clouds of heaven one like a son of man, and he came even to the Ancient of Days . . . and there was given him dominion and glory and a kingdom,' etc. In the Daniel vision this figure resembling a son of man or man serves as collective representation of the ' Saints of the Most High,' for whom the final Kingdom of God is destined (Daniel vii. 18, 27), i.e. he represents the elect nation. Later on, however, as we see by the Jewish writing known as the Similitudes of Enoch (xlvi. 1, 3, lxix. 26–27, 29), the prophecy gave rise in certain circles to what can only be called a new and higher line of Messianism, of which the central figure is a heavenly pre-existent Man, who is to sit on a ' throne of glory ' and to whom ' the sum of judgment ' is to be given. As not a few passages in the gospels echo this conception, and describe the Son of man

as ' sitting at the right hand of Power ' and ' coming with the clouds of heaven ' (Mark xiv. 62, Luke xxii. 69, Mark viii. 38, xiii. 26 ; Luke xviii. 8, xxi. 27, etc.), it seems best to connect the term ' Son of man ' with the Daniel passage. Jesus, as we shall see later, found in the Daniel prophecy a language in which to express his unfaltering assurance that in life and death he brings salvation to his nation. ' Son of man ' therefore denotes him as the Elect of God, the predestined Messiah, and it is in the light of this conception that the present claim is made for him in the Christian tradition. Jesus forgives sins because he is the Man to whom judgment is committed and who brings the Kingdom of God.

It should be noted, however, that Dr. Rudolf Bultmann and other scholars consider the discussion of forgiveness in the above passage to be a later doctrinal accretion to the original story. According to Bultmann the words ' When he saw their faith ' in ver. 20 were followed originally by ' He said to the paralytic man, Rise,' etc. in ver. 24. But if the words ' Your sins are forgiven you ' in ver. 20 were not a part of the original narrative, it fails to appear why the incident became the occasion for such doctrinal elaboration. Consequently we must see in the forgiveness-declaration of Jesus the core of the original narrative. If anything is of later origin, it will rather be the words from ' Jesus addressed them ' in ver. 22 down to ' power on earth to forgive sins ' in ver. 24, which turn wholly upon a form of argument. The claim of Jesus to forgive would then be primary : the argument by which the claim is enforced would be secondary, the product of early Christian controversy. In view of this possibility the question whether Jesus *at this early stage* used the term ' Son of man ' in its Messianic sense ceases to be important. (See below, p. 59.)

v. 27–32 : JESUS AND THE OUTCASTS

On going outside after this he noticed a taxgatherer called Levi 27 sitting at the tax-office and said to him, ' Follow me ' ; he 28 rose, left everything and followed him. Levi held a great 29 banquet for him in his house ; there was a large company present of taxgatherers and others who were guests along with them. But the Pharisees and their scribes complained 30 to his disciples, ' Why do you eat and drink with taxgatherers

31 and sinners ? ' Jesus replied to them,
> ' Healthy people have no need of a doctor, but those who
> are ill :

32 I have not come to call just men but sinners to repent-
> ance.'

(Cf. Mark ii. 13–17.)

The second challenge of Jesus to the orthodoxy of his time
lay in his attitude to taxgatherers and ' sinners.' A case arose
in consequence of his summons to the taxgatherer **Levi**. If we
take the call ' **Follow me** ' to be equivalent to the summons
formerly addressed to Peter and to the sons of Zebedee (v. 10–11),
we may interpret the gathering which Levi now convenes at his
house as a putting into practice of the principle of ' catching
men.' Jewish religious sentiment, however, is shocked by the
presence of Jesus at a promiscuous banquet, and the Pharisees
and their scribes, as custodians of the principle of strict religious
separateness, complain to his disciples.

The name **Pharisees** literally signifies ' the separated ones,'
and may point either (1) to the avoidance by this party of everything that the Law pronounced unclean, or (2) to the fact that
in 163 B.C. the Hasidim, the party from which the Pharisees
had sprung, broke with Judas Maccabaeus and committed
themselves to a purely religious policy.[1] In any case a Pharisee,
according to the Jewish definition, is ' one who separates
himself from all uncleanness and from eating anything unclean.'
According to Josephus, the Pharisees ' are accounted in matters
of ancestral ordinances to exceed all others in punctiliousness '
(*Life*, 38).

The **taxgatherers** with whom Jesus here makes friends would
be mostly underlings of Antipas, employed to levy tariffs and
other dues on merchandise passing into Galilee along the *Via
maris*, or road to the Mediterranean. The profession was suspect
in Judaism because of the contaminating contact into which its
members were brought with Gentile traders, and therefore was
recruited only from the less reputable classes in the community.
Hence ' taxgatherers and sinners ' is a conventional expression
for persons outside the pale of law-abiding Judaism, and even
in Greek writers like Lucian the taxgatherer appears in dubious
company. To the Pharisees therefore the conduct of Jesus

---

[1] See G. F. Moore, *Judaism*, vol. i, pp. 60–2.

signified a letting down of the barriers which, particularly in the matter of ceremonial purifications and tithes, separated the people of God from the world. 'Why do you eat with tax-gatherers and sinners ? ' A Jewish treatise expressly says that ' the disciple of the learned . . . must not sit at table in the society of the ' Am- ha- ' Aretz,' i.e. those who are ignorant or careless of religious usages (*Berakoth*, 43). The fear was that in such company the pious would be offered food from which the tithes had not been properly separated.

Jesus' reply to the charge is that these ostracized classes represent the sick in soul to whom he is sent, and whom specially he desires to win for the Kingdom of God. ' Healthy people have no need of a doctor, but those who are ill.' A physician to souls, Jesus will not, like the Pharisees, wait for sinners to come to him, but will go to them, seeking them out in their haunts. Thereby he refuses to recognize the so-called ' hedge of the Law ' with which Jewish orthodox sentiment had surrounded itself. Over against the Pharisaic idea of salvation by segregation he sets up the new principle of salvation by association (cf. xix. 9–10). A redemptive passion inspires him, to which, on the admission of Jewish scholars like Mr. Montefiore, there is no parallel in Judaism.

v. 33–39 : JESUS AND FASTING

They said to him, ' The disciples of John fast frequently and offer 33
    prayers, as do the disciples of the Pharisees ; but your
    adherents eat and drink.' Jesus said to them,   34
      ' Can you make friends at a wedding fast while the bride-
      groom is beside them ?
    A time will come when the bridegroom is taken from them, 35
      and then they will fast at that time.'
He also told them a parable :   36
    ' No one tears a piece from a new cloak and sews it on an
      old cloak ;
    otherwise he will tear the new cloak,
      and the new piece will not match with the old.
No one pours fresh wine into old wineskins ;   37
    otherwise the fresh wine will burst the wineskins,
      the wine will be spilt and the wineskins ruined.
No, fresh wine must be poured into new wineskins.   38

39   Besides, no one wants new wine [immediately] after
drinking old ;
    " The old," he says, " is better." '

(Cf. Mark ii. 18–22.)

The Law required fasting only upon one day in the year, viz.
the Day of Atonement, but Pharisaism had introduced the
practice of frequent abstinence, and sought to impose it upon all
orthodox Jews. In the parable in xviii. 9–14 the Pharisaic ideal
appears as a fasting on two days of the week, i.e. on Mondays and
Thursdays, though, as Jewish scholars point out, the requirement
applied only to special seasons of prayer, such as the autumn
droughts. We must therefore suppose that the criticism here
directed against Jesus occurred during one of those special
periods. Why did Jesus' disciples eat and drink on days when
the disciples of John, like all strict Pharisees, observed the
customary rules ?

Jesus answers that the regulations in question have no binding
force upon his disciples. ' Can you make friends at a wedding
fast while the bridegroom is with them ? ' The fasting laws are
not consistent with that consciousness of God which for Jesus
and his disciples constitutes the joy of life and the very soul of
religion. While not opposed to fasting as a sincere and inward
discipline (Matthew vi. 16–17), he refuses to regard it as appropriate to the situation in which he and his companions are proclaiming the ' glad news ' of the Kingdom. Public opinion
exempted from fasting the happy circle of the bridegroom on
the wedding-day, lest they should diminish the bridegroom's joy,
and so Jesus declares that rigours such as the followers of John
practised are wholly out of place in the circle in which he lives.

But what about the words which follow ? ' A time will come
when the bridegroom is taken from them.' As they stand, these
words can only refer to Jesus' death and the break-up of his
circle. Did Jesus then at this time allude to the prospect of
his death ? The possibility that he did so is certainly not to be
excluded. But there is nevertheless some ground for asking
whether the words as originally spoken by Jesus referred to
himself and not rather to John. The followers of John had
suffered the loss of their earthly head. He had been violently
reft from them (iii. 20), and therefore they had real grounds for
fasting. In that case Jesus is explaining sympathetically the

fasting-practice of the followers of the Baptist, while at the same time he is maintaining the freedom of his own. The tradition, however, allegorizing the figure of the Bridegroom, has applied the saying directly to Jesus as the Messiah (cf. Matthew xxv. 1), and taken it as a justification of the Tuesday and Friday fasts by which the Christian community soon began to commemorate its Lord.

Two parables now follow which in their present context illustrate the incompatibility of the gospel of Jesus with the institutions of Judaism. The first runs in Mark : ' No one stitches a piece of unseasoned cloth on an old coat, otherwise the piece filled in takes away from the coat,' etc. (Mark ii. 21). If Jesus uttered this parable in connexion with fasting, it might admit of any of the three following explanations : (1) John's disciples have been inconsistent. Though belonging to the new age in which the Kingdom is preached (xvi. 16), they have gone back to Judaism, and patched up a compromise with it. (2) Jesus' disciples, having once been emancipated, cannot attach themselves again to the Jewish rites except at the cost of their new-found freedom. (3) John's disciples cannot adopt the new liberty of the followers of Jesus, since to do so would be to disrupt the system under which they live. The first explanation, however, is improbable, because there is no evidence that John's disciples had accepted the principles of the new age, which Jesus teaches. The second is improbable, because the old cloak in the parable cannot well refer to the liberty of the gospel, but only to the conservative institutions of Judaism. On the whole, therefore, the third explanation is to be preferred, and it consorts best with the peculiar Lukan form of the parable : ' No one tears a piece from a new cloak,' etc.

The second illustration, ' No one pours fresh wine into old wineskins,' etc., may be a defence of Jesus' disciples for not going back to Judaism, or it may be an explanation why John's disciples do not accept the new principles of the gospel. In the former case the meaning will be : the new consciousness of God in which Jesus and his disciples live and move and have their being cannot find adequate expression under the old forms, but must create new institutions for itself.

A third illustration—not supplied by Mark—is added by Luke in ver. 39 : ' No one wants new wine after drinking old,' etc. Here we have an unmistakable reference to the disciples of the Baptist, who are satisfied with the old ways and cannot be expected to change them.

It is possible that the above parables were originally uttered in other connexions to illustrate, for example, the completely new life which Jesus asked of those whom he brought to God. In this case the meaning would be : Faith calls for life in a new spirit, not for a mere patching up of the old character.

vi. 1–5 : Jesus and the Sabbath—First Incident
vi.

1 One sabbath it happened that as he was crossing the cornfields his disciples pulled some ears of corn and ate them, rubbing
2 them in their hands.   Some of the Pharisees said, 'Why
3 are you doing what is not allowed on the sabbath ? '   But Jesus answered them, 'And have you never read what
4 David did when he and his men were hungry ?   He went into the house of God, took *the loaves of the Presence* and ate them, giving them to his men as well—bread that no one is
5 allowed to eat except the priests.'   And he said to them, 'The Son of man is Lord even over the sabbath.'

(Cf. Mark ii. 23–28.)

The disciples of Jesus, by plucking ears of corn on a Sabbath and, as Luke adds 'rubbing them in their hands,' lay themselves open to the charge of reaping and threshing on the holy day.   That this was no merely vexatious charge appears by the Mishna which, enumerating thirty-nine works which are forbidden on the Sabbath, expressly condemns ' Whoso ploughs and sows, reaps and binds sheaves, threshes and winnows, and sorts and grinds and sifts and kneads and bakes,' etc. (*Shabbath*, vii. 2).   Jesus replies, ' Have you never read what David did ? ' and cites the occasion during his wars with Saul when the king of Israel went to the sanctuary at Nob and requisitioned for himself and his troops 'the loaves of the Presence' which the Law reserved for the priests (1 Samuel xxi. 1–6).   The Jewish Midrash *Yalkut* explains that David acted here under circumstances which endangered life.   Jesus would appear to take the same ground.   David acted from necessity, and therefore did not break the Law.   For the same reason the disciples, who have acted under constraint of hunger, are not to be condemned.

Mark represents the conclusion of Jesus as being that ':the sabbath was made for man, not man for the sabbath : so that the Son of man is Lord even over the sabbath ' (Mark ii. 27-28). Luke, like Matthew, omits the first sentence, which stresses the humanitarian purpose of the Sabbath-law, and which has Talmudic parallels in such sayings as, ' The Sabbath is given over to you, and not you given over to the Sabbath ' (*Yoma,* 85b). On the other hand, he retains the second word, and here again we encounter the title Son of man. ' **The Son of man is Lord even over the sabbath.'** In its present form the saying can only mean that Jesus, as the Messiah to whom judgment is committed and who brings the Kingdom of God (see above, under v. 17-26), has the right to supersede the Sabbath-law, or to declare in what sense it is to be kept. Thus once again the Church asserts Christ's authority for the liberty which it enjoys with respect to the holy day.

It is sometimes argued that Jesus cannot have uttered either this saying or the similar word in v. 24 in the present form and context. The reason is that in *Mark* every other occurrence of the title ' **Son of man** ' is subsequent to Peter's confession of Jesus as the Messiah (Mark viii. 29). That Jesus should not unveil the secret of his calling until the development of events and the imminent prospect of his rejection and death required him to render final account to others of the historic significance of his work, above all, of his extraordinary engagement to bring Israel to God, is in itself probable enough. Hence many scholars urge that here and in v. 24 Jesus, using his native Aramaic speech, meant ' Son of man ' (*barnasha*) in its ordinary human sense of ' man,' not in its special sense as equivalent to ' Messiah,' saying in the one case that ' Man has authority to forgive sins,' and in the other, that ' Man has rights which take precedence over the sabbath.' If the two sayings go back to Jesus, it is possible that he meant them in this sense. But if they represent the language which his followers used to formulate the nature of his authority, the above explanations become inept. For certainly the Christian community never intended the words to advance such claims on behalf of men.

vi. 6-11 : JESUS AND THE SABBATH—SECOND INCIDENT
Another sabbath he happened to go into the synagogue and teach. 6
Now a man was there who had his right hand withered,

7   and the scribes and Pharisees watched to see if he would
     heal on the sabbath, so as to discover some charge against
8   him. He knew what was in their minds ; so he told the
     man with the withered hand, ' Rise and stand forward.'
9   He rose and stood before them. Then Jesus said to them,
     ' I ask you, is it right on the sabbath to help or to hurt,
10   to save life or to kill ? ' And glancing round at them all in
     anger he said to the man, ' Stretch out your hand.' He
11   did so, and his hand was quite restored. This filled them
     with fury, and they discussed what they could do to Jesus.

                                        (Cf. Mark iii. 1–6.)

The scene is a synagogue in some unmentioned town, and the
occasion is provided by the presence of a man with a paralysed
hand. The lost gospel of the Nazarenes explained that the
man was a stone-mason who depended for his living upon the
use of his hands, and represented him as saying to Jesus, ' I
pray thee, restore me my health that I may not shamefully
beg for food.' The critics are observing Jesus closely in the
hope of detecting him in some offence against the Sabbath.
Jesus, aware of their purpose, takes up their unspoken challenge,
and raises the whole question of the Sabbath-law.

Summoning the man to come forward where he will be seen,
Jesus says to the Pharisees : ' I ask you, is it right on the
Sabbath '—here the question of his ' authority ' becomes
explicit—' to help or to hurt, to save life or to kill ? ' Nothing
could better illustrate the uncompromising positiveness of Jesus'
whole conception of moral obligation than the issue here formulated. Jesus will recognize no alternative to the doing of good
except the doing of evil. The refusal to save life is tantamount
to the taking of it. Thereby he invalidates at one stroke
the do-nothing attitude, which, under cover of the principle
of not working on the Sabbath, his contemporaries mistook for
obedience to the will of God. The Pharisees sanctioned on
the Sabbath acts which were necessary to save life. ' Every
doubt with regard to life thrusts the Sabbath aside ' (*Yoma*,
viii. 6). But they would have contended that here, as in vi. 1,
there was no danger in waiting till the Sabbath was over. Jesus,
on the other hand, declines to regard the Sabbath-law as pro-
hibitive in any sense of humanitarian duties, and heals the
man forthwith.

Two observations may be made on the subject of the five preceding sections :

(1) Three times, viz. in v. 30, v. 33, and vi. 2, the arguments of the Jewish critics are either addressed to the disciples of Jesus or concern their actions. Hence Dr. Bultmann and others argue that the incidents in question reflect not historical situations in the life of Jesus but later controversies, in which Christians were engaged with adherents of the Baptist or other Jews. But while it may be admitted that such later controversies imparted special interest and point to the incidents in question, it is surely unnecessary to deny them a basis in the authentic records of Jesus.

(2) In none of the above incidents does Jesus actually repudiate or make a breach with the Law. He comes into conflict with its official interpreters, but only as regards deductions which they have unwarrantably made. Nevertheless the ' authority ' with which he discards the traditional interpretations of his opponents creates a widening gulf between him and them, and Mark says that the Pharisees now joined with the Herodian party in a plot to kill him (Mark iii. 6 ; cf. Luke vi. 11). Jesus replies to this move by drawing the circle of his adherents into closer relations with himself.

vi. 12-19 : THE CHOOSING OF THE TWELVE

It was in these days that he went off to the hillside to pray. 12
He spent the whole night in prayer to God, and when day 13
broke he summoned his disciples, choosing twelve of them,
to whom he gave the name of ' apostles ' : Simon (to 14
whom he gave the name of Peter), Andrew his brother,
James, John, Philip, Bartholomew, Matthew, Thomas, James 15
the son of Alphaeus, Simon (who was called ' the Zealot '),
Judas the son of James, and Judas Iscariot (who turned 16
traitor). With them he came down the hill and stood on 17
a level spot. There was a great company of his disciples
with him, and a large multitude of people from all Judaea,
from Jerusalem, and from the coast of Tyre and Sidon, who
had come to hear him and to get cured of their diseases.
Those who were annoyed with unclean spirits also were 18
healed. Indeed the whole of the crowd made efforts to 19
touch him, for power issued from him and cured everybody.
(Cf. Mark iii. 13-19.)

Mark's insertion of the appointment of the Twelve at this juncture suggests a counter-move of Jesus to the growing alienation of the synagogue leaders (Mark iii. 6). Luke mentions that Jesus went off to the hillside to pray, and spent the whole night in prayer to God. The selection of the Twelve at daybreak has thus a special solemnity imparted to it.

It is plain from ver. 13 that the apostles form an inner circle within a larger body of disciples. Their special commission is not mentioned, but will be explained later (ix. 1 f.). The list of names corresponds with Mark's, except that in the third quaternion Judas the son of James takes the place of the disciple whom Mark calls ' Thaddaeus,' and Matthew ' Lebbaeus, whose surname is Thaddaeus.' The same Judas appears in the other Lukan list in Acts i. 13, and this shews that Luke derived his names from another source than Mark, and that not all lists of the apostles exactly agreed.

Three of the Twelve, viz. Simon, James, and John, are already known to us (v. 1-11). Luke has not hitherto mentioned Andrew, and of the other eight none of our evangelists tells us anything, unless Matthew—called in Matthew x. 3 ' the tax-gatherer '—be identical with Levi. Luke mentions Peter, i.e. ' Cephas ' or ' Rock,' as the surname of Simon. It was a custom of Jewish Rabbis to give their disciples surnames : thus in the Mishna tractate *Aboth*, ii. 10, Rabbi Johanan speaks of one pupil as ' a plastered cistern,' i.e. a learner who never forgets a fact, and of another as ' a welling spring.' Luke does not state when Simon received his particular cognomen. According to one account it was when he confessed Jesus as Messiah (Matthew xvi. 18). According to another it was at his first coming to Jesus (John i. 42). Probably the later service of Simon in rallying the Church after the Crucifixion (cf. xxii. 31-32) gave permanent and indelible significance to the name. The force of Zealot as surname of the second Simon is uncertain. The Zealots as a party do not appear in Josephus earlier than A.D. 66, when John of Gischala organized his faction of extreme militarists. But extreme anti-Roman opinions existed before that time, and Simon may have shared them, or the name may merely indicate his zeal for the Law (cf. Galatians i. 14, Acts xxi. 20). The surname Iscariot remains an enigma. It may represent *'ish Kiryoth*, Hebrew for ' man of Kiryoth.' It is less likely that it stands for the Latin *sicarius* (' assassin '),

though that name was known in Palestine, or for *Sycharites,*
meaning ' man of Sychar.'

With these Twelve Jesus comes down to the level ground, so
that the Sermon which now follows takes place, not as in
Matthew on the hillside but on the plain. To the disciples,
in presence of a larger audience representing the nation, Jesus
delivers the promises (20–26), principles of conduct (27–42),
and warnings (43–49), which constitute his ' doctrine,' the
teaching which, as we have seen, came to men with authority.

The structure and contents of the Sermon are taken by
Luke from Q, and reappear with modifications in Matthew
v.–vii., but our first evangelist has greatly expanded the discourse
by the inclusion of cognate items from other parts of Q and
from other sources. (See Introd., p. xxiv.)

vi. 20–26 : BEATITUDES AND WOES

Then, raising his eyes he looked at his disciples and said : 20
  ' Blessed are you poor !
    the Realm of God is yours.
Blessed are you who hunger to-day !   21
  you shall be satisfied.
Blessed are you who weep to-day !
  you shall laugh.
Blessed are you when men will hate you,   22
when they will excommunicate you and denounce you and
    defame you as wicked on account of the Son of man ;
  rejoice on that day and leap for joy !   23
  rich is your reward in heaven—
  for their fathers did the very same to the prophets.
But woe to you rich folk !   24
  you get all the comforts you will ever get.
Woe to you who have your fill to-day !   25
  you will be hungry.
Woe to you who laugh to-day !
  you will wail and weep.
Woe to you when all men speak well of you !   26
  that is just what their fathers did to the false prophets.'
                     (Cf. Matthew v. 1–12.)

The Beatitudes in Luke are four in number, and are prefaced
by the words, **Raising his eyes he looked at his disciples and said.**

Their purpose is to congratulate the disciples on the felicity which awaits them as the inheritors of the Kingdom of God. At present the followers of Jesus are poor, hungry, sorrowful, persecuted, but all these conditions will be reversed through the advent, now eagerly awaited, of the Reign of God. By the fact that they are formulated in the second person, the Lukan beatitudes bring the poverty, hunger, and tears of which they speak into direct relation with the character of the disciples, and so conserve the *religious* sense which attaches to these terms in Israel. Matthew, who throws the beatitudes into the third person, and so generalizes them, contrives to guard their religious significance by adding to ' poor ' the qualifying phrase ' in spirit,' and by inserting ' righteousness ' as object after ' hunger.'

The word blessed represents an Aramaic expression literally signifying ' O the good fortune of those who,' etc. Thus the beatitudes fittingly introduce the deliverance of one who preached ' glad tidings ' to poor folk (iv. 18). The good fortune of the persons addressed lies in the assurance given to them that the Realm of God, of which prophets and saints have dreamed, will be theirs. The Realm or Kingdom of God is here contemplated in its historic prophetic sense. The saints in Israel had always been conscious that under the existing order the evidence of God's sovereignty in the world was far from complete. It was possible for the sceptic to point to the rampant evils of the time, the sins of the mighty and the sufferings of the innocent, and to say to Israel ' Where is your God ? ' (Psalm xiv. 1, xlii. 3, 9–10, lxxiii. 1–11, lxxvii. 7–10, lxxx. 4–7, etc.). The saint could only answer that God had for wise ends not yet taken His power to Himself, but that His reign would come. A supernatural order would arise in which usurping evil would be judged and removed, and God would be visibly revealed as Saviour of His people. (See the writer's *Christ's View of the Kingdom of God*, pp. 24–43.) As this conception of the perfected rule of God had risen on the horizon of the ancient prophets and apocalyptists in proportion as their apprehension of God's redeeming will was strong and clear, so for Jesus in his fully realized consciousness of Sonship to the Father the Realm of God has acquired a nearness and actuality by which it fills the whole foreground of his mind, and he offers it as immediate object of faith and hope to his times.

First, this Realm is offered to the **poor** (cf. Isaiah lxi. 1, Luke

iv. 18), by whom are meant those who, under injustice, loss, and contempt, have set their hope on God and remained loyal to His will. The conditions of Oriental society, where the poor have to go without human justice, are presupposed. Compare Psalm xl. 17, where the psalmist, after referring to his oppressors, says, ' But I am poor and needy, yet the Lord thinketh upon me ; Thou art my help and my deliverer ; make no tarrying, O my God.' Compare also Psalm xxxiv. 6, lxxii. 2–4, 12–14, etc. The term ' poor ' therefore has a religious as well as an economic significance. It denotes those in whom adversity has wrought a sharpened desire and an enlarged capacity of spiritual good, and Jesus who has found a warmer welcome for his word among these humbler sections of society now signalizes their receptivity of spirit as the primary condition of receiving the Kingdom of God. (See also Introd., pp. xxv.–xxvi.)

A similar good fortune awaits those who **hunger** and who **weep** under the present era of sin, when God's sovereignty is still unrealized, still only an object of hope. The hunger and the tears here alluded to are not exhausted or even properly explained by reference to outward conditions, for in Israel it is known that man does not live by bread alone, and sorrow goes deeper than to the sense of earthly want. The hunger is for God, for the vindication of divine justice, for conformity to the divine will. The tears are for the tragedy of sin, for the evils wrought by alienation from God in Israel and in the world. Compare Ezekiel ix. 4, where a mark of God's favour is set on the foreheads of those ' who sigh and weep for all the abominations that are done in the midst ' of Jerusalem. Both hunger and sorrow are combined in Psalm xlii. 3 : ' My tears have been my food day and night, while they continually say to me, *Where is your God ?* ' Not always or everywhere does the world's sin produce the kind of sorrow of which Jesus speaks. Sometimes it inspires only bitterness or revolt. But it is not to the bitter but to those whom the sorrows of earth move to genuine tears [1] that the joy of the Realm of God is promised.

Many, doubtless, of Jesus' hearers had come to think of that Realm in terms of liberation from the foreign yoke of Rome and of the restoration of national glory, but Jesus lays all the emphasis on the spiritual or inward character of redemption.

---

[1] Cf. Virgil's ' Sunt lacrimae rerum et mentem mortalia tangunt ' (*Æneid* i. 462).

The fourth beatitude, **Blessed are you when men will hate you,** etc., points forward to the time when disciples will be excommunicated from Israel through their acceptance of Jesus as the Son of man. As sharing the sufferings of the prophets, they will attain like the prophets the life of the Kingdom of Heaven. The future reference of this blessing, and particularly its allusion to Jesus as the **Son of man,** shews that its present form owes something to the later sufferings of the Christian community at the hands of the Jews.

The beatitudes are followed in Luke by four Woes on the rich, the satisfied, the complacent, the well-reputed among men. The persons so described have received their portion of good in the present world, but having abused their power and oppressed the innocent and the godly, they forfeit all hope of 'comfort' when the Kingdom comes. The situation implied both in the beatitudes and in the woes is, as Dr. Easton observes, thoroughly Palestinian. 'The disciples of ver. 20 are really members of the struggling, poverty-stricken Jewish church. Moreover the rich men of vers. 24–26 are presupposed to be religious leaders, a state of affairs that existed only in Palestine.' But it is doubtful if the woes should be ascribed to Jesus. (1) They are absent in Matthew, and therefore cannot certainly be ascribed to Q, for the writer of Matthew, as we see by xxiii. 13, 15, 16, 23, 25, 27, 29, etc., was not averse to such sayings. (2) They are simply inverted forms of the beatitudes, and may be therefore only a Jewish-Christian commentary on the latter. The sentiments expressed are in the spirit of that church. Compare James i. 9, ii. 1 f., v. 1–6, and Introd., pp. xxv–xxvi.

vi. 27–36 : The Law of Love

27   ' I tell you, my hearers,
       love your enemies, do good to those who hate you :
28   bless those who curse you, pray for those who abuse you.
29   If a man strikes you on the one cheek,
       offer him the other as well ;
      if anyone takes your coat,
       do not deny him your shirt as well ;
30   give to anyone who asks you,

and do not ask your goods back from anyone who has
taken them.

As you would like men to do to you,   31
so do to them.

If you love only those who love you, what credit is that 32
to you ?

Why, even sinful men love those who love them.

If you help only those who help you, what merit is that 33
to you ?

Why, even sinful men do that.

If you only lend to those from whom you hope to get some- 34
thing, what credit is that to you ?

Even sinful men lend to one another, so as to get a fair
return.

No, you must love your enemies and help them,   35
you must lend to them without expecting any return ;
then you will have a rich reward,
you will be sons of the Most High—
for he is kind even to the ungrateful and the evil.

Be merciful,   36
as your Father is merciful.'

(Cf. Matthew v. 38-48.)

From the beatitudes the Lukan sermon proceeds to develop
the principle to which all must conform who would enter into
the Kingdom of God, viz. the principle of Love, by which is
meant no mere emotional sentiment but the most active and
unlimited benevolence. The connexion of the teaching now
given with the preceding promises of the Kingdom would seem
to be that, in order to enter the Kingdom, men must seize and
appropriate forthwith the life which belongs to that Kingdom by
making God's own will and spirit the regulative principle of
conduct. The abruptness of the transition at ver. 27 suggests
either that the Q source followed by Luke supplied no intermediate link between the beatitudes and the principle of loving
enemies, or that Luke has allowed something to drop out. In
favour of the latter alternative stands the antithetic **But I tell you,**
which suggests that Jesus is rectifying some current misinter-
pretation of the will of God such as we find in Matthew v. 38 or
43, and it has been argued that Luke's source actually contained
some of the material reproduced in Matthew v. 20-37, but that

Luke omitted it from lack of interest in legal controversy. It is more probable that Luke has simply followed his source, and that Matthew's argument is due to elaboration of the source by aid of other materials.

In vers. 27-31 the range or scope of the principle of love or active benevolence is disclosed. So far from regulating action by regard for the deservingness of others, Jesus says to his followers ' Love your enemies.' This in a society which legitimated the extremest hatred of the Roman power and sought to bring in the Kingdom by force of arms is sufficiently remarkable. The extremest form that goodwill can take is prescribed. Hatred, cursing, abuse are to be answered with actions, desires, and prayers which aim solely at the good of the offender, and this not primarily in order to disarm his hostility, though the power of love to transform the spirit of hatred is implied, but in order never to demit under any circumstances the obligation to seek the good of men. Nowhere does it appear more clearly that Jesus claims lordship not merely over a man's conduct but in the inmost recesses of his nature. Concrete instances are cited in vers. 29-30. ' If a man strikes you on the one cheek . . . if anyone takes your coat.' Insult and injury in the most affronting forms, viz. personal violence and robbery on the highway, are contemplated. In these cases the injured person is not to retaliate or to shew a spirit of revenge. He must rather offer the other cheek, surrender the remaining garment. In the parallel in Matthew v. 38-41 three cases are taken : (1) personal insult as here, (2) vexatious litigation aimed at the confiscation of property, (3) conscripted service demanded by military or other authority. In each case the injured party is required not merely to be submissive but to go beyond the terms of what is demanded of him. It is obvious that the principle of non-resistance here inculcated implies no declining or shirking of moral issues but contrariwise a fuller acceptance of those issues than would be possible where the normal instinct to refuse or to strike back was indulged. To strike back, to repel injury by injury, is really an evading of the moral situation created by the offender's ill-will. Jesus, who never evades, never takes the line of least resistance, will only consider the situation to be saved when the injury is accepted to the full extent and in a spirit of inextinguishable goodwill. The words were literally meant, and should be literally understood.

In the same spirit the followers of Jesus are to **give to anyone who asks.** The man who asks of us is entitled to receive. A Christian is not at liberty to turn a suppliant away, though the mind which requires love to be the principle of action prescribes also what love will devise. Yet even here a literal response— compare the Bishop and Jean Valjean in Hugo's *Les Misérables*— will not seldom be the true fulfilment of the command. So also the followers of Jesus are to forgo recovery of goods where restitution is withheld, and generally to act upon the rule ' As you would like men to do to you, so do to them.' This principle in the negative form was part of the popular religious ethic as we see by Tobit iv. 15, ' That which you hate, do to nobody,' and by the maxim of Hillel, ' What to thyself is hateful, to thy fellow thou shalt not do.' [1] But Jesus goes far beyond it when he substitutes the positive form of the precept for the negative, for now it becomes not a mere principle of justice or a rule of guarded action but a boundless inspiration to good.

Did Jesus find the principle of non-resistance already indicated in the character of the Lord's Servant in Deutero-Isaiah ? In Isaiah l. 6 the Servant says, ' I gave my back to the smiters, and my cheeks to them that plucked off the hair ; I hid not my face from shame and spitting.' The analogy is close, and it may be therefore that Jesus saw in non-resistance the principle which all must follow who would serve God's purpose of redemption. But the principle is adopted, not because it is scriptural, but because it is rooted in the nature of love, in the will to good itself. For the sake of this will to good all personal revenge, greed, self-seeking must be renounced, and even where the situation is more complex, involving other considerations than those of personal defence or honour, the same principle of benevolence, pure and unlimited, is still to be the rule of action.

In vers. 32-36 the non-limiting of the principle by any consideration of **reward** is emphasized. Current morals assumed the sufficiency of being kind where a response was forthcoming, though occasionally a nobler principle finds utterance, as in *Aboth* i. 3, ' Be not as slaves that minister . . . with a view to receiving recompense . . . and let the fear of Heaven be upon you.' Jesus desires a higher merit in his followers than that which accrues from loving, helping, and lending to those from

[1] For other Jewish forms of the saying see Dalman, *Jesus-Jeshua,* p. 226.

whom requital can be expected. True religion in the sight of
God implies a *plus* upon these canons, and in ver. 35 return
is made to the duty of loving and helping enemies. Why are
Jesus' followers to love their enemies? Because thus **you
will be sons of the Most High**—for he is kind even to the ungrateful and the evil. Here at last the great argument attains
its climax. Jesus desires his followers by surrender to, and
oneness with, the mind of God to realize the divine potentiality
of human nature, which implies the regulation of life here and
now by the same mercy which inspires the actions of God.
Conscious of the blessedness of himself living in harmony with
the Spirit of the Father, he yearns to draw his followers into
the same blessedness, combining the favour of God with likeness
to God, and shewing itself in love. In the Old Testament we
find acknowledgment that the earth is full of the *hesed* or
' lovingkindness ' of the Lord. Jesus gives this gracious aspect
of the created order a precedence over every other, emphasizing
the divine patience with the undeserving, and finding in it the
only final norm of life. **Be merciful** is in Matthew ' be perfect,'
i.e. accept nothing short of the full ideal as it is in God.

vi. 37–42 : Of Judging

37   ' Also, judge not, and you will not be judged yourselves :
    condemn not, and you will not be condemned :
    pardon, and you will be pardoned yourselves :

38   give, and you will have ample measure given you—
    they will pour into your lap measure pressed down,
        shaken together, and running over ;
    for the measure you deal out to others will be dealt back
        to yourselves.'

39 He also told them a parabolic word :
    ' Can one blind man lead another ?
    will they not both fall into a pit ?

40   A scholar is not above his teacher :
        but if he is perfectly trained he will be like his
        teacher.

41 Why do you note the splinter in your brother's eye and fail
42   to see the plank in your own eye ? How dare you say to
    your brother, " Brother, let me take out the splinter that

is in your eye," and you never notice the plank in your own
eye ? You hypocrite ! take the plank out of your own eye
first, and then you will see properly to take out the splinter
in your brother's eye.'

(Cf. Matthew vii. 1-5, xv. 14, x. 24-25.)

In these verses a particular application of the principle of
love is made. Contemporary religion was full of censoriousness,
but over against this Jesus says : Judge not (now), and you will
not be judged yourselves (at the last day). In the present
context the words imply that the service of God, the Merciful
One, implies on man's part a forgiving, liberal spirit that ' thinks
no evil.' The thought that men must forgive if they wish to
be forgiven runs through and through the teaching of Jesus
(cf. Mark xi. 25, Matthew vi. 14-15, etc.), and rests not on any
bargaining of man with God, but rather on the principle that
God's gifts come only to those through whom they can find
an outlet to others. Consequently the conception of a self-
contained, self-centred virtue is excluded, and in ver. 38 the word
about the measure, which elsewhere is applied with regard to
receptive hearing of the Word (Mark iv. 21 f.), is made the
standard of liberality in giving. The liberal giver to men
receives in turn from God ' measure pressed down, shaken
together, and running over.'

The saying ' Can one blind man lead another ? ' is introduced
by Luke as a *mashal* or parabolic word, and occurs in Matthew,
not in the Sermon but in a later discourse. In the present
context, where they are preceded and followed by warnings
against censoriousness, this and the other saying ' A scholar
is not above his teacher,' etc., must be explained with Dr.
Easton as meaning that the harsh critic of others ' cannot
really benefit the objects of his criticism.' A man cannot rise
above the principles which he has been taught, and if he has
derived his norm of life from an unworthy teacher, he will
pass on the same imperfection to others. Both words, however,
admit of a wider application than belongs to them in this
setting. The context of the second is plainly artificial. The
scholar who is perfectly trained is here the product not of Christ's
teaching but of some purblind censorious guide, higher than
whom he does not attain (contrast the setting in Matthew x.
24-25). In vers. 41-42 the principle of not judging is resumed,

and an illustration which would be familiar in the carpenter's shop at Nazareth is used. ' Why do you note the splinter in your brother's eye ? ' etc. The faults which religious people ignore in themselves, while criticizing the failings of their neighbours, are like planks of wood compared to tiny specks. Reform must begin with one's own character, for only in a changed and reborn spirit, inspired by a love like God's, will true perception exist of the character of others.

vi. 43–45 : OF CHARACTER AND CONDUCT

43   ' No sound tree bears rotten fruit,
         nor again does a rotten tree bear sound fruit :
44   each tree is known by its fruit.
     Figs are not gathered from thorns,
         and grapes are not plucked from a bramble-bush.
45   The good man produces good from the good stored in his
         heart,
     and the evil man evil from his evil :
     for a man's mouth utters what his heart is full of.'
                   (Cf. Matthew vii. 16–21, xii. 33–35.)

The stipulation that personal sincerity is the one condition of benefiting others is enforced by the illustration : each tree is known by its fruit. Thorns produce not figs but thorns. Brambles produce not grapes but brambles. So men cannot raise others above the level to which they themselves have attained. They cannot communicate what they do not possess. They cannot inspire others to issues better than those to which themselves are dedicated. Fruit here means personal influence. If character is unsound its influence is unsound. The principle is summed up in ver. 45, where the good man produces good from the good stored in his heart, and the bad man correspondingly. The need of a renewed nature is therefore manifest. Only if the heart is loving and merciful and purified by active desire for the highest good of others will it promote the purposes for which Jesus calls his disciples.

vi. 46-49 : OF HEARING AND DOING

'Why call me, "Lord, Lord!" and obey me not ? Everyone 46
who comes to me and listens to my words and acts upon 47
them, I will show you whom he is like. He is like a man 48
engaged in building a house, who dug deep down and laid
his foundation on the rock ; when a flood came, the river
dashed against that house but could not shake it, for it
had been well built. He who has listened and has not 49
obeyed is like a man who built a house on the earth with
no foundation ; the river dashed against it and it collapsed
at once, and the ruin of that house was great.'

(Cf. Matthew vii. 21, 24-27.)

The saying in ver. 46 formed with the Parable of the Two
Builders the conclusion of the Sermon in Q. Followers or
hearers of Jesus acknowledge his authority by calling him
' Sir ! ' or ' Master ! ', but such difference does not constitute
genuine adhesion to him. For a capital illustration of this
point see xviii. 18-23, where an aspirant to eternal life addresses
Jesus as ' Good Master ! ' but fails to fulfil the condition which
Jesus lays down. Therefore Jesus says Why call me ' Lord,
Lord ! ' and obey me not ? In the parallel (Matthew vii. 21-23)
the saying has reference to the Judgment Day. Professing
disciples will on that day claim that in the name of Jesus they
prophesied, cast out demons, and performed miracles, but these
claims will not procure an entrance into the Realm of God, if
the disciples have not done the will of the Father who is in
heaven. For a commentary on the saying compare 1 Corinthians
xiii. Early Christians were everywhere prone to lay the stress
on outward gifts like speaking with tongues, prophesying, and
healing, and to forget the absolute duty of love. To both
Matthew and Luke the title Lord has a larger significance than
originally attached to it on the lips of the disciples in Galilee.
Jesus is Lord of his Church as the risen, glorified One, who is
present in the worship of his people, and whose name is a summons to adore (cf. Philippians ii. 5-11). But just because the
title Lord has received this vast extension of meaning, the
Church must continually realize afresh wherein true devotion
to Christ consists.

This is defined in ver. 47. A disciple is one who acts upon

73

Jesus' words, carries out his will, makes the teaching of Jesus the foundation of life and character. Such a disciple is like a man engaged in house-building who dug deep down and laid his foundation on the rock, whereas the disciple who has not obeyed is like a man rearing a house without foundation. In the parable as given by Luke the contrast between the two builders lies not as in Matthew in the different nature of the sites which they choose, but in the fact that the one does, and the other does not, go beneath the surface to the rock. The sudden flooding of the dry bed of a wadi is a frequent phenomenon in Palestine, and figuratively represents the swift coming of judgment upon a thoughtless soul. Jesus warns his followers to prepare for judgment by integrating into their lives the truths which he has taught.

In view of the swiftness with which Jesus saw the Judgment Day to be approaching, his ethical teaching, particularly in such matters as not resisting evil, renouncing property, and abandoning home and kindred is often described as *Interim-Ethic*, i.e. as a rule applying only to a situation in which the present world is conceived to be near its end. But though Jesus placed the life of men against the background of eternity and judgment, his ethical requirements are not to be explained as thereby out of relation to the normal constitution of human nature in the world. Non-resistance to evil, for example, has its motive not in the nearness of the Judgment Day but in the nature of love itself. And disciples are asked to renounce possessions and family not because possessions and family will soon be things of the past but in order that they may ' go and spread the news of the Reign of God ' (ix. 57-62, xii. 32-33, etc.). Jesus is not commending an ideal of perfected religious living which has only a temporary and provisional relation to the Kingdom of God. Rather does he mean that ' one who did not come into genuine fellowship with God now would have no hope of happy admission into the divine presence when the Kingdom was finally established ' (Case, *Jesus*, p. 438). To enter the Kingdom is, in fact, to live by the power and in the spirit of the Father-God. (See further the present writer's *Christ's View of the Kingdom of God*, pp. 102-21.)

vii. 1–10 : The Faith of a Gentile Soldier

vii.

When he had finished what he had to say in the hearing of the 1
people, he went into Capharnahum.

Now there was an army-captain who had a servant ill whom
he valued very highly.   This man was at the point of death ; 2
so, when the captain heard about Jesus, he sent some 3
Jewish elders to him, asking him to come and make his
servant well.   When they reached Jesus they asked him 4
earnestly to do this.   ' He deserves to have this favour
from you,' they said, ' for he is a lover of our nation ; it 5
was he who built our synagogue.'   So Jesus went with 6
them.   But he was not far from the house when the captain
sent some friends to tell him, ' Do not trouble yourself,
sir, I am not fit to have you under my roof, and so I did not 7
consider myself fit even to come to you.   Just say the word,
and let my servant be cured.   For though I am a man under 8
authority myself, I have soldiers under me ; I tell one man
to go, and he goes, I tell another to come, and he comes,
I tell my servant, " Do this," and he does it.'   When Jesus 9
heard this he marvelled at him, and turning to the crowd
that followed he said, ' I tell you, I have never met faith
like this anywhere even in Israel.'   Then the messengers 10
went back to the house and found the sick servant was
quite well.

(Cf. Matthew viii. 5–13.)

This incident, which, as we see by Matthew viii. 5–13, was
derived from Q, and in Q followed the great Sermon of Jesus,
is located in Capernaum.   The **army-captain** who, hearing of
Jesus, sends representatives to intercede on behalf of his sick
servant, is a Gentile officer of native troops or police serving
under Antipas.   In Matthew he comes to Jesus in person ;
in Luke he uses the ' elders ' or civic heads of the Jewish community as intermediaries, and these in pressing his claims explain
that the centurion is **a lover of our nation, who built our synagogue.**   As Jesus is hastening to the centurion's house, a second
deputation meets him.   The centurion is reluctant that Jesus
should condescend to cross the threshold of a Gentile, and
pleads that if he will but **say the word**, the sick servant will

be healed. It is obvious that here we have the distinctive feature which singles out this episode as an illustrious instance of faith. The Gentile officer has learned in his professional experience as a soldier the power of the word of command. He is prepared to accept the word of Jesus as the sufficient guarantee of what he asks, and Jesus hails this attitude as remarkable : ' I have never met faith like this anywhere even in Israel.'

That Jesus encountered instances of a rare and beautiful faith in persons who, like this officer or the Syrophoenician woman (Mark vii. 24-29, Matthew xv. 22-28), were outside the pale of Israel, is credible enough. It is interesting, however, that in both of these cases the tradition makes the healing take place at a *distance* from Jesus and through implicit trust in his *word*. This suggests that the aspect of these incidents which appealed to the early Church was one through which they became prophetic of the Church's mission to the Gentiles. Jesus came to the Jews in person : to the Gentiles he comes only through the preaching of the word (cf. Acts x. 32-33, 36-42 ; xi. 17-18, xiii. 7, 48-49, etc.).

vii. 11-17 : RAISING OF THE WIDOW'S SON AT NAIN

11 It was shortly afterwards that he made his way to a town called
12 Nain, accompanied by his disciples and a large crowd. Just as he was near the gate of the town, there was a dead man being carried out ; he was the only son of his mother, and she was a widow. A large crowd from the town were with
13 her. And when the Lord saw her, he felt pity for her and
14 said to her, ' Do not weep.' Then he went forward and touched the bier ; the bearers stopped, and he said, ' Young
15 man, I bid you rise.' Then the corpse sat up and began to
16 speak ; and Jesus gave him back to his mother. All were seized with awe and glorified God. ' A great prophet has appeared among us,' they said, ' God has visited his people.'
17 And this story of Jesus spread through the whole of Judaea and all the surrounding country.

(Luke alone.)

Nain, with which the above tradition is associated, is not else-where mentioned in the gospels or in the Bible, but may correspond with the modern village of Nein, which lies south of Nazareth on a hill overlooking the plain of Esdraelon and the valley of Jezreel. The motive of Jesus' act is pity for the stricken mother whose only son, a youth, is being carried to his grave. Jesus lays his arresting touch on the bier, and when the cortège stops, he raises the dead man by the power of his word and restores him to his mother. The title the Lord which Luke employs in ver. 13 has peculiar fitness in this context, where Jesus appears clothed with that exalted power over life and death by which he becomes the object of his Church's faith and worship (Philippians ii. 10). In Mark this title is never given to Jesus on earth. Luke, on the other hand, uses it very frequently (see x. 1, 41 ; xi. 39, xii. 42, xiii. 15, xvii. 6, xix. 8, 31 ; xxii. 61, etc.).

The effect of the miracle follows in vers. 16-17. The statement, a great prophet has appeared among us, means probably that Jesus recalled to his contemporaries the achievements of Elijah or Elisha. Certainly the form of the story supports that view, for it embodies features of Elijah's raising of the son of the widow of Zarephath (1 Kings xvii. 17-24) and of Elisha's raising of the son of the Shunnamite (2 Kings iv. 17-22, 32-37). That ' God has visited his people ' need not imply that in the popular judgment the Messianic days have come, but only that a prophet has appeared (compare ix. 18-19). Luke's knowledge of the incident is due to his Palestinian source. Whether originally the tradition was symbolical, referring to a spiritual resurrection, is a question upon which different views have been taken. A somewhat similar incident is reported by Philostratus in his life of the heathen philosopher Apollonius of Tyana (iv. 45).

vii. 18-23 : THE QUESTION OF JOHN THE BAPTIST

John's disciples reported all this to him. So John summoned ¹⁸₁₉ two of his disciples and sent them to ask the Lord, ' Are you the Coming One ? Or are we to look out for someone else ? ' When the men reached Jesus they said, ' John the Baptist 20 has sent us to you to ask if you are the Coming One or if we are to look out for someone else ? ' Jesus at that moment 21 was healing many people of diseases and complaints and evil spirits ; he also bestowed sight on many blind folk. So he 22 replied, ' Go and report to John what you have seen and heard ; that *the blind see*, the lame walk, lepers are cleansed, the deaf hear, the dead are raised, and *to the poor the gospel* 23 *is preached*. And blessed is he who is repelled by nothing in me ! '

(Cf. Matthew xi. 1–6.)

Reports of the work of Jesus reach the Baptist who, though in prison (iii. 19–20), is able to communicate with the outer world through his disciples. In the question ' Are you the Coming One ? ' the expression ' Coming One ' must refer to the Messiah, not, as is sometimes represented, to Elijah as the expected of the Jewish nation. The phrase (cf. iii. 16, Hebrews x. 37) goes back perhaps to Psalm cxviii. 26 : ' Blessed be he who comes in the name of the Lord,' perhaps to the vision in Daniel vii. 13 of one who comes with the clouds to receive an everlasting kingdom. John asks in effect whether Jesus is the Messiah, ' or are we to look for someone else ? '

This question—which must be historical inasmuch as no later age would ascribe to John a mood of doubt so compromising to himself—calls for explanation. Upon the traditional view that John recognized the Messiahship of Jesus from his baptism, if not from an earlier time, the question indicates that the prophet's faith had wavered, and this doubtless was how Luke understood it. Imprisoned, frustrated, lonely, John abandons himself to disappointment. But while such a change of mood is psychologically explicable, the theory on which it hangs scarcely coheres with all the facts. If John had before this time recognized Jesus as the Messiah, would his disciples have continued as a separate order with their own customs (v. 33) ? And would Jesus say, as he does in ver. 28, that ' the least in the Realm of God ' is greater than John ? Hence John's question is to be interpreted rather as betokening, not the collapse of an earlier faith, but a first, and as yet doubtful, approach of his mind to the real facts regarding Jesus' work in the cause of religion. Certainly this interpretation agrees better with the statement (cf. Matthew xi. 1) that the inquiry was elicited by reports of what Jesus had done.

The answer of Jesus is to point to the character of the work itself. ' Go and report to John what you have seen and heard.' Luke enhances the force of this appeal by representing Jesus as at the moment engaged in healing and in expelling demons. Thereby he secures that the words about the blind, the lame, etc., shall be understood literally. The message that 'the blind see, the lame walk,' etc., echoes Isaiah xxxv. 5-6, where such phenomena appear as part of the great transformation or renewal of life which comes with the era of redemption. Thus, though not answering John's question directly, Jesus points to significant evidence from which John may draw the proper conclusion, while the concluding words, 'Blessed is he who is repelled by nothing in me,' drop the hint that John may find reason to think that in Jesus ' not only the new era has come, but the Man ' (Klostermann).

That the Baptist's approach to Jesus at this point was one of many signs by which Jesus was confirmed in the consciousness of his own calling may be reasonably believed. Guided by the voice of God within his own soul, Jesus came face to face at moments with strange external verifications of the thoughts to which his inner experience pointed. But, as the present passage shews, the main evidence on which he grounded his unique sense of responsibility was objective. The powers attending his work for the rebirth of Israel gave proof of a destiny unshared and a responsibility undivided with other men. His historical relation to the Baptist was, as we shall see, more complex and various than the single episode of the Baptist's question would lead us to suppose. Jesus, pondering the historical significance of the whole work of John, and in particular the mystery of his own baptism at John's hands, was led to see in John the promised Elijah, so that later when he was confronted with the question ' Why do the scribes say that Elias comes before the Christ ? ' he was ready with an answer (Mark ix. 11-13).

vii. 24-35 : JESUS AND JOHN THE BAPTIST

When John's messengers had gone, he proceeded to speak to the 24
    crowds about John :
      ' What did you go out to the desert to see ?
      A reed swayed by the wind ?
    Come, what did you go out to see ?   25
      A man arrayed in soft robes ?

Those who are gorgeously dressed and luxurious live
in royal palaces.

26 Come, what did you go out to see ?   A prophet ?
Yes, I tell you, and far more than a prophet.

27 This is he of whom it is written,
Here I send my messenger before your face,
to prepare the way for you.

28 I tell you, among the sons of women there is none greater
than John, and yet the least in the Realm of God is greater

29 than he is.' (On hearing this all the people and the taxgatherers acknowledged the justice of God, as they had been

30 baptized with the baptism of John ; but the Pharisees and
jurists, who had refused his baptism, frustrated God's
purpose for themselves.)

31 ' To what then shall I compare the men of this generation ?
What are they like ?

32 Like children sitting in the marketplace and calling to one
another,
" We piped to you and you would not dance,
we lamented and you would not weep."

33 For John the Baptist has come, eating no bread and
drinking no wine,
and you say, " He has a devil " ;

34 the Son of man has come eating and drinking,
and you say, " Here is a glutton and a drunkard,
a friend of taxgatherers and sinners ! "

35 Nevertheless, Wisdom is vindicated by all her children.'
(Cf. Matthew xi. 7–19.)

The question of John is followed by a catena of sayings about
that prophet, derived from the Q source. These sayings, which
cannot all be assigned to any single occasion, witness to the
profound impression which the Baptist had made on the mind
of Christ. In the first group (vers. 24–28) Jesus recalls to a
thronged audience, only too prone to forget spiritual impressions,
the extraordinary greatness of the spell which John had exercised
upon the nation's mind. What was the secret of this spell ?
' What did you go out to the desert to see ? ' It was plainly no
ordinary man whose voice reverberating through the land caused
men to lay down their tasks and to flock to the desert. What
then was John ? ' A reed swayed by the wind,' an obsequious

instrument of the popular will? No, John's stand against the complacency, the pride, the shallowness of his age negatived all such ideas. Was he then ' a man arrayed in soft robes,' a friend of kings who Polonius-like whispered flattery into a monarch's ear? No, John rebuked Antipas as Elijah rebuked Ahab (iii. 19-20). What then was he? A prophet, a voice of God to his age? Jesus answers, ' Yes, and far more than a prophet,' for with John the promise of redemption began to be translated into actuality. John is the promised Elijah, the inaugurator of the day of salvation, ' he of whom it is written, Here I send my messenger before your face, to prepare the way for you ' (cf. i. 16-17, i. 76, iii. 4).

The above passage, taken as it stands, presupposes on Jesus' part not merely the highest estimate of John—' Among the sons of women there is none greater than John '—but a consciousness of the *finality* of his own mission to Israel. In other words, it presupposes the Messiahship of Jesus. From the standpoint of this consciousness Jesus sees in the work of John a mission historically preparatory to his own, by which his own task and path have been made plain. For not only had John filled Israel with religious expectancy, but he had at Jordan discovered Jesus to himself. On the other hand, the saying which follows in the second half of ver. 28 is from a different standpoint. All past standards here appear as abrogated through Jesus' possession of the ' mystery ' of the Kingdom of God. Jesus, as he thinks of the new spiritual life which has come to his followers through himself, declares that even ' the least in the Realm of God,' even the humblest of his own disciples, ' is greater than he is.' This pronouncement, which implies that John still declines the revelation preached by Jesus, agrees with the situation revealed in the Baptist's question, but it can scarcely have been uttered coincidently with the statement in ver. 27 that the Baptist is the promised Elijah. Vers. 24-27 must therefore be assigned to a different situation from ver. 28, perhaps to a later period when the ambiguities connected with John's earlier position had been cleared away.

The short section which follows (vers. 29-30) turns upon the reception which John had received in Israel. The people as a whole, including the lapsed class of taxgatherers, were powerfully stirred by John, and their repentance and acceptance of baptism was a striking proof that they acknowledged the justice of God, who does not rebuke a nation's sins in vain. (For the Jewish idea of the ' justifying of the judgment ' of God see Dalman, *Jesus-Jeshua*, pp. 214–16.) But while the masses in Israel recognized John's authority to be from God, the Pharisees and jurists, by declining baptism, put a divine opportunity from them, and so frustrated the purpose of God. As commonly understood, these words are part of a discourse of Jesus regarding John. In Dr. Moffatt's translation they are taken as an explanatory parenthesis subjoined to vers. 27–28 or prefixed to vers. 31–35. Though absent from the corresponding section in Matthew, they have a parallel in Matthew xxi. 32, and are therefore Q material. We may regard them as sayings of Jesus inserted here to explicate the rest of the section, particularly the enigmatic words about wisdom being vindicated by her children (ver. 35).

A third group of Q sayings (cf. Matthew xi. 16–19) follows in vers. 31–35. Jesus acknowledges that himself and John, different as have been the methods of their approach to Israel, have experienced similar fortunes. The formula ' To what shall I compare ? ' forms a customary introduction to Rabbinical parables. Here Jesus illustrates the negative attitude of his contemporaries to John and to himself by referring to the games of ' children in the marketplace.' A group with a flageolet proposes to play at a wedding or a festival, but their playmates will not join in or dance to the music. Then it is proposed to play at holding a funeral, but here again the mourners receive no encouragement from their fellows. The application of the parable to the generation of John and Jesus is then made. John, the great ascetic, called Israel to austerities of penance, and his contemporaries judged him mad, possessed by a demon. Jesus, the Son of man, came—see under v. 33–39 —not frowning on social life but entering freely and fully into it, and men dubbed him glutton and tippler, friend of taxgatherers and sinners (v. 27–32). Thus Israel defeats the divine intention alike as expressed in John and in Jesus. On the other hand, Jesus asserts that the divine Wisdom—cf. Proverbs i. 20 : ' Wisdom calls aloud in the streets, and lifts her voice in the squares, crying from the busy markets. . . . O heedless ones, how long will you choose to be heedless ? ' etc.—while stultified by the pettish and unreasonable attitude of Israel as a whole, is vindicated by all her children, i.e. by those who like the taxgatherers in ver. 29 hearkened to John, or like the disciples have cast in their lot with Jesus (cf. Matthew xi. 25–27, Luke x. 21–22, Matthew xiii. 16–17, Luke x. 23–24). The parallel to ver. 35 in Matthew has ' works ' in place of ' children.' It is possible that the two readings go back to different but related Aramaic expressions, but no attempts to demonstrate this point have succeeded.

The above sayings owe their preservation to the necessity pressing on the early Christian community to regulate aright its relations with the society which still adhered to the doctrines of John the Baptist (cf. Acts xviii. 24–28, xix. 1–7).

vii. 36–50 : Jesus and the Penitent Woman

One of the Pharisees asked him to dinner, and entering the 36 house of the Pharisee he reclined at table. Now there was 37 a woman in the town who was a sinner, and when she found out that Jesus was at table in the house of the Pharisee, she brought an alabaster flask of perfume and 38 stood behind him at his feet in tears ; her tears began to wet his feet, so she wiped them with the hair of her head, pressed kisses on them, and anointed them with the perfume. When his host the Pharisee noticed this, he said to 39 himself, ' If he was a prophet he would know what sort of a woman this is who is touching him ; for she is a sinner.' Then Jesus addressed him. ' Simon,' he said, ' I have some- 40 thing to say to you.' ' Speak, teacher,' he said. ' There 41 was a moneylender who had two debtors ; one owed him fifty pounds, the other five. As they were unable to pay, 42 he freely forgave them both. Tell me, now, which of them will love him most ? ' ' I suppose,' said Simon, ' the man 43 who had most forgiven.' ' Quite right,' he said. Then 44 turning to the woman he said to Simon, ' You see this woman ? When I came into your house,

> you never gave me water for my feet,
> while she has wet my feet with her tears and wiped them
>   with her hair ;
> you never gave me a kiss,   45
>   while ever since she came in she has kept pressing
>   kisses on my feet ;
> you never anointed my head with oil,   46

while she has anointed my feet with perfume.
47   Therefore I tell you, many as her sins are, they are for-
     given, for her love is great ; whereas he to whom little is
48   forgiven has but little love.' And he said to her, ' Your
49   sins are forgiven.' His fellow guests began to say to them-
50   selves, ' Who is this, to forgive even sins ? ' But he said to
     the woman, ' Your faith has saved you ; go in peace.'

(Luke alone.)

This narrative, which comes from the L source, illustrates
the thought with which the preceding section concludes, that
Jesus is a friend of sinners. As Jesus reclines at table in the
house of the Pharisee Simon, a woman in the town who was a
sinner enters the room and takes her stand behind him. Apparently such intrusions were familiar in Oriental households,
for the woman's entrance provokes no comment. Klostermann
compares the custom in the *Arabian Nights* of uninvited
persons entering a house wherever they hear music. Simon
would suppose the woman to be a beggar seeking food or alms,
and as such, despite her character, not to be turned away.
But the fit of weeping with which she throws herself down
behind Jesus, letting her tears fall on his feet, and then impulsively
loosening her hair to wipe them off, kissing his feet over and
over, and then anointing them with perfume, argues a different
purpose. Simon, who has not forbidden the woman's entrance,
is inwardly offended by Jesus' permission of such extravagant
demonstrations. If he was a prophet he would know what sort
of a woman this is, etc. Jesus, who divines his thoughts, now
seeks by the story of the Two Debtors to reveal the true meaning
of the woman's act, and to present her in a wholly other character
than Simon imagines.

The narrative does not state that the woman was one whom
Jesus had previously rescued from a life of sin and brought to
God. If we assume that she was such, her act will be construed
as one of unbounded *gratitude* for a forgiveness already bestowed,
of which her love is the result and proof. In that case Jesus'
word in ver. 48 is simply the confirmation of a pardon which
she knows herself already to possess. But if she now came to
him for the first time, encouraged by his attitude towards others
of her class, her action is primarily one of *confession*. It is the
expression of bitter sorrow for sin, and the love of which ver. 47

speaks is the ground of the forgiveness which is there bestowed. It is in this sense that Catholic expositors have understood the incident. But in favour of the first of the two assumptions stands the parable of the two debtors which Jesus uses to bring Simon to a better understanding of the incident. The principle of the parable is that gratitude to the forgiver is in proportion to the sins forgiven, and its application in the present case depends upon the woman having *already* received pardon. Simon assents to the principle that a great forgiveness evokes a great gratitude, but as one who, though well-meaning, has never known in his own religious experience the whole reality of the forgiveness which this woman has received, he has not grasped the significance of her reaction to it. To bring this home to Simon is the purpose of the application given to the parable in vers. 44-47. If the unity of the section as a whole is to be maintained, we cannot suppose that Jesus in these words intends to rebuke Simon for a lack of courtesy to himself. Rather will he, by contrasting the unbounded devotion of the woman with the formal politeness which was all that the circumstances required of Simon, teach the latter to see in the woman one who though greatly sinning has been greatly transformed. Clearly that is the point of ver. 47 : ' her sins are forgiven, for her love is great.' The woman's love becomes on this interpretation the *proof* of her forgiveness, not its ground. The closing vers. 49-50 (cf. v. 20-24) probably reflect the use made of the incident in early Christian controversy.

The unity of the passage has been disputed by scholars, but it is difficult to see how the argument can dispense with the parable in vers. 40-43. More difficulty is presented by the application given to the parable in vers. 44-46. These verses, by seeming to indict the conduct of Simon, introduce a second motive into the story, and therefore it is not improbable that they represent an elaborative addition to the parable. The incident of the anointing exhibits a certain parallelism to the other anointing of Jesus which takes place at Bethany in the last week of his life (Mark xiv. 1-9, Matthew xxvi. 6-13). In both narratives ' an unnamed woman enters the house of a Simon in order to anoint Jesus at a feast from an alabaster vase of myrrh ' (Klostermann). But the woman at Bethany is not a sinner, and does not anoint Jesus' feet with her tears nor wipe them with her hair. Later tradition, however, as we see

by John xii. 1–8, has partially combined the features of the
two episodes and so led to their identification. Possibly the
alabaster flask and perfume in Luke's narrative are features
derived from the other story. In that case the anointing of
Jesus in the original form of Luke's narrative was simply with
a woman's tears.

viii. 1–3 : WOMEN WHO MINISTERED TO JESUS

viii.

1 Shortly afterwards he went travelling from one town and village
to another preaching and telling the good news of the Reign
of God ; he was accompanied by the twelve and by some

2 women who had been healed of evil spirits and illnesses,
Mary called Magdalene (out of whom seven daemons had

3 been driven), Joanna the wife of Chuza the chancellor of
Herod, Susanna, and a number of others, who ministered
to him out of their means.

(Luke alone.)

Ver. 1 is editorial, and prepares for the next section which
recounts the Parable of the Sower. Vers. 2–3, which are special
to Luke, assert that Jesus in his journeyings was accompanied
not only by the Twelve but by a number of devoted women
whom he had healed or delivered from demons. Mary of
Magdala, a village on the south-west shore of the Galilean
Lake, has been popularly, but on no sufficient grounds, identified
with the penitent sinner in vii. 36–50. The seven daemons
point to some peculiarly obdurate form of possession ; the idea
of a succession of relapses into which she had fallen (cf. xi. 24–26)
is less probable. Joanna reappears in xxiv. 10. Nothing else
is known of her or of her husband Chuza, the chancellor of
Antipas. Susanna appears only here. Allusions to women
are a feature of Luke's gospel (cf. Introd., page xix), but the
specification of names in the present passage suggests that
Mary, Joanna, and Susanna were prominent figures in the
Palestinian church, and may, perhaps through the circle of
Philip's daughters at Caesarea (Acts xxi. 8–10), have been
personally known to the evangelist.

viii. 4–8a : THE PARABLE OF THE SOWER

As a large crowd was gathering and as people were resorting to   4
  him from town after town, he addressed them in a parable.
‘ A sower went out to sow his seed.   And as he sowed,   5
    some seed fell on the road and was trampled down,
    and the wild birds ate it up ;
  some other seed dropped on the rock,   6
    but it withered away when it sprang up because it had
    no moisture ;
  some other seed fell among thorns,   7
    and the thorns sprang up along with it and choked it ;
  some other seed fell on sound soil,   8a
    and springing up bore a crop, a hundredfold.’

(Cf. Mark iv. 1–9.)

With the parable of the Sower begins the second of the
longer sections which Luke has taken over from Mark. The
section extends from viii. 4 to ix. 50. In the parable Luke
follows Mark closely except for certain omissions and modifications of phrase intended to produce a smoother and conciser
narrative. All three evangelists represent the parable as
addressed to a thronged audience, which indicates that, like the
Sermon in vi. 20–49, it is interpreted as a deliverance or manifesto
of Jesus to the nation. The details of the story, describing the
varying fortunes of seed cast on a wide field, are simple, and
require no comment. That truth is like a seed sown in the heart
is a commonplace of religious and moral literature. ‘ Behold,
I sow my Law in you, and it shall bring forth fruit in you. . . .
But our fathers, who received the Law, observed it not . . . and
perished, because they kept not that which had been sown in
them ’ (2 Esdras ix. 31–33). ‘ Reason has not (the same)
operative force in all men. The soul of the hearer must be
wrought first into a state of preparedness by the training of
habit, like land which is to foster seeds ’ (Aristotle, *Nicomachean
Ethics*, x. 9, 6). It is important, however, to determine the
special motive and purpose with which Jesus used the parable.
What situation in his life does it reflect ?

Here it may be observed that in the source the parable
follows a section (Mark ii. 1–iii. 35) in which Jesus has begun
to encounter opposition. Over against his authority reactionary

forces have started up, expressing themselves in charges of blasphemy, madness, and sorcery (Mark ii. 7, iii. 21, 22). It cannot be supposed that this opposition did not profoundly affect the Saviour's hope of bringing the whole nation to accept his revelation. He who at first had sought an entrance for the good news of the Kingdom into every heart now sees the prospect of success, at least under existing conditions, to be limited to a receptive minority of his hearers, and thus an historical situation arises with which the parable of the Sower stands in fair accord.

On this interpretation Jesus, face to face with the unbelief or relapse of large sections of the Galileans, falls back upon the fact that in the order of nature the sower, while casting his seed everywhere, reaps only a part of what he has sown. The seed is cast without discrimination, but only in the sound soil does it produce a crop, i.e. of lives delivered from sin and renewed by the power of God. By the analogy from nature Jesus reconciles the two facts : (1) of his own unfaltering assurance of possessing the secret of salvation for Israel, and (2) of his failure under present conditions to persuade more than a fraction of the nation. The salvation of Israel becomes the salvation not of the whole number but of an elect.

viii. 8b–15 : THE INTERPRETATION OF THE PARABLE

8b When he said this he called out, ' He who has an ear, let him
9   listen to this.' The disciples questioned him about the
10   meaning of the parable ; so he said, ' It is granted you to understand the open secrets of the Reign of God, but the others get it in parables, so that

for all their seeing they may not see,
and for all their hearing they may not understand.

11 This is what the parable means. The seed is the word of God.
12   Those " on the road " are people who hear ; but then the devil comes and carries off the word from their heart,
13   that they may not believe and be saved. Those " on the rock " are people who on hearing the word welcome it with enthusiasm, but they have no root ; they believe for a
14   while and fall away in the hour of trial. As for the seed that fell among thorns, that means people who hear but who go and get choked with worries and money and the

pleasures of life, so that they never ripen. As for the seed 15
in the good soil, that means those who hear and hold fast
the word in a good and sound heart and so bear fruit sted-
fastly.'

(Cf. Mark iv. 10–20.)

The importance of the parable of the Sower is marked (1)
by the warning which is appended to it (ver. 8b), and (2) by
the controversy to which it gives rise (vers. 9–10). The words
'He who has an ear,' etc., indicate that a hidden or esoteric
truth is contained in the parable which only the spiritually
alert will be able to grasp, and similarly the explanation offered
in ver. 10 alludes to 'mysteries' or revealed truths of the
Kingdom which are disclosed only to disciples. But the section
creates difficulties which are not easily resolved.

The question asked by the disciples in Mark iv. 10 concerns
'the parables' in general. Matthew xiii. 10 takes this vague
inquiry to be equivalent to asking why Jesus uses parables in
his popular teaching. Luke understands the question to relate
entirely to the parable of the Sower. The answer given by
Jesus to the disciples is, 'It is granted you to understand the
open secrets of the Reign of God, but the others get it in parables.'
Open secret or 'mystery'—the word is frequent in the Pauline
epistles (cf. 1 Corinthians ii. 7–12, xiii. 2, xv. 51–54 ; Ephesians
i. 9, iii. 3, v. 32, vi. 19), but in the gospels occurs only here—
is a technical expression for a divine truth which, hitherto undis-
closed, is now matter of revelation. What then is the 'mystery'
or 'open secret' or 'revelation' which Jesus announces with
regard to the Reign of God ? Obviously it cannot relate to the
apocalyptic belief that the Reign comes supernaturally and in
the future, for this was matter of ordinary everyday acceptance.
Rather must Jesus be alluding to truths imparted in his own
teaching, which obviously forms the source of whatever special
religious insight his followers have acquired. Here we may
recall what was said above under iii. 21–22 and iv. 14–30 regarding the revelation which came to Jesus at his baptism, and
which constituted the ground of his mission. Jesus offers to
his nation not a new doctrine of the Kingdom of God but a new
conception of God's will which, if received, will bring the goal
indicated by the Kingdom of God into measurable, indeed into
immediate, relation with the lives of men. This revelation the

disciples have received, but others do not comprehend it. They do not see that loving enemies, meeting evil with good, putting away selfishness, becoming ' sons of God ' by a rebirth of the spirit (vi. 27–36), represent the mode in which the Reign of God actualizes itself in human life. Ver. 10 accordingly will mean that while the disciples have received Christ's revelation, to others it remains an enigma which can be offered only in stories or by aid of analogies from the world of nature and of sense.

But if we accept this explanation of the ' mysteries ' of the Kingdom, can we follow Luke in the further statement, taken over from Mark, that Jesus speaks parables to the people so that for all their seeing they may not see, etc. ? These words recall Isaiah vi. 9 f., where the prophet is bidden to go to Israel and to ' make the mind of this people dull . . . and to close up their eyes, lest their eyes see, lest their ears hear, lest their minds understand, and their health be restored.' What meaning can such words have on our Lord's lips ? It is intelligible that Jesus should, after *failure* to bring home the truths of the Kingdom to the people at large, say sadly that the parabolic teaching had only too literally fulfilled the prophecy in Isaiah : the parables had remained parables, their meaning had not been grasped. But it is inconceivable that Jesus devised his parables to hide the truth from the many. Mark's language, if it implies this, must be set down to some misapprehension of the Isaiah-passage as quoted by Jesus, or to some theorizing of the parables. The probability of the latter explanation appears when we consider (1) that elsewhere in Mark Jesus uses parables to *assist* the understanding of the many, and even explains their purpose (Mark iv. 33, vii. 14–17) ; (2) that the prophecy in Isaiah vi. 9 f. was extensively employed in early Christianity to explain the historical enigma of Israel's rejection of Christ (cf. Romans xi. 8–10, John xii. 39–41). We have here therefore two theories of the parables which are not on the same plane, and which it is not possible to harmonize. The first, according to which the parables were adapted to the understanding of the hearers, alone does justice to the mind of Christ. The second, as taken over by Luke from Mark iv. 12, has its basis in a deterministic philosophy put forward to explain the unbelief of Israel.

We understand our Lord therefore, in speaking of the ' open

secrets ' of the Reign of God, to be referring to the revelation
which he announces, and through which the Kingdom of God
becomes an immediate quickening reality in man's life. This
secret of salvation, though grasped by his disciples, remains
incommunicable to the many, who can think of redemption only
in external ways. To this majority Jesus is and remains a
teller of stories. Consequently the parable of the Sower points
to the salvation of an elect rather than of the whole people of
Israel. To this idea the detailed exposition of the parable
given in vers. 11–15 is to be subordinated. The parable is here
allegorized. The seed is the gospel message. Ver. 12 refers
to the secular type of hearer, in whose profane heart (cf. Esau,
Hebrews xii. 16) the word of repentance gets no chance. Ver. 13
alludes to visionaries who catch enthusiastically at every
symptom of the Messianic times, but do not connect the Kingdom
with present life and duty (cf. John vi. 66). Ver. 14 points to
divided natures, which never fully respond to Christ because
their souls are steeped in worldly cares and pleasures (cf. xviii.
23–27). With the good hearers of ver. 15 compare vi. 43, 47 f.

viii. 16–18 : HIDDEN TRUTHS SHALL YET BE REVEALED

' No one lights a lamp and hides it under a vessel or puts 16
  it below the bed ;

  he puts it on a stand so that those who come in can see
  the light.

For nothing is hidden that shall not be disclosed, 17
  nothing concealed that shall not be known and revealed.

So take care how you listen ; 18
  for he who has, to him shall more be given,
    while as for him who has not, from him shall be taken
    even what he thinks he has.'

(Cf. Mark iv. 21–25.)

This section, which is taken over with slight alterations from
Mark, stands in close conjunction with the foregoing discussion.
Jesus has spoken of the truth being hidden from the many,
and Mark takes occasion to bring in other sayings about hidden
mysteries, which indicate that things now ignored will yet be .

openly revealed. ' No one lights a lamp and hides it under a vessel or puts it below the bed.' The lamp is put on the stand or bracket fixed to the wall where all may see it. So the secret of God's Kingdom, which Jesus knows himself to possess, and which he has revealed to his followers, is not destined to be permanently obscured from the larger part of the nation. *Magna est veritas et praevalebit.* Hence a warning to the disciples to give careful heed to the message that they may be able to instruct others : ' he who has, to him shall more be given.' Spiritual insight grows with exercise, and ceases where there is no appropriation of imparted truth.

The saying about the lamp, and the proverb ' He who has,' etc., which Luke has here taken over from Mark, occurred also in the Q source. The Q versions are given in xi. 33 (cf. Matthew v. 15) and xix. 26 (cf. Matthew xxv. 29). Sayings which are thus twice quoted in a gospel, once from Mark and once from Q, are known as *doublets.* They are mostly aphorisms, and indicate the teaching which was most widely diffused in the early period. The lamp in Matthew v. 15 refers not to the message of the Kingdom but to the ' good works ' of disciples. In Luke xi. 33 it refers to Jesus as a ' sign ' to his generation. The other saying, ' He who has,' etc., appears in Matthew xxv. 29, and in Luke xix. 26 in connexion with the use of entrusted ' gifts.'

viii. 19–21 : JESUS AND HIS FAMILY

19 His mother and brothers reached him but they were unable to
20   join him for the crowd. Word was brought to him that
     ' your mother and brothers are standing outside ; they
21   wish to see you.' But he answered, ' My mother and
     brothers are those who listen to the word of God and obey it.'
                                  (Cf. Mark iii. 31–35.)

This episode is given by Luke in dependence upon Mark, but for once n a different context. In Mark it occurs in a context which records how Jesus, face to face with the opposition of the synagogue authorities and others, drew more closely round himself the circle of his adherents. Luke, who omits the statement that the family of Jesus came out to restrain him because of the popular rumour that he was deranged (Mark iii. 21), leaves the coming of his mother and brothers without other motive than that they wished to see him. Hence a less severe cast is imparted to the answer of Jesus in ver. 21. Jesus states that for the sake of the Kingdom of God he has made choice of another family. ' My mother and brothers are those who listen to the word of God and obey it.' Thus Jesus illustrates in himself the renunciation which he afterwards requires of all who will follow him (ix. 59–62, xiv. 26, etc.).

viii. 22–25 : THE STORM ON THE LAKE

It happened on one of these days that he embarked in a boat 22 alone with his disciples and said to them, ' Let us cross to the other side of the lake.' So they set sail. During 23 the voyage he fell asleep. But when a gale of wind came down on the lake and they were being swamped and in peril, they went and woke him up. ' Master, master,' they cried, 24 ' we are drowning ! ' So he woke up and checked the wind and the surf ; they ceased and there was a calm. Then he 25 said to them, ' Where is your faith ? ' They marvelled in awe, saying to one another, ' Whatever can he be ? He gives orders to the very winds and water, and they obey him ! '

(Cf. Mark iv. 35–41.)

The use of a boat is a feature of quite a number of incidents in the tradition, and has been thought, though perhaps on insufficient grounds, to indicate that our Lord's freedom of movement on land was at this time seriously restricted. The present crossing of the Lake takes the company on to non-Jewish soil. Sudden squalls descending on the Lake from the neighbouring hills are a phenomenon of the region, and on this occasion the skiff in which the company is sailing is seriously endangered. Luke gives the disciples' cry a turn which removes the imputation that the sleeping Jesus did not care, and after the storm is quelled by his command, he softens Jesus' rebuke of his panic-stricken followers by substituting ' Where is your faith ? ' for Mark's ' Why are you afraid like this ? Have you no faith ? ' The final point of the incident is given in the disciples' question, ' Whatever can he be ? ' etc., which indicates that the disciples here, as elsewhere, were thrust back upon the supernatural for an explanation of Jesus' personality.

The question ' Where is your faith ? ' exhibits clearly where the heart of the religious experience recorded in the section is to be sought. The disciples, as those to whom had been committed the task of proclaiming the Kingdom of God, should have had sufficient confidence in God to believe that those whom He had called to this office He would also preserve (cf. xiii. 31–33). The transcendent calm of Jesus, by which he rises above the powers and terrors of the natural elements, is the central datum, and constitutes a vital part of the mystery of his personality as enshrined in the faith of his followers. The latter were not content merely to remember and reassert the truths which Jesus uttered, but constantly emphasized the numinous element in his personality whereby they had been convinced that the supernatural power of God was with him. The incident therefore has a highly symbolical value.

viii. 26–39 : THE GERGESENE DEMONIAC

26 They put in at the country of the Gergesenes, on the shore facing
27 Galilee. As he stepped out on land he was met by a man from the town who had daemons in him ; for a long while he had worn no clothing, and he stayed not in a house but
28 among the tombs. On catching sight of Jesus he shrieked aloud and prayed him with a loud cry, ' Jesus, son of God
29 most High, what business have you with me ? Do not torture me, I beg of you.' (For he had charged the unclean spirit to come out of the man. Many a time when it had seized hold of him, he had been fastened secure in fetters and chains, but he would snap his bonds and be driven by the daemon
30 into the desert.) So Jesus asked him, ' What is your name ? ' ' Legion,' he said, for a number of daemons had entered him.
31 And they begged him not to order them off to the abyss.
32 Now a considerable drove of swine was grazing there on the hillside, so the daemons begged him for leave to enter them.
33 He gave them leave, and the daemons came out of the man and went into the swine ; the drove rushed down the steep
34 slope into the lake and were suffocated. When the herdsmen saw what had occurred they fled and reported it to the town

and the hamlets. The people came out to see what had 35 occurred and when they reached Jesus they discovered the man whom the daemons had left, seated at the feet of Jesus, clothed and sane. That frightened them. They got a report 36 from those who had seen how the lunatic was cured, and 37 then all the inhabitants of the surrounding country of the Gergesenes asked him to leave them, they were so seized with terror. He embarked in the boat and went back. The man 38 whom the daemons had left begged that he might accompany him. Jesus, however, sent him away, saying, 'Go home 39 and describe all that God has done for you.' So he went off to proclaim through the whole town all that Jesus had done for him.

(Cf. Mark v. 1-20.)

The district in which Jesus now lands on the eastern shore of the Lake is named in the best and most ancient MSS. of Mark the country of the 'Gerasenes.' In Matthew the best ancient authorities read 'Gadarenes' (Matthew viii. 28). In Luke the bulk of MSS. exhibit one or other of the same two readings, but one important group has **Gergesenes**, and this reading is adopted by most modern editors. It is quite certain, however, that this preferred reading goes back only to Origen, the Christian scholar and theologian of Alexandria in the early third century, who, finding 'Gerasenes' and less commonly 'Gadarenes' in the MSS. known to him, pronounced against both readings as geographically unsuitable (Gerasa being about 50 miles and Gadara 6 or 7 miles south-east of the Lake shore), and suggested Gergesa—the modern *Kursi*, about half-way down the eastern side of the Lake—as the place where the incident occurred. If this identification be correct, 'Gerasenes,' the original reading in Mark, will have been due to popular confusion of names, and 'Gadarenes' will represent an attempt to improve the geography.

Luke's description, **A man from the town who had daemons in him**, indicates a condition of melancholic mania, associated with extreme antisocial and suicidal frenzy. The man has fled from human society, and finds a ghoulish pleasure in haunting the rock-hewn graves on the hillside, where night and day he shrieks and gashes himself with stones (Mark v. 5). The predilection of demons or unclean spirits for such regions is copiously illustrated in ancient literature, both Jewish and

Greek. It was reputed a sign of madness when anyone spent the night in a place of graves, or rent his garments, or destroyed what people gave to him. The story of the exorcism recalls the earlier incident in iv. 33–36, and shews the tendency of the tradition to a stereotyped formality in the narratives of such cures. 'What business have you with me?' for example, is common to both narratives. For the entreaty 'Do not torture me' compare Philostratus, *Life of Apollonius*, iv. 25: 'The phantom pretended to weep, and entreated him not to torture it, nor to compel it to declare what it was.' On this occasion Jesus at the first approach of the maniac orders the evil spirit to come forth. The demon tries to break the spell imposed by Jesus, whom he recognizes as the Son of God most High (cf. iv. 34, 41), at whose approach the demons must depart to the abyss of punishment (Revelation ix. 1–11). A dogmatic conception of the Messianic lordship of Jesus over the demons has undoubtedly contributed to the featuring of the story, but underneath this theoretical presentation can be seen the process by which the great Healer sought to lead a disorganized mind back to a sense of its true personality. 'What is your name?' he asks. The man answers 'Legion,' believing that a whole invading army of demons is in him, and by the sequel it would appear that in some manner he associates the persecuting spirits with a drove of swine grazing there on the hillside, and is persuaded that if the demons would leave him for the swine, he would be delivered from the fearful terrors which impend him. To what extent the episode of the swine represents a later imaginative elaboration of the story must be left undecided. That demons can transfer themselves to other creatures was matter of common belief. Klostermann quotes an Aramaic-Jewish exorcistic formula : 'Be gone. . . . Go out, fly forth . . . you powers of darkness. . . . Make off, and fall upon the gazelles upon the mountain.' The tradition represents Jesus as consenting to the demoniac's idea about the swine, thus freeing him from the power of his obsession, whereupon a wild stampede of the herd carries it over the cliff. When the people of the district, alarmed by reports of this event, come out to make inquiries, they find the demoniac seated at the feet of Jesus, clothed and sane.

It is sometimes suggested that the entreaty of the terrified Gergesenes that Jesus leave their country signifies that the time

is not yet ripe for Jesus to bring the gospel on to heathen soil.
In view, however, of our uncertainty as to the part which popular
imagination has played in the elaboration of the narrative, this
idea cannot be pressed. An interesting feature is the request
of the restored man to accompany Jesus, and the answer of
Jesus that he go home and declare there what God had done for
him. Jesus undoubtedly attached a special evidential value
to the healing of demoniacs (cf. xi. 20), but whether the removal
of the ban of secrecy, which is so distinct a feature in other
records of healing (v. 14, viii. 56), had on this occasion anything
to do with the fact that Jesus was on *heathen* soil, is at best
doubtful.

viii. 40-56 : The Daughter of Jairus and the Sick Woman on the Way

On his return Jesus was welcomed by the crowd ; they were all 40
looking out for him. A man called Jairus came, who was 41
a president of the synagogue, and falling at the feet of Jesus
entreated him to come to his house, for he had an only 42
daughter about twelve years old and she was dying. As
Jesus went the crowds kept crushing him, and a woman 43
who had had a hemorrhage for twelve years which no one
could cure, came up behind him and touched the tassel of 44
his robe. Her hemorrhage instantly ceased. Jesus said, 45
' Who touched me ? ' As everyone denied it, Peter and
his companions said, ' Master, the crowds are all round you
pressing hard ! ' Jesus said, ' Somebody did touch me, for 46
I felt power had passed from me.' So when the woman saw 47
she had not escaped notice, she came trembling, and falling
down before him she told before all the people why she had
touched him and how she had been instantly cured. ' Daugh- 48
ter,' he said to her, ' your faith has made you well ; depart
in peace.' He was still speaking when someone came from 49
the house of the synagogue-president to say, ' Your daughter
is dead. Do not trouble the teacher any further.' But 50
when Jesus heard it he said to him, ' Have no fear, only
believe and she shall get well.' When he reached the house 51
he would not allow anyone to come in with him except Peter
and James and John, and the child's father and mother.

H

52 Everyone was weeping and bewailing her, but he said, ' Stop
53 weeping ; she is not dead but asleep.' They laughed at him,
54 knowing that she was dead. But he took her hand and
55 called to her, ' Rise, little girl.' And her spirit returned, she
got up instantly, and he ordered them to give her something
56 to eat. Her parents were amazed, but he charged them not
to tell anyone what had happened.

(Cf. Mark v. 21–43.)

Here again Luke abbreviates Mark considerably. The object
of the section is to shew how Jesus, despite the opposition and
unbelief which had arisen in many quarters, continued, wherever
faith was manifested, to shew himself the Physician and Saviour
of Israel. Jairus, who comes forward amid the throng awaiting
Jesus on his return to Galilee, is a president of the synagogue,
i.e. head of the local sanhedrin or court of elders which exercised
supervision over the worship and life of the community. His
only daughter, aged twelve, is dying, and he asks Jesus to come
to him in his need. At this moment a woman, suffering from
an incurable hæmorrhage, which inflicted ceremonial uncleanness
demanding expiation (Leviticus xv. 25–27), takes advantage of
the crowd surrounding Jesus to touch the *zizith* or sacred fringe
of tassels which Jesus, like every Jew, wore attached to his robe
in token of consecration to the God of Israel (Numbers xv. 38–41).
The sufferer is persuaded that Jesus can cure her, and as she
cannot speak of her trouble she trusts to an unnoticed act of
faith to procure the necessary benefit. Jesus, however, conscious that power had passed from him, i.e. that the contact
established with him was due to no accidental jostling but to
some sufferer's desire for healing, insists that the person declare
the fact, whereupon the woman makes a full confession, and
Jesus answers, ' Daughter, your faith has made you well, depart
in peace.' Nowhere is it better illustrated that ' faith,' as Jesus
taught and required it, must avow itself and become fully persuaded of the divine *will* to grant the blessings which it seeks.
The incident, therefore, has a highly symbolical value.

The interest of the narrative now returns to Jairus. The
message comes that his daughter is dead : 'Do not trouble the
teacher any further.' A distinctly limited conception of the
power of Jesus is here indicated, and it is in face of this supposed
limitation that Jesus now acts. Unbelief is reflected not only

in the messenger's word but in the clamorous demonstrations
in the house and in the scornful laughter with which the assurance of Jesus ' She is not dead but asleep ' is received.   Despite
this unbelief, Jesus' word ' Have no fear, only believe ' is carried
to a triumphant issue.   Reaching the house, he will have no one
enter the room except the believing parents and three of those
disciples to whom the ' open secret ' of the Reign of God has
been revealed.   Then in the presence of the unfaltering faith of
the inner circle Jesus commands the child to rise.   The strong
contrast in which faith here appears over against unbelief makes
the incident an appropriate conclusion to the teachings which
form the first half of this chapter.   Some have seen in the word
' She is not dead but asleep ' a hint that the original incident
was a raising of one not already dead but only *in articulo mortis*.
The injunction of silence in ver. 56 can only have been interpreted
by the evangelists as a sign that Jesus desired such incidents to
pass quietly, but some scholars have taken this feature as
evidence that the incident in question was not part of the
common or public tradition in the earliest days.

ix. 1–6 : The Mission of the Twelve

ix.

Calling the twelve apostles together he gave them power and 1
  authority over all daemons as well as to heal diseases.   He 2
  sent them out to preach the Reign of God and to cure the
  sick.   And he told them, ' Take nothing for the journey, 3
  neither stick nor wallet nor bread nor silver, and do not
  carry two shirts.   Whatever house you go into, stay there 4
  and leave from there.   Whoever will not receive you, leave 5
  that town and shake off the very dust from your feet as a
  testimony against them.'   So they went out from village to 6
  village preaching the gospel and healing everywhere.

(Cf. Mark vi. 7–13.)

The sending out of the Twelve—whom Luke here names
apostles—would seem from Mark to have taken place at a com-
paratively advanced stage in the Galilean ministry.   The work
of Jesus has extended in ever-widening circles throughout
Galilee, and Jesus feels that a crisis is imminent (cf. Matthew x.

23). Simultaneously, the opposition of the authorities portends that the period of opportunity will be none too long. For both reasons the despatch of the trained assistants, to whom he has committed the open secret of the Kingdom, seems an urgent necessity.

Luke states in agreement with Mark that Jesus now **gave them power and authority over all daemons**, but he adds that they were **to heal diseases.** The emphasis on demon-possession as constituting the primary challenge to the preachers of the direct power of God in human life is an undoubtedly historical feature of the commission. In ver. 2 the commission is renewed in the form, **preach the Reign of God**, i.e. proclaim the immediate will of God to make an end of evil, both moral and physical. In ver. 3 it is stipulated that the apostles shall **take nothing for the journey**, i.e. shall make no special preparations. The business is urgent, and the time is short. Wallet, bread, money, are unnecessary. It is possible that the disciples had represented to Jesus that they were ill-provided with clothes and shoes. Jesus answers that what they have will suffice ; they do not need a second shirt, or footgear other than the sandals in which they stand (Mark vi. 9). Curiously Luke, with Matthew x. 10, negatives the staff, which Mark's account permits. This suggests that Matthew and Luke were influenced here by another tradition, probably Q, and illustrates how variations occurred in the primitive reports of Jesus' words.

With the above regulations compare the practices which, according to Josephus (*Wars*, ii. 8. 4), the Essenes followed in their journeyings : ' They go in to those whom they have not previously seen as though they were their closest friends. Therefore, on their journeys they carry nothing with them except arms on account of robbers. . . . And neither garments nor shoes do they change until they are torn, etc.' The brotherhood of Jesus bears no arms of any kind.

In vers. 4–5 Jesus assures the disciples that their needs will be supplied. They will be welcomed into friendly houses—Matthew x. 11 suggests that they will discover these by inquiry—whose inmates are waiting for the Kingdom, and there, like Elijah at Zarephath, they must stay, content with such hospitality as is offered till their work is done. Where, on the other hand, they are not received, where opposition to their message develops, they must quit that town, but not before they have made it plain to the inhabitants that the guilt of rejecting the messengers of the Kingdom lies at their door. The Jews considered that the soil under the feet of Gentiles, with its waters, its dwellings, and its ways, was polluted. Hence the gesture 'Shake off the very dust from your feet' may be a token that Israelites unfriendly to the Kingdom are no better than heathen. In ver. 6 the course of the mission is briefly described.

Whether ver. 4 implies that the disciples were not to preach in public places, but to confine themselves to an indoor or house-to-house propaganda, is uncertain. It is possible that such a policy was followed. Luke omits to notice that the disciples went out in pairs. See further x. 1–12, the sending out of the Seventy.

ix. 7–9 : HEROD HEARS OF JESUS

When Herod the tetrarch heard all that was going on, he was 7 quite at a loss ; for some said that John had risen from the dead, some that Elijah had appeared, and others that 8 one of the ancient prophets had arisen. Herod said, 'John 9 I beheaded. But who is this, of whom I hear such tales ? ' And he made efforts to see him.

(Cf. Mark vi. 14–16.)

The stir caused by the mission of the Twelve draws upon Jesus the attention of Herod Antipas, the tetrarch of Galilee. The latter, who has already suppressed John the Baptist, is alarmed at the spread of a religious movement, the political consequences of which he does not foresee. Hence the perplexity into which he falls. Herod hears the popular rumours alluded to in vers. 7–8. He is realist enough not to credit the report that John has reappeared. But he is disquieted notwithstanding, and Luke represents that he made various efforts to see Jesus.

The beliefs cited in vers. 7–8 are instructive. The rumour that John had risen from the dead implies that Jesus was popularly thought to have taken up and continued the unfinished work of John. Both were preachers of righteousness, and both warned the nation of judgment to come. It is conceivable that this particular rumour emanated from circles in which Herod's suppression of John was not forgotten, and to which the appearance of Jesus immediately after John seemed an act of God. The second rumour, that Elijah had appeared, turns on the fact that Jesus prepares the nation for the coming of God in His Kingdom, so fulfilling the rôle assigned by prophecy to Elijah. The third rumour, as given by Mark, is that Jesus is 'a prophet, like one of the old prophets.' This is interpreted by Luke to mean that in Jesus one of the ancient prophets had arisen, i.e. that in Jesus the golden age of prophecy had revived. In the time of Simon Maccabaeus and later, we find the nation waiting for 'a faithful prophet' to arise and declare the will of God (i Maccabees xiv. 41 ; cf. Deuteronomy xviii. 15), and such a prophet Jesus seemed to be. Note that none of the popular rumours identifies Jesus with the *Messiah*.

It is possible that at this time there came to Jesus through certain Pharisees the sinister intimation, which Luke records at xiii. 31–33, that Herod had designs against Jesus' life. If so, additional point is imparted to the retirement of Jesus across the Lake at this juncture, and to the popular excitement to which his action gives rise.

ix. 10–11 : The Return of the Twelve. Jesus Retires across the Lake

10 Then the apostles came back and described all they had done to Jesus. He took them and retired in private to a town
11   called Bethsaida, but the crowds learned this and followed him. He welcomed them, spoke to them of the Reign of God, and cured those who needed to be healed.

(Cf. Mark vi. 30–34.)

When the Twelve returned from their mission with reports of what they had done, Luke says that Jesus took them and retired in private to Bethsaida. Bethsaida, lying at the north end of the Lake, just across the Jordan, was within the tetrarchy of Philip and therefore safe from Herod's interference. The crowds, hearing of this retirement, set themselves in pursuit, and Jesus, after giving them welcome, spoke to them of the Reign of God and cured those who were in need of healing.

Luke has here condensed the narrative of Mark and thereby obscured certain features of the situation. According to Mark, the crossing of the Lake was motived by Jesus' desire to give the disciples rest. This desire is frustrated by the multitude who circumvent the Lake on foot. The result is that when Jesus lands, instead of finding rest, he sees the shore lined with folk. Nevertheless, far from shewing disappointment, ' He was moved with compassion for them, because they were as sheep without a shepherd, and he began to teach them many things ' (Mark vi. 30–34). Only later, after the feeding of the multitude, do Jesus and his disciples pass on to Bethsaida (Mark vi. 45). Luke has therefore telescoped the events of this journey.

Was there any reason, apart from the desire of rest, which led Jesus to undertake this retreat beyond the frontiers of Galilee ? Here account must be taken of the extraordinary action of the Galilean crowds. Why, if Jesus had only temporarily retired from Galilee, did the crowds undertake so long and exhausting an expedition, when *ex hypothesi* they would shortly see him back in their own domains ? Such considerations suggest that some serious menace to Jesus from Herod Antipas had recently occurred. Jesus' departure signified, or was popularly understood to signify, a withdrawal from the soil of Galilee, and the motive of the crowds was fear that they might not see him again. This would explain the compassion of Jesus as he saw the throng on the shore. It would explain his thought that they were being left like sheep without a shepherd. It would explain also why he now turned his face towards Bethsaida, which lay beyond Herod's jurisdiction. We may assume therefore that to Jesus the end of the Galilean ministry was already in sight.

ix. 12–17 : THE FEEDING OF THE FIVE THOUSAND

Now as the day began to decline the twelve came up to him and 12 said, ' Send the crowd off to lodge in the villages and farms around and get provisions there, for here we are in a desert place.' He said to them, ' Give them some food yourselves.' 13 They said, ' We have only got five loaves and two fish. Unless—are we to go and buy food for the whole of this

14 people ? ' (There were about five thousand men of them.)
    He said to his disciples, ' Make them lie down in rows of
15 about fifty.' They did so, and made them all lie down.
16 Then taking the five loaves and the two fish and looking
    up to heaven he blessed them, broke them in pieces and
17 handed them to the disciples to set before the crowd. And
    they all ate and had enough. What they had left over was
    picked up, twelve baskets full of fragments.

                                          (Cf. Mark vi. 35–44.)

The narrative follows Mark, but again with considerable
abbreviation. Jesus has spent the day in teaching and healing.
Evening comes, and still the crowds are hanging on his lips.
The concern of the disciples that a disorganized multitude should
not pass the night without food or shelter in the wilderness is
natural. But Jesus will not dismiss these ' sheep ' until he has
given them some singular token of his ' compassion.' ' Give
them food yourselves ' must have recalled the disciples sharply
to a sense of the responsibility which Jesus had delegated to
them with respect to the Galilean masses (ix. 1 f.). The stores
in hand are cited—' five loaves and two fish '—but the disciples
are not sure that Jesus' unspoken intention is not that they
' go and buy ' more adequate supplies elsewhere. Jesus dismisses the latter suggestion, and orders that the people be
made to recline in groups of fifty on the sward. People reclined
at meals in those days, after the fashion of the Roman *triclinium*,
on cushions surrounding a low table.[1] Here the grassy hillside
does duty alike for tables and for cushions.

The account of the incident bears a considerable resemblance
to certain Old Testament narratives, particularly to Elisha's
feeding the people in 2 Kings iv. 42–44, and there can be little
doubt that the latter narrative has contributed something to
the terms of the Christian tradition. One remarkable feature,
however, characterizes the tradition under all the forms in
which it has come down (Mark vi. 35–44, Matthew xiv. 15–21,
Luke ix. 12–17, John vi. 3–13, Mark viii. 1–9, Matthew xv. 32–38).
Not one of the six narratives states in so many words that Jesus
multiplied the food. This is left to be inferred from the statement that ' all ate and had enough,' and that twelve baskets of
fragments were taken up. The omission to note the multiplica-

---

[1] The Roman word was adopted into Aramaic in the form *triklin*.

tion is interesting, because it indicates that the main interest
of the original narrative lay not in the realm of physical miracle
but in another quarter. It is to be noted that all six narratives
specify the ritual actions with which Jesus accompanied the
giving of the food. First, he blessed, or gave thanks for the
loaves and fishes ; secondly, he broke them in the eyes of all ;
thirdly, he handed them to the disciples to give to the people.
This is the same ritual with which at the Last Supper he gave
the bread and the cup, and suggests that the repast in the
wilderness had, like the Supper, a primarily symbolic or sacramental character. Either—for these are the only alternatives
—the transaction in the wilderness resembled that at the
Supper, or the tradition of the early followers of Jesus assumed
a parallelism. In either case, the Feeding is invested with a
markedly sacramental significance. The bread is symbolic
(cf. John vi. 26-65). Jesus is giving to his adherents a ' sign '
or token of their unity or solidarity with himself in the family
or household of God (cf. viii. 21). He is pointing to the Feast
in the Kingdom of which they will later partake (cf. xiii. 29,
xiv. 15, xxii. 15-18). The ' miracle ' aspect of the incident is
on this interpretation a secondary feature of the tradition.

The religious symbolism which we have thus found reason to
regard as the fundamental element in the story of the Feeding
is thrown into high relief if, following the suggestion made in
the preceding section, we interpret Jesus' retirement across the
Lake as virtually the end of the Galilean ministry. The breaking
of the bread in the wilderness will then represent the last gesture
of Jesus to his Galilean followers. Henceforth his path and
theirs diverge. Jesus must deliver his message at Jerusalem,
and to Jerusalem he will now go, cost what it may.

ix. 18-20 : Peter Confesses Jesus as the Christ

Now it happened that while he was praying by himself his 18
disciples were beside him. So he inquired of them, ' Who
do the crowds say I am ? ' They replied, ' John the Baptist, 19
though some say Elijah and some say that one of the ancient
prophets has arisen.' He said to them, ' And who do you 20
say I am ? ' Peter replied, ' The Christ of God.'

(Cf. Mark viii. 27-29.)

At this point Luke, who has been following Mark, passes over the entire section Mark vi. 45–viii. 26. Thereby he not only drops from his record a number of Galilean incidents which Mark assigns to this period, but he gives no hint of certain wanderings which Jesus undertook about this time in the vicinity of Tyre and Sidon, in the Decapolis, and in the north country bordering on Mount Hermon (Mark vii. 24, 31, viii. 27). These journeyings with his disciples indicate a period of suspense in Jesus' mind, during which he was deeply pondering the nature of his commission to Israel. Was he sent to Israel and to Israel alone ? Then why his rejection at the hands of the nation's leaders ? (Cf. Matthew xv. 24, Mark vii. 27.)

Luke, by saying nothing about these wanderings, leaves the Confession of Peter, which marks the close of the period, without geographical or other explanation. He says simply that while Jesus was praying—this notice is peculiar to Luke (cf. iii. 21, vi. 12, ix. 29, etc.)—his disciples were beside him, and he inquired of them, etc. According to Mark, the question was asked on the road to ' the villages of Caesarea Philippi,' i.e. in the far north, near the southern roots of Hermon, and within the territory of Philip who had rebuilt the city of Paneas and named it Caesarea in honour of the Emperor. The district was redolent of the ancient Amorite worship of the Baalim and of the Greek rites of Pan, introduced after Alexander's conquest of the region. Near the city Herod the Great had erected a temple for the worship of Rome and Augustus. See Sir G. A. Smith's *Historical Geography*, pp. 473 f.

The question of Jesus was propounded in full view of recent happenings in Galilee, including possibly the menace to his life from Antipas. What under these circumstances was to be thought of his work and of its issues ? Jesus, who has never till now unsealed his lips even to his disciples on the subject of his Messianic calling, feels that the time has come to throw off his reserve, and he begins by asking, ' Who do the crowds say that I am ? ' The answers given by the disciples coincide with the rumours discussed above under ix. 7–9, and need not be re-examined. We note again the conspicuous absence of the verdict that Jesus is the *Messiah*. Hence it is to be concluded that Jesus had not spoken publicly of the secret of his vocation, nor had the outward aspects under which he appeared suggested to the Galileans any of those attributes which they were accustomed to connect with the Deliverer of Israel.

When, however, Jesus turns to the inner circle of the disciples and asks, ' And who do you say that I am ? ' the verdict which was missing on the part of the nation is at once forthcoming. Peter, as spokesman of those with whom Jesus has shared his most intimate thoughts of the will of God, pronounces him forthwith the Christ of God, so formulating for the first time the momentous confession which was to become the basis of the Christian Church. According to this confession Jesus stands alone. He is above the prophets. He is the *final* messenger of God to Israel, the Anointed One to whom judgment is committed, and through whom the Reign of God comes.

The confession of the disciples, as thus given in the tradition, springs from a spiritual sympathy through which their minds, under the daily tuition of Christ, had travelled along a path convergent with his own. Jesus from his baptism or from an early period in his ministry recognized that in his knowledge of God he stood alone. No other in his nation shared his experience. Hence he has been deeply confirmed in his resolution to be himself the Deliverer of his people (see above, under iii. 21-22, iv. 14-30). Now the confession of his disciples comes as another intimation from the Father in heaven that he has rightly judged that Father's will ; compare Matthew xvi. 17 : ' Blessed art thou, Simon Bar-jona, for flesh and blood hath not revealed it unto thee,' etc. Jesus at last knows that his work, despite seeming frustration, has not been in vain, and the assurance confirms him in going forward to whatever fate awaits him at the hands of the nation. With Peter's confession the second or Messianic period proper in the Ministry begins.

ix. 21-27 : FIRST PREDICTION OF THE MESSIAH'S SUFFERINGS

Then he forbade them strictly to tell this to anyone. The Son 21 of man, he said, has to endure great suffering, to be rejected 22 by the elders and high priests and scribes, to be killed, and on the third day to be raised.

He said to all, ' If anyone wishes to come after me, let him deny 23 himself, take up his cross day after day, and so follow me ;

24   for whoever wants to save his life will lose it,
       and whoever loses his life for my sake, he will save it.
25   What profit will it be for a man to gain the whole world
26   and lose or forfeit himself ? For whoever is ashamed of
       me and my words, of him will the Son of man be ashamed
       when he comes in his glory and in the glory of the Father
27   and of the holy angels. I tell you plainly, there are some
       of those standing here who will not taste death till they see
       the Reign of God.'

                                  (Cf. Mark viii. 31–32, 34–38.)

The tradition represents Jesus as commanding the disciples
not to disclose his Messiahship. The statement that he forbade
them to tell this to anyone cannot mean that he declined the
Messianic title, but only that his reasons for not encouraging
false expectations on the part of the people remained unchanged.
Moreover, it was now plain to Jesus that his work for Israel
could only be achieved through suffering. This was an aspect
of his personal destiny for which there was no place in current
Messianic beliefs.

Rejected and despised, and *yet* the Messiah ! Nay, rejected
and despised, and *therefore* the Messiah ! This is the Christian
' mystery ' into which Jesus' mind has been now initiated, and
into which he must initiate his followers. Judaism had never
ascribed to the Messiah a destiny of personal suffering. The
Rabbis indeed spoke of the Messianic ' woes ' or pangs, but the
sufferings to which they alluded appertained not to the Messiah
himself but to the inhabitants of the earth who should witness
the convulsions through which the Messianic age would be born
(cf. Mark xiii. 7–8, 14–20). Again, Judaism was familiar with
the idea of vicarious suffering as portrayed in the Servant of the
Lord (Isaiah lii. 12–liii. 12), but it is not certain that in Jesus'
time the Servant was identified with the Messiah. Even where
he is so identified, as in the Targum to Isaiah xlii. 1, ' Behold
my Servant, the Messiah,' it is instructive to note that ' the passages which refer to the humiliation of the Servant are interpreted
of the people of Israel,' and that only ' those which speak of the
glory of the Servant are referred to the Messiah ' (G. H. Box,
Religion and Worship of the Synagogue, p. 51 ; cf. G. F. Moore,
Judaism, vol. i, p. 229). On the other hand, Jesus, in bringing
the Kingdom of God to Israel, now knows himself appointed for

humiliation, hatred, and rejection, and the conception of a Messiah who fulfils his destiny through *suffering* becomes from this time onwards a recurrent note in his teaching.

This conception that the Messiah must suffer and die is expressed in a series of passages (Mark viii. 31, ix. 31, x. 32-34), and shews that Jesus definitely aligned his destiny with that of the Suffering Servant of Isaiah liii. He begins to speak of his death as having a redemptive purpose with reference to the nation. The underlying thought is that the salvation of Israel, which Jesus had sought to effect by his message, but which the greater part of the nation had hitherto resisted, will yet be accomplished by his *death*. He who at the first had sought to win the nation by the preaching of the ' glad tidings ' (iv. 18-21) now sees that repudiation and scorn, as signified by the threat from Antipas and by the implacable hostility of the religious leaders, await him, and he accepts this destiny as the price which he must pay for finishing his work. His death is a ransom for Israel.

Side by side with these predictions of suffering we now find increasing emphasis upon the future or supernatural aspect of the Reign of God. Here Jesus turns to the prophecy in Daniel vii. 13-14 as towards a great light. In the prophet's vision of the everlasting Kingdom which is bestowed on the saints of the Most High in the person of a ' Son of man,' Jesus finds a language in which to depict the final outcome of his own redeeming and expiatory work (Mark viii. 38, ix. 1, xiii. 26, xiv. 61-62). These references to the coming on clouds of the Son of man imply that, as the hope of winning the nation to an immediate acceptance of the Kingdom of God had waned, Jesus, while still proclaiming God's instant purpose to redeem His people, was led to throw a greater stress on the reserved or future aspects of that purpose, and here the prophecy in Daniel offered language for his thought.

We may now proceed to the details of the present section, beginning with ver. 22, **the Son of man has to endure great suffering.** Jesus takes to himself definitely the office of the Man through whom the divine Kingdom comes to Israel (on the title ' Son of man ' see above, under v. 17-26). After rejection by the Sanhedrin, he has to be killed, and on the third day— Mark says ' after three days '—to be raised. This is doubtless a case in which the original prediction of Jesus has been conformed to the later events in which it was fulfilled. But that Jesus declared himself appointed for suffering and death, and saw in this destiny a decree of the divine will, is certain, nor with the Psalms before us need we doubt that he spoke with joyous confidence of resurrection. Compare, for example, Psalm xvi. 8–11 : ' I keep the Lord at all times before me . . . and so my heart and soul rejoice, my body rests secure ; for thou wilt never let me sink to death. . . . Thou wilt reveal the path of life . . . to the bliss of being close to Thee for ever.' The effect of the prediction upon the disciples is astounding. Mark records that Peter immediately remonstrated, and that Jesus sharply rebuked him for not perceiving the mind of God on this matter (Mark viii. 32–33). Luke omits this episode, but records after Mark certain solemn words by which Jesus made it plain that his disciples must not only witness but share the Messiah's sufferings.

These words—' **If anyone wishes to come after me, let him deny himself** '—are to be understood as addressed primarily to the *disciples*. If Mark thinks of the crowd as in the audience (Mark viii. 34), and if Luke says that Jesus spoke **to all**, this is because the Christian Church sees in the sacrifice here demanded a requirement which applies to all who would follow Christ. But in its sharp, literal sense the demand connects primarily with an historical crisis in the lives of the disciples. Jesus is going up to Jerusalem to claim the city for God and for His Kingdom. Will his disciples turn back for the sake of lands or houses or kindred, or will they abjure every selfish interest in order to be loyal to him ? The expression **come after me** is to be taken literally in this context. So with the words **take up his cross.** The disciples must not only forswear selfish interests, but they must be prepared to suffer on crosses, if need be, like condemned slaves at the hands of the Roman soldiery. The phrase ' carry the cross ' is not found in the older Rabbinical literature,[1] but crucifixion was familiar, and its associations for ordinary ears are well expressed in a sentence of Cicero, who says that the very name of cross should not be thought of, seen, or heard in good Roman society. Luke's addition of **day after day** shews that he is spiritualizing the thought of the cross. In its original sense the demand of Jesus is equivalent to a man's

[1] I.e. in a metaphorical spiritual sense, but for Jewish familiarity with the cross as an instrument of punishment see Dalman, *Jesus-Jeshua,* pp. 185–92.

putting of the hangman's rope about his neck. Thus only can the disciple follow Christ, for the path which he treads now is the path of martyrdom.

The solemn demand is enforced by the words, 'For whoever wants to save his life shall lose it.' Jesus does not distinguish a higher and a lower *nature* in a man as Paul does when he sets the mind and the flesh in opposition. To Jesus a man's life or personality is a single entity, which is lost or won according as it is given to lower or higher aims. Here the competing issues are between present earthly safety and the future prize of the Kingdom. The disciples may cling to lands or houses, or to ease and security, but in so doing they will be throwing away their interest in the Kingdom of God, and 'what profit will it be for a man' to keep what he has, nay, 'to gain the whole world' at such a cost? For the Reign is about to be revealed. The Son of man will be disclosed to men's eyes in his glory, or true character as the Elect of God, on whose bidding the angels wait—here the suggestions supplied by the vision in Daniel come clearly to the surface—and then he will blush for those who refused here the sacrifice which he asked.

It is possible that here again traditional language has influenced the record of Jesus' historical expressions. But that at this crisis he called on his followers to abandon everything for the Kingdom of God admits of no doubt. Jesus depended on his disciples' loyalty, and this loyalty meant their going with him to Jerusalem and sharing his fate. But along with, and forming the reverse side of, this renunciation, Jesus points to the certain coming of the Kingdom. 'There are some of those standing here who will not taste of death till they see the Reign of God.' That Jesus should look to see this consummation reached within the experience, and before the eyes, of the generation for which he had laboured and suffered was natural and inevitable. The same strain of expectation recurs in xxi. 32 and in Mark xiv. 62. Those standing here mean the disciples as representing the contemporary world. Jesus looked therefore to the near future for the fulfilment of the purpose signified to him in his revelation from God. He expected the supernatural Kingdom of God to become a fact (cf. Mark ix. 1), or, if death came before his work was finished, he expected to come again from God (cf. Matthew xvi. 28), in terms of the prophecy in Daniel, to bring about its accomplishment.

ix. 28–36 : THE TRANSFIGURATION

28 It was about eight days after he said this, when he took Peter,
29 John, and James, and went up the hillside to pray. While
he was praying the appearance of his face altered and his
30 dress turned dazzling white. There were two men con-
31 versing with him, Moses and Elijah, who appeared in a
vision of glory and said he must go through with his death
32 and departure at Jerusalem. Now Peter and his companions had been overpowered with sleep, but on waking up
they saw his glory and the two men who were standing
33 beside him. When they were parting from him, Peter said
to Jesus, ' Master, it is a good thing we are here ; let us
put up three tents, one for you, one for Moses, and one for
34 Elijah ' (not knowing what he was saying). As he spoke,
a cloud came and overshadowed them. They were awe-
35 struck as they passed into the cloud, but a voice came from
the cloud, ' This is my Son, my Chosen one ; listen to him.'
36 When the voice ceased, they found themselves alone with
Jesus. And in those days they kept silence and told nobody
anything of what they had seen.

(Cf. Mark ix. 2–9.)

The careful dating of the Transfiguration—Mark placing it six
days, and Luke about eight days after the last event—is instructive. It indicates that the tradition recognized a close connexion
between this episode and some preceding experience, in other
words, held the Transfiguration to a cause or explanation within
that experience. What then is the connexion ? Certain ancient
commentators, observing that the Transfiguration follows the
prediction, ' There are some of those standing here who will not
taste of death till they see the Reign of God ' (ix. 27), took it to
be the fulfilment of that prediction. But this explanation
cannot be sustained. The Transfiguration cannot be equivalent
to the coming of the Reign of God, since at a later date Jesus
still alludes to that Reign as future (xxi. 27–28, 31–32 ; cf. xxii.
16, 18, 69).

But while the Transfiguration is not a fulfilment of this particular prediction, the tradition presents it as the sequel or
resultant of the experiences described in ix. 18–27. The announcement that Jesus must suffer and die had stunned his

disciples and deprived them of any point of support in traditional Messianic ideas. But from this bewilderment they are delivered a week later by experiences as the result of which they see Jesus *glorified* by this predicted destiny of suffering (ix. 29-32). At the same time they are conscious of a Voice—the *Bath Qol* or ' daughter of the voice ' of God—proclaiming Jesus to be indeed God's Son, to whom they must listen (ix. 34-35). By thus transferring their thoughts from the older Messianic ideas to a new centre in a Christ exalted through suffering, the Transfiguration becomes the complement and verification of Peter's Confession at Caesarea Philippi. In both Confession and Transfiguration the ' mystery ' of the personality of Jesus occupies the foreground. In both Peter is prominent, and tries to divert Jesus from going to Jerusalem, for is not this, as Origen said, the meaning of his desire to remain upon the Mount (ix. 33 ; cf. Mark viii. 32) ? In both the Death of Jesus is a determining conception (ix. 22, 31). In both Jesus is declared the Chosen of God (ix. 20, 35). Confession and Transfiguration are thus like the parallel limbs of a double rainbow against the dark sky of the Messiah's fortunes.

When, however, we turn to details and particularly to the question of what constituted the historical basis of the representation, we are on more difficult ground. According to the tradition, Jesus took Peter, John, and James, and went up the hillside. A season of retreat seems indicated, during which Jesus initiates into a deeper understanding of his destiny a group of disciples who on other occasions also appear as special recipients of his confidence. What follows would seem to be of the nature of a vision seen in a trance. While he was praying—Luke alone mentions this point, so that according to his presentation the ensuing experience is a vision of Christ in prayer—the appearance of his face altered. The changed aspect under which the disciples presently behold him (ver. 32) is anticipated and explained as wrought by an objective transformation of his person, nor can there be any doubt as to the nature of this symbolism. Judaism knows of a heavenly life in a body of dazzling light : cf. Daniel xii. 3, and especially Enoch cviii. 11, ' And now I will summon the spirits of the good who belong to the generation of light, and I will transform those . . . who in the flesh were not recompensed with such honour as their faithfulness deserved. And I will bring forth in shining light those who have loved My holy

I

name . . . and they shall be resplendent.' When therefore it is stated that the face of Jesus altered and his dress turned dazzling white (cf. Enoch lxii. 16), the meaning is that a heavenly radiance, as of one triumphant over death, surrounds the praying Christ. As for Moses and Elijah who appeared in a vision of glory, etc., Judaism probably included these two historical figures among the men who, after suffering, ' have been taken up ' (2 Esdras vi. 26). They are intimately associated in Jewish thought with the coming of the Messiah (Malachi iv. 4–5), and if the disciples in their vision see them by the side of Jesus, a psychological explanation may be found in the working of this idea upon their subconscious mind. But it is sufficient to suppose the narrative, here as elsewhere, to be symbolical, a way of saying that Jesus, in speaking of his suffering, had cited the fortunes, and perhaps the vicarious sufferings, of Moses and Elijah as prophetic of his own. Cf. Revelation xi. 3–10.

The vision of the disciples is associated with a waking up in ver. 32. Luke alone mentions the sleep and the awakening. Peter ejaculates, ' Master, it is a good thing we are here ; let us put up three tents,' etc. The point of the explanation not knowing what he was saying is that Peter, according to the tradition, did not understand that what he now beheld was a heavenly mystery. He thought that Jesus and his companions were ' in the body,' and therefore in need of earthly habitations. But here again the symbolism owes something to Peter's historical reluctance to let his Master go on to Jerusalem to die. At this moment, however, a cloud, symbolizing the divine Presence, came and overshadowed them (cf. Exodus xiii. 21–22). Does this feature reflect the heavy shadow cast on the disciples by the thought that Jesus must die, out of which darkness comes in turn a stronger, diviner assurance that he is the Christ ? A voice came from the cloud, ' This is my Son, my Chosen one.' As at the Baptism the voice of God had revealed Jesus to himself (' Thou art my Son,' iii. 22), so now the same voice reveals him to his followers. But the revelation is subject to the condition that they ' listen to him.' This proviso has here a very special point. Recalling the prediction of Moses in Deuteronomy xviii. 15, ' The Lord thy God will raise up unto thee a prophet . . . like unto me ; unto him you shall hearken,' it summons the disciples to lay to heart what Jesus says about his *death*. Hitherto they have resisted that teaching. Now they see it to be involved in the very nature of the Messiah's office. The Transfiguration thus signifies the Christianization of the Messianic idea.

While the Transfiguration narrative is thus, as it stands, highly symbolical, an historical basis is discernible in some experience, perhaps a vision of Christ in prayer, through which his words about the suffering which awaited him flashed upon the disciples' minds with a new insistence and reality, recalling significant things which he had said about Moses and Elijah, and opening a momentary vista of what lay beyond the veil of time and sense. Jesus may during recent days have spoken much of these men who had been ' taken up ' as witnessing to the fact that he too must be taken up (ix. 51). As the tradition stands, it implies that the disciples saw Jesus for the moment in the light in which his Church was to see him after the Resurrection. Hence some scholars have actually interpreted the Transfiguration as the projection back into Jesus' life of a vision of the Risen Lord. But it can be urged that without the kind of experience here depicted the disciples would have been unable later to comprehend the Resurrection. On the other hand, the statement that in those days they kept silence and told nobody anything of what they had seen is a plain admission that the new Messianic ideas to which they had been introduced did not become operative until after Jesus' death.

ix. 37-42 : THE EPILEPTIC CHILD

Next day, when they came down the hill, a large crowd met him. 37 ' Teacher,' shouted a man from the crowd, ' look at my 38 son, I beg of you, for he is my only boy, and a spirit gets 39 hold of him till he suddenly shrieks ; it convulses him till he foams ; indeed it will hardly leave off tearing him to pieces. I begged your disciples to cast it out, but they could 40 not.' Jesus answered, ' O faithless and perverse generation, 41 how long must I still be with you and bear with you ? Fetch your son here.' Before the boy could reach Jesus, the daemon 42 dashed him down and convulsed him, but Jesus checked the unclean spirit, cured the boy, and handed him back to his father.

(Cf. Mark ix. 14-29.)

There is a startling contrast between the Transfiguration and the episode which follows. From the exalted experience on the hilltop Jesus and his followers come down again to a world of suffering and need, and Jesus is distressed beyond measure by the failure of his disciples to afford help in a poignantly trying situation. The father of a boy suffering from epileptic seizures has implored them to exorcize the evil spirit, and these men whom Jesus had sent to cast out demons (ix. 1–2) have stood impotently by. On demons and their reputed causation of nervous and mental disorders see above, under iv. 31–44 and viii. 26–39. In the present instance demonic causation of the malady is seen in the terrifying shrieks and convulsions of the child. Jesus asks that the boy be brought. A paroxysm occurs as he is coming, but Jesus checked the unclean spirit, and gave the boy back to his father, sound and well.

Luke has abbreviated the story as told by Mark. He omits *inter alia* the altercation between the disciples and the crowd, and the instruction of the disciples regarding the cause of their failure. Luke, therefore, spares the disciples. But he retains as central feature of the incident the outspoken reproach, ' O faithless and perverse generation,' etc., which recalls Deuteronomy xxxii. 5. Doubtless the disciples are included in this indictment as much as the miracle-loving and gaping crowd. Jesus has given abundant evidence of God's immediate will to terminate the reign of the demons, but men will not believe it. In the words ' How long must I still be with you and bear with you ? ' (cf. Numbers xiv. 27) there lies the thought that God's intervention in history through Jesus will be brief. The opportunity comes, but it passes.

ix. 43–45 : SECOND PREDICTION OF THE PASSION

43 And all were astounded at this grand display of God. But while
44   all marvelled at all he did, he said to his disciples, ' Let these
      words sink into your ears : '' the Son of man is to be betrayed
45   into the hands of men.'' ' But they did not understand this
      saying—indeed it was kept a secret from them, to prevent
      them from fathoming it—and they were afraid to ask him
      about this saying.

(Cf. Mark ix. 30–32.)

The display of divine power in the cure of the epileptic child impresses all, and Jesus takes occasion to remind his disciples anew of the necessity of his death.   In the context the prediction means that the glorious deeds of Jesus, at which the people marvel, must not deceive the disciples as to the true course of Jesus' history (Zahn).   Therefore he calls for attention : ' Let these words sink into your ears.'   The form of the prophecy, ' the Son of man is to be betrayed into the hands of men,' seems to imply a tradition independent of Mark ix. 31.   It is briefer and more mysterious, and therefore, as Dr. Easton observes, the misunderstanding of the apostles, alluded to in ver. 45, becomes more comprehensible.   They share the blindness elsewhere attributed to ' those outside ' (viii. 9-10).

ix. 46-48 : A Dispute about Precedence

A dispute arose among them as to which of them was the greatest. 46
Jesus knew the dispute that occupied their minds, so he 47
took hold of a little child and set it by his side ; then he 48
said to them,
  ' Whoever receives this little child in my name receives me,
    and whoever receives me receives him who sent me.
  For it is the lowliest of you all who is great.'
                          (Cf. Mark ix. 33-37.)

Disputes of the disciples as to which of them was the greatest characterize the period succeeding Jesus' decision to go to Jerusalem, and reflect ardent anticipations of the Messianic triumph to be achieved there by Jesus.   By way of rebuke Jesus took hold of a little child and set it by his side.   This gesture is sometimes explained by saying that the child in its humility and freedom from worldly ambition is an example of what a disciple ought to be.   But this interpretation scarcely consorts with the application, ' Whoever receives this little child in my name receives me.'   ' Receiving ' a child is not equivalent to becoming like a child.   Hence we should find the purpose of the gesture in Jesus' desire to turn away his disciples' minds from thoughts of ambition to thoughts of *ministry*.   Instead of coveting place and power, they should think of the weak and dependent ones with whom Jesus has identified himself, and by protecting, serving, and loving whom they will receive Christ and his Father, since 'whoever receives me receives him who sent me.' For the criterion stated in the words, 'it is the lowliest of you all who is great,' compare the admission made by a modern Jewish scholar : 'The Rabbis were never weary of preaching humility and its greatness. . . . But the combination of humility with *service* . . . was a special characteristic of the religion of Jesus, and a new thing when he preached it ' (C. G. Montefiore, *Synoptic Gospels*, vol. i, p. 218). (Cf. also Mark x. 45.)

ix. 49–50 : An Exorcist outside the Ranks

49 John said to him, ' Master, we saw a man casting out daemons
in your name, but we stopped him because he is not a
50   follower of ours.' Jesus said to him, ' Do not stop him ;
he who is not against you is for you.'

(Cf. Mark ix. 38–40.)

This episode connects well with the last, inasmuch as it also contains a rebuke to a disciple. But whereas vers. 46–48 are directed against self-seeking, the present passage is rather an indictment of intolerance. Some one—perhaps an adherent of Jesus, though not a disciple in the full sense (cf. ix. 23)—is observed by the Twelve to be exorcizing demons by use of the name of Jesus—the possession of a ' name ' was considered to convey spiritual powers (cf. Acts xix. 13–16)—and John says, ' We stopped him because he is not a follower of ours.' Jesus' answer is to forbid such intolerance on the ground that such a man cannot be an enemy. At a time when the name of Jesus was proscribed (Mark iii. 22), it required courage to use it in public. Moreover, was a man to be interdicted whose only fault was that in his own way, and without perhaps the power to render other service, he practised love to those who needed it (Zahn) ? Jesus will have none of this persecuting zeal. ' Do not stop him, for he who is not against you is for you.' For an inverse form of the same saying, spoken in an altogether different context, see on xi. 23.

IV. JESUS ON THE WAY TO JERUSALEM (ix. 51-xix. 28)

ix. 51-56 : THE SAMARITAN VILLAGERS

As the time for his assumption was now due, he set his face 51
for the journey to Jerusalem. He sent messengers in 52
front of him. They went and entered a Samaritan village
to make preparations for him, but the people would not 53
receive him because his face was turned in the direction of
Jerusalem. So when the disciples James and John saw 54
this, they said, ' Lord, will you have us bid *fire come down
from heaven and consume them*? ' But he turned and 55
checked them. Then they journeyed to another village. 56
(Luke alone.)

A long section begins here (ix. 51-xviii. 14) in which Luke
makes no use of Mark, and which, because of the prefixed
statement that Jesus now set his face for the journey to Jerusalem,
is commonly called the ' Perean section ' or ' Travel narrative '
of Luke. But these descriptions are not really applicable to
the whole of the contained material, for (1) many items in this
section reflect Galilean surroundings, and are assigned by
Matthew to the Galilean period, (2) as late as xvii. 11 Jesus is
still passing between Samaria and Galilee, (3) Perea is suggested
only by Mark x. 1, and the crossing of the Jordan in that passage
is of demonstrably later date than the bulk of the matter incorporated in this section. The impression that a journey formed
the occasion of all the incidents included in ix. 51-xviii. 14
probably originated in Luke's mind from the circumstance that
the first incident relates to a projected crossing of the Samaritan
frontier (ix. 52-53), while the next also implies that the company
was in motion (ix. 57). Since, however, other references to a
journeying of Jesus occur in the section (x. 1, 38, xiii. 22, 33
xiv. 25, xvii. 11), we may take the whole to constitute for Luke
a record of sayings and doings of Jesus on the way to
Jerusalem.

The material of the section is drawn partly from Q and
partly from L. (For the items peculiar to Luke see Introd.,
p. xviii.) The evangelist, by commencing the section with
the words, As the time for his assumption was now due (cf. ix.
31), places all its contents under the solemn shadow of the

Cross. By ' assumption ' he means the Ascension of Jesus or the whole Passion-history conceived as a transition from the earthly to the heavenly life.

Disciples sent by Jesus entered a Samaritan village to make preparations for him. According to Josephus ' it was a custom of Galileans proceeding at the feasts to the holy city to journey through Samaritan territory ' (*Antiq.* xx. 6. 1). But relations were not cordial between the Jews and the schismatic race, which after Nehemiah's reforms followed the apostate priest Manasseh and set up a rival temple on Mount Gerizim. The Jews despised ' the foolish nation that dwells in Shechem ' (Ecclesiasticus i. 25), and the Samaritans repaid them with scorn. Josephus records that once in the Samaritan village of Gema ' a Galilean, one of a large company of Jews journeying to the festival, was murdered ' (*Wars*, ii. 12. 3). So here the Samaritans decline to receive Jesus because his face was turned in the direction of Jerusalem, and the hot-blooded James and John wish to retaliate by invoking fire to come down from heaven and consume them. But when the wish is referred to Jesus, Jesus turned and checked them. The company passes on to another village, but whether in Samaria or in Galilee is not stated.

A number of ancient authorities exhibit a longer text in the above passage. After ver. 54 many add, ' As Elias did ' (cf. 2 Kings i. 10–12). Similarly, after ' checked them ' in ver. 55 a number add, ' And said, you know not of what spirit you are, for the Son of man did not come to destroy but to save men's lives.' This longer text underlies the English Authorized Version, but has no foundation in the best Greek MSS. How did a longer and a shorter text arise in the passage ? One answer is that the additional words in the longer text came in under the influence of the second-century heretic Marcion, who, denying all connexion between the gospel of Jesus and the religion of the Old Testament, glossed the words of Jesus so as to make them an explicit repudiation of Elijah's methods. Another suggestion, supported by Zahn, is that the longer text represents what Luke wrote, and that ecclesiastical revisers cut it down to prevent the passage playing into the hands of Marcion. The latter theory is most improbable. The longer text may be due simply to homiletical elaboration of the incident in some early Christian quarter.

ix. 57–62 : CONDITIONS OF DISCIPLESHIP

And as they journeyed along the road a man said to him, 'I will 57
follow you anywhere.' Jesus said to him,   58
   'The foxes have their holes,
      the wild birds have their nests,
         but the Son of man has nowhere to lay his head.'
He said to another man, 'Follow me '; but he said, 'Let 59
me go and bury my father first of all.' Jesus said to him, 60
'Leave the dead to bury their own dead ; you go and spread
the news of the Reign of God.' Another man also said to 61
him, 'I will follow you, Lord. But let me first say good-bye
to my people at home.' Jesus said to him, 'No one is any 62
use to the Reign of God who puts his hand to the plough
and then looks behind him.'

                (Cf. Matthew viii. 19–22.)

For the demands here made by Jesus see above, under ix.
21–27. The words **as they journeyed** point to the time when
Jesus was leaving Galilee for Jerusalem. The first man voluntarily offers to go with Jesus. Jesus warns him that, though
the wild creatures have their dens and nests, ' the Son of man,'
the Messiah who brings the Kingdom of God, ' has nowhere
to lay his head.' The saying reflects a time when Jesus was
proscribed, and dared not settle anywhere (cf. ix. 52–53). The
second man is called by Christ, but asks permission first to
bury his father, whose death presumably had just occurred.
Jesus, whose claims take precedence even over the sacredest
earthly obligations—cf. Mark x. 21—answers, ' **Leave the dead
to bury their dead ; you go and spread the news of the Reign
of God.**' The ' dead ' here are the spiritually dead, who had
not received the high vocation addressed to this man, and to
whom the requisite funeral rites could in this case be safely left.
The saying points to a time when Jesus had relinquished the
hope of rousing all the Galileans to life. The third man—this
case is special to Luke—volunteers service like the first, but
like the second makes conditions. Jesus refuses him permission
to say good-bye to his people. ' **No man is any use to the Reign
of God,**' i.e. as a preacher of the gospel, ' **who puts his hand to
the plough and then looks behind him.**' The impossibility of a
man driving a straight furrow while looking backwards is

obvious. Jesus is thinking of those who would follow him from mixed motives or with divided affections.

Vers. 57–60 are from Q, and are paralleled in Matthew viii. 19–22, where also a journey of Jesus is given as the occasion. But in Matthew the journey is merely to Gadara, which is less suitable.

x. 1–16 : The Mission of the Seventy

x.

1 After that the Lord commissioned other seventy disciples, sending them in front of him two by two to every town and
2 place that he intended to visit himself. He said to them, ' The harvest is rich, but the labourers are few ; so pray the Lord of the harvest to send labourers to gather his
3 harvest. Go your way ; I am sending you out like lambs
4 among wolves. Carry no purse, no wallet, no sandals.
5 Do not stop to salute anybody on the road. Whatever house you enter, first say, " Peace be to this household ! "
6 Then, if there is a soul there breathing peace, your peace will rest on him ; otherwise it will come back to you.
7 Stay at the same house, eating and drinking what the people provide (for the workman deserves his wages) ; you
8 are not to shift from one house to another. Wherever you are received on entering any town, eat what is provided for
9 you, heal those in the town who are ill, and tell them, " The
10 Reign of God is nearly on you." But wherever you are not received on entering any town, go out into the streets of
11 the town and cry, " The very dust of your town that clings to us, we wipe off from our feet as a protest. But mark this,
12 the Reign of God is near ! " I tell you, on the great Day it will be more bearable for Sodom than for that town.
13 Woe to you, Khorazin ! woe to you, Bethsaida ! Had the miracles performed in you been performed in Tyre and Sidon, they would long ago have been sitting penitent in sackcloth
14 and ashes. But it will be more bearable for Tyre and Sidon
15 at the judgment than for you. And you, O Capharnahum! *Exalted to heaven ? No, you will sink to Hades !*
16 He who listens to you listens to me,
he who rejects you rejects me,
and he who rejects me rejects him who sent me.'
(Cf. Matthew ix. 37–38, x. 7–8, 10–16, 40 ; xi. 21–23.)

Luke has already in ix. 1–6 recorded after Mark certain missionary instructions which Jesus gave to the Twelve. Here he reports from Q (cf. Matthew x. 7–8, 10–16) another similar set of sayings. But whereas in Matthew the two series are presented in combination as addressed to the Twelve, Luke introduces the second series by the statement that the Lord commissioned other seventy disciples, sending them, etc. That Jesus would utilize the services of other disciples besides the Twelve is, of course, entirely probable. That their appointment should afterwards be largely forgotten in the special honour due to the Twelve is equally probable. Yet it is possible that the number 70, as given in Luke's source, whether Q or L, is symbolical in origin. Seventy is in Genesis x. the number of the nations of the earth, and if the missionaries, who in the first Christian age went out to the Gentile lands (Acts xi. 19–21, etc.), adopted as their rule the injunctions which the Lord had given to an originally undefined group of disciples, this would account for these injunctions becoming known in certain quarters as his words to ' the Seventy,' i.e. to the missionaries to the Gentile world, and would explain the assigning to them of precepts which in Matthew are assumed to have been given to the Twelve. Some ancient authorities read 72 instead of 70. The same variation occurs in our ancient authorities for Genesis x. (the Hebrew having 70 nations, and the Septuagint version 72), and in the Jewish tradition regarding the number of the translators who produced the Septuagint version.

The Seventy are to go out two by two (cf. Mark vi. 7) into the towns and districts which Jesus intended to visit. Jesus felt that the coming of the Reign of God waited upon the repentance of Israel, and the task of awakening the thousands of souls who were yet unreached lay heavily on his heart. ' The harvest is rich, but the labourers are few,' etc. (cf. Matthew ix. 37–38). But while Israel is ripe for the mission, Jesus plainly reveals that fierce opposition awaits the missionaries from the side of the religious authorities : ' I am sending you out like lambs among wolves ' (cf. Matthew x. 16). Does the word ' lambs ' imply the pacific counsels which the disciples are to follow, e.g. ' Love your enemies, do good to those who hate you,' etc. (vi. 27–29) ? On ver. 4 see above on ix. 3. The injunction ' Do not stop to salute anybody on the road ' deprecates the losing of time in mere civilities, for Oriental ceremonial was wont to be diffuse. We are reminded of Elisha's words to Gehazi in 2 Kings iv. 29, possibly also of the fate of the unnamed 'man of God' in 1 Kings xiii. In vers. 5–6 (cf. Matthew x. 12–13) the salutation 'Peace be to this household,' which is to be used wherever a doorstep is crossed, is declared to be no formality, but to have objective value wherever it is cordially bestowed and received. Even where it is spurned, the goodwill of the messenger will recoil with blessing on his own head. On vers. 7–9 see on ix. 4. The messengers will be offered hospitality by friendly Israelites, for 'the workman deserves his wages' (cf. 1 Corinthians ix. 14), and they must accept it gladly and thankfully. The counsel 'Eat what is provided for you' would be remembered specially because of its bearing on the difficult questions about food which arose later, when Christian missionaries, trained in Jewish ways and customs, crossed to heathen soil. On the announcement, 'the Reign of God is nearly on you,' see above, under iv. 14–30 and viii. 9–15. The proclamation stresses the finality of the revelation and of the opportunity given to Israel in Jesus. On vers. 10–11 compare what is said above on ix. 5. The doom which awaits the impenitent cities of Israel 'on the great Day,' i.e. at the swiftly approaching Judgment, is enforced by reference to Sodom, for Sodom above all cities had outraged the 'messengers' of God (Genesis xix. 1 f.). Nevertheless, as Sodom did not enjoy the spiritual advantages offered to Israel in Jesus, its sentence will be lighter than that of the Jewish cities.

In vers. 13–15 Luke records certain judgments pronounced by Jesus on a trio of Galilean towns. The sayings (which are from Q) are placed by Matthew in another context (Matthew xi. 20–24). 'Woe to you, Khorazin! woe to you, Bethsaida!' Khorazin is identified with a ruined site two miles north-west of Tell-hum or Capernaum. Bethsaida has been referred to in ix. 10. The gospels tell us nothing of a work of Jesus in Khorazin. This word therefore shews how far from complete, as a record of Jesus' activities, our evangelical tradition is. Of a work in Bethsaida the only trace is in Mark viii. 22–26. Apparently the two cities had remained impenitent, and Jesus compares them to their disadvantage with 'Tyre and Sidon,' which, if they had witnessed the miracles wrought in the Galilean cities (cf. vii. 19–23), would long ago have been sitting penitent in sackcloth and ashes. Tyre and Sidon, lying so close to Galilee with their mixed Graeco-Syrian populations, would be bywords for heathen degradation. Jesus says that these cities are less guilty than the proud cities of Galilee. For ancient prophetic denouncements of Tyre see Isaiah xxiii. and Ezekiel xxvi.–xxviii. 'And thou, O Capharnahum ! ': the third city of the group, and principal theatre of Jesus' work, is arraigned for spiritual pride, making it deaf to Jesus' appeal. Shalt thou be 'exalted to heaven ? No, you will sink to Hades ! ' The words recall the prophetic oracle about Nebuchadnezzar, 'How art thou fallen from heaven, O day-star, son of the morning ! ' Do Capernaum people think they will go to heaven, sharing the rapture of the saints ? On the contrary, they are taking the way that leads to death, exclusion from God's presence. The closing words, 'He who listens to you listens to me,' etc. (cf. Matthew x. 40 f.) revert to the mission of the disciples and emphasize that the disciples are ambassadors of Christ and God, who offer the sole terms of the divine salvation. The saying illustrates Jesus' sense of the absolute finality of his mission.

x. 17-20 : The Return of the Seventy

The seventy came back with joy. 'Lord,' they said, ' the very 17 daemons obey us in your name.' He said to them, 'Yes, 18 I watched Satan fall from heaven like a flash of lightning. I have indeed given you the power of *treading on serpents* 19 and scorpions and of trampling down all the power of the Enemy ; nothing shall injure you. Only,   20
    do not rejoice because the spirits obey you ;
    rejoice because your names are enrolled in heaven.'
                        (Luke alone.)

The Seventy returned with elation, exclaiming 'Lord, the very daemons obey us in your name.' The exorcizing of demons was not, as it happens, included in the commission given to them by Jesus, but it is over-subtle on this ground to interpret the joy of the disciples as due to their success having exceeded expectation. The reply of Jesus, 'Yes, I watched Satan fall from heaven,' is sometimes explained as a warning against spiritual pride, in this case the pride of the disciples in the success which they had achieved. But it is better taken as a wholehearted acknowledgment by Jesus of the greatness of that success. Jesus reverts in thought to his temptation in the wilderness, when he saw the power of Satan to be in principle overthrown, or more probably he alludes to a vision which he had contemporaneously with the disciples' mission : ' While you were away, I saw Satan fall, etc.' The passage is of great historical interest as marking the significance which Jesus attached to the disciples' mission. Satan, ' the prince of the power of the air ' (Ephesians ii. 2 ; cf. vi. 12), has been dethroned. He falls from ' heaven,' i.e. from the sky or air, like a meteor or lightning-flash extinguished in darkness (cf. Revelation xii. 9–10). However small in themselves the results of the disciples' work have been, Jesus sees them to be symptomatic of a new era in religious history. ' I have indeed given you the power of treading on serpents and scorpions,' etc. The words echo Psalm xci. 13. ' Serpent ' (cf. Genesis iii. 1 and Revelation xii. 9) is symbolic of Satanic power, nor can there be any doubt that here and in the words ' trampling down all the power of the enemy ' Jesus is speaking of the demons as representing the subtlest craft of the enemy of souls in human life. Nevertheless, the success of the disciples is welcomed by Jesus not for its own sake but as a divine verification of his choice of his disciples. God has signally honoured his confidence in these men, and there-fore Jesus says : ' Do not rejoice because the spirits obey you, but rejoice because your names are enrolled in heaven.' Here speaks a consciousness for which, as Dr. Easton says, ' the exist-ence of a people prepared for the coming of the Kingdom and already registered as its citizens ' is an accomplished fact. The results of the mission are a proof to the disciples of their inherit-ance in the Realm of God. For the metaphor of the book of life compare Exodus xxxii. 32, Isaiah iv. 3, Enoch xlvii. 3, civ. 1, Revelation xx. 15. With ver. 20 compare Matthew vii. 21–23.

x. 21–24 : THE THANKSGIVING OF JESUS

21 He thrilled with joy at that hour in the holy Spirit, saying, ' I praise thee, Father, Lord of heaven and earth, for con-cealing this from the wise and learned and revealing it to

the simple-minded ; yes, Father, I praise thee that such
was thy chosen purpose.' Then turning to the disciples
he said,

 ' All has been handed over to me by my Father ;   22
  and no one knows who the Son is except the Father,
  or who the Father is except the Son,
  and he to whom the Son chooses to reveal him.'
Then turning to the disciples he said privately,
 ' Blessed are the eyes that see what you see !   23
For I tell you many prophets and kings have desired to 24
  see what you see,
 but they have not seen it ;
and to hear what you hear,
 but they have not heard it.'
     (Cf. Matthew xi. 25-27, xiii. 16-17.)

The phrase at that hour—the parallel in Matthew xi. 25 shews
that this note of time rests on Q—indicates that the great
utterance here recorded connects with some definite event, and
doubtless, as Luke suggests, with the return of the disciples.
Jesus is moved to an extraordinary height of emotion. He
thrilled with joy in the holy Spirit, and just as at his baptism
the Spirit was associated with a personal consciousness of
divine Sonship, so here the ecstasy of Jesus leads up to an
expression of that Sonship which is unique in the Synoptic
literature.

The thanksgiving begins with the acknowledgment ' I praise
thee, Father,' indicating that God has ordered everything for
good. The Fatherhood of God is the starting-point of the
consciousness of Jesus. It was through an overwhelming
experience of the Father-love of God that Jesus had been led
to give himself to the saving of his nation (iii. 22). ' He felt
that he was unique in having seen God as he had seen Him. . . .
The abyss which, in this respect, separated him from other men
seemed to him not a reason for doubt but an indication of a
unique vocation ' (Berguer). But the God with whom Jesus
thus lives in closest communion is at the same time the Lord
of heaven and earth, whose power and wisdom are expressed
in all His appointments. Marcion in the second century made a
separation between the Father-God of Jesus and the Creator-
God of the Old Testament, but no basis exists for this distinction

in the religion of Jesus. The ground of the thanksgiving is God's action in concealing this from the wise and learned and revealing it to the simple-minded. It is not stated what it is that is thus reserved from the wise and made known to the simple, but we shall be right in connecting the saying with the revelation or 'mystery' given to Jesus, which, though repudiated by the theologians and scholars of the day, has been grasped by the devout faith of the disciples and has made them victorious over Satan and the demons (x. 17). The blindness of the Scribes and Pharisees must have distressed Jesus, but he takes comfort in the thought that God has willed it for gracious ends : ' Yes, Father, I praise thee that such was thy chosen purpose.' For in the fact that the revelation is given to the ' simple-minded,' there lies the hope that it will one day be grasped by all.

In ver. 22, in words addressed to the disciples, the foundations of the consciousness of Jesus come still more clearly to light. Jesus knows that all the truth necessary for the carrying out of his great commission has, despite the opposition of the wise and learned, been granted to him by God, and this truth has been the secret of the disciples' success. ' All has been handed over to me by my Father ' : Jesus knows that everything that has been revealed to him, and that he reveals to others, is from God. The words ' and no one knows who the Son is except the Father ' take us back to the experience of Jesus at his baptism, which made a separation between him and other men, consisting as it did in the revelation to Jesus of the Messianic mystery. Here then the underlying filial consciousness of Jesus, of which we have spoken above (see under iii. 21-22, iv. 1-13, ix. 18-20), comes at last to open expression. If Jesus did not possess from the start a sense of the absolute uniqueness of his own experience of the Father, the recognition has been forced on him by his peculiar fortunes and by his extraordinary engagement to bring Israel to God, and it involves not only that God is the source of Jesus' knowledge of himself as the Messiah, but also that, because of this knowledge, Jesus is uniquely commissioned to declare God to Israel. So to the above declaration is added : ' or who the Father is except the Son, and he to whom the Son chooses to reveal him.' There exists thus between the Father and the Son a relation into which no other enters, and Jesus, in his awareness of being authoritatively called to declare God to men, utters the felicitation of the disciples recorded in vers. 23–24.

These verses—' **Blessed are the eyes that see what you see,'** etc.—are, like vers. 21–22, from Q, and imply that in the ministry of Jesus the prophecies of the Messianic age are fulfilled. Something is happening to which the whole past history of revelation has led up. ' **I tell you many prophets and kings have desired to see what you see,'** etc. Among the prophets referred to will be Moses, Isaiah, Micah, Zechariah ; among the kings David, Solomon, Hezekiah.

The circumstance that the Messianic mystery is revealed not to the learned but to the simple marks the difference between the gospel of Jesus and systems which, like Gnosticism, offer the divine secrets only to an intellectual few. The Christian mysteries are accessible to the lowly, and therefore are potentially within the reach of all. But did Jesus utter ver. 22 in the form in which we have it ? The question arises because some ancient authorities (Justin, Marcion, Eusebius, and others) quote the words (1) with the past tense ' knew ' instead of ' knows ' ; (2) with the clauses transposed, so that the Son's knowledge of the Father precedes the Father's knowledge of the Son. Some scholars consider that the past tense ' knew ' represents the original form of the saying, implying as it does that Jesus' knowledge of God is something which has come to him historically in time ; and from the varying order of the clauses relating to Father and Son they conclude that one or other of these clauses represents an ancient interpolation into the text. Thus von Harnack would reconstruct the original text as follows : ' No one has come to know who the Father is except the Son, and he to whom the Son wills to reveal Him.' According to this scholar Jesus did not come to reveal himself but only God the Father. Dr. Easton, on the other hand, suggests as the original : ' No one has known who the Son is except the Father, and he, etc.' If there is any ground for such reconstruction of the text, the suggestion of Dr. Easton would seem preferable, for the burden of the whole thanksgiving surely is that God has unveiled the Messianic secret to Jesus and, through him, to his humble followers. For a defence of the traditional text see Dr. James Denney's *Jesus and the Gospel*, pp. 236–47.

x. 25–37 : The Question of the Lawyer and the Parable of the Good Samaritan

25 Now a jurist got up to tempt him. ' Teacher,' he said, ' what am
26 I to do to inherit life eternal ? ' He said to him, ' What is
27 written in the law ? What do you read there ? ' He
replied, ' *You must love the Lord your God with your whole
heart, with your whole soul, with your whole strength, and
with your whole mind. Also your neighbour as yourself.*'
28 ' A right answer ! ' said Jesus ; ' *do that and you will live.*'
29 Anxious to make an excuse for himself, however, he said to
30 Jesus, ' But who is my neighbour ? ' Jesus rejoined, ' A
man going down from Jerusalem to Jericho fell among
robbers who stripped and belaboured him and then went off
31 leaving him half-dead. Now it so chanced that a priest was
going down the same road, but on seeing him he went past
32 on the opposite side. So did a Levite who came to the spot ;
33 he looked at him but passed on the opposite side. However
a Samaritan traveller came to where he was and felt pity
34 when he saw him ; he went to him, bound his wounds up,
35 pouring oil and wine into them, mounted him on his own
steed, took him to an inn, and attended to him. Next
morning he took out a couple of shillings and gave them to
the innkeeper, saying, '' Attend to him, and if you are put to
any extra expense I will refund you on my way back.''
36 Which of these three men, in your opinion, proved a neigh-
37 bour to the man who fell among the robbers ? ' He said,
' The man who took pity on him.' Jesus said to him, ' Then
go and do the same.'

(Cf. Mark xii. 28–34 ; Matthew xxii. 34–40.)

Luke's statement that the lawyer rose to tempt Jesus implies
that his question was a lure intended to draw Jesus, if not into
some anti-legal, at least into some self-contradictory or impracticable pronouncement. ' What am I to do to inherit life
eternal ? ' i.e. the life of the Kingdom or age to come, was a
natural question to put to a teacher whose unvarying theme
was the Reign of God, and who constantly spoke of those who
should obtain an entrance into it. If the lawyer's motive was
not ingenuous, the answer of Jesus must have been a disappointment to him. ' What is written in the law ? What do you read

there ? ' directs him back upon his own professed sources of religious insight, and forces him to be his own judge. (Compare Mark x. 2–9, etc.)

The reply ' You must love the Lord your God with your whole heart . . . also your neighbour as yourself ' combines Deuteronomy vi. 5 with Leviticus xix. 18, and the fact that this synthesis of precepts is accredited to the lawyer suggests that contemporary teachers, in attempting to summarize the Law in one or two brief sentences, had reached agreement upon this formula. The need of reducing the 613 commandments of the Law (365 negative and 248 positive ordinances) was obvious : it comes to the surface in the gospel discussions about small and great, light and weighty commandments (Matthew v. 19, xxiii. 23 ; Mark xii. 28). The Talmud states that Hillel put forth a single rule (see under vi. 27–36) and said : ' This is the whole Torah, all else is commentary.' In the present case Jesus approves the insight revealed in the summary. For a man to give to God the principal place in affection, worship, work, and thought, and to treat his neighbour as he would have others to treat himself, is indeed the way to life. The scribe, however, is unsatisfied. Anxious to make an excuse for himself—did he disapprove of Jesus' attitude to taxgatherers or of his words about foreigners (vii. 9) ?—he asks, ' But who is my neighbour ? '

Jesus replied to this guarded inquiry not with a definition of neighbour but with an illustration of neighbourly conduct which thrusts the question forward into the realm of conscience and humanity. ' A man going down from Jerusalem to Jericho fell among robbers,' etc. Jesus reminds his questioner that suffering and need exist in the world, and asks in effect what he is going to do about it. The priest and the Levite in the story, though they ought to have been the first to come to the succour of the stricken man, especially as, being a Jew, he came under the strictest definition of the term ' neighbour,' leave it to ' a Samaritan traveller ' to do the human and the needful thing. The noble example of the Samaritan contains within it the real answer to the lawyer's question. The narrow striving for a definition of neighbour fades out of sight before the spectacle of a man's generous action to a stricken fellow-mortal. ' Which proved a neighbour to the man ? ' If this is, as it is, the real question, the application is obvious : ' then go and do the same.'

The parallel in Mark xii. 28–34 is from a different source.

The question is different, and the answer, combining the two principles of love to God and man, is assigned to Jesus. From this some have inferred that Jesus was the first to give this answer to the question wherein religion consists. But the inference is unnecessary. Judaism may of itself have reached the definition. It was left to Jesus to shew how it applied.

x. 38–42 : MARY AND MARTHA

38 In the course of their journey he entered a certain village and
39 a woman called Martha welcomed him to her house. She had a sister called Mary, who seated herself at the feet of
40 the Lord to listen to his talk. Now Martha was so busy attending to them that she grew worried ; she came up and said, ' Lord, is it all one to you that my sister has left me to do all the work alone ? Come, tell her to lend me a hand.'
41
42 The Lord answered her, ' Martha, Martha, Mary has chosen the best dish, and she is not to be dragged away from it.'

(Luke alone.)

Luke's authority did not give the name of the village where Jesus was entertained by Martha. The fourth evangelist, writing at a later period, says that it was Bethany, and identifies Mary with the woman who anointed the Lord in the house of Simon the leper (John xi. 1–2, xii. 1–3 ; Mark xiv. 3). The incident (which is from L) has for its point the defence of Mary, who seated herself at the feet of the Lord to listen to his talk, against Martha, who is unduly solicitous to provide material entertainment. The things of the Spirit to which Mary devotes herself are declared to be more important than other things (cf. xii. 22–23). Therefore Jesus does not allow the well-meant but unfair complaint of Martha that Mary is negligent of the duties of hospitality. " Martha, Martha, Mary has chosen the good part "—Dr. Moffatt translates ' the best dish,' seeing here a play upon words—' which shall not be taken from her.' The supreme office of hospitality is to bring to the Lord's teaching an attentive and lowly heart. Compare the Mishna tractate, *Aboth* i. 4 : ' Let thy house be a meeting-house for the wise ; and powder thyself in the dust of their feet, and drink their words with thirstiness ' (Taylor).

Dr. Moffatt's translation in vers. 41-42 follows a Western text. Other ancient authorities are more diffuse, inserting after ' Martha, Martha ' the words ' You are worried and troubled about many things,' and then adding either (1) ' but one thing is needful,' i.e. the care of the spiritual life should take precedence of every other concern, or (2) ' but few things are needful,' i.e. a simpler entertainment than Martha offers would suffice. Some authorities have the curious reading, ' But few things are needful, or only one,' which represents a combination of (1) and (2).

xi. 1-4 : THE LORD'S PRAYER

xi.

He was praying at a certain place, and when he stopped one of   1
his disciples said to him, ' Lord, teach us to pray, as John
taught his disciples.'   He said to them,   2
  ' When you pray, say, Father,
  thy name be revered,
  thy Reign begin ;
    give us our bread for the morrow day by day,   3
    and forgive us our sins,
      for we do forgive everyone who has offended us ;
    and lead us not into temptation.'
                  (Cf. Matthew vi. 9-13.)

The statement that Jesus' own practice of prayer moved the disciples to ask for instruction in the devotional life is peculiar to Luke, and rests on some tradition regarding the Lord's Prayer which the evangelist found in Palestine.   The words ' Teach us to pray as John taught his disciples ' indicate that in the milieu of this tradition the followers of John were known to follow set forms of prayer given them by their master.   John, as we know from v. 33, emphasized fasting, and as fasting was connected with special seasons of intercession (see under v. 33-39), rules and prescriptions of prayer would be a natural accompaniment.

The Lord's Prayer as given by Luke is short, and lacks the liturgical fullness which it exhibits in Matthew vi. 9-13.   Whereas in Matthew it is offered as an example of prayer, in Luke it is presented as a form to be used : ' When you pray, say.'   The opening invocation ' Father ' implies that prayer is to be entered upon in child-like humility and with child-like trust (see below on xi. 11–13).   The follower of Jesus is to put away from his thoughts of God all that is not compatible with the divine Fatherhood, therefore all hard thoughts of God's will (compare Mark x. 5–6, Luke vi. 35–36, xviii. 6–8, and contrast xix. 21). Judaism acknowledged God as Father (see above, p. 23), but Jesus has given to the thought a new intense reality and a universally regulative force and scope. 'Abba' was Jesus' name for God (xxiii. 34, 46), and passed from him to his followers, marking a primordial recognition of the Christian spirit : compare Romans viii. 15 and Galatians iv. 6 : 'God has sent forth the spirit of his Son into your hearts, crying " Abba ! Father ! " '

The first petition, ' **Thy name be revered,**' reminds us that God has given us a revelation of Himself in history. His ' name ' or revealed character constitutes the holiest trust committed to the Jew, and the profanation of the name is the worst of sins (cf. Malachi i. 11–12).   If now Christ has added new depths to that revelation by presenting God under the aspect of the heavenly Father, his disclosure, so far from diminishing the dread in which the holy name is to be held, calls for increased reverence : compare I Peter i. 17, ' If you call on Him as Father, who without respect of persons judges according to each man's work, pass the time of your sojourning in fear.'   But the tense of the verb in the original suggests that the hallowing of the divine Name which is referred to points, like the coming of the Reign, to a definite revelation of God in the future by which all men will be brought to acknowledge His holy character and purpose, and for this consummation the followers of Jesus are to pray.   On the second petition, ' **Thy Reign begin,**' see under iii. 3–6, 21–22, vi. 20–26.   The Reign of God is the supreme object of Jesus' work and passion, the goal to which all his activities are directed.   In place of this petition some ancient authorities read : ' Thy holy Spirit come on us and purify us.'   This is doubtless a gloss, though some scholars think it represents what Luke originally wrote.

From these petitions, which are connected with God's honour and sovereignty, the prayer passes to the disciples' need of daily sustenance : ' **Give us our bread for the morrow.**'   The Greek expression translated ' for the morrow ' is difficult, and in antiquity was often taken to denote ' that which transcends (ordinary) substance ' or ' that which has relation to our essential nature'; therefore 'heavenly, spiritual, non-material' bread, the bread of life in the Eucharist. So Jerome renders the petition in Matthew by the words : ' Panem nostrum supersubstantialem da nobis hodie.' In Luke, however, he writes ' panem nostrum quotidianum,' ' our daily bread,' and this is the sense which on philological grounds most scholars now attach to the Greek word. Literally it signifies ' bread for the morrow.' Christians, meeting for worship in the evening, would naturally think of their daily bread as being bread for the following day. The additional phrase ' day by day' is not in Matthew.

The fourth petition, ' And forgive us our sins, for we do forgive everyone who has offended us,' connects the receipt of divine with the exercise of human forgiveness (compare vi. 37, Matthew v. 23-24, vi. 14-15, xviii. 18-19, 32-35, etc.). The clause ' for we forgive, etc.,' states not the ground on which God bestows forgiveness but the ground on which man can receive it. The gifts of God can only flow to us as we become a channel for them to others. Forgiveness, if it is the first of God's gifts to us through Christ, is the first duty which the Christian owes to his fellow-men. The last petition, ' And lead us not into temptation,' does not prejudge the question as to the source and cause of temptation. Enough that the Christian, knowing his weakness, knowing also that the world into which he goes is full of ' trial,' should pray to be delivered and given the victory. At a later time the origin of temptation became a real question in Christian circles. The author of the epistle of James alludes to such a controversy when he writes in i. 13-17 : ' Let no one who is tried by temptation say, My temptation comes from God. God . . . tempts no one. Everyone is tempted as he is beguiled . . . by his own desire. . . . All we are given is good . . . descending from above, from the Father.' It seems to the present writer that the Lord's Prayer clearly underlies this discussion in James.

The Prayer contains echoes of Jewish prayers, and is indeed based on the sacrosanct language of the Synagogue litanies. Two prayers in particular, the Kaddish and the Shemoneh-Esreh (or ' Eighteen Benedictions '), shew affinities. With the first and second petitions of the Prayer compare the statements in the Talmudic treatise *Berakoth* (40b) : ' Any benediction which omits mention of the Name is no benediction,' and ' Any

benediction which omits the Kingdom is no benediction.' The
Kaddish and the Shemoneh-Esreh prayers contain no petition
for bread. It is interesting that Jesus, who would not countenance the production of bread out of stones (iv. 3–4), teaches men
to pray for it, and to expect it by God's blessing on their labours.

xi. 5–13 : THE FRIEND AT MIDNIGHT, AND WORDS ABOUT PRAYER

5 And he said to them, ' Suppose one of you has a friend, and
you go to him at midnight and say to him, " Friend, let me
6 have three loaves ; for a friend of mine travelling has come
7 to my house and I have nothing to set before him." And
suppose he answers from the inside, " Don't bother me ; the
door is locked by this time, and my children are in bed
8 with me. I can't get up and give you anything." I tell you,
though he will not get up and give you anything because
you are a friend of his, he will at least rise and give you
9 whatever you want, because you persist. So I tell you,
ask and the gift will be yours,
seek and you will find,
knock and the door will open to you ;
10 for everyone who asks receives,
the seeker finds,
the door is opened to anyone who knocks.
11 What father among you, if asked by his son for a loaf,
will hand him a stone ?
Or, if asked for a fish, will hand him a serpent instead
of a fish ?
12 Or, if asked for an egg, will he hand him a scorpion ?
13 Well, if for all your evil you know to give your children
what is good,
how much more will your Father give the holy Spirit
from heaven to those who ask him ? '
(Cf. Matthew vii. 7–11.)

The parable of the Importunate Friend is peculiar to Luke,
and teaches the value of ' pains, patience, and perseverance ' in
prayer. The story, which is narrated not without humour,
shews that persistent application will in ordinary human circumstances obtain results which a less resolute course of action

would not achieve. A man asleep at midnight with his house locked up is not likely to bestir himself to help a friend on whom a guest has been unexpectedly thrust, but if the friend persists and takes no denial, the other will presently grant him what he asks. So Jesus teaches that persistent and believing prayer will unfailingly bring a reward.

' Ask and the gift will be yours, seek,' etc. If any distinction is to be made between the three injunctions here given, it may be done by paraphrasing them as follows. There are things in God's gift which a man has never had : therefore ' ask.' There are things which he has had but which have been lost : therefore ' seek.' There are doors which he longs to see opened, opportunities which he would fain possses : therefore ' knock.' In each case an answer will be given. To shew further that earnest men will not ask a particular blessing, and be put off with something else, Jesus makes use of the illustrations in vers. 11–13 : ' What father among you, if asked by his son for a loaf, will hand him a stone ? ' etc. The appeal is to earthly fatherhood as a shadow of the divine, and the argument is what logicians call *a minori ad majus*. The instances ' loaf—stone,' ' fish—serpent,' ' egg—scorpion,' are taken because of the superficial resemblance of the contrasted things. But if no earthly parent would thus horribly deceive a child, will God, when man asks a blessing, put him off with some mocking substitute ? No ! ' If for all your evil you know to give your children what is good '—the sinfulness of human nature, the fact that men are imperfect both in motive and in action, is recognized by Jesus. His teaching shews no trace of a doctrine of Adamic guilt or inherited transgression, but there is an open-eyed admission of what Judaism calls the ' evil impulse ' in man. But the evil impulse does not preclude that the normal parent will give his children what is good. ' How much more then will your Father ' —in whom good exists not fragmentarily but in all perfection— ' give the holy Spirit from heaven to those who ask him ? ' We should have expected ' give good things,' and so it is in Matthew vii. 11. Luke or his source has spiritualized. The holy Spirit is selected because it is the gift of gifts, the supreme object of man's need.

No one ever gave such assurances to prayer as Jesus. Vers. 11–13 indicate how he approached the thought of the divine Fatherhood, and it is not a little significant that he who taught that stones were not to be turned into bread, teaches here that bread will not be turned into stones.

xi. 14–23 : THE BEELZEBUL CALUMNY

14 He was casting out a dumb daemon, and when the daemon had gone out the dumb man spoke. The crowds marvelled,
15 but some of them said, ' It is by Beelzebul the prince of
16 daemons that he casts out daemons.' Others by way of tempting him demanded he should give them a Sign from
17 heaven. He knew what they were thinking about, so he said to them,

' Any realm divided against itself comes to ruin,
house after house falls down ;
18 and if Satan is divided against himself,
how can his realm stand ?
You say I am casting out daemons by Beelzebul ?
19 If I cast out daemons by Beelzebul,
by whom do your sons cast them out ?
Thus they will be your judges.
20 But if it is by the finger of God that I cast daemons out,
then the Reign of God has reached you already.
21 When the strong man in armour guards his homestead, his
22 property is undisturbed ; but when a stronger man attacks and conquers him, he seizes the panoply on which he relied and divides up the spoil.
23 He who is not with me is against me,
and he who does not gather with me scatters.'
(Cf. Mark iii. 22–30, Matthew xii. 22–30.)

The narrative (which is from Q—cf. Matthew ix. 32–34, xii. 22–30) connects the Beelzebul accusation with the exorcism of a demon by Jesus. The demon is associated with some nervous or mental disorder inhibiting the speech-centres, and is therefore called a dumb daemon. Jesus orders the spirit out, whereupon the man, being delivered from his obsession, recovers his speech. But the popular sensation produced by the cure is marred by two expressions of unbelief : (1) the insinuation ' It is by Beelzebul the prince of daemons that he casts out daemons ' ; (2) the complaint that Jesus has not yet produced a satisfactory sign from heaven. It is to the first of these accusations that Jesus addresses himself in vers. 17–23. The second is reserved for later treatment in vers. 29–32.

The Beelzebul charge implies that Jesus performs his exorcisms by sorcery or *magic*. Compare Justin Martyr's statement (*Dialogue*, lxix.) : ' They dared to say that he was a magician and a deceiver of the people.' The accusation acquires plausibility through the popular notion that Satan disguises himself as an angel of light. In Mark iii. 22–30, where another tradition is followed, the charge is made by the scribes, and the motive is to prejudice and ruin the influence of Jesus. For that reason the answer of Jesus in Mark leads up to the terrible saying about the blasphemy of the holy Spirit (Mark iii. 28–29), which Luke records on another occasion (xii. 10). The name **Beelzebul** is perplexing. It is sometimes explained as a Jewish distortion of ' Baal-zebub,' the name of the god of Ekron in 2 Kings i. 2, but it is not apparent why the name of this Philistine god should be appropriated to the prince of demons, unless the name was confused with a similar Jewish-Aramaic word meaning ' enemy,' and thus transferred to the enemy of souls. But while the name Beelzebul occurs in the gospels, neither it nor Beelzebub is found in Jewish literature as a name for Satan. Hence it is perhaps better to drop all reference to the god of Ekron, and to explain Beelzebul etymologically as signifying ' lord of dung,' i.e. the Baal or lord or divinity, meaning Satan, to whom the heathen offer idolatrous sacrifices. Outside the gospels the names which occur for the head of the demons are Sammael, Ashmedai, and Beliar (cf. 2 Corinthians vi. 15).

By way of answer to the charge Jesus points : (1) to the illogical character of the charge itself (vers. 17–18). ' **Any realm divided against itself comes to ruin**, etc. If, according to the Jewish taunt, Jesus expels demons by infernal agency, it means that Satan is divided against himself, i.e. he consents to the dismemberment and collapse of his realm, which is inconceivable. Neither Jesus nor his hearers can think of evil as consenting to its own destruction. (2) He cites the current practice of exorcizing demons among the Jews (ver. 19), and asks, ' By whom do your sons cast them out ? ' ' Your sons ' here means simply ' others among yourselves, other Israelites.' The charge of sorcery or of being in league with Satan must fall equally on these other exorcists, and exposes the accusers to their judgment.

(3) Jesus shews that, as evil is too malignant to be thought self-destructive, its defeat can only be explained as the work of a higher power. The demons yield only to God, the reign of Satan only to the Reign of God (vers. 20–22). ' If by the finger of God I cast daemons out ' ; ' finger of God '—Matthew has ' Spirit of God '—is an Old Testament expression, occurring with reference to the plagues of Egypt in Exodus viii. 19 : ' The magicians said to Pharaoh, This is the finger of God.' On Jesus' lips it means either ' through the putting forth of God's power,' or ' by God directing me to this work of saving souls from Satan.' The conclusion in either case is that ' the Reign of God has reached you already.' Though the Reign has not come in all its fullness, its powers are at work and its triumph is secure. Satan is being driven back on final overthrow. This thought is further enforced by the parable in vers. 21–22. Jesus compares Satan to an armed man defending a house. His property is undisturbed until a stronger man comes against him, captures his armaments, and carries off his goods. The spoil is here the persons whom Satan has possessed by demons, but whom Jesus has delivered : compare Isaiah liii. 12 : ' He shall divide the spoil with the strong.' Ver. 23, ' He that is not with me is against me,' etc., connects well with the principle that there is no middle course between evil and good, darkness and light, Satan and God. At the same time the saying looks back to the accusers of Jesus mentioned in ver. 15, ' He who does not gather with me scatters.' No neutral attitude towards Jesus and the Kingdom of God is possible. The metaphor ' gather—scatter ' is probably from the herding of flocks.

xi. 24–26 : The Way of Evil Spirits

24 'When an unclean spirit leaves a man, it roams through dry places in search of refreshment. As it finds none, then it
25 says, '' I will go back to the house I left,'' and when it comes
26 it finds the house clean and in order. Then it goes off to fetch seven other spirits worse than itself ; they go in and dwell there, and the last state of that man is worse than the first.' (Cf. Matthew xii. 43–45.)

This interesting section about the ways and habits of demons has a parallel in Matthew xii. 43–45, and is therefore Q material.

In the setting in which Luke places it, it illustrates the principle
that only the power of God can drive out Satan, only the Kingdom of Heaven can oust the tyranny of evil. But it suggests
also that, unless the soul which has been delivered from demons
is kept and held by God, it will relapse to its former condition
or to a worse. 'When an unclean spirit leaves a man, it roams
. . . then it says, I will go back,' etc. The details of the passage
reflect the current imagination regarding demons. When
expelled, they rove about in dry places, i.e. in the desert which
is their special habitat. But, desiring refreshment, they revisit
the house from which they came. A passage from a later
apocryphal writing (Clementine Homilies, ix. 10) well illustrates
this point : 'Being spirits and having the desire for foods and
drinks and intercourse, but not being able to indulge because
they are spirits and lack the necessary organs, they enter into
the bodies of men.' Finding the heart which he left empty,
i.e. not possessed by the power of God, the demon 'goes off
to fetch seven other worse spirits,' and together they resume
control of the man. This calling in of allies reflects the belief
that every demon wishes to share his triumph, and to avoid a
second exorcism. Jesus may have addressed the warning
either to individuals whom he had delivered, or to the nation
which had only been partially reformed by the preaching of
John and of himself. For the idea of seven demons compare
Mary of Magdala (viii. 2), and with the warning 'the last state
of that man is worse than the first' compare the admonition
in John v. 14.

xi. 27–28 : THE WOMAN IN THE CROWD

While he was saying this, a woman shouted to him out of the 27
crowd, 'Blessed is the womb that bore you, and the breasts
you sucked ! ' But he said, 'Blessed rather are those who 28
hear and who observe the word of God ! '

(Luke alone.)

The cry of the woman, 'Blessed is the womb that bare thee,'
etc., means literally 'How happy must be the mother of such
a son ! ' and it is to be understood as an acclamation of the
Messiahship of Jesus. So at anyrate the tradition probably

regarded it. Compare the Jewish sayings, cited by Wetstein :
' Whoso saw Moses, said : Blessed is she who bore him ' (*Shemoth
Rabba*, xlv.), and ' Blessed is the hour in which the Messiah
was created : blessed is the womb from which he came forth '
(*Pesikta*, 12b). The reply of Jesus, ' **Blessed rather are those
who hear and observe the word of God !** ' directs the minds of
his hearers from natural to spiritual thoughts of blessedness,
and like the word in Mark iii. 32–35 (Luke viii. 19–21) it indicates
that the family of God takes precedence of all earthly relation-
ships. This Lukan passage forms indeed a parallel to Mark iii.
32–35. Note that both stories appear in immediate sequence
to the Beelzebul charge.

xi. 29–32 : The Sign of Jonah

29 **As the crowds were thronging to him, he proceeded to say,**
    ' This is an evil generation : it demands a Sign,
        but no Sign will be given to it except the Sign of
        Jonah ;
30   for as Jonah was a Sign to the Ninivites,
        so shall the Son of man be to this generation.
31   The queen of the South will rise at the judgment with
          the men of this generation and condemn them ;
        for she came from the ends of the earth to listen to
          the wisdom of Solomon,
        And here is One greater than Solomon.
32   The men of Ninive will rise at the judgment with this
          generation and condemn it ;
        for when Jonah preached they did repent,
        and here is One greater than Jonah.'
                (Cf. Matthew xii. 38–42.)

    This section has been prepared for by the statement above
in xi. 16 that some of Jesus' auditors, ' by way of tempting
him, demanded he should give them a Sign from heaven.' The
demand implies that nothing which Jesus had done constituted
in the popular view a satisfactory proof of the religious authority
which he claimed. For the Jewish belief in miracle as the proper
evidence of the divine compare 1 Corinthians i. 22 : ' Jews
demand signs, while Greeks require a rational explanation of

the universe.' The conception that extraordinary ' signs '
would attend the person of the coming Deliverer of the nation
was deeply ingrained in the Jewish mind, and seemed adequately
supported by the miracles wrought on behalf of Moses (Exodus
vii. 9), Gideon (Judges vi. 17–22, 36–40), Hezekiah (2 Kings
xx. 8–11), and other men of God.

The answer of Jesus to this demand is ' **This is an evil generation ; it demands a Sign.'** Judaism considered that the age of
the Messiah would be unprecedentedly wicked. If this thought
was in Jesus' mind, his words would imply that the contemporary
generation was sign enough to itself. What he condemns is
the blindness of his race to spiritual evidence. In Mark viii. 12
he says that no Sign will be given to his generation. According
to Luke, who here follows Q (cf. Matthew xii. 39), he says,
' **No Sign will be given except the Sign of Jonah.'** Does this
signify (1) that as Jonah preached repentance to the Ninivites,
so Jesus preaches repentance to Israel ; or (2) that as Jonah
was miraculously delivered from death in the deep, so Jesus
will be raised from the grave (cf. Matthew xii. 40) ; or (3) that
as Jonah, being raised, came to Ninive, so Jesus comes again
to his generation on the clouds of heaven ? The first explanation
accords best with the mind of Jesus, though not conforming to
the terms of the Jewish demand ; if Jesus meant the sign of
Jonah in this sense he was in effect refusing what his critics
sought. Jesus, however, enters into no explanation beyond
saying, ' **As Jonah was a Sign to the Ninivites, so shall the Son
of man be to this generation.'** Luke probably interpreted the
word in accordance with the second or third of the above
explanations : the Resurrection or the Return on clouds of the
Son of man is the grand corroboration of the claims which
Jesus makes upon mankind.

The references to the Queen of Sheba and to the men of
Ninive tax the Jews with their heinous indifference to the
revelation given in Jesus. ' **The Queen of the South '** came
from the ends of the earth to hear the disclosure of divine truth
made by Solomon, and ' **here is One greater than Solomon.'**
' **The men of Ninive '** repented at the preaching of Jonah, and
' **here is One greater than Jonah.'** The contemporaries of Jesus
will at the Day of Judgment be convicted and put to shame by
the brilliant example of those who under far less favourable
conditions, indeed in heathen darkness, acted upon the evidence

which was granted to them, and shine for ever as instances of spiritual earnestness and zeal. How supreme Jesus' consciousness of his own mission is appears by his setting of his own claims above those of Israel's kings and prophets.

xi. 33–36 : Words about the Lighted Lamp

33   ' No one lights a lamp to put it in a cellar or under a bowl,

       but on a stand, so that those who come in can see the light.

34   Your eye is the lamp of the body :

     when your eye is sound,

       then the whole of your body has light,

     but if your eye is diseased,

       then your body is darkened.

35   (Look ! perhaps your very light is dark.)

36   So if your whole body has light, without any corner of it in darkness, it will be lit up entirely, as when a lamp lights you with its rays.'

       (Cf. Mark iv. 21, Matthew v. 15, vi. 22–23.)

The saying ' No one lights a lamp,' etc., occurred above in viii. 16, and there, where it was derived from Mark, it referred to the ' open secret ' or revelation of Jesus which, though temporarily concealed from the many, would yet illuminate all minds. Here the saying comes from Q (cf. Matthew v. 15), and refers to Jesus himself. Men demand a ' Sign,' and do not see that Jesus in his own character and destiny is the portent which God offers to Israel. But what they now ignore will be brilliantly demonstrated. In ver. 34 another saying from Q (cf. Matthew vi. 22–23) equates the lamp with the soul's faculty of discerning truth : ' Your eye is the lamp of the body.' When an eye is normal and healthy (Matthew understands this to mean free from the taint of selfishness or cupidity) it registers true impressions. If contrariwise the eye is diseased the body remains unlighted. So Jesus warns his hearers against trifling with conscience. The light of the soul may be quenched. Ver. 36 seems to mean : if men will not refuse the light or evidence which is granted them at some particular point (e.g. on some particular duty), they shall have all the illumination which they require for life and conduct. The point of the whole section is that men have received in Jesus all the sign which they ought to expect. If they do not recognize the sign, it is because of the shutting of their eyes.

xi. 37–54 : JUDGMENTS ON THE PHARISEES AND SCRIBES

When he finished speaking, a Pharisee asked him to take a 37
meal in his house ; so he went in and lay down at table.
The Pharisee was astonished to see that he had not washed 38
before the meal, but the Lord said to him, 39
   ' You Pharisees do clean the outside of the cup and the
      plate,
      but your inner life is filled with rapacity and malice.
   Foolish men ! did not He who made the outside make 40
      the inside of things too ?
   Better cleanse what is within ; then nothing will be 41
      unclean for you.
   But woe to you Pharisees ! 42
      you tithe mint and rue and every vegetable,
      but justice and the love of God you disregard ;
      these latter you ought to have practised—without
      omitting the former.
   Woe to you Pharisees ! 43
      you love the front bench in the synagogues
      and salutations in the marketplaces.
   Woe to you ! 44
      you are like unsuspected tombs ;
      men walk over them unawares.'
One of the jurists said to him, ' Teacher, when you say 45
this you are insulting us as well.' He said, 46
   ' And woe to you jurists ! you load men with irksome
      burdens,
      and you will not put a single finger to their burdens.
   Woe to you ! you build tombs for the prophets whom 47
      your own fathers killed :
      thus you testify and consent to what your fathers 48
      did,
      for they killed and you build.

49 This is why the Wisdom of God said, " I will send them prophets and apostles, some they will kill and some they
50 will persecute " ; it was that the blood of all the prophets shed from the foundation of the world might be charged
51 upon this generation, from the blood of Abel down to the blood of Zechariah who was slain between the altar and the House of God—yes, I tell you, it will all be charged upon this generation.
52 Woe to you jurists ! you have taken the key that unlocks the door of knowledge ;
       you have not entered yourselves,
       and you have stopped those who were entering.'
53 After he had gone away, the scribes and Pharisees commenced to follow him up closely and cross-question him
54 on many points, lying in ambush to catch a word from his lips.
       (Cf. Matthew xxiii. 25–26, 23, 6–7, 27–28, 4, 29–32, 13–14.)

The statement that Jesus was invited to a Pharisee's house and there delivered the teaching contained in vers. 39–52 represents probably a conjecture, not altogether happy, as regards the place and time of these Q sayings. The Pharisee observes with disfavour that Jesus had not washed before the meal, i.e. had not performed the ceremonial hand-laving customary among strict Jews : compare Mark vii. 1–3, ' The Pharisees decline to eat till they wash their hands up to the wrist in obedience to the tradition of the elders.' Water was in ordinary cases merely poured upon the hands ; dipping was not resorted to except in the case of sacrificial food. As the regulations in question were based not on the Law but on the unwritten Tradition, Jesus could discard them without setting the Law aside. ' The Pharisees,' says Josephus, ' have imposed upon the people many laws taken from the tradition of the fathers, which are not written in the Law of Moses ' (*Antiq.* xiii. 16, 2). But the Pharisaic attitude to these observances may be gauged from the statement in the Mishna tractate *Sanhedrin* xi. 3 which says that ' It is more serious to offend against decrees of the scribes than against decrees of the Law.' The argument was that if it is heinous to ignore precepts of the Law, which are obscure, how much more heinous to ignore interpretations, by which these same precepts have been made clear !

In his reply Jesus says nothing about the laving of hands, but condemns insistence on the washing of vessels, etc., when the ' inner life is filled with rapacity and malice.' God's ideal for Israel prescribes the pure heart (Psalms xxiv. 3–4, lxxiii. 1), but the Pharisees by their inordinate concern for ceremonial purity are overlooking that ' He who made the outside made the inside of things too,' i.e. God looks at the heart. The ordinary text in ver. 41 runs, ' Give alms of what is within,' i.e. of what is within your power, instead of rapaciously taking from others, and this will effect a real cleansing of you in God's eyes. But this is not very appropriate in the context, and Dr. Moffatt adopts Wellhausen's conjecture that the underlying Aramaic signified ' Cleanse what is within,' i.e. make purity of heart your aim, and this will ensure every other kind of cleanness : compare Matthew v. 8. From this the argument passes in ver. 42 to expose the glaring inconsistency between the Pharisaic scrupulousness in tithing the most trivial products of the garden and their neglect of what in Matthew are called ' the weightier matters of the Law,' viz. justice and the love of God : compare Micah vi. 8, ' What does the Lord require of thee but to do justly and to love mercy and to walk humbly with thy God ? ' Jesus does not remove the tithing obligation, but he insists that first things shall have first place. The words ' These latter you ought to have practised,' etc., are absent in one or two ancient authorities, and may have come into Luke from Matthew xxiii. 23. In ver. 43 the vanity of the Pharisees is indicted. In the synagogue they seek the seats nearest to the ark and pulpit, and in places of business they expect reverential greetings. But what are the Pharisees who thus set themselves up for paragons ? ' You are like unsuspected tombs,' i.e. unmarked graves on which men stumble by accident and are defiled (Numbers xix. 16). Men meet you, regard you as models of religious devotion, and never dream of the corruption which festers in your hearts. The corresponding saying in Matthew xxiii. 27 compares the Pharisees to whitewashed, i.e. to marked, graves. It was the Jewish custom to whiten graves with calcium at the approach of Passover, so that pilgrims might not stumble at unawares upon them. The reference in Matthew therefore is to the specious exterior of the Pharisees, the fine profession under which unsuspected vices are concealed.

The transition to the Woes on the Scribes is provided by

ver. 45, which is special to Luke. In Matthew the denunciations apply without distinction both to the Pharisees and to the professional experts on whose judgments they leaned. Here the Scribes are arraigned primarily because by the innumerable regulations which they have derived from the unwritten tradition—compare the above quotation from *Sanhedrin* xi. 3—they ' load men with irksome burdens,' but do not put out a finger to help them in their struggles. Religion is thus made hard for the masses : contrast Jesus' own appeal, ' Come to me, all who are labouring and burdened. . . . Take my yoke . . . for my yoke is kindly ' (Matthew xi. 28–29). In vers. 47–48 Jesus ironically alludes to the scribal cult of the old-time prophets. Statues were forbidden in Israel, but other forms of memorial were possible. ' You build tombs for the prophets,' because they are dead and can no longer disturb you. But your fathers killed them, and you would serve in the like manner any living prophet who comes among you. In ver. 49 this thought is enforced by a quotation from some lost Wisdom-book, unless the expression ' Wisdom of God ' here means simply ' God in His wisdom,' in which case Jesus may have had in mind not a Wisdom-writing but the prophecy in Jeremiah vii. 25–26. In vers. 50–51 the application is made. Jesus charges the existing generation with the accumulated guilt of ' the blood of all the prophets shed from the foundation of the world.' The existing generation is indicted, because it is on this generation that the Last Judgment comes (xxi. 32) : compare Isaiah xxvi. 21, ' The Lord cometh forth . . . to punish the inhabitants of the earth for their iniquity ; the earth also shall disclose her blood, and shall no more cover her slain.' Jesus possibly expected of his age some unprecedented manifestation of wickedness (cf. xi. 29). Abel (Genesis iv. 10), reckoned here a prophet of God, is the first martyr of whom Scripture speaks. Zechariah (2 Chronicles xxiv. 21–22) is reckoned the last because 2 Chronicles stands at the end of the Hebrew canon of Scripture. Jesus assumes the solidarity of the nation, past and present, in the guilt of rejecting the messengers of God. The final indictment of the Scribes takes the form ' You have taken the key that unlocks the door of knowledge.' By laying the emphasis on the wrong things the Scribes have obscured the will of God. Claiming to open the scriptures, they have really closed the book, ' made the knowledge of God impossible ' (Easton). The ' knowledge ' in question

concerns primarily the Kingdom (viii. 10). The Scribes have
not entered the Kingdom themselves (vii. 29–30), and the people
who would have entered they have systematically discouraged.

xii. 1–12 : On Fearlessness of Confession

xii.

Meanwhile as the crowd was gathering in its thousands till they   1
trod on one another, he proceeded to say to his disciples first
of all, ' Be on your guard against the leaven of the Pharisees,
which is hypocrisy.

    Nothing is hidden that shall not be revealed,   2
      or concealed that shall not be made known.

    So all you utter in the dark will be heard in the light,   3
      and what you whisper in chambers will be proclaimed
        on the housetops.

I tell you, my friends,   4
    have no fear of those who kill the body but after that can
      do no more ;

    I will show you whom to fear—   5
fear Him who after he has killed has power to cast you
      into Gehenna.

    Yes, I tell you, fear Him.

Are not five sparrows sold for two farthings ?   6
    Yet not one of them is forgotten by God.

But the very hairs on your head are all numbered ;   7
    fear not, you are worth far more than sparrows.

I tell you, whoever acknowledges me before men,   8
    the Son of man will acknowledge him before the angels
      of God ;

and he who disowns me before men   9
    will be disowned before the angels of God.

Everyone also who says a word against the Son of man 10
    will be forgiven for it,
    but he who blasphemes against the holy Spirit will never
      be forgiven.

When they bring you before synagogues and the magistrates 11
and authorities, do not trouble yourselves about how to
defend yourselves or what to say, for the holy Spirit will teach 12
you at that hour what you should say. '

(Cf. Matthew x. 26–33, 17–20.)

Jesus here addresses the disciples in the presence of a thronged audience. There is a fitness in this presentation because in the criticism levelled by Jesus against the ' false guides ' the nation as a whole is interested and the future of religion is at stake. The disciples are exhorted to be wary of ' the leaven of the Pharisees.' The word ' leaven ' on Jewish lips usually indicates something sinister or malignant (cf. Exodus xii. 15, 1 Corinthians v. 6–8), and Luke here takes it to refer to the hypocrisy of the Pharisees. So understood, the warning of Jesus might be explained to mean : ' you, my disciples, have no right to condemn the dishonesty which is the mark of Pharisaic religion, if on your own part you hold back the truth through fear of consequences.' But it is simpler to understand Jesus to be merely cautioning his followers against the unsleeping enmity of the Pharisees, whose pseudo-religious zeal is exerting itself to the utmost to suppress the new truth.

Over against the machinations of the Pharisees Jesus assures his disciples that ' nothing is hidden that shall not be revealed.' At present the disciples are forced to speak only in dark corners and not to raise their voices above a whisper, but a time comes when the truth will receive the greatest publicity. Therefore Jesus urges courageous confession. The Pharisees may threaten the disciples' lives, but their souls are in God's hands. The warning, ' Fear him who after he has killed has power to cast into Gehenna,' is directed primarily at the enemies of the truth, but the disciples are not exempted, since, if fear seals their lips, they endanger their spiritual life. Gehenna, the Ge-Hinnom or ' Valley of Hinnom ' lying to the south-west of Jerusalem, was polluted by fire-worship and human sacrifice in the reign of Ahaz (2 Kings xvi. 3, 2 Chronicles xxviii. 3), and in consequence of this desecration was set apart as the place where the offal of the city should be burned. Hence, in course of time, the name came to be applied to the place of future punishment : compare Jeremiah vii. 31–33, Isaiah lxvi. 24, and Enoch xxvii. 1, ' This accursed valley is for those who are accursed for ever . . . who utter with their lips against the Lord unseemly words and of His glory speak hard things.'

But while Jesus does not conceal the dread aspect of the divine being in its reaction against sin and apostasy, the ground on which he calls his followers to fearless testimony and service is the infinite love of God. Never has faith in the individualizing love of God risen to higher expression than in the saying about the sparrows and in the assurance, ' the very hairs on your head are all numbered.' Whereas philosophers have striven to attain to the idea of God by a process of abstracting from all the particular interests, sorrows, wants, cares, and sufferings which have to do with human life, Jesus, taking the opposite way, seeks the fullness and glory of the divine being in the completest identification or integration of that being with all that concerns the lives of his creatures. God, because He is God, is interested in everything that affects His creatures, and therefore on their part the completest trust is necessary. On the saying in vers. 8–9, ' I tell you, whoever acknowledges me before men, the Son of man will acknowledge him,' etc., in which a supreme application of the principle of trust is made, see above, p. III.

In ver. 10 there comes an obscurer saying : ' Everyone also who says a word against the Son of man will be forgiven for it, but he who blasphemes against the holy Spirit will never be forgiven.' In this form and context the word has been explained as meaning that ' Whereas others, who are not disciples, may be pardoned for misunderstanding and therefore speaking against the Son of man, you disciples, if you resist and so blaspheme the holy Spirit, which is given to you (cf. ver. 12) and prompts you to confess me, will never be forgiven.' But this forces an unnatural sense upon the word ' blaspheme,' and therefore it is better to understand the saying as meaning : ' Jesus will accept patiently and forgivingly men's misrepresentations of himself, but the calumnies of men against the Spirit, which speaks in his faithful disciples, he will not condone.' Upon this view the word is one of strong encouragement, and Jesus confirms it by saying : ' When they bring you before synagogues,' etc.—the disciples might well quail at this prospect if they depended upon themselves alone—' do not trouble yourselves about how to defend yourselves or what to say.' When the disciples have been faithful, and having done all they stand before the courts on trial for their lives, they may trust God to give them the right word to say : ' the holy Spirit will teach you at that hour what you should say.' Jesus thus encourages faithful disciples to think of the Spirit as their proper counsellor and guide. For a fuller working out of this thought of the ' Paraclete ' compare John xiv. 26, xv. 26, xvi. 7–15.

But while a certain meaning can thus be extracted from ver. 10, it is doubtful if the saying appears here in its original form or context. It happens that Mark iii. 28–29 preserves a similar saying : ' All sins shall be forgiven to the sons of men . . . but whoever blasphemes against the holy Spirit is never forgiven.' The Mark-saying with its contrast between other sins and the blasphemy against the Spirit (i.e. the misrepresenting of good as evil, the putting of Satan in the place of God, Mark iii. 22) is natural and easily understood. The Luke-saying, which is from Q (cf. Matthew xii. 32), and contrasts words spoken against the Son of man with blasphemy against the Spirit, wears by comparison an artificial aspect. Is it possible that the Mark-saying and the Q-saying represent right and wrong translations of the same original word ? Let us suppose an original Aramaic sentence with the three elements, ' sins or evil words '—' son of man '—' forgiven.' The tradition followed by Mark took the connexion to be ' Sins or sinful words (on the part of any) son of man will be forgiven.' The tradition underlying Q took it to be ' Sins or sinful words (against *the*) Son of man will be forgiven.' The two renderings diverge upon different senses of the term *barnasha* (see above, under vi. 1–5). The Q rendering is artificial. Mark is certainly right.

xii. 13–21 : Covetousness. The Rich Fool

13 A man out of the crowd said to him, ' Teacher, tell my brother
14 to give me my share of our inheritance ' ; but he said to him, ' Man, who made me a judge or arbitrator over your
15 affairs ? ' Then he said to them, ' See and keep clear of covetousness in every shape and form, for a man's life is not part of his possessions because he has ample wealth.'
16 And he told them a parable. ' A rich man's estate bore
17 heavy crops. So he debated, "What am I to do ? I have
18 no room to store my crops." And he said, " This is what I will do. I will pull down my granaries and build larger
19 ones, where I can store all my produce and my goods. And I will say to my soul, ' Soul, you have ample stores laid up for many a year ; take your ease, eat, drink and be merry.' "
20 But God said to him, " Foolish man, this very night your

soul is wanted ; and who will get all you have prepared ? "
So fares the man who lays up treasure for himself instead 21
of gaining the riches of God.'

(Luke alone.)

The request, ' Teacher, tell my brother to give me my share,'
etc., is in keeping with the Oriental custom of going to the
religious authority for judgment in legal matters. In Judea,
where Scripture and religious tradition constituted the only
fount of law, every Rabbi might be called upon to give decisions,
and the appellant in this case doubtless hoped to obtain from
Jesus a verdict favourable to his plea. But while at a later
period appeals were not infrequent from the Law of Moses to
the Christian ' Evangelion ' (B. Sabbath, 116a), Jesus acknowledges no call to adjudicate upon such cases. He is interested
only in the prior question of the soul's relation to God. Hence
the answer, ' Keep clear of covetousness in every shape and
form.' The obsession of the mind by property may become so
insistent as to blind men to all higher concerns of life, and
therefore it must be eradicated. ' A man's life is not part of
his possessions because he has ample wealth.' In other words,
abundance of goods is no warrant for supposing property to be
the chief end of man. Against death and the issues of the
hereafter the man of property is as naked and defenceless as
the man who is poor. This now is the point of the parable
in vers. 16-21. The Rich Man in the story is concerned solely
to hoard the increasing wealth that flows to him from his estates.
He provides larger house-room for his commodities, and thinks
that thereby his future is ensured. His advice to himself,
' Take your ease, eat, drink, and be merry ' is purely selfish,
purely hedonistic, but the pathetic folly of it lies less in the
hedonism than in the expectation that the future belongs to
him at all. The same night God says, ' Foolish man, your soul
is wanted,' and poor indeed, as he goes to meet his God, is the
man whose only trust and possession is in goods which he cannot
keep. ' So fares the man who lays up treasure for himself,'
whose wealth inspires only egoistic confidence, and who does
not discover the deceptiveness of his hopes (viii. 14) until it is
too late to repent. Jesus would have men invest their affections
in things that are eternal (xvi. 9), and for the sake of these
renounce every form of avarice.

xii. 22–31 : AGAINST WORLDLY CARE.

22 To his disciples he said,
> ' Therefore I tell you,
>> do not trouble about what you are to eat in life,
>> nor about what you are to put on your body;
23 >> life is something more than food,
>> and the body is something more than clothes.
24 > Look at the crows ! they neither sow nor reap,
>> no storehouse or granary have they,
>> and yet God feeds them.
> How much more are you worth than birds ?
25 > Which of you can add an ell to his height by troubling
>> about it ?
26 >> and if you cannot manage even this, why trouble over
>> other things ?
27 > Look how the lilies neither spin nor weave ;
>> and yet, I tell you, even Solomon in all his grandeur
>> was never robed like one of them.
28 Now if God so clothes grass which blooms to-day in the
field and is thrown to-morrow into the furnace, will he not
29 much more clothe you ?   O men, how little you trust him !
So do not seek food and drink and be worried ; pagans
30 make food and drink their aim in life, but your Father
31 knows quite well you need that ; only seek his Realm, and
it will be yours over and above.'

(Cf. Matthew vi. 25–33.)

Worldliness—such is the connecting-link between this block
of Q sayings and the foregoing parable—may take other forms
than the amassing of earthly goods.   The principle that a man's
life is not dependent upon his possessions (xii. 15) should rule
out anxiety about trivial matters of food or dress.   The disciples,
required to commit themselves to a life of faith (cf. ix. 3, 23–25),
should trust the Father to provide for them.   Appeal is made
to God's care for His lesser creatures, and here again Jesus
accentuates the close relation in which the being of God exists
to the life of His created universe.   The analogy between man,
the responsible moral agent, and the thoughtless creatures of
the wild holds good, of course, only within limits.   Yet in the

one point which is of importance here the analogy is sound. The Providence which watches over the birds can be trusted to protect the disciple who at the call of duty faces hunger and privation (ver. 24). The needlessness of anxiety under such circumstances is enforced by the humorous consideration that worry will not enable a man to 'add an ell to his height,' or, as the words may equally well be translated, add an ell to his length of days (cf. ver. 20). At ver. 27 the thought passes from food to the cognate topic of clothing, and God's care for His universe is again emphasized, but this time to bring out not His comfortable provision for His creatures but His design of beauty. ' The lilies neither spin nor weave, and yet . . . even Solomon in all his grandeur was never robed like one of these.' Solomon is selected because externally he is the most resplendent figure in the Old Testament. But if a purpose of beauty is discernible even in the grass of the field, which to-morrow in the form of turf or stubble is thrown as fuel into some rough oven, cannot God be trusted to look after the habiliments of those who risk being reduced to rags in His service ? Questions of food and drink may well concern pagans who do not know the heavenly Father—witness the later work of the Greek writer Athenaeus on the ' Banquet Philosophers '—but for those who know the Father such concern and suspense of mind are needless. ' Only seek his Realm,' [1] and the other things will be provided. Spiritual well-being takes precedence over, and is the root of, all other well-being. The Realm of God, the objective end of God's redeeming purpose for mankind, is the one thing for which disciples are called to strive. The little flock of Jesus, as it abandons earthly interests for the sake of preaching the gospel, is assured that it is the Father's will, His direct pleasure or purpose, to bring His Kingdom in.

xii. 32–34 : EARTHLY AND HEAVENLY TREASURE

' Fear not, you little flock, for your Father is delighted to give 32
you the Realm.

Sell what you possess and give it away in alms, 33
make purses for yourselves that never wear out :

[1] The meaning is : ' Submit yourselves absolutely to the sway of God.'

get treasure in heaven that never fails,
    that no thief can get at, no moth destroy.
34   For where your treasure lies,
    your heart will lie there too.'

                       (Cf. Matthew vi. 19–21.)

Since it is the will of God to bring in His Kingdom (xii. 32),
and the time is at hand (ix. 27), the followers of Jesus (ix. 23–25)
should transfer their affections from the old to the new order,
and should convert earthly possessions into heavenly. The
injunction dates probably from the crisis when Jesus summoned
the disciples to follow him to Jerusalem. The disciples may
have hesitated. What were they to do with their belongings ?
Were they to sell the things and to take the money with them ?
Jesus answers, ' **Sell what you possess and give it away in alms** '
(O. Holtzmann, *Life of Jesus*, p. 358). No purse or treasure is
worth having which is at the mercy of burglar or moth. ' Moth '
reminds us that Oriental hoardings are often in the form of
rugs or tapestries. ' **Get treasure in heaven.**' The nature of
this treasure is not defined, except indirectly in the reference to
almsgiving (cf. xvi. 9). The disciples must in any case detach
their affections from the present world, for what a man prizes
has the effect of reducing his life to its own measure. ' **Where
your treasure is, your heart will lie there too.**' Only by the
sacrifice of earthly possessions will the minds of the disciples
be prepared to welcome the Kingdom (Easton).

Faith in God, then, as Jesus teaches it, means a trust so
absolute that earthly guarantees of well-being are not only
needless but must be positively discarded. Property, the
holding of possessions, is not merely superfluous, but imposes a
limitation upon the power and grace of God.

xii. 35–40 : The Coming of the Son of Man

35 ' Keep your loins girt and your lamps lit, and be like men who
36   are expecting their lord and master on his return from
     a marriage-banquet, so as to open the door for him at
37   once when he comes and knocks. Blessed are those servants
     whom the lord and master finds awake when he comes !
     I tell you truly, he will gird himself, make them recline

at table, and come forward to wait on them. Whether he 38
comes in the second or the third watch of the night and finds
them thus alert, blessed are they ! Be sure that if the 39
householder had known at what hour the thief was coming,
he would not have allowed his house to be broken into.
So be ready yourselves, for the Son of man is coming at an 40
hour you do not expect.'

(Cf. Matthew xxiv. 43-44.)

If the followers of Jesus have turned their affections to the
coming Kingdom of God, they will feel it incumbent upon them
to watch and pray. The injunction, ' **Keep your loins girt** '
—Oriental raiment was long and needed to be tucked up for
every purpose requiring active exercise—recalls Exodus xii. 11,
where the children of Israel at the redemption from Egypt
stood in readiness for action with shoes on their feet. The
metaphor implies that the disciples too are entering into a new
supernatural inheritance at the Messiah's coming. For the
added words, ' **and your lamps lit**,' compare Matthew xxv. 1.
The parable of the Watching Servants, ' **Be like men who are
expecting their lord**,' has a parallel in the closing sentences of
the great apocalyptic discourse in Mark xiii., and undoubtedly
reflects a late hour in the Master's life. The lord of the servants
is absent at a marriage-banquet, and as the festivities may be
prolonged, the hour of his return is uncertain. Consequently
there is a temptation to his servants to be slack : compare
1 Thessalonians v. 1-10. In the evangelist's day the prorogation
of the Messiah's return would be explained as in Acts iii. 20-21.
Meantime, the Church had its task in the present, and this
called for continual vigilance. The parable is allegorical, for
no earthly master ' **will make his servants recline at table, and
come forward to wait on them**,' but Jesus the Messiah comes
' not to be served but to serve, and to give his life as a ransom '
(Mark x. 45 ; cf. Luke xxii. 27). Ver. 38, with its reference
to the second and third watches, indicates a consciousness
on the part of the Church that the Lord's return to reign may be
delayed. On the Jewish reckoning the second watch of the
night is from 10 p.m. to 2 a.m., the third from 2 a.m. to 6 a.m.
Ver. 39 is another parable hinting the need of vigilance (cf.
Acts xx. 28-31). The moral of the section is summed up in
the words, ' **the Son of man is coming at an hour you do not**

expect.' Christians must not speculate regarding times and
seasons, but pursue their practical task in season and out of
season. (Compare Mark xiii. 30, 32.)

xii. 41–48 : Wise and Foolish Servants

41 Peter said, ' Lord, are you telling this parable for us, or is it
42 for all and sundry ? ' The Lord said, ' Well, where is the
trusty, thoughtful steward whom the lord and master will set
over his establishment to give out supplies at the proper
43 time ? Blessed is that servant if his lord and master finds
44 him so doing when he arrives ! I tell you plainly, he will
45 set him over all his property. But if that servant says to
himself, " My lord and master is long of arriving," and if
he starts to beat the menservants and maidservants, to eat
46 and drink and get drunk, that servant's lord and master
will arrive on a day when he does not expect him and at
an hour which he does not know ; he will cut him in two
and assign him the fate of unbelievers.

47   The servant who knew his lord and master's orders and
        did not prepare for them,
      will receive many lashes ;
48   whereas he who was ignorant and did what deserves a
        beating,
      will receive few lashes.
    He who has much given him
      will have much required from him,
    and he who has much entrusted to him
      will have all the more demanded of him.'
                      (Cf. Matthew xxiv. 45–51.)

Peter's question in ver. 41, which occurs in Luke alone, indicates an interest in determining whether the rules of watching
(xii. 36–40) and renunciation (xii. 31–35) apply to all Christians
or exclusively to the Apostles. The answering parable, which
Luke derived from Q (cf. Matthew xxiv. 45–51), does not formally
dispose of this point, but by implying that ' the lord and master '
has appointed officers over his establishment, it gives the rules
in question a special relevance to the Apostles. ' Where is the
trusty, thoughtful steward whom the lord and master will set over

his establishment ? ' etc. Theologians, Catholic and Reformed, find here a proof that Christ himself institutes the ministry. ' Unto this catholic, visible Church Christ hath given the ministry, oracles, and ordinances of God, for the gathering and perfecting of the saints,' etc. (*Westminster Confession of Faith,* xxv, 3). But the ministry so constituted exists for service, ' to give out supplies,' i.e. to feed the flock (Acts xx. 27–28, 1 Timothy iii. 1–4, iv. 14–16 ; 2 Timothy ii. 24–25 ; John xxi. 15–17, etc.). This moral the parable works out (vers. 43–48) under forms derived from the practice in Oriental households. The faithful servant is promoted to larger responsibility. The unfaithful, tyrannical, slothful, and drunken servant, who takes advantage of his lord's prolonged absence to work his own selfish will, is executed as a traitor. Punishment is made proportionate to knowledge, for some stewards have less advantage in this respect than others (vers. 47–48 ; cf. 1 Timothy v. 17). ' He who has much given him will have much required from him,' etc. For a similar saying compare xix. 26.

Whether the original parable referred to the Apostles or had a larger bearing is not determinable. But Luke, by hanging it upon Peter's question, clearly takes it to mean that, while sacrifice and watchfulness are obligatory upon all followers of Christ, they are demanded in a peculiar degree of his ministers. (Compare 1 Corinthians ix.)

xii. 49–53 : A PREDICTION OF THE PASSION

'I have come to throw fire on earth.   49
   Would it were kindled already !
I have a baptism to undergo.   50
   How I am distressed till it is all over !
You think I am here to make peace on earth ?   51
   No, I tell you, it is dissension.
After this there will be five at issue in one house,   52
   three divided against two and two against three,
father against son and *son against father*,   53
mother against daughter and *daughter against mother*,
mother-in-law against daughter-in-law and *daughter-in-law against mother-in-law*.'

                 (Cf. Matthew x. 34–35.)

The warnings given to the disciples in the last section lead up naturally to the crisis which now impends for Jesus himself. Vers. 49–50 contain perhaps one of the best-preserved of Jesus' predictions of his Passion : ' **I have come to throw fire on earth.**' The ' fire ' is the flame of righteousness in a nation-wide move-ment of repentance toward God. But as the next words, ' **Would it were kindled already,**' shew, this purpose of Jesus to inaugurate the great Repentance of Israel has been opposed, and Jesus sees that suffering awaits him : ' **I have a baptism to undergo.**' The deep waters of trial must go over the soul of Jesus, and he longs that the ordeal were past. Judaism knew of the Messianic ' Woes ' or ' Pangs,' but had not reckoned that they fell on the Messiah. In vers. 51–53, Jesus dismisses the Jewish dream of a Messianic age of peace. ' **You think I am here to make peace on earth ? No, I tell you, it is dissension.**' Before the Kingdom of God can truly come there must be a sifting of Israel, a ferment of mind disrupting the bonds of social and national life, and fulfilling the prophecy of Micah vii. 6. ' **There shall be five at issue in one house,**' etc. In Micah, where the dis-sensions are a sign of an evil condition of Israel calling for divine judgment, the antagonism proceeds in each case from the younger generation, ' son against father, daughter against mother,' etc., and so it is also in Matthew x. 34–35. In Luke the clash and repulsion of older and younger generations are mutual. Jesus recognizes sorrowfully that the Messianic peace can only come *now* through tension and elimination. With vers. 51–53 compare the passage about the swords in xxii. 35–38, and with 49–50 compare the Greek legend of Prometheus, whose gift of fire to men brought doom upon himself.

xii. 54–59 : THE CRITICAL ISSUES OF THE TIME

54 And to the crowds he said,

      ' When you see a cloud rise in the west,
         you say, '' There is a shower coming,''
         and so it is ;

55   when you feel the south wind blow,
         you say, '' There will be heat,''
         and so it is.

You hypocrites, you know how to decipher the look of 56
    earth and sky ;
    how is it you cannot decipher the meaning of this
      era ?
And why do you not yourselves settle what is right ?   57
Thus, when you go before the magistrate with your opponent, 58
do your utmost to get quit of him on the way there, in case
he hales you before the judge ; then the judge will hand you
over to the jailer and the jailer will throw you in prison.
I tell you, you will never get out till you pay the last farthing 59
of your debt.'

                 (Cf. Matthew xvi. 2–3, v. 25–26.)

The first part of the present section—which is from Q—occurs
in Matthew in answer to the request for a ' sign ' from heaven.
Jesus addresses the crowds, and indicts them for blindness to the
spiritual phenomena of the time.   Accustomed to derive weather-
lore from ' the look of earth and sky,' they fail to see in contemporary history the proof that the Kingdom of God draws
near.   Hypocrites means that, while professing religious zeal
and an honest desire to be enlightened, they shut their eyes to
facts.   ' How is it you cannot decipher the meaning of this era ? '
Did the ' sign ' lie in the moral evils of the age, or in the appearance of John calling the nation to repentance, or in Jesus' own
announcement of the Kingdom ?   Recall in this connexion the
passages vii. 24–27, 31–35, xi. 29–32, and compare xx. 1–8.   In
ver. 57 Jesus rounds on his audience and asks, ' Why do you not
yourselves settle what is right ? '   His hearers know for themselves that repentance is urgent and in what it should consist.
They know God's just demand as it applies to their own conduct.
Why then do they wait for ' signs ' ?   The ultimate appeal of
Jesus is thus to conscience, to man's moral nature, in which the
authority of his will is surely registered.   That *immediate*
repentance is necessary is the point of vers. 58–59.   Everyone
admits the advisability of a man, against whom judgment is
sure to go, settling a case out of court rather than risking a judicial
verdict.   So Jesus urges his generation to make its peace with
God.   The parable serves in Matthew v. 25–26 to illustrate the
putting away of unbrotherly feeling, but Luke conserves better
its original design and force.

xiii. 1–9 : THE URGENCY OF REPENTANCE

xiii.

1 It was at this time that some people came to tell him about the Galileans whose blood Pilate had mingled with their sacrifices.

2 But he replied to them,
   ' Do you think, because they suffered this, that these Galileans were worse sinners than the rest of the Galileans ?

3   I tell you, no ;
      unless you repent you will all perish as they did.

4   Or those eighteen men killed by the fall of the tower at Siloam ?—
      do you think they were worse offenders than the rest of the residents in Jerusalem ?

5   I tell you, no ;
      unless you repent you will all perish as they did.'

6 And he told this parable. ' A man had a fig tree planted in his vineyard ; he came in search of fruit on it but he

7 found none. So he said to the vinedresser, '' Here have I come for three years in search of fruit on this fig tree without finding any ; cut it down, why should it take up space ? ''

8 But the man replied, '' Leave it for this year, sir, till I dig

9 round about it and put in manure. Then it may bear fruit next year. If not, you can have it cut down.'' '

                                                    (Luke alone.)

Nothing else is known of these **Galileans whose blood Pilate had mingled with their sacrifices.** The Galilean populace, however, ever since the rising under Judas in A.D. 6, contained elements that were ' inclined to revolution, naturally disposed to change, and fond of sedition ' (Josephus, *Life*, 17), and if Pilate, procurator of Judea since A.D. 26, sent troops against certain pilgrims, whom he suspected of insurrectionary designs, and slaughtered some of them in the act of bringing their sacrifices to the Temple, it would be in keeping with his character and with his procedure on another occasion when he dispersed a Jerusalem mob by the batons of his soldiers (Josephus, *Wars*, ii. 9, 4). What motive the informants had for bringing the massacre of the Galileans under the notice of Jesus is not stated.

His answer, however, suggests that they had sided against the victims, from which we infer that they had raised no problem of unmerited suffering, but rather, when they heard Jesus speak of judgment hanging over the nation, had asked if the fate of these Galileans was to be considered a case in point. Jesus in reply declares it inept to fasten on this case at a time when God was displeased with the whole nation. The supposition that the Galileans were ' **worse sinners than the rest of the Galileans** ' is rejected, but the warning, ' **'unless you repent you will all perish as they did,**' indicates that the Roman power may yet prove the instrument of divine justice upon the whole people. In ver. 4 Jesus himself cites another incident by which to enforce the same lesson. The ' **eighteen men killed by the fall of the tower at Siloam** ' could not be supposed to be specially wicked persons whose evil designs had brought upon them a well-deserved punishment. They were like other people in Jerusalem, and the whole country ought to take warning. The reason why disaster in such cases falls on certain persons and not on others is not considered.

The parable of the Fig Tree—which like the above warnings is from the L source—points the same moral that Judgment is nigh. A fig tree which is planted not on ordinary soil but in a vineyard is obviously an object of special culture and care. When therefore the owner can say, ' **Here have I come for three years in search of fruit without finding any,**' it is natural that he should condemn the tree as a useless burden to the land. But even then the vinedresser will say, ' **Leave it for this year, sir,**' in the hope that further care and attention may lead to improved results. The meaning of the parable is that there is a limit to the divine patience with men. Jesus is conscious of giving Israel a last opportunity of repentance. The time is short, the call peremptory, the issues irrevocable. Zahn and others allegorize the story. The vineyard is Israel (cf. Isaiah v. 1 f., Jeremiah ii. 21, Psalm lxxx. 8, etc.), the fig tree is Jerusalem, the three years are the period since John rang out his summons to repentance, the vinedresser is Jesus, the extra year of grace is Jesus' ministry (cf. iv. 18). But such exegesis over-elaborates the intention of the story. The parable suitably concludes a section (xii. 13–xiii. 9) of which the dominant idea has been that the Last Judgment is near and the present course of history drawing to its close.

xiii. 10–17 : HEALING OF A CRIPPLE WOMAN

10 When he was teaching in one of the synagogues on the sabbath,
11 there was a woman who for eighteen years had suffered
weakness from an evil spirit ; indeed she was bent double
12 and quite unable to raise herself. Jesus noticed her and
called to her, ' Woman, you are released from your weakness.'
13 He laid his hands on her, and instantly she became erect and
14 glorified God. But the president of the synagogue was
annoyed at Jesus healing on the sabbath, and he said to the
crowd, ' There are six days for work to be done ; come
during them to get healed, instead of on the sabbath.' The
15 Lord replied to him, ' You hypocrites, does not each of you
untether his ox or ass from the stall on the sabbath and lead
16 it away to drink ? And this woman, a daughter of Abraham,
bound by Satan for all these eighteen years, was she not to
17 be freed from her bondage on the sabbath ? ' As he said
this, all his opponents were put to shame, but all the crowd
rejoiced over all his splendid doings.

(Luke alone.)

This is the only point in the later ministry of Jesus at which
he is found teaching in a synagogue. The place is unnamed,
but was probably in Galilee. The attribution of the woman's
bowed and helpless condition to an evil spirit is a secondary
feature, for the usual symptoms of possession are absent, and
the action of Jesus does not recall the ordinary procedure at an
exorcism. As on another occasion (vi. 6–11), Judaism is scan-
dalized by the seeming breach of the Sabbath-law. The president of the synagogue, in a remonstrance addressed to the congre-
gation but really aimed at Jesus, cites Deuteronomy vi. 13,
' Six days shalt thou labour, and do all thy work.' The contention is that, as in the present case there was no danger to life in
waiting until the Sabbath was over, Jesus had broken the Law.
This interpretation of the Sabbath-law Jesus rejects with heat.
' You hypocrites ! does not each of you untether his ox or ass ? '
etc., i.e. ' you undo the bonds of your draught-animals to refresh
them, and you feel that in this there is no infringement of the
holy day, but you protest against the release of a human creature,
a daughter of Abraham, from bonds which Satan—the source
of the evil spirit—has clamped upon her not for a day but for

eighteen years!' 'Hypocrites' suggests, as usually, a false religiosity, a simulation of devotion to the Law, when the real motive is antipathy to Jesus. On the claim made for the Sabbath see above, under vi. 6-11.

xiii. 18-21 : PARABLES OF THE MUSTARD-SEED AND THE LEAVEN

So he said,   18
   ' What is the Reign of God like ?
   to what shall I compare it ?
It is like a grain of mustard-seed which a man took and put 19
into his orchard, where it grew up and became a tree, and
the wild birds roosted in its branches.' He added, ' To what 20
shall I compare the Reign of God ? It is like dough which 21
a woman took and buried in three pecks of flour, till all of it
was leavened.'
                (Cf. Matthew xiii. 31-33, Mark iv. 30-32.)

This pair of little parables stood together in the Q source (cf. Matthew xiii. 31-33) and serves to illustrate certain aspects under which Jesus presented the Kingdom of God. The formula ' What is so-and-so like ? ' was customary in Biblical and Rabbinical style : cf. Isaiah xl. 18, ' To whom then will you liken God ? Or what likeness will you compare to Him ? ' In Luke the two parables are joined to the preceding section by the words, So he said, and the connexion of thought is—the impression made on the crowd by Jesus' ' splendid doings ' (xiii. 17) has revealed a sympathy through which Jesus is encouraged to speak of the ultimate triumph of his mission. This connexion of ideas, however, is not to be pressed. The formula, ' The Reign of God is like,' etc., does not suggest necessarily that the thing described in the parable is equated with the Kingdom. All that is implied is that the Kingdom has aspects or relations which are illustrated in the story (Bultmann, p. 112).

' A grain of mustard-seed ' (*Sinapis nigra*) is a proverbially small thing, but the growth of the plant is phenomenal, attaining at times to a height of 10 to 12 feet. The parable therefore connects the Reign of God with some process or principle of phenomenal growth or expansion, and Luke doubtless took this to be the spread of the Church on earth. From small beginnings the Christian society extends over the world, and Luke may even have thought of the ' wild birds ' which settle in the branches as the Gentile peoples who have been brought to Christ. It is possible that our Lord intended the parable in a similar sense to foreshadow the increase of those who should repent and receive his message. In that case the seed will be the ' mystery ' or revelation taught by Jesus, which the hearers receive into obedient hearts, or—since Jesus elsewhere uses the figure of the mustard-seed to signify ' faith ' (Matthew xvii. 20, Luke xvii. 6)—it will refer to the believing earnestness with which the hearers appropriate the message.

The second illustration, ' like dough which a woman took,' etc., presents the same message or the same principle of faith as a leavening process working in the hearts of men. The Jews were accustomed to use ' leaven ' or dough as a metaphor for the power of evil (see under xii. 1), and if Jesus employs it here to indicate rather the transforming influence of goodness, it is because he regards good as mightier than evil. Luke probably took the parable to apply to the marvellous diffusion of the Christian faith in society. Jesus meant probably the invincible inward power of righteousness. Both parables express the thought that, though the present effects of our Lord's teaching seemed meagre, nevertheless ' at the advent of the Kingdom a very great number of persons would be found prepared ' (Easton).

xiii. 22–30 : THE NARROW WAY

22 On he went, teaching from one town and village to another, as
23 he made his way to Jerusalem. A man said to him, ' Is it
24 only a few, sir, who are saved ? ' So he said to them, ' Strive to get in through the narrow door, for I tell you many will
25 try to get in and not be able, once the master of the House has got up and closed the door. You may stand outside and knock at the door, crying, "Lord, open for us," but he will
26 answer you, "I do not know where you come from." You will then proceed to say, " But we ate and drank in your presence,
27 and you taught in our streets !" "I tell you," he will say, "I
28 do not know where you come from ; *begone every one of you, you evildoers.*" There you will wail and gnash your teeth, to see Abraham, Isaac, Jacob and all the prophets inside the

Realm of God and yourselves put outside. Yes, and people 29
will come *from east and west* and north and south to their
places at the feast within the Realm of God.
    Some are last who will be first,   30
    and some are first who will be last.'
             (Cf. Matthew vii. 13–14, 22–23 ; viii. 11–12.)

The introductory verse, by reminding us that Jesus is on the
way to Jerusalem, directs our thoughts afresh to the final issues
of his work, and hence gives added point to the interlude which
here finds place. The question, ' Is it only a few who are saved ? '
taken with the rejoinder of Jesus, makes it plain that the Realm
of God connotes not merely a condition of present blessedness
but a transcendent future world of good, into which only those
who are morally in earnest will enter. The questioner probably
reasoned that if the mysterious veil which hid the glories of the
future could be removed, his faith would be helped. Jesus,
however, who has never stressed the glories of the Kingdom but
always and only the moral conditions of entrance, dismisses the
question with the general warning, ' Strive to get in through the
narrow door.' The thought of the ' Two Ways ' of life and
death, and of the narrowness of the way to life, was familiar to
his hearers : compare Jeremiah xxi. 8, ' Behold, I set before you
the way of life and the way of death ' ; 2 Esdras vii. 6–7, ' A
city has been built . . . and it is full of all good things, but its
entrance is narrow. . . . There is but one path . . . such that
it makes room for only one man's steps.' The narrow door
obviously means the way of repentance and surrender to God,
and in the word **strive**, which suggests the strenuous efforts of
the athlete in the stadium (1 Corinthians ix. 24–27), the audience
is warned that only an unfaltering earnestness will obtain
entrance into the Kingdom. The statement that ' many will
try to get in and not be able ' cautions against a belated repentance. The time is short, and as there is an hour by which the
ordinary householder expects his family to be indoors, so there
is a time when God will close the gate of life, and those who
come knocking after that will be treated as intruders.

Vers. 24–30, which consist wholly of Q material, shew us by
what sayings of Jesus the early Christian community reminded
itself of the seriousness of life's issues. Men will plead before
the Judgment-throne of Christ, ' We ate and drank in your pres-

ence, and you taught in our streets.' But to have seen and to
have companied with the Lord in the flesh will not confer any
privilege, where there has been no turning of the soul to righteousness. The Judge will say to the late-comers, ' **Begone every one
of you evildoers !** ' For a more detailed presentation of the
same teaching compare Matthew vii. 21–23. The statement,
' **People will come from east and west,**' etc., is subjoined in
Matthew viii. 11–12 to Jesus' encomium on the faith of the
Gentile centurion. The Jews took it for granted that the
banquet with Abraham and the patriarchs and prophets of Israel
would be for Jews, and that discomfiture and the ' wailing and
gnashing of teeth ' would be reserved for the Gentiles. Jesus
warns them that the parts will be reversed. The test will be not
national birthright or hereditary privilege, but character and
conduct, and the application of this criterion will have surprising
results. ' **Some are last who will be first,**' etc. Israel has had
an advantage over other peoples in point of time and also in the
superior greatness of its opportunities, but this will not avail at
the Judgment in default of personal righteousness.

xiii. 31–33 : The Threat of Herod Antipas

31 Just then some Pharisees came up to tell him, ' Get away from
32   here, for Herod intends to kill you.' ' Go and tell that fox,'
    he replied, ' I cast out daemons and perform cures to-day
    and to-morrow, and on the third day I complete my task !
33   But I must journey on, to-day, to-morrow, and the next
    day ; it would never do for a prophet to perish except in
    Jerusalem ! '

(Luke alone.)

The threat from Antipas must have come while Jesus was still
in the tetrarch's dominions, and as it presupposes that the
activities of Jesus were still at their height, it is best assigned
to the period when Herod's attention was first attracted towards
him (Mark vi. 14–16). The sinister intimation, ' **Get away from
here, for Herod intends to kill you,**' is delivered by aid of certain
Pharisees whom Herod on this occasion finds willing instruments
of his purpose. Whether the tetrarch intended to put his threat
into execution, or thought only to intimidate Jesus, may be left

undetermined. The subtilty of the stratagem is not lost on Jesus, who dubs the tetrarch ' that fox,' and bids the informants report to Herod that he will not be intimidated. He has a work to do for God which, until it is accomplished, renders him inviolate. ' To-day and to-morrow and the third day ' expresses the fullness and roundedness of the span of time which is allotted to Jesus. ' I cast out daemons and perform cures to-day and to-morrow '—it was the miracles of Jesus which had drawn on him the attention of Herod (Mark vi. 14)—' and on the third day I complete my task.' Nevertheless, it is now clear to Jesus that his days in Galilee are numbered. Herod's requirement that he move on only confirms a higher purpose which has made the whole life of Jesus the life of a wanderer. ' I must journey on, to-day, to-morrow, and the next day ' (cf. ix. 58). For to Jerusalem alone belongs the unenviable privilege of bringing the messengers of God to their doom. There is irony in the words, ' It would never do for a prophet to perish except in Jerusalem,' but, as the next section shows, Jesus based his prognostication on the facts of the nation's history.

xiii. 34-35 : THE APOSTROPHE TO JERUSALEM

' O Jerusalem, Jerusalem, slaying the prophets and stoning those 34 who have been sent to you ! How often I would fain have gathered your children as a fowl gathers her brood under her wings ! But you would not have it ! *See, your House* 35 *is left to yourselves.* I tell you, you will never see me till the day comes when you say, *Blessed be he who comes in the Lord's name.*'

(Cf. Matthew xxiii. 37-39.)

The lament, ' O Jerusalem, Jerusalem,' is placed in Matthew xxiii. 37-39 at the close of Jesus' long indictment of the Pharisees. This position, which reserves it almost to the end of Jesus' work in Jerusalem, is very suitable, but as Luke seldom or never varies the order of his sources, we must infer that his authority connected the lament with the threat from Antipas ; in other words, his authority here was not Q *simpliciter*, but Q combined with L materials (Introd., page xix f.). Jesus is grieved over the city's tragic record in ' slaying the prophets and

stoning those who have been sent to her.' If anywhere a welcome
should have been accorded to the messengers of the Kingdom, it
was in Jerusalem : cf. Isaiah lii. 7, ' How beautiful upon the
mountains are the feet of him that . . . publisheth salvation,
that saith unto Zion, Thy God reigneth.' But the city remains
impenitent and unmoved. The words, ' How often I would fain
have gathered your children,' presuppose that Jesus has made
repeated efforts to win Jerusalem, and suggest that his work
there was by no means confined to a single visit. Jesus now
predicts the city's destruction. ' Your house is left to yourselves,'
i.e. God's glory will move elsewhere. Did Jesus think of this
doom as coming by means of the Roman legions ? It is probable
that he did. The closing word, ' You will never see me till the
day comes when you say, Blessed is he who,' etc., can only be
taken as Jesus' last word to Jerusalem. Therefore its position
here in Luke is quite unsuitable. Jesus, leaving Jerusalem,
means that he comes no more till he ' comes in the Lord's name,'
i.e. till he comes to reign (cf. Revelation i. 7). Nowhere is it
stated more uncompromisingly that Jesus alone holds the secret
of peace for Judea. He alone can avert national destruction.
See later on xix. 41–44.

xiv. 1–6 : THE MAN WITH THE DROPSY

xiv.

1 Now when he entered the house of a ruler who belonged to the
Pharisees to take a meal, they watched him closely. In
2 front of him there was a man who had dropsy ; so Jesus
3 asked the jurists and Pharisees, ' Is it right to heal on the
4 sabbath or not ? ' They held their peace. Then Jesus took
5 hold of the man and cured him and sent him off. ' Which
of you,' he said to them, ' when an ass or an ox has fallen
into a well, will not pull him out at once upon the sabbath
6 day ? ' This they could not dispute.

(Luke alone.)

The invitation extended to Jesus by a synagogue-president
belonging to the Pharisees gives the company, who would all
be of the Pharisee's class, an opportunity of observing Jesus at
close range. From the suspicion with which they eye his conduct

towards the dropsical man it would appear that the latter was not a guest but some intruder who, following Oriental custom (cf. vii. 37), had taken advantage of the open door to solicit alms or food. The question, ' Is it right to heal on the Sabbath or not ? ' revives the issue stated in vi. 9, and the challenge in ver. 5 recalls the similar challenge in xiii. 15. It is not clear that strict Jews would have conceded the lawfulness of rescuing ' an ass or an ox ' from a well on the Sabbath. But it is characteristic that Jesus makes the argument turn not on a legal scruple—he is satisfied on the legal point (Mark ii. 27)—but on the dictates of humane feeling, a consideration which the company cannot entirely dismiss.

xiv. 7–14 : On being Humble and Loving

He also told a parable to the guests, when he observed how they 7 picked out the best places. ' When anyone invites you to a 8 marriage-banquet,' he said, ' never lie down in the best place, in case a more distinguished guest than yourself has been invited ; then the host will tell you, " Make room for him," 9 and you will proceed in shame to take the lowest place. No, when you are invited, go and recline in the lowest place, 10 so that when your host comes in he will tell you, " Move higher up, my friend." Then you will be honoured before your fellow guests.

For everyone who uplifts himself will be humbled, 11
    and he who humbles himself will be uplifted.'
He also said to his host, ' When you give a dinner or supper, 12 do not ask your friends or your brothers or your relatives or your rich neighbours, in case they invite you back again and you get repaid. No, when you give a banquet, invite the poor, 13 the maimed, the lame, and the blind. Then you will be 14 blessed ; for as they have no means of repaying you, you will be repaid at the resurrection of the just.'

The presence of Jesus at the Pharisee's table provides Luke, or his authority, with the opportunity of introducing certain parables or sayings of Jesus which have reference to banquets and places at feasts. This setting is a little artificial, and it is just possible that the words, he told a parable to the guests, etc., ran originally in Aramaic ' He spoke a parable about guests.'

The object of the parable is to inculcate humility : compare Proverbs xxv. 6–7, of which the parable is simply a dramatic application. The order of precedence at an Oriental banquet was punctiliously observed. Jesus therefore uses the humiliation which inevitably overtakes an over-ambitious and self-assertive guest to point the moral that humility alone constitutes worthiness in the eyes of God : compare Romans xii. 3 and Philippians ii. 1–11. ' Everyone who uplifts himself will be humbled and he who humbles himself will be uplifted.' The promotion and degradation here referred to take place at the Judgment. A parallel to the above parable is inserted by certain Western authorities into the text of Matthew at xxi. 28, where it is introduced by the admonition : ' Seek from being little to grow, and from being greater to become less.'

The second parable (vers. 12–14) turns on the social practice of inviting to feasts only equals, friends or relatives or well-to-do neighbours, who can reciprocate the favour. Jesus urges the opposite course : ' Invite the poor, the maimed,' etc., those who cannot repay your kindness, and from whom the proud and ambitious turn with social and physical repugnance. Those who take this course ' will be repaid at the resurrection of the just.' The Resurrection of the Just was a cardinal article of religious belief among the Pharisees (cf. Acts xxiii. 6–8, xxiv. 14–15), and Jesus insists on the superiority to worldly considerations to which the holders of such a belief should rise. For similar teaching see vi. 32–35 and xvi. 9 ; for the opposite practice and its consequences compare xvi. 19–31.

xiv. 15–24 : The Messianic Banquet

15 Hearing this, one of his fellow guests said to him, ' Blessed is he
16 who feasts in the Realm of God ! ' Jesus said to him,
' There was a man who was giving a large supper, to which
17 he had invited a number of guests. At the hour for supper
he sent his servant to tell the guests, " Come, things are all
18 ready." But they all alike proceeded to decline. The first
said to him, " I have bought a farm and I am obliged to go
19 and look at it. Pray consider me excused." The second
said, " I have bought five pair of oxen and I am going to try
20 them. Pray consider me excused." Another said, " I have

married a wife ; that is why I cannot come." The servant 21
went and reported this to his master. Then the master of
the house was enraged, and said to his servant, " Quick, go
out to the streets and lanes of the town and bring in the poor,
the maimed, the blind, and the lame." When the servant 22
announced, " Your order has been carried out, sir, but there
is still room," the master said to the servant, " Go out to 23
the roads and hedges and make people come in, to fill up my
house. For I tell you that not one of those who were invited 24
shall taste my supper." '

(Cf. Matthew xxii. 1-10.)

A guest at the table, impressed by the reference to the Resurrection (ver. 14) and thinking to give the conversation an edifying
turn, ejaculates ' Blessed is he who feasts in the Realm of God ! '
For the Jewish idea of the Messianic banquet, see xiii. 28-29.
The answer of Jesus, conveyed in the form of a story, is that a
sentimental interest in the Kingdom of God may exist without a
real desire to enter that Kingdom when the invitation to do so
is given. For the double summons given to the privileged
guests in the story, compare the Jewish Midrash quoted by Zahn,
which records, in proof of the high social standing claimed by
the people of Jerusalem, that no one of them goes as guest to a
banquet until he has been repeatedly called. In the present
parable the invited guests fully intend to be present at the
Supper, indeed cannot imagine themselves absent, yet when, in
accordance with Oriental etiquette, the host's servant arrives
to say, ' Come, things are all ready '—Jesus stresses the *immediacy* of God's will to bring in His Kingdom—they find themselves unable to accept. Lands, oxen, wives—compare, for the
last-mentioned, Deuteronomy xx. 7—interpose themselves
between the guests and the Supper, whereupon the disappointed
host turns elsewhere. ' Go out to the streets and lanes,' he says
to his servant, ' and bring in the poor, maimed,' etc., i.e. those
who are not so rich and satisfied with this world as to despise
the invitation. When the servant, who this time is successful,
reports that ' there is still room,' the host says, ' Go to the roads
and hedges,' i.e. to the waifs and strays of society, and make
them come in. He cancels the invitation to the original guests,
and fills the house with others.

The parable, as it stands, is clearly allegorical. No single

servant would be able to summon in person all the guests invited
to an ordinary feast, but Luke or his source is thinking of Christ.
Christ comes to the chosen people with the revelation (see under
iii. 21–22 and vi. 20–26) that the time is fully come and the
Kingdom of God has drawn near, but finds the religious leaders
of that people absorbed in worldly interests. While, however,
these leaders reject the summons, Jesus finds a welcome among
the poor, who press into the Kingdom (cf. iv. 18, vi. 20, xvi. 16).
A peculiar feature of the parable in Luke is the double extension
of the open invitation in vers. 21 and 23. The ' poor,' i.e. the
humble and earnest in the land, are first called. Then the
invitation is extended to the denizens of the ' roads and hedges,'
i.e. to the lapsed mass of ' taxgatherers and sinners ' (v. 30–32).
Luke, however, probably understood by the roads and hedges
the outer Gentile world, and for this reason, as Dr. Easton notes,
this part of the servant's commission remains still unfulfilled
when the parable closes. For this larger mission of the ' Servant,' which was still only in prospect when Jesus lived on earth,
compare Isaiah xlii. 6 and especially xlix. 5–6 : ' It is too light
a thing that thou shouldst be My servant to raise up the tribes
of Jacob. . . . I will also give thee for a light to the Gentiles.'

xiv. 25–35 : THE CONDITIONS OF DISCIPLESHIP

25 There were large crowds travelling with him ; so he turned
and said to them,

26 ' If anyone comes to me and does not hate his father and mother
and wife and children and brothers and sisters, aye and his
own life,
he cannot be a disciple of mine ;

27 whoever does not carry his own cross and come after me,
he cannot be a disciple of mine.

28 For which of you wants to build a tower and does not first
sit down to calculate the expense, to see if he has enough

29 money to complete it ?—in case, after he has laid the foundation and then is unable to finish the building, all the spectators

30 start to make fun of him, saying, " This fellow started to

31 build but he could not finish it." Or what king sets out to
fight against another king without first sitting down to
deliberate whether with ten thousand men he can encounter

the king who is attacking him with twenty thousand ?   If he 32
cannot, when the other is still at a distance he will send an
embassy to do homage to him.

So with everyone of you who will not part with all his 33
 goods—
 he cannot be a disciple of mine.

Salt is excellent indeed ; but if salt becomes insipid, what 34
will restore its flavour ?   It is no use for either soil or dunghill, 35
it is flung out.   He who has an ear let him listen to this.'

(Cf. Matthew x. 37-38.)

The sayings in this passage, particularly those in vers. 26 and
33, follow appropriately upon a section which has shewn how
property and home and family ties interpose themselves between
men and the call of God.   If we assume that the crowds who
travelled with Jesus consisted in part of pilgrims and others
who wished to continue in his company but had no clear sense
of his aim in going to Jerusalem, the extension to them of the
demand, ' If anyone comes to me,' etc., by which he had
already sifted the inner circle of his disciples (ix. 23-26, 57-62),
becomes intelligible.   On the nature of this demand see under
ix. 21-27 and 57-62.   The requirement to hate father and
mother, etc., means that the extremest violence must be offered
to one's own affections and inclinations in cases where family
ties conflict with personal allegiance to the call of Christ.
Natural feelings must in such a case not only be denied but
slain.

In the illustrations in vers. 28-32 the situation is viewed from
the standpoint of Christ himself.   ' Which of you wants to build
a tower ? ' etc.   Jesus intends to inaugurate the Messianic era
at Jerusalem, and for this purpose he requires effective followers.
Otherwise he resembles the man who, beginning to build a tower
without forecasting the cost, is compelled to abandon operations
and to become a laughing-stock.   Obviously the parable means
not simply that Jesus' disciples must be prepared for sacrifice
but that Jesus must see that they are so prepared.   So with the
second illustration, ' What king sets out to fight against another
king ? ' etc.   (Compare here xi. 21-23.)   Jesus, who is battling
against the kingdom of Satan, needs not camp-followers but
soldiers !   Otherwise there is no alternative but to conclude an
ignominious peace.   For the criterion applied in ver. 33, ' Who

will not part with all his goods cannot be a disciple of mine,' compare xii. 33–34 and discussion there.

In vers. 34–35 the proverbial qualities of salt are used to enforce the same inexorable demand. Salt, as those who had practised fish-curing on the Galilean Lake would know from experience, is an excellent thing so long as it retains its function, e.g. its property of preserving perishable matter from decay. Lacking this property—the reference may be to some spurious substitute which was offered on the market—the commodity is valueless even as a fertilizer for the land. So Jesus can do nothing with followers who lack the essential salt of character. The saying comes from Q (cf. Matthew v. 13), and has a parallel in Mark ix. 50. By comparing the present context with the Mark passage it is seen that ' salt ' means here the capacity or willingness to make sacrifice. Only if disciples possess this sacrificial quality will Jesus be able to conduct his cause to victory.

xv. 1–10 : THE LOST SHEEP AND THE LOST COIN

xv.

1 Now the taxgatherers and sinners were all approaching him to
2 listen to him, but the Pharisees and the scribes complained,
3 ' He welcomes sinners and eats along with them ! ' So he
4 told them this parable, ' Which of you with a hundred sheep,
   if he loses one, does not leave the ninety-nine in the desert
5 and go after the lost one till he finds it ? When he finds it
6 he puts it on his shoulders with joy, and when he gets home
   he gathers his friends and neighbours : " Rejoice with me,"
7 he says to them, " for I have found the sheep I lost." So,
   I tell you, there will be joy in heaven over a single sinner
8 who repents, more than over ninety-nine good people who
   do not need to repent. Or again, suppose a woman has
   ten shillings. If she loses one of them, does she not light
9 a lamp, and scour the house and search carefully till she
   finds it ? And when she finds it she gathers her women-
10 friends and neighbours, saying, " Rejoice with me, for I
   have found the shilling I lost." So, I tell you, there is joy
   in the presence of the angels of God over a single sinner
   who repents.'

(For vers. 3–7, cf. Matthew xviii. 12–14.)

Chap. xv. consists of three parables united by the single motive of illustrating the joy felt in heaven when a sinner repents and is brought to God. The first has a parallel in Matthew xviii. 12–14. The second and third are peculiar to Luke. Mr. Montefiore notes the changed aspect under which repentance appears in this chapter as compared with preceding sections. ' The theme is not, Repent while there is yet time, but how good repentance is and how beloved of God.' While holding this doctrine to be in harmony with Rabbinic teaching, the Jewish scholar admits that the practical lesson which is drawn by Jesus, and which is exemplified in his own relations with sinners, is new and original. The attraction exercised by Jesus, the fact that sinners were all approaching to listen to him, indicates, he says, a note which is sounded neither in the Old Testament nor in the Talmud. The teaching of Jesus ' did not palter with, or make light of sin, but yet it gave comfort to the sinner ' (*Synoptic Gospels*, vol. ii, p. 520). On the charge brought against Jesus that ' He welcomes sinners and eats along with them,' see above on v. 27–32.

The first parable, which by the shepherd's joy in recovering the lost sheep teaches that there is ' joy in heaven over a single sinner who repents,' requires us to look away from the ninety-nine, the small flock which remains safe in the pasture, and to concentrate attention on the wanderer. The point which Jesus would make is the value of the individual soul to God (cf. Isaiah xl. 11), which value he declares to be absolute. The satisfaction or emotion which attaches to the safety and well-being of the flock as a whole does not excuse for leaving the wanderer to its fate, and does not diminish but enhance the joy with which the lost one is found. Whether any persons answer to the description of ' good people who do not need to repent ' is not considered. Jesus need not be here speaking in irony, but only focusing attention on the salvation of the obviously *lost*. The parable occurs in Matthew xviii. 12–14, but in that gospel the context identifies the lost sheep not with a lost sinner but with a lapsed member of the Christian community who must be tenderly restored. The second parable, the Lost Coin, enforces the meaning of the first. The appeal, ' Does she not light a lamp ? ' suggests perhaps the part which *truth* plays in this task of recovering lost souls. Jesus knows that he has a revelation to proclaim, to which even the lost will respond. (Compare viii. 16, xi. 33, etc.)

xv. 11–32 : Parable of the Lost Son

11 He also said : ' There was a man who had two sons, and the
12   younger said to his father, " Father, give me the share of the
      property that falls to me." So he divided his means among
13   them. Not many days later, the younger son sold off every-
      thing and went abroad to a distant land, where he squandered
14   his means in loose living. After he had spent his all, a
      severe famine set in throughout that land, and he began to
15   feel in want ; so he went and attached himself to a citizen
16   of that land, who sent him to his fields to feed swine. And
      he was fain to fill his belly with the pods the swine were
17   eating ; no one gave him anything. But when he came to
      his senses he said, " How many hired men of my father
      have more than enough to eat, and here am I perishing of
18   hunger ! I will be up and off to my father, and I will say to
      him, ' Father, I have sinned against heaven and before you ;
19   I don't deserve to be called your son any more ; only make
20   me like one of your hired men.' " So he got up and went
      off to his father. But when he was still far away his father
      saw him and felt pity for him and ran to fall upon his neck
21   and kiss him. The son said to him, " Father, I have sinned
      against heaven and before you ; I don't deserve to be called
22   your son any more." But the father said to his servants,
      " Quick, bring the best robe and put it on him, give him a
23   ring for his hand and sandals for his feet, and bring the
24   fatted calf, kill it, and let us eat and be merry ; for my son
      here was dead and he has come to life, he was lost and is
25   found." So they began to make merry. Now his elder son
      was out in the field, and as he came near the house he heard
26   music and dancing ; so, summoning one of the servants, he
27   asked what this meant. The servant told him, " Your brother
      has arrived, and your father has killed the fatted calf because
28   he has got him back safe and sound." This angered him,
      and he would not go in. His father came out and tried to
29   appease him, but he replied, " Look at all the years I have
      been serving you ! I have never neglected any of your
      orders, and yet you have never given me so much as a kid,
30   to let me make merry with my friends. But as soon as this
      son of yours arrives, after having wasted your means with
31   harlots, you kill the fatted calf for him ! " The father said

to him, " My son, you and I are always together, all I have
is yours. We could not but make merry and rejoice, for 32
your brother here was dead and has come to life again, he
was lost but he has been found." '

(Luke alone.)

With the third parable we come closer to the heart of Jesus'
teaching about the value of the individual soul to God. No
emotion which attaches to the recovery of a lost animal or a
lost thing can equal the joy of recovering a lost *son*, for here
there enters into the reckoning not only the grief of the father
at the loss of his son, but the tragic situation of the son himself
when he discovers that he has put himself out of his father's
house and forfeited his filial status. The story should be read
not as allegory but as an illustrative incident from ordinary
human life. Jewish wisdom counselled fathers against premature disposition of their property (Ecclesiasticus xxxiii. 19).
Therefore, if the father in this story consents to his son's wish,
and gives him his third (Deuteronomy xxi. 16–17), the human
fallibility of the material out of which the parable is constructed
is amply evidenced. The rest of the story, the boy's departure
to the far country—the hearers of Jesus would at once think of
Alexandria or Rome or other foreign metropolis with a Jewish
colony—and the subsequent stages of his collapse and ruin
would be sufficiently familiar. What the final stage of the
youth's misfortunes, when he has become swineherd to a Gentile
master, would signify to Jewish ears may be gauged from the
saying (*Baba Kama*, 82b), ' Cursed is the man who keepeth
swine.' Now comes the point of the story. Half-starved and
envying the swine their diet of carob-pods, the son comes to his
senses. While the motive which turns his thoughts homewards
is his misery, nevertheless conscience is alive. He feels that he
has sinned and forfeited the rank of son. But in proposing, when
he returns, to take a hired man's place, he does not know the
extent of his father's love. He is not prepared for the extraordinary demonstration of that love in ver. 20. All he can
utter at the moment is, ' I have sinned against heaven and before
you and do not deserve to be called your son.' So much needs
to be said, for apart from such confession of guilt the return of
the son is merely nominal. But the suggestion to take a hired
man's place is never spoken. It is crowded out by the father's

overwhelming eagerness to reinstate the lost one. ' Quick, bring the best robe and put it on him.' The son is clothed with the garment reserved for an honoured guest, he is given the ring and the sandals which are the badge not of slavery but of sonship, his return is celebrated by a feast. So by a touching incident from human life Jesus would illustrate the love of God towards sinners returning to Him, and defend his own attitude towards the lapsed among his nation who have lost their status as sons of God and whom he seeks to lead homewards to the Father. Do legalists contend that the wicked, having chosen their way, must take the consequences ? Jesus will remind them that the God who gave the Law says also, ' As I live, I take no pleasure in the death of the wicked, but that the wicked turn from his way and live ' (Ezekiel xxxiii. 11). The argument is from man to God. Will an earthly father, in the case of an erring lad, treat the past as though it had never been ? And will not God, to whom every penitent is a son who ' was dead and has come to life, was lost and is found ' ?

The second half of the story (vers. 25-32) introduces a seemingly new motive centring in the relation of the elder son to the prodigal. Scholars who take it as axiomatic that the parables of Jesus contain only a single motive are disposed to regard these verses as a later accretion to the story. But it may be well asked whether Jesus, speaking to Pharisees who discountenanced his mission to the lost, would have depicted the Prodigal's return without stigmatizing in some measure the unforgiving attitude of those whom he was specially addressing. For this reason the Elder Brother episode appears not an after-thought but an integral part of the original conception of the parable. The gloom and suspicion of the brother are necessary to throw into proper relief the father's joy at the wanderer's return. Moreover, so long as we restrict our attention to the purely human character of the illustration, no difficulties need occur. The elder son's resentment at being forgotten (vers. 25-28), his complaint that his years of upright service have gone unrecognized (ver. 29), his impatience at the prodigal being made the hero of the hour (ver. 30), are all features of a *human* situation in which the father has not been altogether free of blame. Yet even so—and here this section of the parable comes to a point— the father will entreat and expect the son to forget his own feelings in the joy of his brother's return. No considerations based on what is ordinarily just and normal, no legalism in fact, should repress the emotion of pity in an hour in which it can be said, ' your brother here was dead and has come to life again, he was lost but he has been found.'

So from the imperfect human love Jesus rises to the love of God. If an earthly father expects his elder son to forget all other feelings in the joy of a brother's return, how much more God ! The parable constitutes a double plea for Jesus' mission to the lost. (1) God Himself welcomes and forgives the repentant sinner, (2) God expects men to do the same. We exceed, however, the limits of what is intended if we make the parable an epitome of the whole gospel, or if from its omission of all reference to the cost of forgiveness we argue that the apostolic message, centring in the death of Christ, had no foundation in the teaching of Jesus. The measure of the gospel is constituted not by any one parable or word but by the sum-total of the aspects under which Jesus is revealed, and if these elsewhere include the sense of a redeeming or expiatory purpose to be effected by the sufferings and death of the Messiah, the parable of the Lost Son, perfect illustration as it is of the joy of God over a sinner's repentance, is not to be pressed to the exclusion of that conception.

xvi. 1–9 : PARABLE OF THE DISHONEST FACTOR

xvi.

He also said to the disciples : ' There was a rich man who had a 1 factor, and this factor, he found, was accused of misapplying his property. So he summoned him and said, "What is this 2 I hear about you ? Hand in your accounts ; you cannot be factor any longer." The factor said to himself, "What am 3 I to do, now that my master is taking the factorship away from me ? I am too weak to dig, I am ashamed to beg. Ah, 4 I know what I will do, so that people will welcome me to their houses when I am deposed from the factorship." So 5 he summoned every single one of his master's debtors. He asked the first, "How much are you owing to my master ? " 6 "A hundred barrels of oil," he said. The factor told him, "Here is your bill ; sit down at once and enter fifty barrels." Then he asked another, "And how much do you owe ? " 7 "A hundred quarters of wheat," he said. "Here is your

8 bill," said the factor, " just enter eighty." Well, the master praised the dishonest factor for looking ahead ; for the children of this world look further ahead in dealing with

9 their own generation than the children of Light. And I tell you, use mammon, dishonest as it is, to make friends for yourselves, so that when you die they may welcome you to the eternal abodes.'

(Luke alone.)

As chap. xv. consists of three parables united by the single motive of defending the mission of Jesus to the outcasts of Israel, so chap. xvi. brings together a group of parables and sayings about the uses of wealth, particularly in relation to the winning or losing of eternal life. The first, the parable of the Dishonest Factor, is introduced by the statement, He also said to his disciples. This would suggest that, in Luke's understanding of it, the parable has to do with the stewardship or ministry (xii. 41–46) which the apostles have received from Christ, though, if we conceive the Pharisees to be present, as they are in chap. xv. and again in xvi. 14–31, the parable will have a less restricted range of appeal. The story itself need not be an *ad hoc* creation of Christ. Some actual incident which was known to the hearers may have provided a basis. In that case the interest will lie not at all in the minor details of the story but in the use to which Jesus puts it.

 Allegorizing methods must in any case be strictly avoided. The rich man who had a factor does not stand for God or for Satan or for anyone except himself. His factor, in turn, is merely a clever and unscrupulous man of the world who, fore-seeing his dismissal from office because of incompetence, and rejecting as impossible the alternatives of manual labour or dependence on charity, contrives adroitly to put his master's debtors under a lasting obligation to himself. Summoning a meeting of these debtors—who may be thought of either as tenants on the estate who have guaranteed the surrender annually of a certain proportion of their wheat and olives, or as purchasers of produce from the manor who have given the factor in lieu of money a bill payable at some future date—he hands back to them the various bills, authorizes the debtors to reduce the figures, and having by this trick pleased and obliged them looks forward to receiving favours at their hands. They

' will welcome me to their houses,' he says, ' when I am deposed.'

So far, all is simple. But now comes ver. 8 : ' the master praised the dishonest factor for looking ahead.' If this is part of the original parable, the ' master ' will be the factor's employer who, despite the audacious immorality of his employee's transaction, cannot but congratulate him on his cleverness. In that case ver. 9 will give the lesson which Jesus drew from the incident, viz. that the disciples ought, *exceptis excipiendis*, to take a lesson from the steward with regard to their own spiritual and eternal interests.

But even if this explanation of the first half of ver. 8 be accepted, some difficulty will still attach to the saying that ' the children of this world look further ahead,' etc. This, by limiting the shrewdness of the worldly-wise to the strictly mundane sphere in which they are ' dealing with their own generation,' introduces into the discussion a spiritual criterion of values which is scarcely in place on the employer's lips. Doubtless with the omission of the limiting clause the words might pass as the employer's. The latter might well observe that rascals like his factor might teach wisdom to the saints. On the other hand, is it possible that the ' master ' in ver. 8 is Jesus ? The story told by Jesus would in that case be limited to vers. 1–7, and the words ' the master praised ' would state that our Lord, isolating from the rest of the story the one quality of the factor's wisdom in looking to the future, held this up as an example to the children of light, i.e. to the Jews who possessed the knowledge of eternal things or to the disciples who had received a special revelation through himself. Here was a man of the world whose fortunes were tottering to a fall. What zeal, what foresight he shewed to ensure an earthly future, a hearth at which to sit down when his day was done ! Should not the children of Light shew an equal foresight with regard to more important things ? But if ver. 8a referred to Jesus, we should expect Luke to have begun ver. 8b in a different way, by the insertion of some such phrase as ' And he said ' or ' He said therefore.'

Does ver. 9, ' I tell you, use mammon,' etc., belong to the original parable, and does it convey the real message which Jesus left with his hearers ? Some scholars have denied this, arguing that this verse allegorizes the parable and unduly narrows the broader application adumbrated in ver. 8. The point is not an easy one to decide, for the L tradition which Luke here follows shews elsewhere a peculiar interest in Jesus' teaching about ' unrighteous mammon ' (xii. 33–34, xvi. 11–12, 19–31), and may have allegorized the parable under the influence of that teaching. But since Mark and Q as well as L represent Jesus as calling his disciples to renounce possessions and give to the poor (Mark x. 21, 23–27, 28 ; Luke xvi. 13), the possibility that he spoke the present parable to enforce that lesson is not to be excluded. ' Mammon ' is an Aramaic expression, literally signifying ' entrusted thing,' and used in a semi-personified sense to indicate money or wealth. The addition, ' dishonest as it is,' implies not that the money in question is ill-gotten but that money ordinarily plays a sinister part in life. It belongs to the present world, which is evil, and for the disciples of Jesus it denotes something alien, something which is not really theirs, and which they must exchange for value of another kind. The suggestion, ' make friends for yourselves,' means ' give the money to the poor.' It is sometimes objected that, as the disciples cannot have possessed much money, we should ignore ver. 1, and regard the parable as originally directed to rich converts like Zacchaeus (xix. 8). But in xii. 33 the disciples appear in possession of some kind of property. Hence there is no impossibility in supposing that here also Jesus called them to give their goods to the poor, ' that when you die '—another reading is, ' when it (i.e. mammon) fails '—' they may welcome you to the eternal abodes.' This probably means, ' that after death the poor whom you have helped may be your advocates with God.' But as the impersonal third plural is often on Jewish lips a mode of reference to God (cf. xii. 20), the meaning may simply be, ' that God may welcome you.' For the ' eternal dwellings ' of the righteous compare xvi. 22, 25, John xiv. 2, Enoch xxxix. 4–5.

xvi. 10–13 : Faithfulness in the Use of Money

10 ' He who is faithful with a trifle is also faithful with a large trust,

and he who is dishonest with a trifle is also dishonest with a large trust.

11 So, if you are not faithful with dishonest mammon, how can you ever be trusted with true Riches ?

And if you are not faithful with what belongs to another, 12
how can you ever be given what is your own ?
No servant can serve two masters :   13
  either he will hate the one and love the other,
  or else he will stand by the one and despise the other—
  you cannot serve both God and Mammon.'

(Vers. 10-12, Luke alone.)

The parable of the Dishonest Factor has attracted to itself in
Luke's source a catena of sayings bearing on faithfulness in
positions of trust, which serve in the present context to
counteract false conclusions from the commendation bestowed
in that parable on the Factor. In ver. 10 a proper conscientious-
ness in minor matters of trust is made the one condition of larger
responsibility (compare xix. 26). Character is a unity, and
he alone 'who is faithful with a trifle is also faithful with a
large trust.' In ver. 11 the principle is applied to the use of
'dishonest mammon' (xvi. 9) in comparison with 'true Riches.'
The conscientious employment of the former is a necessary
preliminary to being entrusted with the latter, which in turn
signifies a sharing in the blessedness, consisting in sonship to
God, which is Jesus' peculiar possession and gift to men (cf. xii.
22-34). In ver. 12 money appears as that which 'belongs to
another,' i.e. it is in no sense a Christian's property, and is
contrasted in the above sense with that which is 'your own.'
Some authorities read 'our own' or 'my own' in place of
'your own,' but these alternatives are unlikely to be right,
not being in the usual manner of Jesus. All three sayings
presuppose that until the followers of Christ have settled the
question of earthly possessions in the way which he requires,
i.e. by divesting themselves completely of mammon in
accordance with xvi. 9, nothing further can be done. Sacrifice
of earthly possessions is the one means by which disciples can
appropriate the Kingdom of God ; see on xii. 32-34. Ver. 13,
'No servant can serve two masters,' which is from Q (cf. Matthew
vi. 24), is to be taken literally. A man may divide his time
between two duties, but he cannot divide his soul or his affections.
'You cannot serve,' i.e. be the absolute property or slave of,
'both God and mammon.' The intensity of the moral passion
of Jesus comes out in the antitheses 'hate—love,' 'stand by
—despise.' For Jesus there is no *via media*.

xvi. 14–15 : Pharisaic Righteousness Impugned

14 Now the Pharisees who were fond of money heard all this, and
15   they sneered at him.   So he told them, ' You are the people
    who get men to think you are good, but God knows
    what your hearts are ! What is lofty in the view of man
    is loathsome in the eyes of God.'

(Luke alone.)

The statement that ' the Pharisees heard all this ' implies
that they were present when the above parable and its
application were spoken, and the indictment which now follows
starts, in the present context, from the principle laid down in
ver. 13 that God and mammon cannot be conjoined. The
Pharisees, it is implied, have tried to reconcile a religious
profession with an avaricious spirit, and have in consequence
fallen to mammon. That the Pharisees were fond of money
is vehemently denied by Jewish scholars, but it is scarcely
likely that so highly influential and dominant a caste was
immune from the temptation to over-estimate prosperity, and
to construe it as a sign of God's acceptance of their works.
Jesus rejects this criterion and the popular applause which it
evoked. ' You are the people who get men to think you are
good, but '—here the hollowness of a profession which sanctioned
greed comes to the front—' God knows what your hearts are '
(cf. 1 Samuel xvi. 7, Psalm cxxxix). It is assumed, here as
elsewhere, that the popular verdict and God's fall apart.

xvi. 16–18: The Law and the Gospel

16 ' The Law and the prophets lasted till John ; since then the
    good news of the Realm of God is preached, and anyone
17   presses in. Yet it is easier for heaven and earth to pass
    away than for an iota of the Law to lapse.
18   Anyone who divorces his wife and marries another
        woman commits adultery,
      and he who marries a divorced woman commits adultery.'

(Cf. Matthew xi. 12–13, v. 18, 32.)

The sayings in this section are abruptly introduced, and
exhibit at first sight only a minimum of interconnexion. Any

formal relationship which they possess comes merely of their all in some measure referring to the Law, or more properly, to the connexion between the Law and the gospel, and this must have been the motive which led to their being con-catenated in the original Q source, the bare bedrock of which here crops with unusual clearness to the surface. Luke, if he did not find this Q material already tacked on to ver. 15 in some document which he followed, must have effected the connexion himself because the sayings illustrated the criticism which in verse 15 is passed on the Pharisees. The point is that the teaching of Jesus, while it confirms the Law, makes a still higher demand.

The Matthew-parallels to the three sayings may here be presented :

Ver. 16, Matthew xi. 12–13 : ' From the days of John the Baptist till now the Realm of heaven suffers violence, and the violent press into it. For all the prophets and the Law prophesied of it until John.'

Cf. Matthew v. 17 : ' Do not imagine I have come to destroy the Law or the prophets ; I have not come to destroy but to fulfil.'

Ver. 17, Matthew v. 18 : ' Till heaven and earth pass away, not an iota, not a comma, will pass from the Law till it is all in force.'

Ver. 18, Matthew v. 32 : ' Anyone who divorces his wife (for any reason except unchastity) makes her an adulteress : and whoever marries a divorced woman commits adultery.'

The first saying in Luke, ' The Law and the prophets lasted until John,' reveals Jesus' consciousness that through the revelation made to him a new era has dawned. ' The good news of the Realm of God is preached,' i.e. men are invited to enter upon the realization of everything of which the Law and the prophets had spoken (cf. x. 23–24), and this proclamation, whether or not it already implies the complete fulfilment of the kingdom of God, definitively marks the final stage in the history of redemption (cf. vii. 28). The gate of redemption has been thrown open, ' and anyone presses in ' (cf. Matthew xxi. 31). The latter statement, which proves the authority of Christ's message by its spontaneous results in life and character, indirectly reproaches the Pharisees for still standing aloof. Luke, or his source, has here simplified a saying which in

Matthew xi. 12–13 occurs in the much more difficult form :
' The Realm of heaven suffers violence,' etc., a statement which
may possibly allude to the misguided zeal of contemporaries
who, stimulated by John the Baptist's preaching (Matthew iii. 2),
wish to bring in the Kingdom of God by armed force instead of
by non-resistance, loving enemies, and waiting patiently upon
God's good time and pleasure (cf. xii. 32).

The second saying, ' **Yet it is easier for heaven and earth to
pass away than for one iota of the Law to lapse,** concedes the
eternity of the Law, and in this context means that the new
revelation which Jesus brings is not to be construed as sub-
versive of it. The saying occurs in Matthew v. 18, and is
historically supported by Jesus' practice of never setting aside
any article of the Law except upon a ground discovered within
the Law itself. Jesus did indeed, as we shall see by the next
saying, abrogate certain permissions of the Law as merely
temporary, but in these cases he grounded his action upon the
express will of God as elsewhere declared in the same Law.
In view, however, of the scribal objection that, since every part
of the Law was equally divine, no one part might be removed
in favour of another, we can only take the saying to mean
that Jesus, where he seems to rescind a principle, is conscious
thereby only of giving fuller and more absolute expression to
the will of God. He is himself the judge of what the Lord desires.

The third saying shews by an illustration how the gospel
reaches above and beyond the Law. The Law permitted a
husband to divorce his wife under specified circumstances
(Deuteronomy xxiv. 1 f.), and this permission, originally intended
to curb the irregular practices of an earlier day, was mistaken
by the scribes for a positive ordinance of God. Jesus rejects
this interpretation (Mark x. 2–12), and declares the Deutero-
nomic law was to be a concession to the ' hard-heartedness ' of
the age to which it was given. Marriage is indissoluble if regard
is had to the original law of God in Genesis ii. 24. Consequently,
' **Anyone who divorces his wife and marries another woman
commits adultery,**' because by the will of God the man is still
joined to his first wife, and if he remarries he violates that bond.
Similarly, ' **he who marries a divorced woman commits adultery** '
because the woman is still bound by the law of God to her
first husband. Ver. 18a corresponds to Mark x. 11 ; ver. 18b
to Matthew v. 32b. On the exceptive clause in Matthew

see Dr. T. H. Robinson's *Matthew* (Moffatt Commentary), pp. 158 f. Jesus is not laying down a principle of civil law for ordinary society, but ' stating how the righteous should act ' (Easton). In God's ideal for men divorce has no place at all. Some scholars have supposed that the saying is in this context allegorical, referring to the inseparability of the Law and the gospel. But this is far-fetched.

xvi. 19–31 : The Rich Man and Lazarus

' There was a rich man, clad in purple and fine linen, who lived 19 sumptuously every day. Outside his door lay a poor man 20 called Lazarus ; he was a mass of ulcers, and fain to eat 21 up the crumbs that fell from the rich man's table. (The very dogs used to come and lick his ulcers.) Now it hap- 22 pened that the poor man died, and he was carried by the angels to Abraham's bosom. The rich man died too, and was buried. And as he was being tortured in Hades he raised 23 his eyes and saw Abraham far away with Lazarus in his bosom ; so he called out, " Father Abraham, take pity on me, 24 send Lazarus to dip his fingertip in water and cool my tongue, for I am in anguish in these flames." But Abraham said, 25 " Remember, my son, you got all the bliss when you were alive, just as Lazarus got the ills of life ; he is in comfort now, and you are in anguish. Besides all that, a great gulf 26 yawns between us and you, to keep back those who want to cross from us to you and also those who want to pass from you to us." Then he said, " Well, father, I beg you to 27 send him to my father's house, for I have five brothers ; let 28 him bear testimony to them, that they may not come to this place of torture as well." " They have got Moses and the 29 prophets," said Abraham, " they can listen to them." " No, 30 father Abraham," he said, " but if someone only goes to them from the dead, they will repent." He said to him, 31 " If they will not listen to Moses and the prophets, they will not be convinced, not even if one rose from the dead."

(Luke alone.)

The parable, both by its position and by its moral, seems to point back to xvi. 9 and to illustrate from the negative side the

principle ' Use mammon to make friends for yourselves.' The
' rich man' is condemned to Gehenna not because of other sins, nor
because being rich is in itself a crime, but because he has neglected
' a poor man called Lazarus outside his door,' thereby losing for
ever an entrance into the ' everlasting habitations ' of the
righteous. Some weight, however, is due to the opinion that in
Luke's Judean source the parable connected not with xvi. 1–9
but with xvi. 15, ' What is lofty in the view of man is loathsome
in the eyes of God.' So understood, the parable taught not a
warning against the selfish use of riches, but the reversal of
earthly conditions at the Judgment and in the future life. The
rich man got all the bliss of life while here ; Lazarus got all the
ills ; but the future life readjusts the disparity. It is possible,
however, that while the parable bore this sense in the source,
Luke has reasserted the original meaning of Jesus. Jesus
does not seem to have proclaimed the reversal of earthly conditions for its own sake, but he certainly condemned selfishness
and championed the cause of the poor.

The story would not seem to have been invented *ad hoc*
by Jesus. There are parallels in Rabbinical literature, and
Professor Gressmann has sought to trace these to an Egyptian
source, represented by the tale of Si-Usire, which relates, on the
evidence of one who had been admitted to the secrets of the
after-life, how a poor man of Memphis who had been buried
without honour was seen clothed in royal linen by the side
of Osiris, while a rich man who had received sumptuous burial
on earth was carried off to Hades. The parable therefore takes
up a familiar theme, but Gressmann considers that the second
half (vers. 27–31) is due to Jesus alone, who will not allow the
reality of the after-life to depend on spiritualistic evidence or
indeed on anything except the clear recognition by conscience
of the ethical demands made by the Law and the prophets.

The story is simple, and in the main calls for little comment.
From the scene on earth, where the rich man lives in luxury,
while poor Lazarus (i.e. Eleazar, ' God helps ') lies at his gate
untended and unhelped, we are transported in ver. 22 to the
world beyond the grave. The poor man, his sorrows ended,
is ' carried by angels to Abraham's bosom,' i.e. to a place by
Abraham's side in that part of Sheol or Hades which is called
Paradise. But while he feasts there with the patriarchs (cf.
xiii. 28–30) the rich man, who has been given ceremonious

burial on earth, descends to that part of the same Hades which is appointed for the punishment of the wicked and is called Gehenna (cf. xii. 5). The description of the two spheres of Paradise and Gehenna is traditional. Compare Enoch xxii. 8-13, where the seer, who asks, ' Why is one separated from the other ? ' receives as answer—' This division has been made for the spirits of the righteous. . . . And this has been made for sinners when they die and are buried in the earth, and judgment has not been executed upon them in their lifetime. Here their spirits shall be set apart in this great pain till the great day of judgment and punishment and torment,' etc. (Charles). Compare also 2 Esdras vii. 36, ' And then shall the pit of torment appear, and over against it the place of refreshment. The furnace of Gehenna shall be made manifest, and over against it the Paradise of delight ' (Box). While Enoch, however, depicts an intermediate state of existence between death and the Judgment, the present parable represents the fate of the two spirits as finally sealed. Vers. 23-25 bring out the complete reversal of relations which has come about in the after-life, and the irrevocableness of the award of God. Abraham reminds the rich man, who has appealed to him as father of the chosen race : ' Remember, you got all the bliss when you were alive, just as Lazarus got the ills.' An unbridgeable gulf now separates the two spheres in which they exist, though they lie within sight of each other or, as Judaism says, only a handbreadth apart.

It is probable that with ver. 26 the traditional *motif* of the parable comes to an end. What follows gives the moral lesson which Jesus would impart. Addressing himself to the query, ' Why then, if the issues of life are so inexorable, does no one come back from the dead to give us warning ? ' he answers that the moral truths spoken to Israel by ' Moses and the prophets ' contain ample evidence of the finality of life's issues and of the character of God's awards. If men will not listen to the Scriptures, ' they will not be convinced, not even if one rose from the dead.' By the fact of the parable being brought to a climax in this application, the impression that Jesus teaches a mere reversal of earthly fortunes is averted. The fate of the rich man and Lazarus secures a moral explanation. The former is condemned for his refusal to shew mercy and justice ; the latter is saved by his righteousness. It is possible that to Luke ver. 31 had the further significance of suggesting that, if the Jews had really listened to Moses and the prophets, they would not have denied the Resurrection of Christ (compare John v. 39–47).

xvii. 1–4 : On Stumbling-blocks and Forgiveness

xvii.

1 To his disciples he said, ' It is inevitable that hindrances should come, but woe to the man by whom they come ; it would
2 be well for him to have a millstone hung round his neck and be flung into the sea, rather than prove a hindrance to
3 one of these little ones ! Take heed to yourselves. If your brother sins, check him, and if he repents forgive him.
4 Even if he sins against you seven times in one day and turns to you seven times saying, " I repent," you must forgive him.'

(Cf. Matthew xviii. 6–7, 15, 21–22.)

It is uncertain under what circumstances Jesus would utter the warning in vers. 1–2. The opening sentence, which stands in Luke alone, states that ' hindrances ' or ' stumbling-blocks '— the word is frequent in the Bible for what misleads or subverts or causes anyone to sin—are in the nature of things unpreventable, but this does not excuse the witting or unwitting authors of such offences. But who are 'these little ones !' whose innocence Jesus espouses in ver. 2, and under what circumstances does he think of them as being injured? As the warning is addressed to his disciples, the ' little ones ' can hardly be identical with these disciples. On the other hand, the parallel sayings in Matthew xviii. 6 and in Mark ix. 42 identify the little ones with those who ' believe.' Under these circumstances we must suppose our Lord to be warning the Twelve against the doing of anything that would injure the souls of their humbler brethren in the faith, and we may conclude the ' hindrances ' to be occasioned by such faults as ambition (cf. ix. 46–48), intolerance (cf. ix. 49–50), negligence (cf. xii. 36–37), or tyrannousness (cf. xii. 45–46). Accordingly, Jesus says to the Twelve, ' Take heed to yourselves,' and a special case illustrating the need of self-scrutiny is cited, viz. ' if your brother sins.' In such a situation the ' stumbling-block ' offered to the weaker brother may take the form either of not pointing out to him the consequences of his sin or of refusing pardon when the fault is confessed. Either course involves serious dangers to the soul of the erring brother, and rather than that a repentant soul should be discouraged Jesus urges a boundless forgiveness. ' If he sins against you seven times in one day '—the Matthew-parallel has ' seventy times seven ' or (some authorities) ' seventy seven times,' reversing Lamech's song of revenge in Genesis iv. 24—' and turns to you seven times saying, I repent, you must forgive him ' (see next section). In Matthew xviii. the demands in this section have become the nucleus of an elaborate code of ecclesiastical discipline.

xvii. 5–10 : THE NATURE OF FAITH

The apostles said to the Lord, ' Give us more faith ! ' The Lord 5 said, ' If you had faith the size of a grain of mustard-seed, 6 you would say to this mulberry tree, " Be uprooted and planted in the sea," and it would obey you. Which of you, 7 with a servant out ploughing or shepherding, will say to him when he comes in from the field, " Come at once and take your place at table ? " Will the man not rather say to him, 8 " Get something ready for my supper ; gird yourself and wait on me till I eat and drink ; then you can eat and drink yourself " ? Does he thank the servant for doing his bidding ? 9 Well, it is the same with you ; when you have done all you 10 are bidden, say, " We are but servants ; we have only done our duty." '

(Luke alone, but for ver. 6 cf. Matthew xvii. 20.)

The connecting-link between this section and the preceding lies in the greatness of Jesus' demand in xvii. 4. The requirement of a forgivingness which knows no limit seems to the apostles impracticable, and they indicate their doubt by saying, ' Give us more faith ! ' Jesus' answer is to repel altogether this idea of the less and more as applied to the nature of faith. Faith is something which, if it exist at all in the true sense, will make any moral duty possible, and an illustration is taken which obviously is to be symbolically understood. ' If you had faith the size of a grain of mustard-seed ' (cf. xiii. 19), ' you would say

o 193

to this mulberry tree,' etc.   The Q parallel in Matthew xvii. 20
has ' hill ' in place of mulberry tree (*morus nigra*), and so also the
other tradition in Mark xi. 23, ' Have faith in God.   I tell you
truly, whoever says to this hill, " Take and throw yourself into
the sea," and . . . believes that what he says will happen, he
will have it done.'   In Mark the hill is the Mount of Olives, on
which Jesus and his disciples are standing, and the words recall
the prophecy (Zechariah xiv. 4) that, when God judges Jerusalem,
' His feet shall stand upon the Mount of Olives . . . and the
Mount of Olives shall be cleft . . . and half of the mountain shall
remove toward the north, and half of it toward the south, etc.'
If this prophecy, applied to the last times, underlies the saying
in Mark, it strengthens the presumption that ' hill ' was the word
used by Jesus.   Luke's variant ' mulberry tree ' will be due to
reminiscence possibly of the cursing of the fig-tree in Mark xi.
12–14, 20–21.   The Zechariah-prophecy further suggests that
what Jesus meant was that real faith, if the disciples possessed
it even in the least degree, would bring in the glories of the
Messianic time.   In place of balking at the forgiveness required
in ver. 4, disciples would find that ' all things are possible to
him who believes.'

Did Jesus originally aim this word at the unforgivingness of
the Jews to the Romans ?   Did he mean that such unforgivingness was retarding the Kingdom of God ?

The illustration, ' Which of you with a servant out ploughing,'
etc., follows without other announcement, and therefore Luke
probably took it to justify the demand of Jesus for a faith
adequate to any task.   The slave-ploughman or shepherd—
he is presumably his master's only ' hand '—does not expect
when he returns from the field to be seated at table and waited
upon by his employer.   He prepares his master's supper before
taking his own, and expects no special gratitude for doing what
he is bound by his position to do.   So with disciples of Christ.
' When you have done all you are bidden, say, We are but servants '—almost all authorities read ' useless servants,' but the
adjective weakens the sense, and is probably a glossing addition
—' we have only done our duty.'   If a connexion exists between
this teaching and vers. 5–6 above, it may be stated thus : Faith
such as Jesus asks of the disciples is a duty which they owe
simpliciter to God.   It is commanded, and there is nothing more
to be said.

But while Luke, or his source, gives the parable this bearing its relevance to the subject of faith is not very clear. Is it not possible that Jesus had in view the legalists of his day, the type of Pharisee whom Dr. Klausner, quoting a Jewish tradition, calls the ' What-is-my-obligation-and-I-will-do-it ' Pharisee (*Jesus of Nazareth*, p. 214) ? Many of Jesus' contemporaries thought to put God in their debt by a meritorious obedience. The best Rabbinical tradition indeed opposed such ideas : compare *Aboth* ii. 9, ' If thou hast practised much Torah, claim not merit to thyself, for thereunto wast thou created ' (Taylor). But, as Mr. Montefiore admits, the excessive emphasis on rewards remained a weak spot in Rabbinical Judaism (*Synoptic Gospels*, vol. i, p. 543). If we take the parable to have been originally aimed against the reward-seeking type of Pharisee (cf. xviii. 11–12), it mitigates the seeming harshness with which the servant is treated, and the lesson will be : ' Whatsoever good a man does, he cannot do more than he owes to God.'

xvii. 11–19 : THE TEN LEPERS

Now it happened in the course of his journey to Jerusalem that 11 he passed between Samaria and Galilee. On entering one 12 village he was met by ten lepers who stood at a distance and lifted up their voice, saying, ' Jesus, master, have pity on 13 us.' Noticing them he said, ' Go and *show yourselves to* 14 *the priests.*' And as they went away they were cleansed. Now one of them turned back when he saw he was cured, 15 glorifying God with a loud voice ; and he fell on his face at 16 the feet of Jesus and thanked him. The man was a Samari- tan. So Jesus said, ' Were all the ten not cleansed ? Where 17 are the other nine ? Was there no one to return and give 18 glory to God except this foreigner ? ' And he said to him, ' Get up and go, your faith has made you well.' 19

(Luke alone.)

The statement that Jesus was passing between Samaria and Galilee explains how a Samaritan is found among the lepers who now supplicate for healing. Here, in contrast with v. 12, there is no breaking of bounds. The lepers preserve their distance (Leviticus xiii. 45 f.), and attract the notice of Jesus merely by their cry. Hence Jesus does not in this case heal by touch, but signifies his assent to the request of the suppliants by saying, ' Go and show yourselves to the priests,' which in the case of the nine Jews would mean a visit to the Temple at Jerusalem, since only after sacrificial rites could the declaration of cleanness be pronounced (Leviticus xiv. 1–8, etc.). What formalities were requisite in the case of the Samaritan is not indicated. The healing of the lepers takes place as they went, i.e. it becomes operative through faith in Jesus' word. The sequel, in which lies the special interest of the narrative, turns on the fact that only one of the ten, a Samaritan, gives thanks to Jesus for the healing which he has received. The response of Jesus, contrasting the gratitude of this foreigner with the forgetfulness of the nine Jews, creates some difficulty for the expositor. Why does Jesus regret the departure of the nine when he has himself sent them to Jerusalem ? And what special grace is conferred on the Samaritan by his word, ' Your faith has made you well ' ? Possibly Jesus, in acclaiming the gratitude of the Samaritan, did not originally so sharply contrast it with the defaulting conduct of the others. The only alternative to this view is to suppose—somewhat arbitrarily, it must be confessed—that in the original tradition of the incident only the Samaritan was healed. The others did not shew the necessary faith.

xvii. 20–21 : THE KINGDOM IN THE MIDST

20 On being asked by the Pharisees when the Reign of God was coming, he answered them, ' The Reign of God is not coming
21 as you hope to catch sight of it ; no one will say, " Here it is " or " There it is," for the Reign of God is now in your midst.'

(Luke alone.)

The Pharisaic demand to know when the Reign of God was coming signifies less a desire to be enlightened than a covert rejection of the kind of evidence on which Jesus had consistently grounded the immediate nearness of the divine salvation. In effect the question is a challenge and a taunt. The Pharisees see no immediate sign of that divine event which Jesus declares to be at hand. Jesus' answer is that his questioners look for proofs in every direction except the right one. ' **The Reign of God is not coming as you hope to catch sight of it.'** The Pharisees expect external signs—the Greek suggests the quest of astronomical or other evidence—by which the nearness of the End may be computed. Such methods of divination were fostered by apocalyptic literature and would be familiar to Jesus' hearers. Jesus on the other hand declares that such evidence will be for ever lacking. ' **No one will say " Here it is " or " There it is," '** for all this signifies a looking away from the fact that ' **the Reign of God is in your midst.'**

The last statement is difficult, and has given rise to conflicting interpretations. (1) It is usually taken as an assertion of the inward or spiritual character of the Kingdom. The Kingdom becomes real for the individual only by the rebirth of himself. It exists solely within the hearts of men. But while our Lord makes the individual's entrance on the Kingdom conditional upon a new birth, this cannot be his meaning here, since he would scarcely say that the Pharisees were reborn. (2) Those who hold that Jesus always and everywhere spoke of the Kingdom in a future, apocalyptic sense, understand him to say here : ' It is vain to look for signs in the sun, moon, and stars, since suddenly and without warning, in the twinkling of an eye, the New Age will appear among you.' But this interpretation forces an unnatural sense upon the words. If Jesus were understood to have meant this, his reporters would surely have employed less ambiguous language. (3) The right interpretation, as the present writer considers, connects the saying with the ' mystery ' or revelation which Jesus has received, and which he declares to men. Jesus is conscious of possessing the secret of salvation, and he and his disciples therefore constitute the present and sufficient ' sign ' of the nearness of the Reign of God. To look past this evidence and to centre attention elsewhere is to miss the object of the quest. The Pharisees will find salvation in the message of Jesus—or they will not find it at all ! The word is a ' parable ' from which the hearers are left to draw their own conclusion.

xvii. 22-37 : THE COMING OF THE SON OF MAN

To his disciples he said, ' There will come days when you will long 22 and long in vain to have even one day of the Son of man.

23   Men will say, " See, here he is ! " " See, there he is ! "
but do not go out or run after them,

24   for like lightning that flashes from one side of the sky
to the other,
so will the Son of man be on his own day.

25   But he must first endure great suffering and be rejected by

26   the present generation. And just as it was in the days of

27   Noah, so will it be in the days of the Son of man ; they were
eating, drinking, marrying and being married, till the day
Noah entered the ark—then came the deluge and destroyed

28   them all. Or just as it was in the days of Lot ; they were

29   eating, drinking, buying, selling, planting and building, but
on the day that Lot left Sodom *it rained fire and brimstone*

30   *from heaven* and destroyed them all.   So will it be on the day

31   the Son of man is revealed. On that day, if a man is on
the housetop and his goods inside the house, he must not go

32   down to fetch them out ; nor must a man in the field *turn
back* (remember Lot's wife).

33   Whoever tries to secure his life will lose it,
and whoever loses it will preserve it.

34   On that night, I tell you,
there will be two men in the one bed,
the one will be taken and the other left ;

35   two women will be grinding together,
the one will be taken and the other left.'

37   They asked him, ' Where, Lord ? '
And he said to them,
' Where the body is lying,
there the vultures will gather.'
(Cf. Matthew xxiv. 26–28, 37–41.)

This section, which is from Q, forms practically the last
citation made by Luke from that document. Apparently the
Q source ended, as we should expect, with predictions of the
Coming of the Son of man. As Luke places it, the section indicates that what was thrown out in a ' parable ' in vers. 20–21 above,
was afterwards ' interpreted ' by Jesus to his disciples. Thus
ver. 22 corresponds with 20, and 23 with 21. But it is impossible
to suppose that the present section is really an interpretation of
the oracle in vers. 20–21. The latter expressly excludes the
thought of any visible sign of the Reign of God being given.

Ver. 24 concedes one. Possibly therefore in ver. 24 the Christian tradition is affected by apocalyptic ideas which it was the purpose of Jesus to discourage.

Ver. 22 indicates a situation in which the disciples, after the death of the Master, will under stress of trial or persecution wish to anticipate the Messiah's return. ' You will long to have even one day of the Son of man ' implies not a desire to summon back the days when Jesus was on earth, but a strained and anxious waiting for the glories of the final period (ix. 27). Under the influence of this mood the disciples will be hypersensitive to rumours, arising locally, that the Messiah has appeared or that the Messianic age has begun. Portents of local origin will be appealed to, and the cry will be raised, ' See, here he is ! See, there he is ! ' The disciples are to be on their guard against such delusions. The coming of the Son of man, though it will occur in the present generation (ix. 27), cannot be hastened, nor will it be local or indistinct in its manifestation but universal and unmistakable, like the lightning-flash which illumines the sky from horizon to horizon. On the point of these warnings see further under xxi. 7-19.

In vers. 26-35 Christians are warned to be ready, since ' the day the Son of man is revealed ' will put the final seal on the destinies of all upon whom it comes. Examples of unpreparedness are cited from the world's condition at the Deluge (vers. 26-27) and from the fate of Sodom in the time of Lot (vers. 28-29). For a parallel warning see 1 Thessalonians v. 1-10. Vers. 31-32 assert afresh the suddenness and inexorableness of the Judgment to be exercised by the Son of man, and the tragedy of Lot's wife is recalled. But these verses in their present form seem ill adapted to the context. The Judgment Day, which will be universal and instantaneous (ver. 24), will leave no time to anyone to think of salving his effects, and therefore it is possible that the saying, ' if a man is on the housetop . . . he must not go down,' referred originally not to the Last Day itself but to perilous times accompanying the destruction of Jerusalem, when it might still seem possible to secure one's earthly belongings (Mark xiii. 14-16). The closing verses obviously refer in their present context to the Judgment Day. Even the closest friends will be separated (vers. 34-35), some to everlasting life, and some to everlasting shame and punishment. The Judgment takes place at night, and therefore the Women at the Mill must be thought of as working after sundown. The inexorableness of the moral issues of life could not be more vividly expressed. The question in ver. 37, asking to know *where* friends will be thus separated, receives as answer that the moral nature of every situation will draw to it the appropriate reward or doom. Like vultures from carrion, judgment is inseparable from the body of sin and death. Some have made the ingenious suggestion that the reference is to the Roman eagles—the insignia of the legions—swooping down on Jerusalem. This would consort with other evidence that Jesus thought of Rome as the predestined executor of the divine justice. But a saying in itself proverbial need not have acquired this special metaphorical significance.

xviii. 1–8 : Parable of the Unjust Judge

xviii.

1 He also told them a parable about the need of always praying
2 and never losing heart. ' In a certain town,' he said,
' there was a judge who had no reverence for God and no
3 respect even for man. And in that town there was a widow
who used to go and appeal to him for " Justice against my
4 opponent ! " For a while he would not, but afterwards
he said to himself, " Though I have no reverence for God
5 and no respect even for man, still, as this widow is bothering
me, I will see justice done to her—not to have her for ever
6 coming and pestering me." Listen,' said the Lord, ' to
7 what this unjust judge says ! And will not God see justice
8 done to his elect who cry to him by day and night ? Will
he be tolerant to their opponents ? I tell you, he will quickly
see justice done to his elect ! And yet, when the Son
of man does come, will he find faith on earth ? '

(Luke alone.)

This little parable has no connexion with the foregoing sections except for the allusion in its concluding verse to the Coming of the Son of man. The lesson inculcated is the need of always praying and never losing heart, a principle applicable to all times, but possessing a special relevance for days such as those to which the disciples were now going forward (xvii. 22), days of ardent longing for their absent Lord's return (vers. 7–8). The story itself needs little commentary. In shewing that a profitable lesson may be drawn from the conduct of a dubious and discreditable character, such as the unjust judge, the parable resembles that of the Dishonest Factor in xvi. 1-7, with which it also agrees in the obvious humour with which it is related.

The centre of interest lies in the application given to the story in vers. 7-8. ' Will not God see justice done to his elect ? ' i.e. to the suffering Church which longs to be saved from its oppressors ? Prayer for final deliverance at the Coming of the Son of man will not go unanswered. The words ' Will he be tolerant to their opponents ? ' are in the original ambiguous. The Greek might be rendered in any of the three following ways : (1) as a statement—' though he keeps them (i.e. his elect) waiting ' ; (2) as a question relating to the elect—' does he delay to help them ? ' ; (3) as a question relating to the enemies of the elect— ' is he patient with them ? ' Dr. Moffatt accepts the third of these interpretations. The first would mean that God defers answering his people for a time, but for gracious ends, lest they should enter unprepared into the last decisive crisis (Zahn). Jesus gives in any case the absolute assurance that the promise of his return will be fulfilled, but in the closing word—' Yet when the Son of man does come, will he find faith ? ' etc.—a certain anxiety regarding the disciples comes clearly to expression. Will the latter have courage and stedfastness enough to hold on under all circumstances to the promise of Christ's Coming ?

xviii. 9-14 : THE PHARISEE AND THE PUBLICAN

He also told the following parable to certain persons who were 9 sure of their own goodness and looked down upon everybody else. ' Two men went up to pray in the temple ; one was a 10 Pharisee and the other was a taxgatherer. The Pharisee 11 stood up and prayed by himself as follows : " I thank thee, O God, I am not like the rest of men, thieves, rogues, and immoral, or even like yon taxgatherer. Twice a week I 12 fast ; on all my income I pay tithes." But the taxgatherer 13 stood far away and would not lift even his eyes to heaven, but beat his breast, saying, " O God, have mercy on me for my sins ! " I tell you, he went home accepted by God 14

rather than the other man ;
    for everyone who uplifts himself will be humbled,
    and he who humbles himself will be uplifted.'
                    (Luke alone.)

The connexion of this parable with the foregoing is confined
to the circumstance that both speak of effectual prayer. But
whereas the preceding parable relates to the prayers of the Church
for the return of Christ, this treats of the sinner's prayer for
pardon. The parable admirably illustrates the method of
inculcating a lesson by contrasting two types of character,
each being brought separately on to the stage. The **Pharisee**
here typifies, doubtless in an extreme form, a self-conscious
virtue, claiming personal merit before God, and disdaining and
condemning all who do not conform to its accepted standards
and canons of religious observance. It must be admitted that
Judaism, though it discouraged the enumeration of personal
merits before God, sometimes lent itself to the kind of language
here attributed to the Pharisee. Strack-Billerbeck quote from
the Palestinian Talmud (*Berakoth*, 4) the prayer of a certain
Rabbi on leaving the house of instruction : ' I thank thee, Lord
my God, . . . that thou hast granted me my portion with
those who sit in the house of instruction and in the synagogues
. . . not in the theatres or in the circus. . . . I make it my
business to inherit Paradise, but they, etc.' For the attitude of
Pharisaism to taxgatherers in particular, see under v. 27–32.
For the claim, ' **Twice a week I fast**,' see under v. 33. The
Pharisees made a special virtue of tithing as well as fasting. The
Law required the tithing only of agricultural produce, but the
Pharisee goes beyond this demand : ' **on all my income I pay
tithes**.' Over against this scrupulous but self-satisfied virtue—
condemned not for its scrupulousness but for its self-confidence
toward God and its censoriousness toward men—Jesus sets the
broken and contrite heart as illustrated in the despised **taxgatherer** who in some inconspicuous corner of the temple-court,
with no thought save of God and of his own wasted life, beats
on his breast and cries, ' **O God, have mercy on me for my sins !** '
Jesus urges that in the taxgatherer's case alone is the prayer
real and therefore effectual. He, rather than the Pharisee, is
accepted by God, for God cannot find entrance to a proud, but
only to a lowly, heart.

At this point ends the long section (ix. 51–xviii. 14) in which Luke has been following other sources than Mark. He now returns to Mark, who serves as his authority down to xviii. 43.

xviii. 15–17 : RECEIVING THE CHILDREN

Now people even brought their infants for him to touch them ; 15 when the disciples noticed it they checked them, but Jesus called for the infants. ' Let the children come to me,' he 16 said, ' do not stop them : the Realm of God belongs to such as these. I tell you truly, whoever will not submit to the 17 Reign of God like a child will never get into it at all.'

(Cf. Mark x. 13–16.)

The motive of the parents who here bring their infants to Jesus is that he may give the children his blessing by laying his hands upon them. Such confidence towards him at a time when his name was proscribed as evil must have touched Jesus and imparts additional point to his rebuke of the disciples. The latter have interfered on the ground that this was no time for parents to intrude their infants on Jesus. What had children to do with the Kingdom of God in which alone Jesus was interested ? Jesus' answer is that the children have much, very much to do with the Kingdom. They represent the one type of those who will enter into it. Therefore to the word, ' **Let the children come to me,**' he adds, ' **for the Realm of God belongs to such.**' The highest life and blessedness, fulfilling the purpose of God for men, is for those, including the children, who have the truly childlike mind. Some quality therefore not possessed by children alone, but capable of indefinite extension, is indicated. Probably Jesus refers to simple and absolute trust in the Heavenly Father's will. As the children have come forward to himself without fear and without reserves, so must grown men accept the revelation of God which he offers to them. Inward division and conflict, distracting aims, discordant purposes, unreality of life, must be surmounted by a new-born vision and acceptance of God through which knowing and being shall again become one. Men must surrender, without misgiving and without reserve, to the absolute sway of God in the heart. In this sense, to ' **submit to the Reign of God like a child** ' is the *sine qua non* of salvation.

xviii. 18–27 : THE RULER'S QUESTION

18 Then a ruler asked him, ' Good teacher, what am I to do to in-
19   herit life eternal ? ' Jesus said to him, ' Why call me
20   " good " ? No one is good, no one but God. You know the
     commands : *do not commit adultery, do not kill, do not steal,
     do not bear false witness, honour your father and mother.*'
21   He said, ' I have observed all these commands from my
22   youth.' When Jesus heard this he said to him, ' You lack
     one thing more ; sell all you have, distribute the money
     among the poor and you will have treasure in heaven ; then
23   come and follow me.' But when he heard that, he was
24   vexed, for he was extremely rich. So Jesus looked at him
     and said, ' How difficult it is for those who have money
25   to enter the Realm of God ! Why, it is easier for a camel
     to get through a needle's eye than for a rich man to get
26   into the Realm of God.' His hearers said, ' Then whoever
27   can be saved ? ' He said, ' What is impossible for men is
     possible for God.'

(Cf. Mark x. 17–27.)

Luke follows Mark, but with slight abbreviations of the
latter's narrative. The questioner is introduced as a ruler,
i.e. a magistrate or member of some local sanhedrin, therefore a
person of social and religious standing. He has heard Jesus
speak of submission to the Reign of God as the one condition
of eternal life (xviii. 17), and now inquires what this submission
means in the way of personal conduct. ' What am I to do to
inherit eternal life ? ' The question is serious, and deference
and respect are indicated in the words ' Good teacher ' with which
he approaches Jesus. Jesus, however, discerning in this style
a somewhat formal and complacent use of the term ' good,' in-
terrupts him, and not till he has directed his questioner's mind
to the one source and measure of all goodness does he take up
the specific inquiry to which he is asked to give an answer. Here
in the interests of clearness two points call for attention.

First, the rebuke, ' Why call me good ? No one is good but
God,' by seeming to exclude the perfect goodness of Jesus
created difficulties for the early Christian consciousness, and led
the writer of Matthew to recast the question in the less challeng-
ing form, ' Why do you ask me about what is good ? ' (Matthew

xix. 16–17). But just for the reason that it created such difficulties the form ' Why call me good ? ' must be original, since
no later age would of itself have put such a question into the
lips of Jesus. On the other hand, it is surely needless to interpret
the words as an admission that Jesus shared the sinfulness of
ordinary humanity. Goodness in the full sense implies not only
the absence of defect but a perfectly unlimited range of moral
activity, and this in the nature of things can belong only to
God. On the other hand, Jesus is never found using the language of the human confessional. There is no echo in his self-
revelation of Psalm li. or of Romans vii. (Compare also vi. 46.)

Secondly, the direction, ' You know the commands,' is serious.
If God is the source of goodness, man must take the rule of life
primarily from Him. The commandments which are quoted
bear on duties to one's fellow-men, and are given in an order
which, since it follows neither Mark x. 19 nor the Decalogue
(Exodus xx. 12 f., Deuteronomy v. 16 f.), but partially recurs in
other New Testament writings (Romans xiii. 9, James ii. 11),
must reflect some current and familiar usage. The contention
that it was possible to keep the whole commandments of God
was freely made by Jewish Rabbis. Thus the Talmud represents a certain Rabbi Eliezer as asking Rabbi Aqiba, ' Is there
anything in all the Torah which I have not kept, so that it
would need to be atoned for by suffering ? ' (*Sanhedrin,* 101a),
and relates that another Rabbi, when a hostile army was at the
gates of his town, went up on to his roof with a book of the Law,
and said, ' Lord of the worlds, if I have failed to follow one single
word of this book of the Law, so let them come in ; but if not,
then let them depart ' (Strack-Billerbeck). The ruler therefore
is not making an unheard-of claim when he says, ' I have observed
all these commands from my youth,' and though we infer that
he has not read into the commandments all the meaning which
Christ took from them (cf. Matthew v. 21 f., 27 f.), yet as this
point is not made in the narrative, we need not read an ironical
meaning into the reply, ' You lack one thing more.' Jesus
accepts the ruler's confession as sincere, and in response to his
obvious desire for a greater satisfaction he lays upon him a new
and higher demand. This demand, which goes beyond the
Decalogue, is one which Jesus has already imposed on the Twelve
as part of what the *gospel* requires (Mark viii. 34) as the way to
life (ix. 23–25).

Why does Jesus ask the ruler to make the sacrifice of his possessions ? Explanation has been sought in the peculiar circumstances of the man's case. Jesus sees in the ruler's wealth a perilous entanglement from which his soul must be delivered. But perhaps a sufficient explanation lies in the statement made in Mark x. 21 that Jesus, looking at the man who had just made so remarkable a confession, ' loved him.' Love always implies an elective purpose, and in the present case it implies Jesus' desire to make the ruler one of his chosen band of apostles. But in order to qualify for this, the man must conform to the demand made by Jesus of all members of that fellowship (ix. 23–25, xii. 33–34, xiv. 27, xvi. 9). On ' sell all you have,' etc., see above under xii. 32–34. Jesus is going up to Jerusalem to proclaim the Reign of God. He and his disciples have divested themselves of every worldly interest and possession, but the ruler, though a candidate for eternal life, rejects these terms.

Mark says that the ruler turned away at this moment, and understands Jesus' sorrowful comment, ' How difficult it is for those who have money,' etc., to have been spoken to the disciples. Luke represents it as addressed to the ruler, perhaps with the idea that the latter will yet change his mind. The corroborative, ' It is easier for a camel to get through a needle's eye,' etc., is a proverbial expression for something which is impossible. Explanations which suppose the ' needle's eye ' to be a small postern-gate in Jerusalem, or which take ' camel ' to be a misreading of a similar word meaning cable or rope, are unwarranted. The statement is literally intended, and by seeming to exclude all hope of a rich man making the venture required for entrance on the Kingdom of God, it rouses the disciples to ask, ' Then who can be saved ? ' Jesus concedes the justice of the question, so long as salvation is envisaged from a merely human standpoint, but his statement that ' what is impossible for men is possible for God ' carried his disciples' thoughts into a realm in which such difficulties are surmounted. We see here that, though Jesus appealed to human volition, he did not isolate that volition or regard it apart from energies and powers which God puts forth in order to bring His Kingdom to pass. A principle, recognized as supernatural though still ethical, enters into and operates upon the human will, so as to make it the instrument of God's purpose. The saying is important as providing a point of connexion between Jesus' teaching and the Pauline conception of the ' Spirit ' as the dynamic principle of Christian life and action.

xviii. 28-30 : THE REWARD OF THE APOSTLES

Peter said, ' Well, we have left our homes and followed you ! ' 29 He said to them, ' I tell you truly, no one has left home or wife or brothers or parents or children for the sake of the Realm of God, who does not receive ever so much more in 30 this present world, and in the world to come life eternal.'

(Cf. Mark x. 28-31.)

The ruler's rejection of the terms offered to him recalls to Peter's mind the sacrifices made by himself and his companions. ' We have left our homes and followed you.'   Jesus rejoins that none who have thus abandoned every human relationship for the sake of the Realm of God will fail to receive ' ever so much more in this present world, and in the world to come eternal life.' The wording in Luke removes the suggestion in Mark that the reward attained by Christians in the present world is a reward in *kind*—' homes, brothers, sisters, mothers,' etc.   It leaves it open to us to place a purely spiritual interpretation upon the promise of Jesus.

xviii. 31-34 : THE PASSION AGAIN PREDICTED

Then he took the twelve aside and told them, ' We are going up 31 to Jerusalem, and all the predictions of the prophets regarding the Son of man will be fulfilled ; he will be betrayed to the 32 Gentiles, mocked, illtreated, and spat on ; they will scourge 33 him and kill him, but he will rise again on the third day.' However, they did not understand a word of this ; indeed 34 the saying was hidden from them, and they did not know what he meant.

(Cf. Mark x. 32-34.)

The section corresponds to Mark x. 32-34, but the wording suggests the influence of another tradition.   Luke has no parallel to the vivid picture in the first half of Mark x. 32. The part which the Gentiles, i.e. the Roman authority, are destined to play in the tragedy of the Crucifixion appears here for the first time, and has relatively greater prominence in Luke than in Mark. As in ix. 22, Luke substitutes ' on the third day ' for the ' after three days ' of Mark's prediction of the Resurrection. Ver. 34 has no parallel in Mark, but corresponds with Luke ix. 45.

xviii. 35-43 : THE BLIND MAN BY THE WAYSIDE

35 As he approached Jericho, it chanced that a blind man was seated
36   beside the road begging. When he heard the crowd passing
37   he inquired what was the matter, and they told him that
38   Jesus the Nazarene was going by. So he shouted, ' Jesus,
39   Son of David, have pity on me ! ' The people in front
     checked him and told him to be quiet, but he shouted all the
40   more, ' Son of David, have pity on me ! ' So Jesus stopped
     and ordered them to bring him, and asked him when he
41   approached, ' What do you want me to do for you ? ' ' Lord,'
42   he said, ' I want to regain my sight.' And Jesus said to
     him, ' Regain your sight, your faith has made you well.'
43   Instantly he regained his sight and followed him, glorifying
     God. And all the people gave praise to God when they saw
     this.

                                      (Cf. Mark x. 46-52.)

This incident brings us to Jericho, which is the last point of halt on the journey of Jesus to the city. Luke omits the name of the blind beggar by the wayside : Mark gives it as Bar-Timaeus. Luke further differs from Mark by placing the incident before the arrival in Jericho, not at the departure. The centre of interest in the section is the faith by which the suppliant, on learning that Jesus of Nazareth is passing, hails him as Son of David, and despite rebuffs from the bystanders keeps on iterating, ' Son of David, have pity on me,' until he gets the boon of sight. ' Son of David ' is not a title elsewhere given to Christ in this gospel or in Mark. Apparently it was a popular designation of Israel's Saviour or Hero, and Jesus, though rejecting it on another occasion as unsuitable (xx. 41-44), accepts it here because of the simple faith of which it is the expression.

Luke adds that the incident deeply impressed the beholders. The reference in ver. 43 to the religious enthusiasm of the crowd —which possibly consisted of pilgrims going up to the Feast— prepares us for the demonstrations which presently accompany the entry to the city.

xix. 1-10 : THE CONVERSION OF ZACCHAEUS

xix.

Then he entered Jericho. And as he passed through it, there was 1 a man called Zacchaeus, the head of the taxgatherers, a 2 wealthy man, who tried to see what Jesus was like ; but he 3 could not, on account of the crowd—for he was small of stature. So he ran forward and climbed into a sycomore 4 tree to get a sight of him, as he was to pass that road. But 5 when Jesus reached the spot he looked up and said to him, ' Zacchaeus, come down at once, for I must stay at your house to-day.' He came down at once and welcomed him 6 gladly. But when they saw this, everyone began to mutter 7 that he had gone to be the guest of a sinner. So Zacchaeus 8 stopped and said to the Lord, ' I will give the half of all I have, Lord, to the poor, and if I have cheated anybody I will give him back four times as much.' And Jesus said of him, 9 ' To-day salvation has come to this house, since Zacchaeus here is a son of Abraham. For the Son of man has come to 10 seek and save the lost.'

(Luke alone.)

The visit of Jesus to Jericho was connected in Luke's special source with two notable episodes : the conversion of a prominent taxgatherer belonging to the town (vers. 1-10), and the utterance of a parable bearing on the Reign of God (vers. 11-28). Zacchaeus (Heb., *Zakkai*, contraction of Zechariah) is introduced as head of the taxgatherers, which probably means that he was contractor-in-chief of local custom-dues. Under a system then widely prevalent, these would be purchased by him *en bloc* and then leased to underlings. As Jericho was the emporium of a large trade, and lay on the principal caravan-route from the East to Judea, the profits of the office would not be slight. Zacchaeus' interest in Jesus would be attracted by what he had heard regarding Jesus' dealings with taxgatherers in other parts of the country (cf. v. 29–32). The refusal of the man of Nazareth to allow social and religious prejudice to interpose between these ostracized members of society and the salvation of God which he preached had earned his gratitude, and in his eagerness to see this friend of his class he resorts to the stratagem of climbing into a wayside tree.

Jesus' knowledge of Zacchaeus was probably attributed by Luke to supernatural insight, but admits perhaps of a simpler explanation. Jesus had enjoined his disciples when they entered any town or village to inquire what local residents would be likely to ' receive ' the messengers of the Kingdom (Matthew x. 11), and the same procedure may have been followed at the approach to Jericho. In any case, the recognition of Zacchaeus and the remarkable overture indicated in the greeting, ' Zacchaeus . . . I must stay at your house to-day,' constitute a turning-point in the man's life and character. The narrative suggests that the great surrender of Zacchaeus as declared in ver. 8 was made while Jesus was still on the way to the taxgatherer's house, and therefore before any considerable interview between guest and host had taken place. It is therefore to be interpreted as the man's spontaneous response to the gracious act of Jesus in voluntarily electing to visit a sinner's abode. Moved by a desire to shew himself worthy of the Master's confidence, Zacchaeus renounces the service of mammon. ' I will give the half of all I have to the poor, and if I have cheated anybody I will give him back four times as much.' The vow indicates the purpose of a changed life in accordance with Christ's demand of altruism (cf. xii. 33, xvi. 9), and wins the acknowledgment expressed in vers. 9–10.

The incident is finely illustrative of the manner in which Jesus deals with the individual, discovering a man to himself, and at the same time revealing what things are interposing between his life and God. The influence of personal contact and association could not be better expressed than in ver. 9, where Jesus says, ' To-day salvation has come to this house, since Zacchaeus here is a son of Abraham.' In face of the indurated prejudice which forbade any dealings with persons like Zacchaeus, Jesus affirms that his own resolve to visit Zacchaeus' house has proved the means of saving him. The ostracized taxgatherer has shewn himself a true son ' of Abraham ' by the revolution of character which has taken place in him. Jesus, by crossing his threshold, has veritably succeeded in bringing the Messianic salvation to a whole household.

xix. 11–28 : THE PARABLE OF THE POUNDS

He went on to tell a parable in their hearing, as he was 11 approaching Jerusalem and as they imagined God's Reign would instantly come into view. 'A nobleman,' he said, 12 'went abroad to obtain royal power for himself and then return. He first called his ten servants, giving them each 13 a five-pound note, and telling them, " Trade with this till I come back." Now his people hated him and sent envoys 14 after him to say, "We object to him having royal power over us." However he secured the royal power and came 15 home. Then he ordered the servants to be called who had been given the money, that he might find out what business they had done. The first came up saying, " Your five 16 pounds has made other fifty, sir." " Capital," he said, 17 " you excellent servant ! because you have proved trust- worthy in a trifle, you are placed over ten towns." Then 18 the second came and said, " Your five pounds has made twenty-five, sir." To him he said, " And you are set over 19 five towns." Then the next came and said, " Here is 20 your five pounds, sir ; I kept it safe in a napkin, for I was 21 afraid of you, you are such a hard man—picking up what you never put down, and reaping what you never sowed." He replied, " You rascal of a servant, I will convict you by 22 what you have said yourself. You knew, did you, that I was a hard man, picking up what I never put down, and reaping what I never sowed ! Why then did you not put 23 my money into the bank, so that I could have got it with interest when I came back ? " Then he said to the by- 24 standers, " Take the five pounds from him and give it to the man with fifty." " Sir," they said, " he has fifty already ! " 25 " I tell you, 26

> to everyone who has shall more be given,
>> but from him who has nothing, even what he has shall
>> be taken.

And now for these enemies of mine who objected to me 27

reigning over them—bring them here and slay them in my
presence.'' '

28 With these words he went forward on his way up to Jerusalem.

(Cf. Matthew xxv. 14–30.)

As the parable follows without any break upon vers. 9–10
Luke understood it to have been spoken to the same circle of
hearers, therefore while Jesus was still in the house of Zacchaeus.
But whereas vers. 9–10 triumphantly assert the actuality,
under the circumstances there described, of the Messianic
salvation, the parable on the other hand warns against premature
imaginings that the Reign of God, the final end of the Messianic
salvation, is to be immediately realized. Jesus spoke the
parable, says Luke, because **he was approaching Jerusalem and
they imagined God's Reign would instantly come into view.**
Instead of any such immediate consummation the parable
predicts an interval of waiting and trial. ' The Messiah is
conceived not as coming but as going ; a lengthy period must
elapse before Jesus' faithful adherents obtain their reward
and the opponents of his kingship meet their punishment '
(Klostermann). That the disciples were under the influence
of apocalyptic excitement about this time appears by Mark x.
35–45, where James and John make their famous request for
right and left places by the side of the Messiah in his glory.

In part, the Lukan parable corresponds with Matthew xxv.
14–30, where also a man going abroad entrusts certain sums
of money to his servants, of whom three are specially mentioned,
and on his return calls for a statement of accounts. With
minor differences the two narratives exhibit a substantial
identity which points to their derivation, within those limits,
from Q or another common source. But the Lukan narrative
has in addition a number of bold features which have no parallel
at all in Matthew. The departing master is a nobleman. He
goes abroad **to obtain royal power,** i.e. to have his succession
to a throne recognized (ver. 12). His subjects, being opposed
to him, try to frustrate his purpose by sending a legation after
him to say, ' **We object to him having royal power over us** '
(ver. 14). In due course the nobleman obtains confirmation
of his title (ver. 15a), and on his return destroys the late rebels
with Oriental ferocity (ver. 27). None of these features appear
in the Matthew-parable, and therefore it is arguable that Luke's

source has here conflated two different traditions : (1) a story of
a prince who, as aforesaid, went abroad to establish his succession-
rights and was repudiated by his subjects (vers. 12, 14, 15a, 27) ;
(2) a story of a trader who, on leaving home, entrusted his capital
to his employees that they might invest and augment it (vers.
13, 15b, 16–26).   In favour of the first of these stories forming
a separate item is the coherency of its parts and the fact that
it seems to reflect the historical fortunes of Archelaus who,
when appointed over Judea by the will of Herod in 4 B.C.,
paid a visit to Rome to obtain confirmation of his title from
Augustus, and had the mortification of seeing his suit opposed
by a deputation of the refractory Judeans (Josephus, *Wars*,
i, 1–6 ; *Antiq.*, xvii, 9–11 ; Schürer, *Jewish People*, vol. ii,
pp. 1–6).   If Jesus spoke a parable of this kind at or near to
Jericho, a special motive would lie in the intimate associations
of that city with Archelaus.   Archelaus had built a palace
and constructed an aqueduct at Jericho (Josephus, *Antiq.*,
xvii, 13, 1), and the purpose of the parable would be to enforce
afresh the thought of Jesus' rejection and of the judgment which
would overtake an impenitent nation.   But the details reflecting
the fortunes of Archelaus may represent not a separate parable
of Jesus but an elaboration which the parable of the Pounds
underwent in the course of its transmission.

In any case, the latter parable has a character and con-
sistency of its own.   Its gist is that disciples of Christ, instead
of indulging day-dreams of Kingdom honours and awards,
ought to exert themselves actively to carry out the will of
Christ.   The first two servants, to whom the departing nobleman has entrusted money, saying, ' **trade with this till I come
back,**' utilize their opportunity and increase their capital five-
fold.   They represent earnest, diligent, and grateful disciples
who remember their Master's commission and earn promotion
by proving themselves qualified for higher responsibilities.
Only disciples who have been faithful will receive honour when
the Reign of God arrives.   Over against these faithful ones
is set in the person of the third servant another type, and as
his case is treated with special detail, it is obvious that the
parable is principally directed against the faults of which he
is the representative.   This third servant can point to no results
of his stewardship.   He has kept the entrusted capital, i.e. he
has refused to part with his office, but he has done nothing

to justify it. Why? ' I was afraid of you,' he says to his master, ' you are such a hard man.' A grudging spirit, taking cover under groundling fears of his master's character, has warped this servant's mind, and made him unfruitful. Even upon his own ground, however, he stands condemned, for had his master really answered to his description, fear should have spurred him, if not to improve the opportunity himself, at least to stand aside in favour of those who would profit by it (ver. 23). Compare *Aboth* ii. 19 : ' The day is short, and the task is great, and the workmen are sluggish, and the reward is much, and the Master of the house is urgent.' What is condemned in the parable on the part of any follower of Christ is the indulgence of a discontented mind rendering him not only sterile in himself but an impediment in the path of others. Such a follower will be deprived, and his stewardship given to better men. For in this matter, despite the popular leaning to a mere arithmetical justice (ver. 25), honour and reward belong to those who acquit themselves well : ' To everyone who has shall more be given, but from him who has nothing, even what he has shall be taken.' While the lesson applies particularly to the apostles in virtue of their special stewardship (xii. 32-38, 41-44), the fact that the number of servants is ten, not twelve, makes it unlikely that Jesus spoke the parable with reference to them alone. Every follower of Christ must remember the test to which his Master subjects him and the judgment which he will pass on his works.

Having thus directed his hearers' minds into more serious channels, Jesus enters on the last stage of his journey.

V. THE MESSIANIC OCCUPATION OF JERUSALEM
(xix. 29-xxi. 38)

xix. 29-40 : THE ENTRANCE TO THE CITY

29 When he was near Bethphage and Bethany at the hill called the Olive-Orchard, he despatched two of his disciples, saying,

30   ' Go to the village in front, and on entering it you will find a colt tethered on which no one ever has sat ; untether it

31   and bring it. If anyone asks you, " Why are you untethering it ? " this is what you will say, " The Lord needs it." '

The messengers went off and found the colt exactly as he 32
had told them. As they were untethering it, the owners 33
said to them, ' Why are you untethering the colt ? ' And
they said, ' Because the Lord needs it.' So they brought it 34
to Jesus, and throwing their clothes on the colt they mounted 35
Jesus upon it. As he went forward they spread their clothes 36
under him on the road ; and as he was now close to the 37
descent from the Hill of Olives all the multitude of the
disciples started joyfully to praise God with a loud voice
for all they had seen, saying,

> ' Blessed be the king who comes in the Lord's name !   38
> Peace in heaven and glory in the High places ! '

Some Pharisees in the crowd said to him, ' Check your 39
disciples, teacher.' But he replied, ' I tell you, if they were 40
to keep quiet, the very stones would shout.'

(Cf. Mark xi. 1–10.)

The road from Jericho to Jerusalem reflects in its physical
features the sternness of the resolve which Jesus now pursues.
It runs over arid, waterless country amid blistered limestone
rocks (see Sir G. A. Smith, *Historical Geography*, p. 264). In
course of time the company arrives at the Mount of Olives, to
which Luke gives the less familiar name of the hill called the
Olive-Orchard. From this height Jerusalem lies less than a
mile to the west. Here prophecy of old time had said that the
divine salvation would appear : ' Jahweh shall go forth . . . and
his feet shall stand in that day upon the Mount of Olives '
(Zechariah xiv. 4). Bethphage, the village confronting Jesus
on the farther or western side of the hill, marked the farthest
extension of Jerusalem in that direction. Bethany, lying to his
left on the south-eastern slope, was a little more than a mile
from the city. Now follows an act which, as reported by the
tradition, signifies Jesus' resolve to enter Jerusalem in a
manner which, if not to the general public and to the authorities,
at least to his own disciples and to other sympathizers will
indicate that he comes as Messiah. Yet not with the pomp and
circumstance with which contemporary imagination clothed
the figure of Israel's Deliverer. The tradition in Matthew
and John states that Jesus acted to fulfil Zechariah ix. 9 :
' Tell the daughter of Zion, Here is your King coming to you,
he is gentle and mounted on an ass, and on a colt, the foal of a

beast of burden.' Rabbinical thought was at a later time much exercised with this prophecy, and according to the Talmud (*Sanhedrin*, 98a), one Rabbi, about A.D. 250, commenting on the contrast between it and the prophecy in Daniel vii. 13, said : ' When Israel is deserving, he (the Messiah) comes with the clouds of heaven ; when it is not deserving, he comes " poor and riding upon an ass." ' The evangelical tradition, however, sees in Jesus' action simply a reflection of the lowly and pacific spirit which governed his whole work in Israel. He comes not as the martial hero of nationalistic expectation but as the Prince of Peace.

The young colt, which the two disciples are to fetch from the village, is one ' on which no one has ever sat.' This is a symbolic touch, indicative of the sacred religious purpose for which the animal is requisitioned. In the event of being interrogated the disciples are to say, ' the Lord needs it,' adding, according to Mark xi. 3, that ' he will immediately send it back.' As a young unbroken colt might be discovered almost by any door, the two disciples have no difficulty in fulfilling Jesus' behest. The colt is brought and caparisoned, and as the procession moves forward, the company ' spread their clothes under him ' as to a king (cf. 2 Kings ix. 13). At the crest of the road the city comes into view, and the company started joyfully to praise God for all they had seen, i.e. for the revelation brought and for the deeds done by Jesus. The hymn, as given in Mark xi. 9 f., takes up the theme of Psalm cxviii. 26. Originally composed as a blessing on pilgrims ascending to worship at Zion, the words have been transferred to the Messiah, a transference which Luke underlines by giving the acclamation in the form, ' Blessed be the king who comes in the Lord's name.' In the second strophe Luke, following a different tradition from Mark, has ' Peace in heaven and glory in the High places,' words which can only mean ' Peace is willed toward man by Him who dwells in heaven, and thus His glory is shewn forth ' (cf. ii. 14). When Pharisees interrupt and ask Jesus to discourage these unseemly demonstrations, Jesus answers in a way which shews how heavily the apathy of Israel weighed upon his heart. ' I tell you, if these were to keep quiet, the very stones would shout.' Compare for commentary the words in x. 21 : ' I praise thee, Father, for concealing this from the wise and learned and revealing it to the simple-minded.' The secret of Jesus must out, and if human lips do not confess it, the flints on the road-bed will find a voice.

xix. 41-44 : JESUS' GRIEF ON BEHOLDING JERUSALEM

And when he saw the city, as he approached, he wept over it, 41 saying, 'Would that you too knew even to-day on what 42 your peace depends ! But no, it is hidden from you ! A 43 time is coming for you when your enemies will throw up ramparts round you and encircle you and besiege you on 44 every side and raze you and your children within you to the ground, leaving not one stone upon another within you— and all because you would not understand when God was visiting you.'

(Luke alone.)

The pacific mode of Jesus' approach—he comes not as Warrior but as Prince of Peace—carrying out the spirit of his own teaching, ' Love your enemies, do good to those who hate you (vi. 27)—gives a peculiar appropriateness to the words which he utters on beholding the city. Jesus knows himself to possess the one secret by which even now the ' peace of Jerusalem '— see Psalm cxxii.—may be secured, and as he sees the city, so unmoved and so inapprehensive of its doom, the sight draws tears from his eyes. **He wept over it, saying, 'Would that you too '** (i.e. you as well as my disciples) **' knew even to-day on what your peace depends ! '** But no ! Jerusalem is uncon- cerned about Jesus' message. Therefore as the Old Testament seer predicted the downfall of ' Ariel, the city where David dwelt,' at the hands of ' a multitude of all the nations ' (Isaiah xxix.), so Jesus forecasts the disaster awaiting Jerusalem at the hands of her ' enemies,' the Roman power. The terms of the prediction, **' your enemies will throw up ramparts round you, and encircle you, and besiege you,'** etc., need not in their present form be later than the event of A.D. 70, for they are drawn largely from Isaiah xxix. 3 and Psalm cxxxvii. 9. Jesus plainly saw the end towards which things were tending in Judea (cf. xxiii. 28 f.). His message to Israel had been a last intervention from the God of peace, but the infatuated city had refused to see it, and Jesus saw Jerusalem borne as by a mill-stream to its doom.

xix. 45–48 : The Temple claimed for God

45 Then he went into the temple and proceeded to drive out those
46   who were selling. ' It is written,' he told them, ' *my house
     shall be a house of prayer*, but you have made it *a den of
     robbers.*'
47 Day after day he taught within the temple. The high priests
     and scribes tried to have him put to death, and so did the
48   leaders of the people, but they could not discover what
     was to be done, for the whole of the people hung upon
     his lips.

(Cf. Mark xi. 15–17.)

Arrived in Jerusalem, the first act of Jesus is to claim the
temple for the purely religious purpose for which it was instituted.
Thereby he inaugurates dramatically and at the very heart of
the nation's life the bloodless revolution which he came to bring
(cf. xii. 49). Israel is summoned anew to worship the Lord God
and to serve Him alone. The degrading secular traffic which
soiled the temple courts is peremptorily forbidden. Luke's
account of the incident is much abbreviated from Mark. Jesus
went into the temple, we read, and proceeded to drive out those
who were selling. The traffic in question was in animals required
for sacrifice. As the Law demanded that these should be free
of certain prescribed faults, it was less risky for worshippers to
purchase victims which had already been passed by the temple
scrutineers than to bring animals of their own which might or
might not answer to prescribed standards. Hence a busy and
lucrative trade went on in the temple courts under the patronage
of the wealthier priestly families, among whom ' the house of
Boethus ' and ' the house of Annas ' were conspicuous. Jesus'
condemnation of the traffic is unqualified : ' It is written,' he
cried, as he expelled the hucksters, ' " my house shall be a house
of prayer " ' (Isaiah lvi. 7), ' but you have made it " a den of
robbers " ' (Jeremiah vii. 11). Here doubtless Jesus was
putting into force sentiments and feelings shared by the vast
majority of pilgrims now thronging the courts. The trade was
unpopular. Dr. Klausner affirms that it was due to certain
worldly sacerdotal groups having acquired control of the shrine
(*Jesus of Nazareth*, p. 314). It is curious that Luke leaves out
the words ' for all nations,' which follow ' house of prayer ' in

Isaiah and in Mark xi. 17. The wider significance attached by
these words to the temple worship would have accorded well
with his universalist sympathies, but apparently he has his eyes
for the moment only on the national aspect of the reform carried
through by Jesus.

Luke's appended statement that day by day he taught within
the temple indicates that Jesus now intended the shrine to become
the centre from which his own revelation should go forth to
Israel. Equally it shews that Jesus at the moment was strong
in popular support. The whole of the people hung upon his lips,
and thus imposed an effective check upon the designs which the
authorities were now forming against his life.

xx. 1–8 : The Authority of Jesus

xx.

One day, when he was teaching the people in the temple and 1
preaching the gospel, up came the priests and scribes along
with the elders. ' Tell us,' they said, ' what authority you 2
have for acting in this way ? Who was it that gave you
this authority ? ' He answered them, ' Well, I will ask you 3
a question. Tell me, did the baptism of John come from 4
heaven or from men ? ' Now they reasoned to themselves, 5
' If we say, "From heaven," he will ask, "Why did you
not believe him ? " And if we say, "From men," the 6
whole of the people will stone us, for they are convinced
John was a prophet.' So they answered that they did not 7
know where it came from. Jesus said to them, ' No more 8
will I tell you what authority I have for acting as I do.'

(Cf. Mark xi. 27–33.)

The religious authorities could not be tolerant of the drastic
invasion of their rights signified by Jesus' occupation of the
temple. The priests were conscious of a frontal attack upon
their prestige, and they were only biding their time to interfere.
One day, as Jesus is preaching in the temple, which is now the
centre from which the gospel goes forth to the nation, the
priests and scribes with the elders, i.e. a deputation of the whole
Sanhedrin, interpose and ask, ' What authority have you for
acting in this way ? ' The reply of Jesus is to propound a counter-

question, upon the answer to which depends his own ultimate
response to their inquiry.

The demand, 'Tell me, did the baptism of John come from
heaven or from men?' is not so remote from the immediate
issue raised by the priests as might at first sight appear. On the
ordinary view Jesus simply repels one query by another. He
cites the parallel case of John, and from the unanswerable
neglect by the religious authorities of that prophet concludes
their absolute want of a title to interpellate himself. In reality
the relation of the one question to the other is more intimate.
The prophetic message of John had awakened Jesus to a sense
of his own mission to Israel. It was when receiving baptism
at John's hands that the voice ' Thou art my Son ' came to him.
Consequently the nature of the authority of Jesus is not only
formally but really bound up with the prior question regarding
John.

What Jesus himself thought of John's authority has already
appeared (vii. 27, 29–30, xvi. 16). But the questioners of Jesus
are taken aback by the dilemma which his counter-query creates
for them. To derive the authority of John from heaven lays
them open to the charge of having opposed the will of God
through their refusal to be baptized. To derive it from men,
i.e. to say that John had no divine authority, is to outrage
public opinion, which at this moment is solidly on the side of
Jesus. In this predicament they answer that they have no
knowledge where John's authority came from. Doubtless they
think this equivalent to declining the relevancy of Jesus' question. In reality, coming from the religious leaders of the nation,
the answer argues them checkmated and leaves the field to
Jesus.

xx. 9–18 : The Parable of the Vineyard

9 Then he proceeded to tell the people the following parable.
   'A man *planted a vineyard*, leased it to vinedressers,
10   and went abroad for some time. When the season came
   round he sent a servant to the vinedressers to receive
   part of the produce of the vineyard, but the vinedressers
11   flogged him and sent him off with nothing. He proceeded
   to send another servant, and they flogged him too, insulted

him and sent him off with nothing. Then he sent still a 12
third, but this one they wounded and threw outside.
Said the owner of the vineyard, "What shall I do? I will 13
send my beloved son; perhaps they will respect him." But 14
when the vinedressers saw him, they argued to themselves,
"Here is the heir, let us kill him, so that the inheritance may
be ours." And they threw him outside the vineyard and 15
killed him. Now what will the owner of the vineyard
do to them? He will come and kill these vinedressers and 16
give the vineyard to others.' When they heard that, they
said, 'God forbid!' But he looked at them and said, 17
'Then what does this scripture mean?—

The stone that the builders rejected
is the chief stone now of the corner.
Everyone who falls on that stone will be shattered, 18
and whoever it falls upon will be crushed.'

(Cf. Mark xii. 1-12.)

Having countered the frontal attack of the Sanhedrists,
Jesus proceeds to carry the war into their camp, and in the
parable of the Vineyard he declares to the people that the religious leaders in Jerusalem have systematically defied every
appeal and representation made to them from God. The
comparison of Israel to a vineyard was hereditary and familiar
(compare Psalm lxxx. 8-16 and especially Isaiah v. 1-7). In
the parable of Jesus, however, the interest is less in the vineyard
than in the vinedressers, to whom it is leased and who here
represent the hierarchy in Israel. These hierarchs, appointed
to foster and promote the spiritual well-being of the nation, have
so far forgotten themselves that the past history of Israel has
been an unbroken record of repulse and defiance meted out to
the messengers whom God has sent. The parable is here clearly
allegorical. The servants are the prophets who, sent to receive
pledges of the spiritual productiveness of Israel, have been
subjected to ever-increasing violence by its unworthy leaders:
note the crescendo of injury and insult in vers. 10, 11, 12.
The same holds true of the reception accorded to God's final
messenger, the Messiah, here described as 'my beloved son'
(iii. 22, ix. 35). The latter is the bearer of a higher revelation
than has come through any of the prophets, and in his case the
rage of the authorities, hitherto confined to slashing and

wounding, rises to a murderous height (xix. 47). ' Here is the heir, let us kill him, so that the inheritance may be ours.' The hierarchs wish to hold Israel not for God but for themselves as their own domain and *peculium*. Hence the doom of deposition and destruction now declared to be at hand. The Lord of the Vineyard will oust and supersede the present unworthy lessees.

It is scarcely likely that vers. 13–16 were uttered in their present form by Jesus. They presuppose the death of Jesus as an already accomplished fact, and the language used suggests the distinctive manner of the Christian Church. But that Jesus did in Jerusalem declare himself to have come from God with an authority possessed by no other before him, and as the bearer of an ultimatum to his nation, need not be disputed. Such a claim would be in keeping with the whole consciousness which had inspired him from his baptism. Nor need we doubt that Jesus saw doom to be descending on the existing administration in Israel, and said that God would ' give the vineyard to others.' Such an announcement might appal and shock the hearers (ver. 16b), but to Jesus the event was certain. Destruction awaited temple and nation at the hands of Rome (xix. 43–44, xxi. 6, 20–22), and power would pass to others. Who these others are is not stated ; see, however, xxii. 28–30, where Jesus promises that his apostles will rule the tribes of Israel. A spiritual revolution is thus announced, and verification is added by appeal to the prediction in Psalm cxviii. 22–23 : ' The stone that the builders rejected is the chief stone now of the corner.' The hierarchy with the scribes and elders have rejected Jesus, but he will yet come to reign (Daniel vii. 13–14). To fall or trip on the stone—i.e. to find a present cause of stumbling or offence in Christ—is to be broken. But to have the stone fall on one—i.e. to continue impenitent until the Judgment—is to be crushed. For the metaphor compare Daniel ii. 34–35.

XX. 19–26 : THE QUESTION OF TRIBUTE TO CAESAR

19 At that hour the scribes and high priests tried to lay hands on him, but they were afraid of the people. They knew
20 he had meant this parable for them. So watching their chance they sent spies who pretended to be honest persons

in order to seize on what he said and get him handed
over to the authority and jurisdiction of the governor.
They put this question to him, ' Teacher, we know you 21
are straight in what you say and teach, you do not look
to human favour but teach the Way of God honestly. Is 22
it right for us to pay tribute to Caesar or not ? ' But 23
he noted their knavery and said to them, ' Show me a shilling. 24
Whose likeness and inscription does it bear ? ' ' Caesar's,'
they replied. ' Well then,' he said to them, ' give Caesar 25
what belongs to Caesar, give God what belongs to God.'
So they could not seize on what he said before the people, 26
and marvelling at his reply they said nothing.

(Cf. Mark xii. 13-17.)

The hierarchy are sensible that in the Vineyard parable
Jesus has struck a deadly blow at their authority. On the
other hand, public opinion, as represented by the mass of
pilgrims in Jerusalem, is on the side of Jesus, so that no attempt
to take him by force can hope for success. Nothing remains
for the hierarchs but to drive a wedge between Jesus and the
people, or at anyrate to divide the ranks of his supporters.
Jesus aims at a Messianic revolution (xix. 45-46, xx. 15-17),
and thus far he has the people with him. But the people expect
deliverance from Rome, and if it can be shewn that Jesus does
not countenance this idea, indeed preaches non-resistance and
love to enemies, popular sympathy will be severely strained.
Sending secret agents therefore to ingratiate themselves with
Jesus, they propound the question, ' Is it right for us to pay
tribute to Caesar ? ' The tribute—a poll-tax levied on every
adult male in Judea ever since that country came under a
Roman procurator in A.D. 6—was notoriously unpopular,
inflicting as it did a brand of servitude on the free people of
God. If therefore Jesus approved the payment, he stood to
lose nationalist sympathies. If on the other hand he dis-
approved, he could be delated to the procurator for treason.
Jesus detects the subtle stratagem, and his sudden demand,
' Show me a denarius. Whose likeness and inscription does
it bear ? ' so breaks up and divides the question that the
dilemma—' God *or* Rome '—no longer appears as absolute.
If coin bearing Caesar's stamp is freely received and used in the
country, it surely implies that Caesar has some kind of rights

in that coin. On the other hand, the righteous claims of God to His people's worship and obedience are in no wise diminished. Consequently Jesus answers ' **Give Caesar what belongs to Caesar and God what belongs to God.**' The two obligations are not contradictory. It is obvious, of course, that Jesus, here as elsewhere, definitely rejects the nationalistic conception of the Kingdom of God. Hence, once his declaration percolates into the nation's mind, it cannot but alienate popular sentiment. On the other hand, the argument deprives the hierarchs of all chance of delating Jesus to the procurator. **They could not seize on what he said before the people, i.e. nothing in Jesus'** utterance constituted a crime of treason.

xx. 27–40 : The Question of the Resurrection

27 Some of the Sadducees came up, who deny any resurrection,
28 and put a question to him. ' Teacher,' they said, ' Moses has written this law for us, that *if a man's married brother dies and is childless, his brother is to take the*
29 *woman and raise offspring for his brother.* Well, there were seven brothers. The first married a wife and
30
31 died childless. The second and the third took her, as indeed all the seven did, dying and leaving no children.
32
33 Afterwards the woman died too. Now at the resurrection whose wife will she be ? She was wife to the seven of them.'
34 Jesus said to them, ' People in this world marry and are
35 married, but those who are considered worthy to attain yonder world and the resurrection from the dead neither
36 marry nor are married, for they cannot die any more ; they are equal to angels and by sharing in the resurrection they
37 are sons of God. And that the dead are raised has been indicated by Moses in the passage on the Bush, when he calls *the Lord " God of Abraham and God of Isaac and God of*
38 *Jacob."* God is not a God of dead people but of living, for
39 all live to him.' Some of the scribes declared, ' Teacher,
40 that was a fine answer.' They no longer dared to put any question to him.

(Cf. Mark xii. 18–27.)

The resurrection of the body represents the only form in which the idea of immortality was received among Jews. The belief had developed late in the religious history of Israel, and it had not found acceptance among all sections of the community. While the Pharisees received it and made it a cardinal article of doctrine, the older-fashioned Sadducees, who clung to the Pentateuch and declined all recent enthusiastic tendencies in religion, rejected it *in toto*. The difference between the two parties is succinctly given in Acts xxiii. 8 : ' While the Sadducees declare there is no such thing as resurrection, angels, or spirits, the Pharisees affirm them all.' Consequently, when the Sadducees raise with Jesus the question of the resurrection, they are merely pursuing a debate begun with, and using weapons already forged against, their Pharisaic antagonists. Any special relevance which the question as addressed to Jesus possesses lies in the fact that Jesus, by rejecting the political dreams of the nation, has flung his hearers upon a wholly other-worldly conception of the Kingdom of God. How then does he interpret this ' Kingdom ' ? What does he mean by the ' resurrection ' with which, herein agreeing with the Pharisees, he associates the Kingdom of God.

The Sadducees on their part are fortified with arguments which in their judgment amount to the *reductio ad absurdum* of the resurrection-belief. Proof starts from the law of levirate marriage according to which, ' if a man's brother dies and is childless, his brother is to take,' etc. (Deuteronomy xxv. 5–6). It is of no consequence to determine whether the law in question was still commonly observed. The law itself left a loophole for objectors (cf. Deuteronomy xxv. 7–10), and in the Israel of the age of Jesus conformity was perhaps more the exception than the rule. Nevertheless, the law was on the statute-book, and this was sufficient ground for the Sadducees to proceed with their argument. They suppose a case where seven brothers in succession marry the same woman, and they demand to know whose wife she will be at the ' resurrection.'

The answer of Jesus, as given in Mark xii. 24, is that the Sadducees, in arguing as they do, ignore ' both the scriptures and the power of God.' Luke, following here a somewhat different tradition, omits these words, but otherwise agrees in substance with Mark. The refutation is two-fold : (1) The Sadducees overlook the total difference which exists between the present life and life in the world to come. Any force which their objection retains it owes to an unwarrantable transference to the future life of conceptions belonging to a world in which death rules, and in which therefore marriage and the births of children must continue. But 'those who are accounted worthy to attain yonder world and the resurrection from the dead '—note that only the righteous here come into consideration—do not marry, 'for they cannot die any more.' Their mode of life is like that of angels, and like the angels they are sons of God. (2) The Sadducees ignore that God, as shewn by the Pentateuch itself, takes His redeemed ones into permanent fellowship with Himself. In proof Jesus appeals to the passage on the Bush (Exodus iii. 1-6), where Moses, the traditional author, speaks of God as still ' God of Abraham and God of Isaac and God of Jacob.' Moses describes those long-dead patriarchs as still the objects of God's loving interest and care. Therefore they still live to Him : ' God is not a God of dead people but of living.' The argument might seem to be purely nominal, turning as it does on the implied use of a verbal tense. In reality Jesus argues from something deeper. God, when He takes His faithful ones into fellowship with Himself, cannot be thought to limit this purpose to the brief span of earthly existence, but wills to create an eternal relation and an eternal bliss.

The same thought that the patriarchs still 'live to God ' occurs in the Hellenistic-Jewish work known as 4 Maccabees, and is therefore probably traditional (Easton). Its force as an argument for bodily resurrection, as distinct from spiritual survival, coheres with the Jewish and Christian refusal permanently to dissociate body and soul, as did the Greeks. Man is a single entity, and the sundering of soul and body which occurs at death cannot be thought of as permanent. There is no thought here of the soul being indestructible *per se*. The future life has its whole ground in God's redeeming will.

xx. 41-44 : Is Christ the Son of David ?

41 But he said to them, ' How can people say that the Christ is
42   David's son ? Why, David himself says in the book of psalms,
      The Lord said to my Lord, " Sit at my right hand,
43   *till I make your enemies a footstool for your feet."*
44   David then calls him *Lord*. So how can he be his son ? '
                        (Cf. Mark xii. 35-37.)

The scribes are represented as pleased with Jesus' refutation of the Sadducees, and further criticism is allowed to drop (vers. 39-40). Jesus, however, now opens fire on them by taking up one of their phrases and asking, ' How can people say that the Christ is David's son ? ' To Jesus this designation of the Messiah is misleading as well as inadequate, and he appeals by way of proof to Psalm cx. 1. ' David himself '—Jesus accepts the view of the authorship of the Psalms current in his age— ' says in the book of Psalms ' something which exalts the Messiah far above the rank usually assigned to the ' Son of David.' He says : ' The Lord said to my Lord, Sit at my right hand,' etc. This forbids to speak of the Messiah only as David's son, for ' David calls him Lord.'

The argument presupposes that the Psalm refers to the Messiah, and this it does in early Christianity, where the words ' Sit at my right hand ' are peculiarly appropriate to the crucified and risen Messiah in whom the Church believes. But while the argument thus reflects the standpoint of apostolic thought, there is no reason for questioning that Jesus explicitly repudiated the tendency of his time to sink the religious functions of Israel's Redeemer in the prevalent conception of a national deliverer. Jesus has never at any time sanctioned a political interpretation of the salvation of God. The argument by no means necessarily involves that Jesus is not of Davidic descent (i. 27, 32, 69 ; ii. 4, etc.). But he will not allow that the Kingdom of God is synonymous with the nationalist dream of Israel.

XX. 45-47 : WARNING AGAINST THE SCRIBES

And in the hearing of all the people he said to his disciples, 45 ' Beware of the scribes ! They like to walk about in long 46 robes, they are fond of getting saluted in the market-places, of securing the front seats in the synagogues and the best places at banquets ; they prey upon the property of widows 47 and offer long unreal prayers. All the heavier will their sentence be ! '

(Cf. Mark xii. 38-40.)

The section follows Mark, and supplements the fuller indictment of Pharisaic hypocrisy which Luke has already inserted from Q (xi. 39–54). Jesus assails the vanity of the professional teachers of the Law, and finally brings the charge against them that ' they prey upon the property of widows,' which may mean that they are dishonest trustees of property committed to their charge, or that they take advantage of the credulity of simple women to enrich themselves and, to offset this in the public eye, ' offer long unreal prayers.' Such a travesty of religion, which combines a name for piety with flagrant self-seeking, will not go unpunished. (Contrast James i. 27.)

xxi. 1–4 : THE WIDOW'S OFFERING

xxi.

1 Looking up he saw the rich putting their gifts into the treasury,
2   and noticed a poor widow putting two little coins in. He
3   said, ' I tell you plainly, this poor widow has put in more than
4   them all ; for these people all contributed out of their surplus,
    but she has given out of her neediness all her living.'

(Cf. Mark xii. 41–44.)

This little section goes closely with the preceding. Over against the scribes who, while pretending earnest piety, make religion a means of self-enrichment, Jesus sets the poor widow who has given all that she possesses to God's service. The treasury, consisting of a row of chests or boxes with trumpet-shaped apertures for the receipt of money offerings, stood round the walls of the Women's Court in the Temple, and the actions of worshippers as they came up would be visible to the bystanders.

xxi. 5–6 : PROPHECY OF THE DESTRUCTION OF THE TEMPLE

5 Some were speaking of the temple with its ornamentation of
6   splendid stones and votive gifts, but he said, ' As for what
    you see, there are days coming when not a stone will be left
    upon another, without being torn down.'

(Cf. Mark xiii. 1–2.)

According to Luke Jesus was still in the temple courts when, in rejoinder to some allusion to the grandeur of the buildings, he gave his judgment that the whole edifice would soon be totally destroyed. With this setting agrees the special mention in Luke of the votive offerings with which the buildings were adorned, for these would be visible only from a position within the courts. In Mark the episode occurs as Jesus is leaving the Temple, and it is to a group of disciples now outside the city and looking back at the Temple from the opposite side of the Kidron valley that he delivers the ensuing discourse on the Signs of the End (Mark xiii. 3). As Luke keeps Jesus within the Temple, and represents him as still there when the discourse is ended (xxi. 37–38), it would seem that he is here dependent on a different tradition from Mark.

The splendour of the **temple** buildings was proverbial in antiquity : ' a temple of immense wealth ' is the description given by Tacitus (*Hist.*, v. 8. 1). The **stones** were huge, some according to Josephus being 25 cubits in length. Herod's reconstruction had begun about 20–19 B.C., the work proceeding at intervals throughout the intervening period, and came to a finish only in A.D. 64, some six years before the destruction. **Votive gifts** had come from many quarters. The Emperor Augustus, says Philo, ' adorned our sanctuary with lavish offerings,' while Herod himself had presented a golden vine (Josephus, *Antiq.*, xv. 11. 3). The more tragic for the splendour of this setting is the prediction now uttered by Jesus : ' **As for what you see, there are days coming when not a stone will be left upon another.**' This doom was literally fulfilled in A.D. 70. The Romans brought up their siege-engines, and ' as the army had now none left either to murder or to pillage . . . Caesar gave orders to raze the entire city and temple to the ground.' So great was the demolition that ' henceforth none visiting the spot would have found reason to believe that the place had ever been inhabited ' (Josephus, *Wars*, vii. 1. 1–3).

For analogies to the prediction in ancient prophecy see Micah iii. 12, Jeremiah xxvi. 6, 18. Jesus saw disaster to be looming over the city and nation which had refused God's overtures of peace in him (xix. 42–44). The impenitence of the nation would involve even the holy Place in ruin. The prediction is not to be regarded as a projection backwards of the event of A.D. 70. Echoes of the same prophecy are heard at the trial of Jesus (Mark xiv. 58, xv. 29), at the accusation of Stephen (Acts vi. 14), and on other occasions (John ii. 19). So

substantial a body of evidence cannot be explained away.
Jesus must have predicted the extinction of the Temple, as part
of the now imminent eschatological drama in which the present
order of history would come to a close.

xxi. 7–19 : Woes Preceding the End

7 So they asked him, ' Teacher, and when will this happen ?
8 What will be the sign for this to take place ? ' He said,
' Take care that you are not misled ; for many will come
in my name saying, " I am he " and " the time is near "—
9 do not go after them. And when you hear of wars and disturbances, do not be scared ; *these have to come* first, but
10 the end is not at once.' Then he said to them, ' *Nation*
11 *will rise against nation, and realm against realm,* there
will be great earthquakes with famine and pestilence here
and there, there will be awful portents and great signs
12 from heaven. But before all that, men will lay hands on
you and persecute you, handing you over to synagogues and
prisons ; you will be dragged before kings and governors
13 for the sake of my name. That will turn out an opportunity
14 for you to bear witness. So resolve to yourselves that you
15 will not rehearse your defence beforehand, for I will give
you words and wisdom that not one of your opponents will
16 be able to meet or refute. You will be betrayed by your
17 very parents and brothers and kinsmen and friends, and some
of you will be put to death. You will be hated by all on
18 account of my name ; but not a hair of your head will
19 perish. Hold out stedfast and you win your souls.'

(Cf. Mark xiii. 3–13.)

In all the Synoptists the prophecy of Jesus regarding the
Temple is followed by a discourse in which, with warnings
appropriate to each stage of the developing drama, the Woes
of the last days (8–19), the final catastrophe in Judea (20–24),
and the End of the world itself (25–36) are successively set
forth. The incentive to the discourse lay, according to Mark,
in a request of four disciples who, taking up the Lord's prediction
about the Temple, asked ' When is this to happen ? What will
be the sign for all this to be accomplished ? ' But as, both in

Mark and Luke, the discourse hangs very loosely to this question,
the destruction of the Temple not being mentioned, and the
argument being almost wholly directed against fallacious expectations of Christ's coming, there is reason to believe that the
material here incorporated by the evangelists must have passed
through some independent stage of development, and many
scholars therefore see in it a Jewish-Christian apocalypse, based
partly on words of Jesus and partly on other traditional materials,
which was drawn up for the instruction of Christians in days
when excited anticipations of the Lord's return were rife, and
which took its present form shortly before or simultaneously
with the catastrophe of the year 70. Whatever may be thought
of this 'Little Apocalypse' theory—and there is a striking
parallel in 2 Thessalonians ii. 1-10—the material forming the
discourse has certainly undergone elaboration. Words of Jesus
have been supplemented from Jewish-Christian apocalyptic
sources. A subsidiary question is whether Luke's differences
from Mark (notably in vers. 20-24) represent a rewriting of
Mark by Luke himself, or rest on a version of Mark's original
source which had subsequently been brought up to date by
reference to current events in which the prophecies were fulfilled.

Part I of the discourse (vers. 8-19) warns the followers of
Jesus against rumours of the Lord's return to which the dis-
turbed conditions of the age would inevitably give rise. The
point of view resembles that of 2 Thessalonians ii. 1-3, written
in A.D. 51. The prediction ' Many will come in my name saying
" I am he " and " the time is near " ' is difficult. Persons who
come in Jesus' ' name ' must be Christians claiming his authority,
but how could such Christians expect to be received as the
returning Messiah ? The difficulty would be removed if the
expression ' I am he ' is understood, as the present writer thinks
it ought to be, as equivalent to ' the Messiah has come.' The
warning would then be identical with that in 2 Thessalonians
ii. 2. The Church is to be on its guard against Christians who,
carried away by contemporary upheavals in the political world,
precipitately raise the cry that Christ has returned and that
the Messianic age has begun. Over against such errors it is
pointed out that ' wars and disturbances have to come first,
but the end is not at once,' i.e. the ominous signs in the
contemporary world precede but do not mark the Messianic
era : in Mark's language, they are only the ' beginning ' of

Woes (Mark xiii. 8.) Therefore Christians must maintain their equilibrium.

As historical basis for such warnings we have the fact of Christ's refusal to speak of times or seasons and his saying, ' The Kingdom of God is not coming as you expect ' (xvii. 20–21). But the prediction that ' nation will rise against nation,' etc., and the references to earthquakes, famine, and pestilence, and to ' awful portents and great signs from heaven,' while they echo the Old Testament (Isaiah xix. 2, Joel ii. 10, 28, 30–31), are not in the manner of Jesus who rebuked the craving for signs, and therefore it is likely that here the discourse reflects not Jesus but the traditional apparatus of ideas with which Jewish apocalypses delineated the World-End (compare 2 Esdras xiii. 30–32). In vers. 12–19 is indicated the conduct required of Christians during these critical times. In spite of persecution and trial before synagogues and even before kings and governors (cf. Acts xxiv. 2, 24, xxv. 6, 23, etc.), they are not to be distracted, but to see in these distresses ' an opportunity to bear witness.' Luke's differences from Mark in vers. 13–15 indicate that he is influenced here by an independent tradition or source. The Christian on trial and anxious how to answer his judges receives the promise, ' I will give you words and wisdom,' etc. (see Mark xiii. 11 and Matthew x. 17–20). In vers. 16–19 Luke again is close to Mark. Family discord and even betrayal (cf. Isaiah xix. 2, Micah vii. 6), and the hatred of all men (cf. Tacitus, *Annals*, xv, 44) are eventualities which have to be faced, but the followers of Jesus are in God's keeping, and their task is plain. ' Hold out stedfast and you win your souls.'

Is there any suggestion here that Christians, whom the Lord has called to love enemies and to wait God's own time and pleasure with regard to the Kingdom, will inevitably become embroiled with their fellow-countrymen who, not content to wait in patience, wish to precipitate the Messianic Reign by force ?

An examination of Luke's language in the above section makes it probable that he drew on his L source. This source was Palestinian in outlook, and this may explain why Luke has no parallel to the statement in Mark xiii. 10 that ' ere the End, the Gospel must be preached to all nations.'

xxi. 20–24 : THE LAST CATASTROPHE IN JUDEA

' But whenever you see Jerusalem surrounded by armies, then be 20
sure her desolation is not far away.   Then let those who are 21
in Judaea fly to the hills, let those who are in the city escape,
and let not those who are in the country come in to the city ;
for these are *the days of the divine Vengeance*, in fulfilment 22
of all that is written in scripture.   Woe to women with 23
child and to women who give suck in those days, for sore
anguish will come upon the land and Wrath on this
people ; they will fall by the edge of the sword, they will 24
be carried prisoners to all nations, and *Jerusalem* will
be *under the heel of the Gentiles* till the period of the Gentiles
expires.'

(Cf. Mark xiii. 14–33.)

Part II of the discourse brings us to a crisis which, though
not yet coincident with the World-End, marks the definite
inauguration of the last times.   In Mark the language used is
cryptic and traditional : ' When you see the appalling Horror
standing where he has no right to stand,' etc.   ' The appalling
Horror ' (lit., ' the abomination which makes desolate ') denotes
in Daniel ix. 27, xi. 31, xii. 11 the idolatrous altar to Zeus
Olympios, which in 168 B.C. Antiochus Epiphanes of Syria
erected in the temple at Jerusalem.   In Mark, however, the
Horror is personified.   Someone, incarnating in himself the
last powers of evil—perhaps a Roman emperor intent like
Caligula on setting up his image in the Temple, perhaps the
Roman legions regarded as a manifestation of Satanic power—
will appear in the holy Place.   For a parallel prediction see
2 Thessalonians ii. 3–4, where Paul insists that before the
return of Christ an Antichrist will reveal himself.   In this
epistle both Antiochus and Caligula have lent features to the
Antichrist, the arch-enemy of God.

In Luke, on the other hand, the prediction is rationalized.
It runs : when ' you see Jerusalem surrounded by armies, then
be sure her desolation is not far away.'   The appalling Horror
is interpreted definitely as the siege of Jerusalem by the Romans
(cf. xix. 41–44).   Luke's differences from Mark at this point
have sometimes been set down to free paraphrase of Mark by
Luke himself, writing with the event of the year 70 in mind.

But many features of the discourse suggest that Luke was influenced by a document representing ' the form Mark's " Little Apocalypse " took in Southern Palestine ' (Easton). Neither in Mark nor in Luke is the catastrophe identified with the final *dénouement* of human history. Terrible times are predicted for Judea, flight of the population to the hills, evacuation of the doomed city : ' these are the days of the divine Vengeance ' foretold in Scripture (Jeremiah v. 29, Hosea ix. 7), when it will go hard with women with infants and little children. In Luke's narrative there is again deviation from Mark in the direction of a greater realism, and the prediction (not in Mark) is added that ' Jerusalem will be under the heel of the Gentiles till the period of the Gentiles expires ' (cf. Revelation xi. 2). The ' period of the Gentiles ' is the period when the heathen power as the executor of judgment will wreak its savage will on impenitent Jerusalem (cf. Daniel viii. 13–14, xii. 7, etc.). The reference to this interval again reminds the reader that the End is not yet. Christians are not to believe that the Fall of the city, whether prospective (as in Luke's source) or past (as from Luke's own standpoint), is identical with the Lord's return.

xxi. 25–38 : THE END OF THE WORLD

25 ' And there will be signs in sun and moon and stars, while on earth the nations will be in dismay with bewilderment *at the roar*
26 *of sea and waves*, men swooning with panic and foreboding of what is to befall the universe. For *the orbs of the heavens*
27 *will be shaken*, and then they will see *the Son of man coming*
28 *in a cloud* with power and great glory. But when these things begin to happen, look up and raise your heads, for
29 your release is not far distant.' And he told them a parable.
30 ' Look at the fig tree and indeed all the trees ; as soon as they put out their leaves, you can see for yourselves
31 that summer is at hand. So, whenever you see all this happen, be sure the Reign of God is at hand.
32 I tell you truly, the present generation will not pass away till
33 all this happens. Heaven and earth will pass away, but my words never.
34 Take heed to yourselves in case your hearts get overpowered by dissipation and drunkenness and worldly anxieties, and so

that Day catches you suddenly like *a trap*. For it will come 35 *upon* all *dwellers on* the face of all *the earth*. From hour to 36 hour keep awake, praying that you may succeed in escaping all these dangers to come and in standing before the Son of man.'

By day he taught in the temple, but at night he went outside the 37 city and passed the night on the hill called the Olive-Orchard. And all the people used to come early in the morning to 38 listen to him in the temple.

(Cf. Mark xiii. 24-37.)

At last in Part III the discourse brings us to the closing act of the world-drama. When the ' period of the Gentiles ' expires, ' there will be signs in sun and moon and stars,' by which the nations, the Gentiles who till now have lorded it over God's heritage, will be apprised of the hour of doom. Comparison of Luke's language with Mark's again shews that Luke follows a separate tradition. Both sources, however, agree in depicting the last crisis as precipitated by a general collapse of the powers of nature. There will be eclipses, meteoric phenomena, earth-quakes : ' the orbs of the heavens will be shaken ' (cf. Joel ii. 30-31). The reference to the sea suggests a tidal wave which overwhelms the world. At creation the sea—always a sinister element to the Jews—was set in its place and bounded (Genesis i. 9). Now it reasserts its mastery and threatens to engulf the land. But at this hour, when the nations swoon with ' panic and foreboding of what is to befall the universe,' the expectant followers of Christ will see ' the Son of man coming in a cloud ' with great power and glory. This is the promised signal for the Messianic Reign to begin (cf. ix. 26-27), and its appearance will be a *Sursum Corda !* to Christians, a pledge that their redemption will no longer be delayed.

It is probable that the prediction in ver. 27 constitutes the authentic historical kernel of the section. Jesus appealed to the ' Son of man ' prophecy in Daniel vii. 13-14 as giving the assurance of his vindication before men and of the ultimate triumph of the Kingdom of God. Hence to his followers the ' Coming ' of the Son of man became synonymous with the end of the world-order. For the rest, while it is possible that Jesus did speak of natural signs preluding that consummation, it is more likely that his followers supplemented his simple prediction

235

about the Son of man with details drawn from the traditional stock of apocalyptic ideas.

The parable of the **Fig-tree** as placed here conveys an added assurance that the cosmic events which have been enumerated are pregnant with promise of the Reign of God. In Mark attention is confined to the single tree : Luke generalizes by including ' all the trees.' As all arboreal nature witnesses in spring to the life of the new season, so the Woes and Signs, with which the proximate age will be rife, prelude the dawning of the Reign of God. And the consummation will take place in living experience. ' **The present generation will not pass away till all this happens** ' (compare ix. 27 and the discussion on that passage). As originally uttered, the word would have reference to the immediate particular issue with which Jesus was concerned, viz. his own revelation as the Son of man, and would not include all the details with which the above discourse has been garnished. But whether he is speaking of his own coming, or only of the doom of Jerusalem, his pronouncement is to be taken as final truth of God. ' **Heaven and earth will pass away, but my words never.** '

The section closes with warnings (vers. 34–36). The historical nucleus here is the admonition to watch and pray for the Son of Man's coming. This charge the community interprets as condemning slackness, drunkenness, and worldly preoccupations (cf. xii. 42–46, and 1 Thessalonians v. 1–10). The Son of man comes suddenly and judges men as he finds them. In view of oncoming perils and woes the followers of Christ must hourly **keep awake, praying** that they may stand before the Son of man.

At this point some ancient MSS. of Luke insert the section on the adulteress, which many other MSS. introduce into the text of John at vii. 53 of that gospel.

VI. THE PASSION HISTORY AND THE RESURRECTION
(xxii. 1–xxiv. 53)

xxii. 1–6 : THE BETRAYAL BY JUDAS

xxii.

1 Now the feast of unleavened bread which is called the passover
2 was near. The high priests and scribes were trying how to get him put to death (for they were afraid of the people),

and Satan entered Judas called Iscariot, a member of the 3
twelve, who went off to discuss with the high priests and 4
commanders how he could betray him to them. They were
delighted and agreed to pay him for it. He assented to this 5
and sought a good opportunity for betraying him to them in 6
the absence of the crowd. (Cf. Mark xiv. 1-2, 10-11.)

The seizure of Jesus by the Jewish authorities was in the end
facilitated by the defection of Judas, who, deserting Jesus, sold
himself to the High-priests and Temple officers of the Levite
patrol. Luke's statement that **the feast of unleavened bread
which is called the passover was near**, explained by Mark xiv. 1,
points to Wednesday as the date, and this Wednesday on the
Synoptic reckoning would be Nisan 13. Jerusalem was at this
time thronged with pilgrims, many of them ardent supporters of
Jesus. The authorities were therefore obliged to proceed with
caution. Jesus must be surprised after sunset when the crowds
drawn by his teaching had dispersed and he was alone on the
Mount of Olives (xix. 37). Even then, as the Mount of Olives,
like all surrounding districts, would be studded with pilgrim
encampments, information of his whereabouts would be necessary. The unexpected desertion of Judas led to a solution of
these difficulties.

Why did Judas betray Jesus? Luke says, **Satan entered
Judas**, thus attributing the act to diabolic inspiration or possession, but how did Judas lend himself to such influences? Here
we can only suppose either that he had abandoned the belief that
Jesus was the Messiah, or that, tired of what seemed to him a
policy of inaction on the part of Jesus, he thought by his disclosure of the Messianic secret to force Jesus to public measures
on behalf of his claim. In the latter case he was in effect
seconding the policy attributed to Satan in the wilderness
temptation. In any case he has renounced Jesus' method of loving
and forgiving and seeking the Kingdom only through rebirth and
the denial of self. The decision to approach the hierarchy may
have dated from the tribute declaration of Jesus in xx. 25.

xxii. 7-13 : PREPARATIONS FOR THE PASSOVER

Then came the day of unleavened bread when the paschal lamb 7
had to be sacrificed. So Jesus despatched Peter and John, 8

saying, ' Go and prepare the passover for us that we may
9   eat it.' They asked him, ' Where do you want us to prepare
10   it ? ' He said to them, ' When you enter the city you will
meet a man carrying a water-jar : follow him to the house
11   he enters, and tell the owner of the house, " The Teacher
asks you, Where is the room in which I can eat the passover
12   with my disciples ? " Then he will show you a large room
upstairs with couches spread ; make your preparations
13   there.' They went off and found it was as he had told
them.

(Cf. Mark xiv. 12–16.)

The time indicated in ver. 6 is the morning of Thursday, the
day preceding Jesus' death. This, according to the Synoptic
chronology, would be Nisan 14. The expression **the day of
unleavened bread when the paschal lamb had to be sacrificed**
(cf. ver. 1) is not technically exact. While the lambs were slain
according to Jewish usage on Nisan 14, the feast of the Azyma
or Unleavened Loaves began strictly only with Nisan 15. But
as the Jewish day was reckoned from 6 p.m., Nisan 14 and 15
would both be represented within the one diurnal period on a
system of reckoning which, like the Graeco-Roman and our own,
calculated the day as from twelve midnight. Hence Josephus,
writing like our evangelists for the wider world, uses the same
expression ' the feast of unleavened loaves which we call Passover.' According to Mark, whom Luke here follows, the meal
which the disciples prepare is the Passover itself. Jesus and his
friends are encamped without the city, but in conformity with a
custom, which Strack-Billerbeck think to have been legally
secured to pilgrims journeying to the Feast, a room in Jerusalem
had been bespoken for them where the sacred rites might be
observed. This seems the best explanation of the sign of the
man carrying a water-jar in ver. 10. Jesus, aware of his enemies'
design to seize him, has made a secret arrangement with an
adherent of his own in Jerusalem. The water-carrier is a slave
of the latter, and is posted at some trysted spot to guide the
disciples to his master's house. Peter and John are now informed
of the sign and despatched with the instruction, ' Go and prepare
the passover for us.' The preparation would include the purchase and slaying of the lamb, the roasting of its flesh, and the
provision of other prescribed articles of food (Exodus xii. 8).

xxii. 14-23 : THE LAST SUPPER

So they prepared the passover, and when the hour came he 14
took his place, with the apostles beside him. He said
to them, ' I have longed eagerly to eat this passover with 15
you before I suffer, for I tell you I will never eat the passover 16
again till the fulfilment of it in the Reign of God.' And 17
he took a cup which was handed to him, gave thanks to
God and said, ' Take this and distribute it among yourselves,
for I tell you I will never drink the produce of the vine 18
again till such time as God's Reign comes.' Then he took 19
a loaf, and after thanking God he broke it and gave it to
them, saying, ' This means my body given up for your sake ;
do this in memory of me.' So too he gave them the cup
after supper, saying, ' This cup means the new *covenant* rati- 20
fied *by* my *blood* shed for your sake. But the hand of my 21
betrayer is on the table beside me ! The Son of man moves
to his end indeed as it has been decreed, but woe to the man 22
by whom he is betrayed ! And they began to discuss 23
among themselves which of them could possibly be going
to do such a thing.

(Cf. Mark xiv. 17-25.)

At this point Luke, whose narrative in the two preceding
sections shews the influence of Mark, passes over to the guidance
of his Judean source and follows it, except for a few Markan
insertions, down to the close of his gospel (see Introd., p. xviii f).
Luke's differences from Mark in the Supper narrative are
conspicuous.

The natural sense of the words ' I have longed eagerly '
(literally, ' With desire I have desired ') is that Jesus, despite
the precautions which he has taken, has dreaded an interference
of the authorities before he could partake of this passover with
the Twelve. He has something to say to the disciples for which
the Passover is the fitting occasion, and his words express
thankfulness that his wish has indeed been granted. (For
another interpretation, favoured by some modern exegetes,
see below.) The words ' before I suffer ' explicate the peculiar
importance attaching to the occasion. Jesus' death is imminent.
For him remains no recurrence of the beloved rite but only
the fulfilment—often depicted as a feast (xiii. 28-29)—to which

239

in Jewish thought the Passover pointed, viz. the consummation
of redemption in the Reign of God. This allusion imparts an
intense prospective direction to all that now follows.[1]

The precise nature of the ritual actions in vers. 17–20 is
rendered somewhat difficult by a complicated textual problem,
on which see below. Taking the text as it stands in all Greek
MSS. except one, we find Jesus making use of two cups. First,
he took a cup which was handed to him, and after giving thanks
he passed it to his disciples saying, ' Take this and distribute
it among yourselves.' As the ritual of the Lord's Supper proper
does not begin until ver. 19, this cup is naturally understood
as belonging to the Passover order, in the context of which
the Eucharist arises. Hence two alternatives. We may
identify the cup with the *first* of four cups which Jewish
tradition prescribes at the Passover. This would be of red wine
mixed with water, and would be blessed with the words, ' Praised
be thou, Jahweh our God, who createst the produce of the
vine.' Or, if the expression this passover in ver. 15 presupposes
the presence in Jesus' hand of the unleavened bread which was
tasted after the preliminary cup, the cup in ver. 17 will be
the *second* Passover cup, which followed the bread. On either
supposition Jesus is still following the order of the Passover
rite, though his words in verse 18, ' I tell you I will never drink
the produce of the vine again,' etc., impart, like the similar
words in ver. 16, a special personal significance to the acts.
In vers. 19–20, however, procedure graduates from the Passover
order into something which later becomes the Eucharist-
observance of the Christian society. He took a loaf, and after
thanking God he broke it and gave it to them—the distribution
and common partaking of the symbolic element are here of
central significance—saying, ' This means my body given up
for your sake.' The relation in which the offered element
of bread stands to the body of Christ is representative or
symbolic. As the Christ who speaks is still a living person,
no existential oneness of his body with the bread can be thought
of. Such an identification will arise later, first in a spiritual-
mystical way in the teaching of Paul and of the Fourth Gospel
and later in a more concrete materialistic fashion. The

---

[1] For a full discussion of the significance of the Supper-narrative the
reader is referred to the brilliant exposition by Dalman in his *Jesus-
Jeshua* (1929), pp. 86–184.

injunction which accompanies, 'Do this in memory of me,' is absent from Mark and Matthew, but agrees with the statement in 1 Corinthians xi. 24–25 (see below). The Greek tense conveys an understanding that the memorial is to be *repeated*. In ver. 20 the Eucharistic cup proper is given with the explanation, 'This cup means the new covenant.' This indicates that under the form of the cup or of the wine within the cup the 'new covenant' is given and appropriated. 'New covenant' takes us back to Jeremiah xxxi. 31, but as a new covenant necessarily presupposes an older one the roots of the conception stretch still farther back to the ancient covenant which God made with Israel at the Exodus (Exodus xxiv. 4–8). That the new covenant like its prototype is instituted by sacrifice appears by the explanatory addition, 'ratified by my blood shed for your sake.' Jesus is conscious that through the shedding of his blood the new covenant of which prophecy spoke becomes for his followers an accomplished fact into the benefits of which they now proleptically enter. His death is not a tragedy simply or a price demanded by fidelity to a cause. It is the means of bringing on, instituting, applying, and sealing a redemption which by his life and word he has sought to effect but which only the final sacrifice of his life will bring to fulfilment. Thus Jesus, according to the evangelical tradition, reads the final purpose of God in his own mysterious fortunes.

The Lord's Supper as thus presented indicates and inaugurates a redemption effected by the death of Christ as a sacrifice. 'Christ knew that his death was at hand. But he believed that by his death the disciples would be saved from the world as were the Israelites from Egypt' (Easton). The rite points to this final redemption; it expresses the solidarity of the disciples with Christ; and it perpetuates the memorial of the sacrifice by which the redemption is won.

Now arise two questions of critical and historical importance:

(1) Does the whole of the above narrative come to us from Luke? The reason for asking this question is that the Greek codex D and a group of ancient Latin versions omit the second half of ver. 19 (beginning with ' given up for your sake ') and the whole of ver. 20. According to this shorter text Jesus used only one cup (ver. 17), the cup came *before* the bread (ver. 19), and neither cup nor bread was explained as pointing to a covenant or to the shedding of Christ's blood. Now, as it is inconceivable

that in so sacred a matter an originally longer text would be accidentally or deliberately truncated, scholars generally assume that the short text of the above authorities represents what Luke wrote, and they consider that vers. 19b–20 are a later addition inserted to remedy the defects of a narrative which, by placing the cup before the bread and by leaving both insufficiently explained, conflicted with existing usage and failed to satisfy the Church. In confirmation of this it should be mentioned that vers. 19b–20 are almost a *verbatim* reproduction of 1 Corinthians xi. 24–25, and hence may have been borrowed from that source. On this view Luke's original text, following his Judean source, made the Supper a prophecy of the Messianic banquet and a symbol of the disciples' fellowship with Christ, but not a representation of his sacrifice or a channel by which the results of that sacrifice are communicated.

(2) Was the meal of which Jesus and the disciples partook really a Passover meal? This question belongs properly to a commentary on Mark, and is only raised here because of a certain ambiguity in Luke xxii. 15. Mark, Matthew, and Luke all represent the meal as the Passover, and are therefore commonly understood to date it on Nisan 14, and the death of Christ on Nisan 15. But this understanding involves the very difficult assumption that the trial and crucifixion of Jesus were carried out after the Feast had begun, and conflicts with the plan ascribed to the authorities in Mark xiv. 1–2.[1] Moreover, the Fourth Gospel deliberately assigns the crucifixion to Nisan 14, and throws back to Nisan 13 the meal of which Jesus partook with the Twelve (John xiii. 1, xviii. 28). In view of the difficulties inhering in the Synoptic account most scholars prefer here the Johannine chronology, and think that the Synoptic identification of the Supper with the Passover meal is due to confusion. The meal of which Jesus partook was not the Passover but the Qiddush, a celebration observed on the eve of Sabbaths and Feasts, and they think that Luke's Judean source supported that view. The words of Luke xxii. 15 they take to mean that Jesus had desired to eat the Passover of that year with his disciples, *but that the desire was not fulfilled.*

[1] Dalman seeks to dismiss these difficulties, and rejects the hypothesis put forward by Chwolson. According to him the Johannine chronology is artificial. The Synoptic account is correct.

But while the Johannine chronology is right in placing the death of Christ on the Passover Day, Nisan 14, it does not follow that the meal on the previous evening was not a Passover. According to Chwolson (whose argument the English reader will find summarized in Klausner's *Jesus of Nazareth*, p. 326), if Nisan 14 fell on the eve of a Sabbath, while strict Pharisees felt obliged to observe the Passover on that eve, it was permissible for others, if they chose, to celebrate it on the evening of Nisan 13. ' Hence Jesus and his disciples celebrated Passover on the Thursday, the 13th of Nisan.' The Synoptic language is on this view correct, and there is no real conflict with the Johannine chronology.

The acceptance of the view that Jesus was crucified on Nisan 14, in one of a cycle of years (A.D. 26–36) in which Nisan 14 fell on a Friday, gives us A.D. 29 as, on the most probable astronomical reckoning, the year of his death.

The narrative of the Supper in Luke closes with an allusion to the presence of the traitor (vers. 21–23), the enormity of whose guilt is revealed by his having accepted table-fellowship with Christ. This incident in Mark *precedes* the Supper. Jesus is conscious of the alienation of Judas and discerns what is in his mind. That he predicts the act without making mention of the guilty person's name constitutes a last appeal to the traitor. The other disciples, not knowing to whom Jesus refers, are mystified and embarrassed.

xxii. 24–30 : GREATNESS AND SERVICE

A quarrel also rose among them as to which of them could be 24
    considered the greatest. But Jesus said to them, 25
    ' The kings of the Gentiles rule over them,
      and their authorities take the name of " Benefactor " :
      not so with you. 26
      He who is greatest among you must be like the youngest,
      and he who is chief like a servant.
      Which is the greatest, guest or servant ? Is it not the 27
      guest ?
      But I am among you as a servant.
    It is you who have stood by me through my trials ; so ⁂
    even as my Father has assigned me royal power, I assign 30

you the right of eating and drinking at my table in my Realm and of sitting on thrones to rule the twelve tribes of Israel.'

(Cf. Mark x. 42–45 ; Matthew xix. 28.)

Luke, following his special source, brings in here an episode which has a parallel in Mark x. 42–45. On the psychology of the question, which could be considered the greatest ? see under ix. 46–48. Jesus declares that the identifying of greatness with privilege or power is Gentile, heathenish, as witness the grandiose titles of honour assumed by former Ptolemaic and Seleucid rulers and by some contemporary princes. Euergetes (' Benefactor ') was a favourite designation of the Ptolemies of Egypt ; Soter (' Saviour ') was another. Over against this confusion of honour with lordship over others, Jesus sets the necessity of self-sacrifice for others' good, and instances his own example : ' I am among you as a servant.'[1] What constitutes Christ's ' service ' is not stated by Luke. He does not, like Mark x. 45, identify it with the giving of Jesus' life as a ransom, nor does he allude explicitly to the Servant of the Lord in Isaiah. He presents Jesus rather as one who, though head of his household and host of his company, has condescended at his table to lowly acts of helpful ministry (cf. John xiii. 1–17). But though Luke does not indicate it, the thought of Isaiah liii. is in the background.

With this teaching the promise in vers. 28–30 is consistent. In the words, ' It is you who have stood by me through my trials,' Jesus acknowledges the fidelity of his disciples throughout the many crises, the assaults, and temptations which Satan has created for him in his ministry. But this experience must have taught the disciples upon what principles alone the honours which they seek, and which he wills them to receive, can be attained. ' Even as my Father has assigned me royal power '— the disciples have surely seen by now on what terms Jesus obtains his crown—' so I assign to you the right of eating and drinking at my table in my Realm (compare Mark x. 35–40) and of sitting on thrones to judge the twelve tribes of Israel.' The disciples have coveted the splendid distinction of being Christ's

---

[1] Dalman thinks that the question of the disciples arose out of the allocation of the places of honour at the Supper-table, and this gives excellent point to our Lord's words.

assessors in his Kingdom, but this is only to be attained as Christ attains his sovereignty, viz. by sacrifice (cf. Philippians ii. 5 f.).

Thus the vision of rewards in the Kingdom, which otherwise would be indistinguishable from a chiliastic dream, is stripped of everything gross and earthly. This is a point not sufficiently emphasized by commentators. Ver. 30 rests on a Q word (cf. Matthew xix. 28).

xxii. 31-34 : THE DESERTION OF THE APOSTLES PREDICTED

' Simon, Simon, Satan has claimed the right to sift you all like 31 wheat, but I have prayed that your own faith may not fail. 32 And you in turn must be a strength to your brothers.' ' Lord,' he said, ' I am ready to go with you to prison and 33 to death.' Jesus said, ' I tell you, Peter, the cock will not 34 crow to-day before you have three times denied that you know me.'

(Cf. Mark xiv. 27-31.)

This section is from Luke's special source, and differs notably from the corresponding narrative in Mark xiv. 27-31. In Mark Jesus says that his flock will be scattered, and adds : ' But after my rising I will precede you to Galilee.' Luke's source excludes, here as elsewhere, all reference to an appearance of the Risen Lord in *Galilee*, but seems nevertheless in ver. 32 to point to some post-resurrection experience of Peter. Looking at Peter, but speaking with reference to the whole company, Jesus says, ' Simon, Simon, Satan has claimed the right to sift you all like wheat.' The events now impending signify a last desperate determination of Satan to break up the fellowship of Jesus and to toss its members to the winds, but—here Jesus addresses himself to Peter alone—' I have prayed that your own faith may not fail.' If these words stood apart from vers. 33-34, they might indicate that Jesus looked to Peter not to give way at all, but in the context of these verses no more is expressed than the hope that Peter having once fled will turn and rally the scattered flock of Jesus. ' You in turn must be a strength to your brothers ' undoubtedly connects in the tradition with the circumstance that Peter first, through a revelation of the Risen Lord (xxiv. 34, 1 Corinthians xv. 5), re-formed the broken ranks of the fellowship of Jesus and consolidated them upon a revived basis of faith.

The prediction of the denial, which Mark reserves till Jesus reaches the Mount of Olives, is assigned by Luke's source to the Supper-room. The disciple is affronted by the Lord's suggestion of his possible defection and answers with his usual bold assurance. Jesus' word ' Peter ' (' thou who art called Rock ') is pregnant with the contrast at this moment between his disciple's high calling and his downfall.

xxii. 35–38 : PURSE AND SWORD

35 And he said to them, ' When I sent you out with neither purse nor wallet nor sandals, did you want for anything ? ' ' No,'
36 they said, ' for nothing.' Then he said to them, ' But he who has a purse must take it now, and the same with a wallet ; and he who has no sword must sell his coat and buy one.
37 For I tell you, this word of scripture must be fulfilled in me : *he was classed among criminals.* Yes, there is an end to all
38 that refers to me.' ' Lord,' they said, ' here are two swords ! ' ' Enough ! Enough ! ' he answered.

(Luke alone.)

This section impressively concludes the words spoken in the Supper-room. Jesus passes to the sorrowful contrast between the sunny Galilean days and the dark prospect which now lies before his disciples. Time was when the disciples, as they went out to the towns and villages of Israel, could expect a welcome (ix. 4). Purse and wallet were superfluous, since everywhere they could count on a hospitable board. ' When I sent you out with neither purse nor wallet, did you want for anything ? ' But these were the days when Jesus, though still unknown to many, could hope that his message, the winsome ' glad tidings ' of the Kingdom, would be universally received. He was not yet ' classed among criminals.' But now the prospect is closed doors, repulse, repudiation. ' He who has a purse must take it now, and the same with a wallet.' But what about the words which follow ?—' And he who has no sword must sell his coat and buy one.' What can ' sword ' signify on the lips of One who said ' I tell you, you must not resist an injury ' ? Here two suggestions are possible. (1) Jesus is speaking literally, but ironically, of a situation in which he is regarded as a dangerous person. His eye perchance has fallen on one or other of his disciples snatching a sacrificial knife and smuggling it out of the room under his cloak, and he says : ' Yes, provide yourselves with swords, at whatsoever cost ! ' (2) Jesus is speaking seriously, but metaphorically. Dangers to life will indeed now be let loose against his faithful band, and they will need to gird themselves for conflict. The sword on this interpretation is not literally intended. Either interpretation would suit well enough with the sad words, ' I tell you, this word of scripture must be fulfilled in me : he was classed among criminals ' (Isaiah liii. 12). The second, however, because it is serious, seems the more likely.

But while these two interpretations, the literal-ironical and the symbolic-serious, naturally suggest themselves, another explanation is sometimes offered, viz. that (3) Jesus meant the sword both literally and seriously. He knew that the penalty in ver. 37 fell on himself. He was classed among criminals by his enemies, by himself, and by the will of God. But the penalty was confined to himself. He wished to save his disciples, to arm them, if necessary, against what might yet prove a murderous attempt upon their lives. But this understanding of the saying clearly conflicts with the sequel. When the disciples, taking him literally, produce their brace of smuggled knives, ' Lord, here are two swords,' Jesus answers ' Enough ! ' While this might mean ' two swords will serve,' it is more probably a dismissal of a childish mistake, meaning ' No more of this ! You have not understood.' Jesus was speaking in parables.

xxii. 39-46 : CHRIST'S PRAYER IN THE GARDEN

Then he went outside and made his way to the Hill of Olives, 39 as he was accustomed. The disciples followed him, and when he reached the spot he said to them, ' Pray that 40 you may not slip into temptation.' He withdrew about a 41 stone's throw and knelt in prayer, saying, ' Father, if it 42 please thee, take this cup away from me. But thy will, not mine, be done.' [And an angel from heaven appeared to 43 strengthen him ; he fell into an agony and prayed with 44

45
46

greater intensity, his sweat dropping to the ground like clots of blood.] Then rising from prayer he went to the disciples, only to find them asleep from sheer sorrow. He said to them, 'Why are you sleeping ? Get up and pray that you may not slip into temptation.'

(Cf. Mark xiv. 32–42.)

The dark premonitions which had gathered round the Saviour's mind during the closing moments in the Supper-room acquire a terrible intensity in the ensuing hour on the Mount of Olives. Luke's source indeed makes no mention of the appalling change which comes over Jesus (Mark xiv. 33), nor does Jesus return three times to pray the same agonized prayer for the removal of his ' cup.' His attitude is collected, his spirit resigned. Yet in the words to the disciples, ' Pray that you may not slip into temptation,' there is the sense of ghostly forces now let loose and boding peril to the souls of the disciples (cf. xxii. 53). Therefore, while withdrawing from them, Jesus remains within call, only ' a stone's throw ' away. Here the final drama of his self-consecration to God enacts itself. ' Father, if it please thee, take this cup away from me.' The ' cup ' is his rejection (cf. Mark x. 38) with its bitter ingredients, the betrayal by Judas, the sense of being accursed—' classed among criminals,' his distressing anxiety lest his disciples should fall away, his consciousness of awful exposure to Satan's power. Jesus shrinks from the cup. Can it be the Father's will that all this should really come to pass ?

There are those who argue from the experience in the Garden that Jesus had not prophesied his *death*, had not even contemplated its possibility. Faced by hostility, he predicted sharp suffering and trial—the Messianic ' pangs '—as the portion of himself and his faithful disciples. But from this trial he would emerge triumphant. God would intervene, and set up His reign. The predictions of death, so argue these scholars, are a projection backwards of the ultimate event. Not till the Supper and the vigil in the Garden did death appear a certainty.

But if Jesus did not predict his death, why should the tradition declare him to have done so ? The Passion brought a new amazing change in men's thoughts of God's redeeming love, and it would have done so even if it had not been fore-announced. Paul's gospel would stand whether Christ *predicted* the Cross or

248

not. That Jesus should foretell his passion and yet shrink from the appalling form which it had now assumed before his mind is explicable, when we do not discount altogether the human nature of Jesus. His prayer is for submission : 'Thy will, not mine, be done.' Vers. 43–44 are absent from many ancient authorities, and are only doubtfully a part of the text. But that the struggle of Jesus' soul was severe is terribly apparent. In ver. 45 the victory has been won. Jesus returning finds the disciples sleeping, as Luke adds, ' from sorrow.' 'Why are you sleeping ? ' he cries. The peril of the disciples is again before him.

xxii. 47–53 : JESUS ARRESTED

While he was still speaking, there came a mob headed by the 47 man called Judas, one of the twelve. He approached in order to kiss Jesus, but Jesus said to him, ' Judas ! would you 48 betray the Son of man with a kiss ? ' Now when the sup- 49 porters of Jesus saw what was going to happen, they said, ' Lord, shall we strike with our swords ? ' And one of them 50 did strike the servant of the high priest, cutting off his right ear. Jesus said, ' Let me do this at least,' and cured him 51 by touching his ear. Then he said to the high priests and 52 commanders of the temple and elders who had appeared to take him, ' Have you sallied out to arrest me like a robber, with swords and cudgels ? Day after day I was 53 beside you in the temple, and you never stretched a hand against me. But this is your hour, and the dark Power has its way.'

(Cf. Mark xiv. 43–50.)

The crisis of which Jesus had spoken was nearer than the dis- ciples imagined. A mob headed by Judas appears, and accord- ing to Mark xiv. 45 the traitor kissed Jesus in accordance with a preconcerted sign. In Luke's source the kiss was prevented. ' Judas ! would you betray the Son of man—the Messiah of God —with a kiss ? ' At this point in Mark Jesus is seized, and the drawing of the sword by one of the company is by way of retalia- tion. In Luke this *coup de force* anticipates the seizure : ' Lord, shall we strike with our swords ? ' Without waiting for an answer a disciple strikes at a slave of the high-priest. Jesus

intervenes with a word—literally, ' Permit thus far '—which
may signify, as in Dr. Moffatt's translation, his will to heal the
wounded man, or may be a command to the disciples to desist
from interference. Luke and John agree in adding the miraculous healing of the slave's wound.

Luke alone states that high-priests, officers of the Levite guard,
and leading Sanhedrists were with the mob. This is probably
an inference from Jesus' remonstrance in vers. 52–53, which
suggests a responsible audience. But the inference goes beyond
what the facts require. Jesus' remonstrance would be in place
if representatives of the Levite police who ordinarily patrolled
the Temple were present. The words from ' Have you sallied
out ? ' to ' stretched a hand against me ' are from Mark. Luke
alone has ' But this is your hour, and the dark Power has its way,'
a reminder of the supernatural forces which are now massed
against the Son of man. Satan has organized his hosts for a
final combat.

xxii. 54–62 : PETER DENIES JESUS

54 Then they arrested him and led him away inside the house of
the high priest. Peter followed at a distance and sat down
55 among some people who had lit a fire in the courtyard and
56 were sitting round it. A maidservant who noticed him
sitting by the fire took a long look at him and said, ' That
57 fellow was with him too.' But he disowned him, saying,
58 ' Woman, I know nothing about him.' Shortly afterwards
another man noticed him and said, ' Why, you are one of
59 them ! ' ' Man,' said Peter, ' I am not.' About an hour
had passed when another man insisted, ' That fellow really
60 was with him. Why, he is a Galilean ! ' ' Man,' said
Peter, ' I do not know what you mean.' Instantly, just as
61 he was speaking, the cock crowed ; the Lord turned round
and looked at Peter, and then Peter remembered what the
Lord had told him, that ' Before cock-crow to-day you will
62 disown me three times.' And he went outside and wept
bitterly.

(Cf. Mark xiv. 53–54, 66–72.)

According to Mark Jesus was immediately conducted before
the high priest. A full meeting of the Sanhedrin is in session,

a formal trial ensues, and Jesus is condemned. Thereafter, in the morning, a renewed consultation is held as a preliminary to bringing Jesus before Pilate. The denial of Peter falls after the trial (Mark xiv. 66-72). Luke's source differs widely from Mark, and has a higher probability on its side. There is no midnight session of the Sanhedrin. Jesus, being seized, is led to the courtyard of the high-priest's house, and there detained till morning. Meantime Peter, who has not fled, follows at a distance and mingles with the throng in the courtyard, thinking to escape notice and to bide his time—perhaps for some *coup de force* in defence of Jesus. But being suspected and questioned he is guilty of a triple denial of his Master. In Luke therefore the denial precedes the trial of Jesus by the Sanhedrin. Different traditions of the episode were apparently current in early days. Thus Mark and Luke's source vary as regards the persons who take Peter to task. In Mark the cock crows twice, in accordance with a prediction of Jesus to that effect (Mark xiv. 30, 68, 72) ; in Luke only once, when Peter has uttered his third denial (xxiv. 34, 60-61). Otherwise the accounts generally agree. Peter, called to deny *himself* (ix. 20-23), denies his Lord instead. He disclaims knowledge of Jesus, is not of his company, does not understand what his accusers mean. As the questions are pressed home, however, the reserves of Peter sensibly weaken. The crowing of the cock, and the fact that the Lord, who is in the courtyard and within earshot of the disciple's disclaimers, at that moment turned round and looked at Peter, bring home to the disciple a sense of what he has done.

xxii. 63-65 : JESUS FLOGGED AND MOCKED

Meantime the men who had Jesus in custody flogged him and 63 made fun of him ; blindfolding him they would ask him, 64 ' Prophesy, tell us who struck you ? ' And many another 65 insult they uttered against him.

(Cf. Mark xiv. 65.)

This passage goes closely with the preceding, indicating by its verbal tenses—which are imperfects—the ' attendant circumstances ' of Peter's denial. Jesus is mocked as a prophet

—in accordance with the forecast in xiii. 33. Mark introduces the episode after the trial and, less probably, attributes the sport to members of the Sanhedrin.

xxii. 66–71 : THE TRIAL BEFORE THE SANHEDRIN

66 When day broke, the elders of the people all met along with the high priests and scribes, and had him brought before
67 their Sanhedrin. They said to him, ' Tell us if you are the Christ.' He said to them, ' You will not believe me
68 if I tell you, and you will not answer me when I put a
69 question to you. But after this *the Son of man will be*
70 *seated at God's right hand* of power.' ' Are you the Son of God then ? ' they all said. ' Certainly,' he replied, ' I am.'
71 So they said, ' What more evidence do we need ? We have heard it from his own lips.'

(Cf. Mark xiv. 55–64.)

Luke's narrative is short, and omits all reference to the legal process by which in Mark the Sanhedrin tried to elicit incriminating evidence from witnesses. The issue is confined to a single question addressed to Jesus : ' Tell us if you are the Christ.' The answer of Jesus in Luke is that the court has prejudged the case : ' you will not believe me if I tell you.' That Jesus can be really the Messiah is to the court unthinkable. Secondly, if Jesus makes the claim, the court will twist his words to a wrong significance. Are they prepared to say *why* they interrogate him ? No, ' you will not answer me when I put a question to you.' Here, on a question of defining what Messiahship means, turns the issue between Judaism and Christianity, and possibly the form of Christ's answer, as given by Luke's source, owes something to this controversy. In ver. 69 Jesus, waiving the objections just urged, answers the question of the court affirmatively and in a manner which leaves no room for any earthly misconceptions of his office. He is the Messiah, but in the heavenly sense of the ' Son of man ' who receives the Kingdom from God alone. ' After this— Jesus assumes that his condemnation and death are certain— the Son of man will be seated at God's right hand of power ' (cf. Mark xiv. 62). Nowhere is it more clearly revealed that

Jesus has found in Daniel vii. 13 the ultimate key to his fortunes, the clue to his mysterious engagement to bring his nation to God. Messiahship is sublimated, stripped of all earthly associations. But as the statement of Jesus, being in the third person, might still seem to point to someone other than himself, the court presses for greater precision : ' Are you then the Son of God ? ' On Jewish lips this title would signify ' the Elect of God.' Jesus, by his reply, which literally means ' You say that I am,' accepts the part denoted by the title, while leaving it to his judges to determine what he means. The admission is seized by the court as final proof of his guilt.

Jesus therefore is condemned as an open claimant to Messiahship. On the title ' Son of God ' see under iii. 21–22. It is not apparent how the claim to Messiahship constituted of itself a capital crime. This consideration would not, however, weigh with an assembly to which on other grounds Jesus was unacceptable. Unless the blasphemy lay entirely in the fact of a human being aspiring to be the *heavenly* One of whom the Scriptures spoke, we are forced to conclude that the Jewish hierarchy and nation, while cherishing a Messianic *hope*, was precluded by its presuppositions from admitting a Messiah in human form. In this connexion Dr. Klausner writes some revealing words. ' The Jews expected the Messiah at any time. Every day there arose false Messiahs. . . . Sometimes the Pharisees and Tannaim supported them, as Rabbi Akiba supported Bar Kokhbah ; but as a rule the Pharisees dreaded the difficult consequences of the Messianic belief in practice. Hence in the older Talmudic literature we find an ambiguous attitude towards the Messianic promises : there is a certain wariness as touching the persons of the Messiahs, but a deep and enthusiastic belief in the Messianic hope itself. When the appointed hour should strike, God would redeem His people by miracles and wonders, and the Messiah would be no more than the instrument of God. Jesus, from the moment of his baptism, looked upon himself as the Messiah : the Messiah was therefore already in the world, and so the kingdom of heaven, the kingdom of the Messiah, was likewise in existence in the world ' (*Jesus of Nazareth*, pp. 402 f.). This the Jewish hierarchy could not admit.

xxiii. 1–5 : JESUS BEFORE PILATE

xxiii.

1 Then the whole body of them rose and led him to Pilate.
2 They proceeded to accuse him, saying, 'We have discovered this fellow perverting our nation, forbidding tribute being
3 paid to Caesar, and alleging he is king messiah.' Pilate asked him, ' Are you the king of the Jews ? ' He replied,
4 ' Certainly.' And Pilate said to the high priests and the crowds, ' I cannot find anything criminal about him.'
5 But they insisted, ' He stirs up the people by teaching all over Judaea. He started from Galilee and now he is here.'

(Cf. Mark xv. 1–5.)

The Jewish Sanhedrin did not possess the *ius gladii* or power to inflict the death-sentence upon an offender. This appertained exclusively to the Roman procurator. If, however, the Messianic claim of Jesus were to come under the cognizance of a Roman court, it must be given a political complexion. Otherwise it would remain among those purely religious questions—' controversies about words and persons and your own Law ' (Acts xviii. 15)—with which no Roman judiciary would ordinarily interfere. Hence the form under which, according to Luke, the Sanhedrin presents its case against Jesus. Jesus is denounced as a fomenter of sedition, the claimant to a native princedom, one who is ' perverting our nation, forbidding tribute being paid to Caesar, and alleging he is king messiah.' Pilate, presented with this indictment—which controverted the facts at every point, though the procurator could not be supposed to know this—confines attention to the one point of the Messianic claim, and asks Jesus, ' Are you the king of the Jews ? ' The answer of Jesus, conforming to his statement before the Sanhedrin in xxii. 70, is literally ' Thou sayest.' He admits the claim because sovereignty is inseparable from Messiahship, but he leaves it to Pilate to decide what construction he is to put on this sovereignty. Pilate declares himself satisfied that no menace to the state is involved : ' I cannot find anything criminal about him.' To this the Sanhedrists retort that the menace to peace created by Jesus throughout Judea is real enough : ' He stirs up the people. He started from Galilee and now he is here.'

A comparison of this narrative with Mark shews a tendency in Luke, if not to darken the guilt of the Jewish Sanhedrin, at least to exonerate considerably the Roman procurator (cf. Acts iii. 13–14). Pilate is accredited with an understanding of Jesus' Messiahship which removes from it every political or earthly feature. This accords with Luke's apologetic purpose in Acts to represent Christianity as politically innocuous and as fully vindicated in this character by a series of official pronouncements. Hence some scholars would see Luke's own hand in the drafting of the false charges attributed to the Sanhedrin in ver. 2. There is, however, no ground for supposing that Luke had not here the support of his Judean source. The Jewish Christians of Palestine, under stress of persecution by their fellow-countrymen, would tend to sympathize with Rome against their apostate nation, and this tendency would colour Luke's source. Jewish apologists contend that Pilate was the real villain. He would be only too ready to crush any Jewish *mahdi* who fell into his hands. But while the tradition favoured by Luke places Pilate in the best light, it does not follow that the Jewish Sanhedrin was not guilty of the atrocious misrepresentations of fact charged upon it in ver. 2.

xxiii. 6–12 : JESUS BEFORE ANTIPAS

When Pilate heard that, he asked if the man was a Galilean, 6 and ascertaining that he came under the jurisdiction of 7 Herod, he remitted him to Herod, who himself was in Jerusalem during those days. Herod was greatly delighted 8 to see Jesus ; he had long wanted to see him, because he had heard about him and also because he hoped to see him perform some miracle. But though he 9 put many questions to him, Jesus gave him no answer. Meanwhile the high priests and scribes stood and accused 10 him with might and main. Then Herod and his troops 11 scoffed at him and made fun of him, and after arraying him in a bright robe he remitted him to Pilate. Herod and 12 Pilate became friends that day—previously they had been at enmity.

(Luke alone.)

The sending of Jesus to the tetrarch Antipas is but an interlude in the trial-drama. Pilate, hearing that Jesus 'started from Galilee,' thinks it diplomatic to refer the case to a quarter in which local or personal knowledge of the facts could naturally be assumed. Herod, however, has little or no knowledge of Jesus. He has listened to gossip, and is curious to see for himself the reputed miracle-worker of his province. The investigation conducted by Herod proves futile from the start. **Though he put many questions, Jesus gave him no answer.** Was it that Antipas by his behaviour to John had put himself for ever beyond the forgiveness of Jesus ? Or did Jesus deem it idle, nay, a sacrilege to discuss sacred matters with a shallow sensationalist ? As the Sanhedrists are present and pressing for an answer to their pleadings, Antipas has to do something. Calling in his bodyguard, he has Jesus arrayed in a resplendent robe and mocked. Thereby he indicates that the Messianic claims of Jesus are a mere jest, undeserving of serious consideration.

An incident which presents the Galilean tetrarch in so dubious a light cannot have owed or contributed much to the apologetic aims of Luke or of his source. Clearly the narrative is controlled by a definite tradition of fact, and the motive for including it in the Passion-drama can only have been its illustrative value as shewing how Jesus was ' despised and rejected ' by his whole nation (cf. Acts iv. 24–28). The conduct ascribed to Antipas is in keeping with what we otherwise know of his character.

xxiii. 13–25 : Jesus Surrendered by Pilate

13 Then summoning the high priests and rulers and the people,
14 Pilate said to them, ' You brought me this man as being an inciter to rebellion among the people. I have examined him before you and found nothing criminal about him, for all
15 your accusations against him. No, nor has Herod, for he has remitted him to us. He has done nothing, you see, that
16 calls for death ; so I shall release him with a whipping.'
18 But they shouted one and all, ' Away with him ! Release
19 Bar-Abbas for us ! ' (This was a man who had been put into prison on account of a riot which had taken place in the
20 city and also on a charge of murder.) Again Pilate addressed
21 them, for he wanted to release Jesus, but they roared, ' To

the cross, to the cross with him ! ' He asked them a third 22
time, ' But what crime has he committed ? I have found
nothing about him that deserves death ; so I shall release
him with a whipping.' But they loudly urged their demand 23
that he should be crucified, and their shouts carried the day.
Pilate gave sentence that their demand was to be carried 24
out ; he released the man they wanted, the man who had 25
been imprisoned for riot and murder, and Jesus he handed
over to their will.

(Cf. Mark xv. 6–15.)

The trial is now resumed before the procurator, and in vers.
13-16, which are peculiar to Luke, Pilate reiterates but with
greater emphasis and formality his already expressed judgment
that Jesus is guiltless of any political crime. The charge that
he has been ' an inciter to rebellion ' has broken down on investigation, and Pilate cites Antipas as additional witness that
Jesus ' has done nothing that calls for death.' But as a pretender
to Messiahship, albeit innocuous, Jesus merits punishment, and
Pilate therefore proposes to scourge him. The suggestion is
greeted with the shout ' Away with him ! Release Barabbas
for us ! ' In vers. 18-22 Luke follows Mark, but maintains the
same attitude to Pilate as has characterized his Judean source.
In Mark Pilate wishes to humour the people : in Luke he is bent
on acquitting Jesus (vers. 20, 22). The clamour for the release
of Barabbas, a political prisoner lying under sentence of death
for complicity in a recent riot involving bloodshed, is meant to
divert Pilate from sympathy with Jesus, and in this it proves
successful. Pilate after a third but unavailing protestation of
his prisoner's innocence succumbs to the popular will. Barabbas
is released, and Jesus is sentenced to die on a cross.

The Barabbas-episode is not a little perplexing. Where are
the supporters of Jesus whose presence before the arrest so
intimidated the hierarchy ? And who constitute the furious
throng which demands the release of Barabbas ? As we cannot
suppose the supporters of Jesus to have melted away or to have
turned their backs on their Leader at the last moment, we can
only conclude that the proceedings have taken them by surprise.
The arrest, trial, and condemnation of Jesus have been expedited
during the darkness and early hours of Friday morning before
the pilgrims camped outside the city had begun to stir. The

rabble who beset the procurator's tribunal may then be explained as partisans of Barabbas who have taken advantage of the amnesty customary at the Feast (Mark xv. 6) to procure the release of their friend. Their clamorous insistence plays into the hands of the Sanhedrists, and expedites the fulfilment of their hopes.

xxiii. 26–31 : THE ROAD TO CALVARY

26 As they led him off they caught hold of Simon a Cyrenian on his way from the country and laid the cross on him to carry

27 after Jesus. He was followed by a large multitude of the people and also of women who beat their breasts and lamented

28 him ; but Jesus turned to them and said, ' Daughters of Jerusalem, weep not for me but weep for yourselves and for

29 your children ! For there are days coming when the cry will be,

> " Blessed are the barren,
>   the wombs that never have borne
>   and the breasts that never have suckled ! "

30 Then will people say *to the mountains, " Fall on us ! " and to the hills, " Cover us."*

31 For if this is what they do when the wood is green, what will they do when the wood is dry ? '

(Luke alone, except for ver. 26.)

Jesus is now handed over to soldiers to be led to the place of execution. For the presence in the narrative of Simon of Cyrene Luke is probably indebted to Mark, whose statement that Simon was ' the father of Alexander and Rufus ' suggests that these two brethren were known to the community for which Mark wrote, and thus accounts for the preservation of the tradition. The burden which Simon is impressed to carry consisted probably not of the upright stake of the cross but of the transverse beam to which the Sufferer's hands were to be affixed, and which was borne in procession as a deterrent to evil-doers. Vers. 27–31 are peculiar to Luke, and exhibit affinities with such another extract from his Judean source as xix. 41–44. Followers of Jesus, mostly women, have gathered, and their demonstrations of grief at what has happened touch him to the heart. There rises before his eyes the coming doom of Jerusalem, and he cries : ' Daughters of Jerusalem, weep not for me, but weep for yourselves and for your children.' In agonies and distresses in which motherhood and the custody of little children will seem the very acme of woe, and people will cry out in the words of Hosea x. 8 for the mountains to fall on them and crush them, Jesus sees a suffering which calls more than his own for tears. The corroborative ' For if this is what they do when the wood is green, what will they do when the wood is dry ? ' recalls Ezekiel xx. 47, and may be proverbial. The subject ' they ' is impersonal, and in the context the words mean either ' If tears are exhausted now, where will relief be found in the greater grief which is coming ? ' or—compare the analogous word 1 Peter iv. 17-18—' If the righteous One who sought Jerusalem's peace must suffer, how can the nation which disbelieved his word escape ? '

xxiii. 32-38 : The Crucifixion

Two criminals were also led out with him to be executed, and 32 when they came to the place called The Skull they crucified 33 him there along with the criminals, one at his right and one at his left. Jesus said, ' Father, forgive them, they do not 34 know what they are doing.' Then they *distributed his clothes among themselves by drawing lots*. The people stood 35 and looked on, and even the rulers sneered at him, saying, ' He saved others, let him save himself, if he is the Christ of God, the Chosen One ! ' The soldiers made fun of him too 36 by coming up and handing him vinegar, saying, ' If you are 37 the king of the Jews, save yourself.' (For there was an 38 inscription over him in Greek and Latin and Hebrew characters,

THIS IS THE KING OF THE JEWS.)

(Cf. Mark xv. 22-32.)

Luke relates the final tragedy with sustained reserve. The circumstances on which he dwells, the crucifixion along with Jesus of the two criminals, the prayer of Jesus for his executioners, ' Father, forgive them, they do not know what they are doing,' the drawing of lots for Christ's garments, the cruel sport of the soldiers, the mockery of the inscription placed on the cross, all these in the dying hour of the Son of man remind us that he was ' numbered with the transgressors ' and ' bore the sins of many.' The place-name Golgotha, literally **The Skull**, was derived probably from the configuration of the spot ; it lay outside the city wall (cf. Hebrews xiii. 12–13), but its location is uncertain. The first half of ver. 34 is wanting in many of our important MSS. and Versions, and cannot be certainly concluded a part of what Luke wrote. The scriptural quotation in the second half of the verse identifies Jesus with the Martyr of Psalm xxii. 18. In vers. 35–37 the hierarchs, the people of the Jews, and the Roman soldiery are all represented as finding in the Cross the complete refutation of the Saviour's claims : **' He saved others, let him save himself, if he is the Christ of God, the Chosen One ! ' :** compare Isaiah liii. 4, ' We esteemed him stricken, smitten by God, and afflicted.' For the Christian answer here to Jewish and world unbelief see 1 Corinthians i. 22–24, 2 Corinthians v. 14–21, xiii. 3–4, etc. To Jews, who make miracle and intervention the proof of God, and to Greeks, who demand the rationalization of the human process, the crucifixion of Jesus seemed the blank negation of all divine purpose in his life. To the Christian Church, on the other hand, the Cross appears the supreme revelation of Omnipotence and of divine Wisdom. ' We preach a Messiah crucified . . . who to those who are called, both Jews and Greeks, is God's omnipotence and God's answer to all questions ' (1 Corinthians i. 23–24).

xxiii. 39–43 : The Penitent Thief

39 One of the criminals who had been hung also abused him, saying, ' Are you not the Christ ? Save yourself and us as well.'

40 But the other checked him, saying, ' Have you no fear even of God ? You are suffering the same punishment as he.

41 And we suffer justly ; we are getting what we deserve for

42 our deeds. But he has done no harm.' And he added,

43 ' Jesus, do not forget me when you come to reign.' ' I tell you truly,' said Jesus, ' you will be in paradise with me this very day.'

(Luke alone.)

Differing from Mark xv. 32, which represents both of the criminals crucified with Jesus as joining in the general execration,

Luke's source made an exception in favour of one of the two who, acknowledging the justice of his own and his companion's doom, protests the innocence of Jesus, thereby confessing faith in the claim for which he dies. To this penitent who appeals for pardon at the Judgment—' Jesus, do not forget me when you come to reign '—Jesus promises immediate entrance into life. (On Paradise see under xvi. 19–31.) Is the tradition which is here recorded in any sense symbolical ? Does it stand for the fact that Jesus by his redeeming work among the outcasts introduced division even among those in Israel who sought the Kingdom by methods of criminal violence ?

xxiii. 44-49 : THE DEATH OF CHRIST

By this time it was about twelve o'clock, and darkness covered 44 the whole land till three o'clock, owing to an eclipse of the sun ; the curtain in the middle of the temple was torn in two. 45 Then with a loud cry Jesus said, ' Father, *I trust my spirit* 46 *to thy hands,*' and with these words he expired. When the 47 army-captain saw what had happened, he glorified God, saying, ' This man was really innocent.' And when all the 48 crowds who had collected for the sight saw what had happened they turned away beating their breasts. As for his *acquaint-* 49 *ances*, they *were all standing at a distance* to look on, with the women who had accompanied him from Galilee.

(Cf. Mark xv. 33–41.)

The crucifixion had commenced at 9 a.m. (Mark xv. 25). It is now twelve o'clock midday, and darkness covered the whole land till three o'clock. This statement, which may have borne originally a symbolical meaning, indicating the sympathy of nature with the sufferings of the Son of man, Luke or his source rationalizes by adding owing to an eclipse of the sun. ' A solar eclipse was of course impossible at Passover time '— which had to coincide with full moon—' but Luke might not have known this ' (Easton). Symbolic also in origin may be the other tradition that the curtain in the middle of the temple was torn in two. The curtain in question separated the Holy Place with its shew-bread, seven-branched candlestick, and altar of incense, from the interior Holy of Holies, the dark and awful chamber which none but the high-priest might enter, and he only on the Day of Atonement. The meaning of the symbolism is obvious. Through the dying of the Son of man the veil between God and man is removed. ' Confidence to enter the holy Presence ' is granted ' in virtue of the blood of Jesus by the fresh, living way which he has inaugurated ' (Hebrews x. 19–20). Mark places the incident after the death of Jesus : Luke makes it coincident with his dying hour. Luke's source contained no mention of the cry of dereliction (Mark xv. 34) with which the Saviour yielded up his life. In the words which it substitutes, ' Father, I trust my spirit to thy hands ' (Psalm xxxi. 5), the supreme surrender is taken on the side not of the anguish and desolation which the vicarious Sufferer endured but of the faith and submission with which he bore his suffering to the end. The army-captain who is looking on is shaken with religious emotion, and his words, ' This man was really innocent,' doubtless prefigured for Luke the coming conversion of the heathen world. In Mark the exclamation takes the form, ' This man was certainly a son of God,' a confession that in Jesus a divine or superhuman personality had been manifested to the world.

xxiii. 50–56 : THE BURIAL

50 Now there was a man called Joseph, a member of council but
51 a good and just man who had not voted for their plan of action ; he belonged to Arimathaea, a Jewish town, and
52 he was on the outlook for the Reign of God. This Joseph
53 went to Pilate and asked him for the body of Jesus. He then took it down, wrapped it in linen, and put it in a tomb
54 cut out of the rock, where no one had yet been buried. It was the day of the Preparation and the sabbath was just
55 dawning. So the women who had accompanied him from Galilee and who had followed Joseph, noted the tomb and
56 the position of the body ; then they went home and prepared spices and perfumes.

(Cf. Mark xv. 42–47.)

The bodies of crucified persons were ordinarily left to hang on the cross. The exception made in the case of Jesus is due to the good offices of a Sanhedrist named Joseph, who belonged to

Arimathea, a Jewish town otherwise unknown, and who like
Symeon in ii. 25 is a sincerely upright Jew on the outlook for
the Reign of God. If according to Luke's source this man,
though a member of the supreme council, had withheld his
vote from the Sanhedrin's plan of action, the motive may be
sought in some kinship of spirit with the Gamaliel of Acts v. 34 f.,
rather than in any real, but unavowed, discipleship to Jesus.
Pilate concedes the request of Joseph, and the body shrouded in
linen is laid by him in a new rock-hewn grave situated probably
on some neighbouring hill-side. The omission of the usual
embalming may be ascribed to the haste imposed on the proceedings by the approach of dusk. **It was the day of the Preparation,** and with sunset, which at this season would occur between
the hours of five and six, the Sabbath would begin. Vers.
55-56 prepare us for the next event in xxiv. 1-7. The women
mark the place of burial in order to perform later the neglected
office of the embalmment. Their names are given in Mark xv.
40, 47.

xxiv. 1-12 : The Women at the Tomb

xxiv.

On the sabbath they rested in obedience to God's command, but 1
on the first day of the week at early dawn they took the
spices they had prepared and went to the tomb. The boulder 2
they found rolled away from the tomb, but when they went 3
inside they could not find the body of the Lord Jesus. They 4
were puzzling over this, when two men flashed on them in
dazzling raiment. They were terrified and bent their faces 5
to the ground, but the men said to them, 'Why do you look
among the dead for him who is alive ? He is not here, he 6
has risen. Remember how he told you when he was still in 7
Galilee that the Son of man had to be betrayed into the hands
of sinful men and be crucified and rise on the third day.' 8
Then they remembered what he had said, and turning away 9
from the tomb they reported all this to the eleven and all the
others. (It was Mary of Magdala, Joanna, and Mary the 10
mother of James who with the rest of the women told this
to the apostles.) But this story of the women seemed in 11
their opinion to be nonsense ; they would not believe them.
Peter did get up and run to the tomb, but when he looked 12

in he saw nothing except the linen bandages ; so he went
away home wondering what had happened.

The concluding chapter of Luke is devoted to the recital of
certain post-resurrection experiences of the disciple community,
and from a literary point of view it represents the final victory
of what may be called the Jerusalem tradition of the Resurrection as distinguished from another and older cycle of testimony
which centred round Peter and an appearance of the Risen One
in Galilee. This Jerusalem tradition has entered into all our
gospels in so far as the latter all start their narratives with an
experience of certain women at the grave of Jesus, but whereas
Mark looks beyond that event to a manifestation of the Lord in
Galilee (Mark xvi. 7), and Matthew actually records such a
manifestation (Matthew xxviii. 16-20), Luke excludes every
reference to Galilee, and confines attention to events local to
Jerusalem or to its immediate vicinity. This can only be
explained by the Jerusalem-Judean provenance of the source
which he followed. See Appendix III for further discussion
of the literary question.

Luke begins with the evidence of the Resurrection which was
granted to certain women at the grave of Jesus. Heavenly
voices proclaimed that the Lord was not among the dead, but
that he had risen. Coming after the Sabbath's rest to embalm
the body of Jesus, the women discover the stone which closed
the entrance to the vault removed, and on entering could not
find the body of the Lord Jesus. This circumstance excites
their wonder, but from all mistaken inferences as to its cause
(cf. John xx. 2, 13) they are delivered by seeing two men—Mark
mentions only one—who flashed on them in dazzling raiment.
This description—see under ix. 28-36—implies the celestial
character of the messengers, and assigns the experience to the
realm of spiritual-supernatural vision. While the women bend
their faces to the ground as if stricken by some blinding light,
there comes to them in their recumbent position a voice rebuking the foolish thought that they would find the Saviour in the
tomb. 'Why do you look among the dead for him who is alive ?
He is not here, he has risen.' Simultaneously a former prediction
of the Lord Jesus is brought vividly to their minds. ' Remember
how he told you . . . that the Son of man had to be betrayed
. . . and be crucified and rise on the third day ' (xviii. 31-33).

This experience of the women at the grave of Jesus is absent from the Resurrection-proofs enumerated by Paul in 1 Corinthians xv. 3-8, and would seem therefore not to have been an invariable part of the *earliest* apostolic tradition. This earliest testimony accentuated a first appearance of the Lord to ' Cephas ' (1 Corinthians xv. 5). On the other hand, the women's experience has become the starting-point of proof in all our gospels. In Mark, indeed, the integration of this element into the narrative is not—so far as the original text of Mark goes—compl te. The women do not relate their experience to anyone because they are afraid (Mark xvi. 8). But while the genuine text of Mark ends abruptly with these words, Luke goes on to state that the women turning away from the tomb reported everything to the eleven. In this way he links up the women's experience with the rest of the narrative. Even here, however, the statement that to the apostles the story seemed to be nonsense is sometimes thought to hint that the experience of the women was not at first usually included among the apostolic proofs of the Resurrection. However that may be, a peculiarity of the Lukan narrative is the form of the message given to the women in vers. 6-7 : ' Remember how he told you when he was still in Galilee,' etc. Reference to an earlier prediction made by Jesus in Galilee takes the place of the promised appearance in Galilee announced in Mark xvi. 7 (cf. xiv. 28). Ver. 12, recording a visit of Peter to the empty tomb (cf. John xx. 1-7), is wanting in the Greek MS. D, and in some Latin versions, and is probably an insertion into Luke from the narrative of John.

xxiv. 13-35 : The Disciples Going to Emmaus

That very day two of them were on their way to a village called 13 Emmaus about seven miles from Jerusalem. They were 14 conversing about all these events, and during their con- 15 versation and discussion Jesus himself approached and walked beside them, though they were prevented from 16 recognizing him. He said to them, ' What is all this you 17 are debating on your walk ? ' They stopped, looking downcast, and one of them, called Cleopas, answered him, ' Are 18 you a lone stranger in Jerusalem, not to know what has been happening there ? ' ' What is that ? ' he said to them. 19

They replied, ' All about Jesus of Nazaret ! To God and
all the people he was a prophet strong in action and utter-
20 ance, but the high priests and our rulers delivered him up
21 to be sentenced to death and crucified him. Our own hope
was that he would be the redeemer of Israel ; but he is dead,
22 and that is three days ago ! Though some women of our
number gave us a surprise ; they were at the tomb early in
23 the morning and could not find his body, but they came to
tell us they had actually seen a vision of angels who declared
24 he was alive. Some of our company did go to the tomb
and found things exactly as the women had said, but they
25 did not see him.' He said to them, ' O foolish men, with
hearts so slow to believe, after all the prophets have declared !
26 Had not the Christ to suffer thus and so enter his glory ? '
27 Then he began with Moses and all the prophets and interpreted to them the passages referring to himself throughout
28 the scriptures. Now they approached the village to which
they were going. He pretended to be going further on, but
29 they pressed him, saying, ' Stay with us, for it is getting to-
30 wards evening and the day has now declined.' So he went
in to stay with them. And as he lay at table with them he
took the loaf, blessed it, broke it and handed it to them.
31 Then their eyes were opened and they recognized him, but
he vanished from their sight. And they said to one another,
32 ' Did not our hearts glow within us when he was talking to
33 us on the road, opening up the scriptures for us ? ' So they
got up and returned that very hour to Jerusalem, where they
34 found the eleven and their friends all gathered, who told
them that the Lord had really risen and that he had appeared
35 to Simon. Then they related their own experience on the
road and how they had recognized him when he broke the
loaf.

(Luke alone.)

Though the women at the grave receive a revelation that the
Lord is risen, they do not see Jesus. This experience, according
to Luke's source, came first to two disciples travelling to
Emmaus, a village described as about seven miles distant from
Jerusalem. As the Emmaus, now 'Amwas, which lay on the
Jerusalem-Joppa road is too remote, and the other similarly
named place, now Kaloniyeh, which Josephus (*Wars*, vi. 6. 6)

mentions as on the same road, is not remote enough to answer
to this description, we must either suppose some inexactness in
the evangelist's figures (60 furlongs instead of 34, the distance
to Kaloniyeh), or abandon the identification of the site. The
two disciples, who are not of the Eleven (cf. ver. 33) but of the
' others ' mentioned in ver. 9, are conversing about all these
events, i.e. the crucifixion of Jesus with the strange sequel in
vers. 1-11, when Jesus himself approached and walked beside
them. If the experience here recorded were judged to go back
originally to a revelation of the Lord in the Spirit, a special point
would be imparted to the statement in ver. 16 that the disciples
were prevented from recognizing him. Luke's source, however,
clearly represented the event as upon the plane of an experience
granted to sense, during which the normal operation of the facul-
ties was suspended in the two disciples. The Stranger questions
them about their discussions. They stop, and after Cleopas—
the other disciple remains unnamed, though later tradition calls
him Simon or fancifully identifies him with Luke himself—has
expressed surprise that anyone living in Jerusalem should be
ignorant of recent happenings there, they reveal their trouble.
' Jesus of Nazaret, a prophet strong in action and utterance '
before God and the nation, whom they had expected to prove
' the redeemer of Israel,' i.e. to deliver Israel from her present
humiliation by bringing in the Kingdom of God, ' is dead.'
Rumours have reached them that he has arisen—here the coher-
ence of this Judean narrative with the women's experience at
the grave comes out plainly—but he has not appeared. Thereupon the Stranger, after rebuking the disciples for their slowness
to believe the prophets, takes them through the scriptures to
show that ' the Christ had to suffer and so enter his glory ' (on
this see under ix. 21-27). The climax comes when the travellers
reach their destination at Emmaus. The Stranger, constrained
to stay with them because the day is over, suddenly places himself at the head of the table, and by certain signs—he took the
loaf, blessed it, broke it, and handed it to them—which recalled
other days and scenes, discloses himself to their astonished eyes
as Jesus, then vanishes from sight. The disciples, thus apprised
that the Resurrection is a fact, and understanding now the
supernatural ardour which the Stranger's words had kindled in
their hearts, return incontinently to Jerusalem, and on rejoining
the Eleven are met by the tidings that ' the Lord had really risen '

(a reference back to vers. 9–11) 'and had appeared to Simon.'
Thereupon the travellers relate their own experience. The
reference in ver. 34 to a revelation of the Risen One to Simon is
interesting. It is a vestigial remnant in Luke's source of the
primitive tradition that Peter was the first to behold the Risen
Lord. But Luke's source did not preserve particulars of the
event, or Luke would have described it.

If, as is probable, the Emmaus-narrative represents a certain
elaboration of some original experience, we may possibly find
the nucleus in vers. 28–31 which associate the revelation of the
Lord with the Eucharist. If such revelations repeated themselves (Acts i. 3–4), the Emmaus incident will have the value of
a condensed representation of post-resurrection history. Whatever the circumstances may have been—and the mysterious
coming and going of the Risen One shews that the ordinary
plane of terrestrial experience has been left behind—the presence
of Christ in word and act is objectively and convincingly guaranteed to his followers. The supernatural, the 'wholly other,'
breaks in upon the ordinary world with results which reconstitute
the faith and life of the Christian community and make the
Resurrection the foundation-stone of the Church.

xxiv. 36–49 : THE APPEARANCE TO THE ELEVEN

36 Just as they were speaking He stood among them [and said
37 to them 'Peace to you ! '] They were scared and terrified,
38 imagining it was a ghost they saw ; but he said to them,
'Why are you upset ? Why do doubts invade your mind ?
39 Look at my hands and feet. It is I ! Feel me and see ; a
40 ghost has not flesh and bones as you see I have.' [With
41 these words he showed them his hands and feet.] Even
yet they could not believe it for sheer joy ; they were lost
in wonder. So he said to them, ' Have you any food here ? '
42 And when they handed him a piece of broiled fish, he took
43 and ate it in their presence. Then he said to them, ' When
44 I was still with you, this is what I told you, that whatever
is written about me in the law of Moses and the prophets
45 and the psalms must be fulfilled.' Then he opened their
46 minds to understand the scriptures. ' Thus,' he said, ' it is
written that the Christ has to suffer and rise from the dead

on the third day, and that repentance and the remission 47
of sins must be preached in his name to all nations, beginning
from Jerusalem. To this you must bear testimony. And 48
I will send down on you what my Father has promised ; 49
wait in the city till you are endued with power from on high.'

(Luke alone.)

The revelation here recorded appears by ver. 36 to have
occurred while Cleopas and his companion were still speaking.
The mode of the Risen One's appearance—he stood among them
suddenly—points again to something transcending all earthly
experience. But to obviate the suspicion that what the terrified
disciples beheld was only a spectre, a product of their own
excited imagination, Luke's source states that distinct objective
proofs of the reality of the Saviour's resurrection-body were
granted. Jesus not only spoke rebuking fear and doubt, but
offered himself to be touched and handled. ' Look at my hands
and feet. It is I l ' Ver. 36b and ver. 40 are wanting in the
Greek MS. D, and in a group of Latin authorities, and are
probably interpolations into the text. In vers. 41–43 the proof
attains its climax. While even now they could not believe for
sheer joy, Jesus asks for food and eats it before the disciples' eyes.
Then he speaks recalling to their minds what scripture had
predicted regarding the Christ. The predictions include his
sufferings—see again under ix. 21–27—his resurrection from the
dead, and the extension of the gospel from Jerusalem to the
Gentile world. The apostles are solemnly invested with the
office of diffusing the gospel to the nations, for which task they
will receive the promised Spirit (Joel ii. 28). But they must
wait in Jerusalem till the promise is fulfilled.

A representation which unites a spiritual-supernatural interpretation of the resurrection-body of Christ (vers. 36a, 37) with
features distinctly material (vers. 39–43) suggests the blending
of two somewhat different types of tradition. The tendency of
Luke's source and of his own mind was to materialize spiritual
experience, and a comparison of the above narrative with
Matthew xxviii. 16–20 makes it probable that in Luke we have
the overlaying of a less by a more corporeal conception of the
Saviour's risen life. Such an admission should not prove a
hindrance to our faith. So long as we recognize, as indeed we
must, that the post-resurrection experiences of the Christian

community were adequate to the production of the amazing revolution which flowed from them in Christian life and character, as well as in Christian conviction, the *nature* of the manifestations of the Risen Lord may be considered relatively unimportant. Sufficient evidence was granted to make the Resurrection the triumph-song of the Christian Church. The reference to the broiled fish in ver. 42 has been sometimes taken as a hint that this episode belonged originally to the tradition of an appearance by the Galilean Lake. Vers. 44–49 we may regard as summarizing much that only came to the disciples over a lengthened period of communion with the Risen Lord. The insistence on Jerusalem as the starting-point of the Christian mission is a primary indication of the Judean character of Luke's source. See further Appendix III.

xxiv. 50–53 : THE ASCENSION

50 He led them out as far as Bethany ; then, lifting his hands, he
51   blessed them. And as he blessed them he parted from them
52   [and was carried up to heaven]. They [worshipped him and]
53   returned with great joy to Jerusalem, where they spent all
      their time within the temple, blessing God.

(Luke alone.)

It would seem from Luke that all the events recorded in chap. xxiv., including the Ascension, fell on the first day of the Resurrection. This, if strictly taken, would rule out from Luke's mind the forty days of which we read in Acts i. 3. It is more probable, however, that Luke has merely omitted to mark the break between the appearance to the Eleven described in vers. 36–49 and a subsequent revelation at Bethany of which his source spoke. The source may not have identified the two experiences. On this hypothesis room would still remain in Luke's scheme for the events to which he later alludes in Acts i. 6–12.

APPENDIX I

WAS LUKE THE AUTHOR OF ACTS AND OF THE THIRD GOSPEL?

OUR answer to the question who wrote the Third Gospel must take account of several lines of evidence, of which the most important are the following :

(1) The authorship of the gospel cannot be determined without reference to its companion-work, the Acts of the Apostles. Both writings are dedicated to the same Theophilus. Both contain prefaces, and the preface to Acts is in language which distinctly looks back to the gospel. Moreover—and this is the point of supreme importance—the two writings exhibit so close an agreement in language, vocabulary, and style as to leave no option to any reasonable mind except to conclude their common authorship. Proof of this statement, turning as it does on countless technicalities of Greek diction and style, cannot be presented here, but will be found in such works as Sir John Hawkins's *Horae Synopticae*, and Dr. A. von Harnack's *Luke the Physician* and *Acts of the Apostles*, etc. Now as Acts contains a number of passages connected with Paul's travels, in which the writer uses the pronoun ' we,' and as these passages exhibit the same characteristics of language and style as the rest of Acts and the gospel, it would seem to follow that the writer of both works was at certain periods of his career an associate and fellow-traveller of Paul, and this conclusion has been unhesitatingly adopted by such scholars as Sir John Hawkins, Dr. von Harnack, Sir W. M. Ramsay, Dr. Moffatt, Canon Streeter, and others.

This argument is indeed resisted by a number of scholars who are on other grounds unsatisfied that the portrait of Paul in Acts can have come from a member of the apostle's staff. Such scholars contend that the ' we ' passages do not necessarily prove the writer of Acts to have been himself a fellow-traveller of Paul, but only to have used the diary or memoranda of such a fellow-traveller (who may of course have been Luke). But

271

this theory involves the assumption that the author of Acts, while rewriting the substance of the Diary in his own peculiar style, failed or for some reason refused to remove the ' we ' pronoun, and this, while not unexampled among ancient historians, is not easily credited to so careful a writer and so serious an historian as the author of Acts elsewhere shews himself to have been. Nor have we the right to say beforehand, with those who hold this theory, that the representation given of Paul in Acts could not have come from a companion of the apostle. We must not press a subaltern's loyalty to his chief to the extent of making him a pure echo of his hero's sentiments. While therefore the authorship of the gospel and Acts by a companion of Paul cannot on the sole basis of the ' we ' passages be said to be proved, it seems on the whole to be a natural inference from the ' we ' sections, taken together with the general harmony of language which the Acts and the gospel display.

(2) While the further step of identifying this companion of Paul with Luke is not to be reached by the above argument, the tradition that he was Luke is in itself credible enough. For Luke, as we know from the apostle's own statements in Colossians iv.14, Philemon 24, and 2 Timothy iv. 11, was with Paul when these passages in his correspondence were dictated ; and if, according to the usual view, these epistles were written during the term of the apostle's captivity in the imperial city, their evidence would agree with the implication of Acts that its writer journeyed with Paul to Rome. The only alternative to holding that the ascription of the gospel and the Acts to Luke rested from the beginning on an independent tradition of origins would be to suppose it the result of a happy guess from the above-named passages in the epistles. Someone searching the lists of companions named here and there by the apostle was able first to isolate the three passages in which Luke is named, and then by successive eliminations of the other names decided that Luke, as he alone remained with Paul when 2 Timothy iv. 11 was written, could alone have been his biographer. This theory is just possible. The passages are :

Colossians iv. 14 : ' The beloved Luke, the physician, greets you ; also Demas.'

Philemon 24 : ' Epaphras, my fellow-prisoner in Jesus Christ, Mark, Aristarchus, Demas, Luke, my fellow-workers, greet thee.'

2 Timothy iv. 11 : ' Luke alone is with me.'

But while this explanation of the connexion of Luke's name with the Acts and the gospel is possible, it is not convincing. The assumption of an independent tradition pointing to Luke as the author is not excluded.

(3) It may be further suggested that the identification of the author of Acts with Luke is confirmed by a comparison of the passages in Acts, where the writer is personally in attendance upon Paul, with the evidence of the latter's epistles as regards the presence of Luke. From the ' we ' passages in Acts we make out that the unnamed author of that work was with Paul from Troas to Philippi on the second missionary journey (xvi. 10–17), from Philippi back by Troas to Miletus on the third journey (xx. 5–15), from Miletus to Jerusalem on the resumption of the same journey (xxi. 1–18), and from Caesarea onwards on the last voyage to Rome (xxvii. 1–xxviii. 16). Now this means that the writer of Acts was not with Paul at Corinth or at Ephesus, the centres from which 1 and 2 Thessalonians, 1 Corinthians, Galatians, and Romans were written ; and with this agrees the fact that Luke's name is not mentioned in any of these epistles. On the other hand, the unnamed writer of Acts was with Paul at Rome, from which on the usual view came Colossians, Philemon, and 2 Timothy iv. 9–12, the epistles in which Luke is mentioned.

But here again the strength of the argument is not so great as might appear at first sight. It is not certain that Colossians and Philemon were written by Paul from Rome. Dr. Adolf Deissmann and other scholars have in recent years contended that these epistles proceeded from an otherwise unrecorded imprisonment of the apostle at Ephesus during his third mission-ary journey.[1] If this view should be sustained, the supposed harmony of Acts with the epistles breaks down, for Acts con-tains no evidence that its author was with Paul at Ephesus. On the other hand, Luke may have been with Paul at Ephesus for at least a period, though Acts is silent on the subject.

(4) Paul's personal references to Luke in his epistles harmonize very fully with the conclusions regarding the author of the Third Gospel and Acts to which an independent study of these writings leads us. For example, a comparison of Colossians iv.

---

[1] For a demonstration of this view the reader can now refer to Professor G. S. Duncan's *St. Paul's Ephesian Ministry* (1929).

ii and iv. 14 shews from Paul's side that Luke was not of ' the circumcision,' in other words, that he was a Gentile by birth : and with this agree the universalist sympathies which are so marked a feature of the author of the gospel and Acts. Again, in Philemon 24 Luke appears as one of Paul's ' fellow-workers,' and it is in such a relation to the apostle, as sharer of his evangelistic and healing activities, that Acts presents its author (cf. Acts xvi. 10, xvi. 13, xxviii. 9–10). Again, Paul, in the passages in his epistles in which he mentions Luke, mentions also as members of his staff Tychicus, Aristarchus, Mark, Jesus Justus, Epaphras, Demas, Crescens, Titus, Trophimus, and Timothy. Four of these, viz. Aristarchus, Timothy, Tychicus, and Trophimus, appear in Acts xx. 4–5 as travelling in company with the writer of that work. Finally, Colossians iv. 14 describes Luke as ' the physician,' and this description is considered to harmonize admirably with the marked attention to disease and to therapeutic processes which is so characteristic a feature of the Third Gospel and Acts. Indeed, Dr. W. K. Hobart in a work published in 1882 on *The Medical Language of St. Luke* undertook to shew from the turn of mind revealed in Luke-Acts and from the many coincidences between the language of these writings and that of the standard Greek medical textbooks that the gospel and the Acts must have been written by a medical man, and his demonstration has been accepted almost without qualification by scholars like von Harnack and Dr. Theodor Zahn.

Yet here again the evidence is not everywhere regarded as cogent. Hobart's argument from the supposed medical vocabulary of Luke-Acts is overstated, and has been seriously damaged by Professor H. J. Cadbury. Hence it is wiser perhaps to let this particular argument drop.

On a review of all the evidence it would appear therefore that Luke's authorship of the gospel and Acts cannot be regarded as absolutely proved. On the other hand, it has on the whole a fair balance of probability in its favour, and may be regarded as the most credible hypothesis.

APPENDIX II

THE BIRTH NARRATIVES IN LUKE'S GOSPEL

It is pointed out above (p. 3) that the close interweaving in Luke of the birth-stories of Jesus and John shews that in the source upon which Luke drew the two cycles of narrative were already combined—in other words, that Luke's authority was Christian. We must now take up in somewhat fuller detail the question of the origin and character of the birth-narratives in order to supplement what is said in the Commentary.

In the first place, the primitive tradition embodied in Mark includes no reference to the Saviour's birth. It opens with the scene at the Jordan, where the call of Jesus as Messiah-Son of God was divinely revealed or certified to his consciousness (Mark i. 1–11), and nothing in the rest of Mark points to portents or signs at his birth by which that call was anticipated or fore-announced. We must therefore assume either that Mark did not find the birth-traditions among the data presented to him, or that he considered them irrelevant to his purpose in writing a gospel. The latter alternative is scarcely probable, but even if we accepted it and supposed Mark to be acquainted with the Virgin-birth of Christ, the fact would remain that the rest of the evangelical history as incorporated in his gospel, and as taken over from him by Matthew and Luke, shews no trace of the conception, indeed seems to exclude it by the attitude which it ascribes to Jesus' kinsfolk at Nazareth (Mark iii. 21 ; cf. John vii. 5) and even by certain actions of Mary herself, though the latter point is doubtful. We must suppose therefore that the birth-traditions circulated originally in independence of the main body of the evangelical narrative. Even apart from Mark, the main body of the New Testament witness to Jesus dispenses with all reference to his birth. While both Paul and the writer of the Fourth Gospel teach the pre-existence of Christ as a divine being (Galatians iv. 4, 2 Corinthians viii. 9, Philippians ii. 6–8, John i. 14, iii. 13, vi. 51, viii. 58, etc.), neither refers to a supernatural birth as the mode of his entrance into the world, though, of course, the idea may be latent in their determination of his person and function.

In the second place, in Matthew and Luke, where the birth-narratives appear, and where they are united, though only partially, with the rest of the tradition, the differences in detail are so considerable as to shew that at the time when these gospels were composed no single narrative of the birth-history was in possession of the field. While the two accounts agree on the central points of the birth at Bethlehem, the occurrence of supernatural signs before and after the event, the names Joseph and Mary, the miraculous character of the birth itself, and the upbringing of the divine Child at Nazareth, they diverge in so far as Matthew leaves it to be understood that Bethlehem was the home of Joseph and Mary (Matthew ii. 1, 22-23), while Luke brings the parents to Bethlehem only in consequence of the census under Quirinius (Luke ii. 1-7). Again, while Matthew associates the birth with the visit of the Magi, the star, the massacre of the innocents, and the flight to Egypt (Matthew ii. 1-21), Luke knows nothing of these events, but records instead the angel's appearance to the shepherds, the song of the heavenly host, the finding of the Child in the manger, the visit of the parents to the Temple, and the words of Symeon and Anna (Luke ii. 8-38). All this seems to shew a freedom of development as regards the central theme of the narratives which has no parallel in the rest of the evangelical tradition except perhaps as regards the post-resurrection history.

The source of Luke's narrative, with which alone we are here concerned, admits of being satisfactorily determined. It goes back to Palestinian Christian circles and, as most scholars believe, to a written document composed in Aramaic or in Hebrew. This appears by the atmosphere of the narrative and by certain features of the Greek style which reflect an underlying Semitic idiom. Moreover, the ideals of piety so exquisitely portrayed in the chief characters of the story, the Messianic hopes revealed in the hymns (i. 14-17, 32-33, 46-55, 68-79, ii. 29-32), and the intimate knowledge of Jewish religious customs which the narratives display, are Jewish-Christian. Finally, the words in i. 65, ' These events were talked of through the whole of the hill-country of Judea,' and in ii. 18, ' All who heard it were astonished at the story of the shepherds,' remove all doubt as to the original home and provenance of the traditions. Luke drew upon a Jewish-Christian source which must have taken shape in Judea in the quiet years before the disastrous

Roman war of A.D. 66–70, which scattered the Christian community in Judea. In rewriting the story, however, he has made great use of the language of the Greek (LXX) version of the Old Testament, besides contributing a number of special features from other sources : see above on i. 34–35 and on ii. 1–2.

On the other hand, Matthew's account will have been based on the tradition as known in Antioch, where the interest in the approach of the Orient to Christ, as reflected in the story of the Magi, would be especially strong.

But while literary criticism thus decides the origin and age of our evangelist's source, it does not enable us to penetrate behind that source to the original data on which the tradition was based. Here, however, it may be confidently asserted that no explanation of these narratives will be truly historical which does not recognize in some degree the influence of Messianic prophecy and of the Old Testament narratives of the births of Isaac, Samuel, and Samson, as well as the presence in primitive Christianity of a powerfully inspired poetic-creative impulse. When we allow for the passionate adoring celebration of the gift of God in His Son which characterized primitive Christian worship, it will be found impossible to limit its activities in Judea or elsewhere to the mere recital of matter-of-fact statements. Faith would, from whatever basis of fact it started, follow the inspiration and guidance of the prophetic suggestions of the Old Testament. Here different minds will incline to different conclusions according as the principal stress is laid on the element of Old Testament prediction or on the existence of factual data, accessible to the primitive community, regarding Jesus' birth. In the former case it is customary to connect the development of these Jewish-Christian narratives with the passage in Isaiah vii. 14 : ' Behold, the maiden shall conceive and bear a son and shall call his name Immanuel,' where the birth-story of the Messiah would seem to be clearly given. But this passage cannot be the *origin* of the Christian conception of the Virgin-birth, since nothing in the prophecy suggests the thought that the divine Child there referred to would not be born in wedlock. In the other case, where stress is laid principally on an independent tradition of fact regarding the Saviour's birth, it is customary to trace the knowledge of the facts to personal sources. Indeed, it is usually argued from ii. 19, ' Mary kept all these things, pondering them in her heart ' (cf. ii. 51), that the mother of

Jesus was the source. But while the hypothesis that the mother of our Lord entrusted to some intimate circle in the community a record of religious experiences of an unusual nature which had come to herself before the birth of her Son is not to be excluded, the fact that she did so is not to be too certainly inferred from Luke's language in ii. 19. The words might mean, ' Whereas the shepherds spread abroad the report of these things, Mary on her part kept her secret to herself.' Consequently, to many scholars it appears that the main stress as regards these narratives should be laid neither on the Old Testament nor on a secure assumption of precise tradition regarding the birth but on intuitive conclusions from the transcendent nature and destiny of One who had been received in the Church as Son of God and of the nature of God. The worshipping recognition of Jesus as divine Messiah, Saviour, Deliverer, the Beloved Son of the Father, is the fact on which not only the whole evangelical tradition but the entire Christianity of the New Testament rests. The acceptance of Jesus Christ as divine Revealer of the Father did not start from the birth-narratives but from his own attributes and character, and therefore it does not depend on the precise interpretation put upon the narratives. As we see by Paul and the writer of the Fourth Gospel, the divine Sonship of the Redeemer may be presented in all its wonder without any reference to the precise mode of his entrance into the world. Hence most theologians are content to leave many questions connected with the details of the birth-narratives open. On the other hand, the religious values enshrined in the narratives must be upheld as integral and vital to the primitive Christian consciousness and so historically constitutive of the Christian attitude to Christ.

APPENDIX III

THE RESURRECTION NARRATIVES IN THE GOSPELS

THE primary evidence for the Resurrection of Christ is not documentary but factual. There is the Christian Church itself which acknowledges no other basis than that ' God raised Jesus on the third day and allowed him to be seen . . . by witnesses '

(Acts x. 40). Apart from astounding experiences adequate to the production of this belief, neither Church nor faith is explicable. There is furthermore the *tone* in which from the beginning the Church delivers its message to the world. Here we have no conjecture or surmise, no chastened mood of hope, no tremulous or courageous ' perhaps,' but a triumphant and ringing and sustained note of certainty. This characteristic of the Church's faith is not to be explained except upon some ground of constitutive fundamental experience.

But this factual evidence, important as it is, throws no light upon the particular nature of the experience. For this we depend on documentary evidence attesting where and how and by whom the Lord was seen. Here our primary authority is the deposition of Paul in 1 Corinthians xv. 1-8, written little more than twenty-five years after the Crucifixion. Not only is this our earliest extant statement regarding the Resurrection-appearances but, coming from one the workings of whose mind we know and whose judgment may be supposed to have been in that age the least biased by popular rumour or fancy, it is less exposed than our other documents to damaging assault by critical analysis. Premising that his affirmations rest on what he has ' received ' (xv. 3) and carry the unanimous consent of all the apostles (xv. 11), Paul specifies six occasions on which the Risen Lord was seen, concluding with the appearance to himself which made him an apostle. The passage has three principal characteristics : (1) it begins with an appearance of the Lord to ' Cephas ' (xv. 5) ; (2) it makes no mention of any experience of women at the grave of Christ ; (3) it offers no explicit account of the mode of the appearances, but by the general tenor of the argument which follows—see especially xv. 35-53—it relegates them to the sphere of ' spiritual,' not material, reality, and to the category of the ' spiritual,' not the carnal, body. That is, the appearances belong to the order of reality which is wholly governed by ' Spirit.'

Scholars rightly find in this passage a proof that the *oldest* apostolic testimony to the Resurrection started from an objective revelation to Peter, but stressed the ' spiritual ' character of the phenomena concerned. Moreover, while the argument from silence is often dangerous—and it ought not to be positively concluded in this case that Paul knew nothing of the women at the tomb—the absence of all reference to them shews that their experience was no universally regulative and unvarying part of the apostolic ' gospel ' (xv. 1–2).

A comparison of 1 Corinthians with the later narratives in our gospels cannot therefore but prove of critical and historical value. If on general grounds of the psychological laws governing the transmission of a body of traditional material, or on evidence contained within the documents themselves, we judge our gospel-narratives to have undergone development, we may find in the Corinthians passage an instrument by which earlier and later elements or strata in these narratives may be distinguished.

(1) While the tradition that the Lord appeared first to Peter has left residual traces in our gospels—compare the predictions in Mark xiv. 28, xvi. 7 (Matthew xxvi. 32, xxviii. 7) and the allusion in Luke xxiv. 34—no actual record of the event appears in any one of them. The original ending of Mark is lost, and we do not know what that gospel went on to relate after xvi. 8, but neither Matthew nor Luke describes any revelation to Peter, while the late appendix to the Fourth Gospel, which mentions Peter, does not bring him in (and then not by himself alone) until the third post-resurrection appearance (John xxi. 14). For some reason the primitive datum of faith that the Lord appeared first to Cephas has been elided from our gospels. As this cannot have happened by oversight, it must be explained in some other way, and here plausible grounds exist for considering that the elision was due to the growing ascendancy of another line of tradition which started not with Peter but with the women at the tomb.

(2) The women's experience at the grave of Jesus, while not included in the Pauline *testimonia*, has established itself in all our gospels as the starting-point of proof. But that it cannot have constituted an unvarying part of the primitive tradition in all its forms appears by its omission from 1 Corinthians, and also to some extent by Mark's statement that the women said nothing to anyone about their experience because they were terrified (xvi. 8). It seems difficult altogether to exclude the possibility that Mark's statement here indicates some want of connexion between the women's testimony and the line of proof which he was *otherwise* following. Mark indeed gives it a connexion with that other line of proof by the statement in xvi. 7 that the divine messenger at the tomb pointed forward to an appearance of the Risen One in Galilee, and Matthew and Luke state that the

women reported their experience to the Eleven. But in Luke all reference to a future appearance in *Galilee* is dropped. We seem therefore to see the stages of a process by which a line of tradition which started with the grave in Jerusalem came to be drawn over another line which started from Peter in Galilee. This does not mean that the women's deposition did not rest upon some actual experience, but only that this evidence was not at first emphasized among accepted proofs of the Resurrection. Afterwards, as we see by Luke's source, it entirely displaces the Galilean tradition.

(3) As contrasted with Paul, who assigns the phenomena presented to consciousness in connexion with the Resurrection to the sphere of what he calls the ' spiritual ' body, our gospels exhibit an increasing tendency to a materialistic presentation of the evidence. In Matthew this tendency is still held considerably in check (cf. xxviii. 17). In Luke, on the other hand, it is almost unrestrained. Luke's source, while retaining such ' spiritual ' features as the mysterious entrance and departure of the Risen One (xxiv. 31, 36), and asserting that the beholders were doubtful to what order of reality the phenomena belonged (xxiv. 37–39), insists also that the manifestations were corporeal. The body of Jesus is not spectral but compact of ' flesh and bones' (xxiv. 39), and to conclude the proof Jesus asks and receives food (xxiv. 41–43). Is this a consistent representation derived from a single fount of tradition ? Do the various statements all lie on the same plane of understanding, or is it the case that both here and in John xx. 19–20, 24–28, experiences of a mystical order, i.e. experiences involving some suspension of the ordinary sense-faculties, have attracted to themselves the features of ordinary sense presentations ? In the light of the Pauline evidence the latter hypothesis is not to be excluded. The tendency of popular tradition is to give a more sensual and physical form to apprehensions of the spiritual consciousness, and this naïver interpretation of the spiritual is specially characteristic of Luke's Judean source.

We conclude then that the gospel narratives of the Resurrection are not constructed out of wholly simple and homogeneous elements. A tradition centring round Peter and Galilee has been partly overshadowed by another tradition starting from the grave at Jerusalem, and the form of evidence appealed to has received a more materialistic cast. Beyond this, purely literary evidence does not enable us to go.   Its operations are confined to the *form* of our documents, but behind these documents lies the actuality of experiences which, whatever their nature was, came to the disciple community with overwhelming power, and made the Resurrection of Christ the irrefragable basis of the Church's living faith.

2.45